I0590427

Letters of

RAINER MARIA RILKE

RAINER MARIA RILKE

In Translations by M. D. HERTER NORTON
Letters to a Young Poet
Sonnets to Orpheus
Wartime Letters of Rainer Maria Rilke
Translations from the Poetry of Rainer Maria Rilke
The Lay of the Love and Death of Cornet Christopher Rilke
The Notebooks of Malte Laurids Brigge
Stories of God

Translated by STEPHEN SPENDER and J. B. LEISHMAN
Duino Elegies

Translated by JANE BANNARD GREENE and M. D. HERTER NORTON
Letters of Rainer Maria Rilke
Volume One, 1892–1910   Volume Two, 1910–1926

RILKE was born in Prague in 1875, the son of a conventional army-officer father and a religious-fanatical mother, who first sent him, most unsuitably, to military school. After that, largely autodidact, he studied philosophy, history, literature, art, in Prague, Munich, Berlin. From his earliest years he wrote verse. In the '90s both *Erste* and *Frühe Gedichte* appeared, short stories, plays. Much of his early work he declined to include in his collected works. In 1899 (which saw the *Cornet*, first version) came the first of two trips to Russia with Lou Andreas-Salomé (*Vom lieben Gott und Anderes*, later to be called *Geschichten vom Lieben Gott*, appeared in December 1900). He married Clara Westhoff in 1901, lived in Worpswede till the birth of their only child, Ruth, moving to Paris in 1902, Clara to work with Rodin, Rilke to write his monograph on him. Between travels in Germany, France, Italy, Spain, Egypt, Scandinavia, and his prodigious letter-writing, the twelve years with Paris as base were productive: *Stundenbuch, Buch der Bilder, Neue Gedichte, Notebooks of M. L. Brigge,* translations of E. B. Browning, Gide, de Guérin. After the outbreak of World War I he lived mostly in Munich, served briefly in army office work in Vienna, and in 1919 went to Switzerland. Here, in the small stone tower of Muzot, he achieved in 1922 the *Duineser Elegien* and the *Sonette an Orpheus,* followed by poems in French and translations of Valéry and others. He died at Valmont near Glion on December 29, 1926, and is buried beside the little church of Raron overlooking the Rhone Valley.

Phot. Henri Martinie, Paris

Rainer Maria Rilke
1925

Letters of
RAINER MARIA RILKE
1910 — 1926

Translated by

JANE BANNARD GREENE
and
M. D. HERTER NORTON

The Norton Library
W · W · NORTON & COMPANY · INC ·
NEW YORK

Note: Certain of the letters in this
volume were first printed in *The
Kenyon Review*, Autumn, 1947

Copyright 1947, 1948 by W. W. Norton & Company, Inc.
First published in the Norton Library 1969

ISBN: 978-0-393-00477-9

Books That Live
The Norton imprint on a book means that in the publisher's
estimation it is a book not for a single season but for the years.
W. W. Norton & Company, Inc.

PRINTED IN THE UNITED STATES OF AMERICA

1 2 3 4 5 6 7 8 9 0

CONTENTS

TRANSLATORS' NOTE	9
INTRODUCTION	11
THE LETTERS	13
NOTES	398
LIST OF CORRESPONDENTS	451
INDEX	453

ILLUSTRATIONS

RAINER MARIA RILKE   *Frontispiece*
        (from Salis, *Rainer Maria Rilkes Schweizer Jahre*)

                                                  Facing page
RILKE WITH MAX REINHARDT AND GERHARD HAUPT-
    MANN   128
        (from *Philobiblon*, 1935)

FACSIMILE OF A FRAGMENT OF THE TENTH ELEGY   129
        (from *Dichtung und Volkstum*, 1936)

RILKE WITH PAUL VALÉRY IN THE GARDEN AT ANTHY 160
        (from *Hommage des écrivains étrangers à Paul Valéry*)

RILKE'S GRAVE IN RARON   161
        (from *Inselschiff*, Christmas, 1936)

7

TRANSLATORS' NOTE

As IN the preceding volume of LETTERS: 1892–1910, all these letters, unless otherwise indicated in the Notes, have been taken from the two editions of the general collection of Rilke's LETTERS, edited by his daughter and son-in-law, Ruth Sieber-Rilke and the late Carl Sieber, and published by Insel-Verlag.

Again we are deeply indebted to Herbert Steiner for his invaluable assistance.

INTRODUCTION

THE present volume of letters covers the years from the completion of *The Notebooks of Malte Laurids Brigge* to Rilke's death in December 1926, nearly five years after he had finished the *Duino Elegies* and the *Sonnets to Orpheus*, his last big works. The period falls into four distinct divisions: the years before the first World War, when a harrowing reaction from the psychological strain of writing the *Malte* drove Rilke in mounting desperation to country after country, to person after person; the wartime period itself, in which the flare-up of excited, almost exalted response quickly gave way to a persisting dismay at the phenomenon of war, what he himself calls the "whole sad man-made complication"; the search in Switzerland, from 1919 to 1921, for congenial surroundings in which to bring to their conclusion the long-despaired-of *Elegies;* and finally, the end of the quest, Muzot, which was to be his home for the brief remainder of his days. So much of what is generally known of the outer events and inner currents of Rilke's life emerges directly from the letters themselves that little need be added.

Letters continued to be as necessary to him both artistically and humanly, as they had been in his youth. They remained always "a kind of transition from the verbal and communicating to the writing of work which is no longer addressed to any single individual."

There is a great increase in the number of his correspondents. The letters to Clara are fewer now and their importance far less. To Lou Andreas-Salomé, on the other hand, he continued to speak most easily and, to the end, it was to her that he turned in moments of crisis. Other major relationships were those with Princess Marie von Thurn und Taxis-Hohenlohe and, in the last years, with Frau Nanny Wunderly-Volkart. Unfortunately the important letters to the latter are at present available only in fragmentary form unsuitable for inclusion here.

The greatest difference between this second volume of correspondence and its predecessor is the subtle but quite conscious shift in Rilke's point of view, a shift to which attention has already been called in the introduction to the first volume and which is best expressed in the poem "Turning" included in the present pages. Having schooled his eye to see with a painter's accuracy, he was now able to bring this acquired objectivity to bear on his inner vision. As a result, there are far fewer visually descriptive passages and a greater preoccupation with psychological and spiritual insights. This is not to say, however, that the letters become dry or abstract. Rilke was above all a poet, constantly seeking more and more precise equivalents for his inner experience in the concrete images of his expression.

One of the most significant indications of Rilke's maturity is the growth of his capacity to learn and to be nourished from a wider variety of experience. No one interest or personality holds the central focus here in the way Rodin did in the earlier years. As he grew older, he enriched his art and his life from many sources: from places —Venice, Egypt, Spain, the Valais; from the ideas of Kassner and Schuler; from a deeply experienced painting of Picasso; from the art of Paul Valéry; the list could never be complete, for with his feeling of love and reverence for life Rilke wanted nothing so much as to become more and more open to all it might bring.

Although during this last third of his life Rilke passed through times of extreme suffering, there are in these letters many positive and ringing affirmations such as were later to receive definitive artistic expression in the *Elegies* and the *Sonnets*. "It is certain that the divinest consolation is contained in humanity itself—", he was able to write in the midst of the first World War; "we would not be able to do much with the consolation of a god; only that our eye would have to be a trace more seeing, our ear more receptive, the taste of a fruit would have to penetrate us more completely, we would have to endure more odor, and in touching and being touched be more aware and less forgetful—: in order promptly to absorb out of our immediate experiences consolations that would be more convincing, more true than all the suffering that can ever shake us to our very depths."

The justly famous letters from Muzot form the richest portion of the entire correspondence. Many are written to young people Rilke did not know and, as in the earlier instance of the *Letters to a Young Poet*, there is in them a tone of authority and eloquence one rarely finds elsewhere. The completion of the *Elegies* resolved the frustrations of many years and freed their author's mind for a new perspective on his own poetry. In response to professional inquiries regarding his work he now returned long, careful commentaries and elucidations that are an invaluable contribution to the understanding of his art. Almost all the letters of this time are imbued with a special quality that can come only with a sense of fulfillment, the same poise of spirit that informs the verses he chose for his epitaph:

> Rose, oh pure contradiction, desire
> to be no one's sleep beneath so many
> lids.

The Letters

[1]

To Clara Rilke   Venice, May 5, 1910
                    On the Day of Ascension, of the "Sensa," formerly the
                    great day of the marriage of Venice with the sea.

It is indeed true . . . I do not write at all, my not writing is
taking on dimensions. But, look, of what importance is my thin
experience (which persists) beside all the intense things that are
befalling you? It would be like conversation, if I wanted to tell
anything; since I have been underway, I do not know how to let
anything important happen to me. I hope the insight will follow,
once I am back in Paris, that after all something or other has taken
place inside *à mon insu.* The only thing that keeps me here is the
possibility of discovering in the libraries still a few particulars
for the life of Carlo Zeno. But in these books and catalogues I am
just as hopelessly inept as when I have to look for a clover leaf or
strawberries. People treat me as if I were a scholar, lay everything
before me, but I sit on the folios just like a cat who merely conceals with her being there what is in them, and at most is pleasantly
aware of the novelty of her situation. And if the lagoon below
beats and beats again on the old marble foundations, my whole
attention goes toward that noise, as if more were to be learned
from it than from the old texts.

With that really everything about me has been said. At Duino
there were friendly days, the understanding with the Princess,
which I instantly recognized in a general way in Paris, proved
warm in detail . . . With Kassner I had three more days there,
then he had to leave; but he will now live in Paris for a time. He is
a little like an examination, and for me it was not the time for passing; I flunked in a gentle sympathetic way at this examination, I
mean just in the particular subjects. On the whole, of course, it
couldn't help being all right. I am happy to have him in Paris in

15

any case. He is something sure, true, really eminently serious. One can test every word against his listening, but for that reason one also doubts every word of one's own. I remember from the physics class that gold never looked less like gold than when one was examining it for the streak it leaves on the touchstone.

Goodbye, dear, be indulgent with me for returning so little for so much. I have no more and remain in debt . . .

[2]

To Princess Marie von Thurn
und Taxis-Hohenlohe

Schloss Janowič
Selčan district, Bohemia
August 30, 1910

I am all absorbed in picturing how this letter will reach you in Duino; I see your little realm up there, the world you are at home in, dense with memories, with its window on the very great; there is something definitive in this arrangement of drawing the near very near, so that the distance may be alone with itself. What is close by means much, and the infinite in this way becomes singularly clear, free of meaning, a pure depth, an inexhaustible store of spiritually usable interspace.

But well as I can imagine all that, I do catch myself hoping in every mail for a card from you, with just this much, that your trip did you good and that you found the days down there the way you like them. Is the Prince with you, and how is Prince Pasha? You must sometimes feel how much I am inwardly continuing the Lautschin life. Prague interrupted me for a few days, I arrived here almost ill, but now everything is going along, yes, I can really say things are somehow going along. Lautschin was a real watershed, now everything is flowing off in another way, I don't know whither, I don't see ahead, I am wholly taken up by springs being suddenly there that are making the most of the new declivity and driving onward. That is not to be understood at all as applying to my work, which is resting, but inside my life something is stirring, my soul is about to learn something, it is beginning with new rudiments, and to me the best thing in all this is to see it so modest. Perhaps I shall now learn to become a little human; hitherto my art has really come into being at the cost of my insisting on nothing but things; that was a stubbornness, I fear, an arrogance too, dear Heaven, and it must have been a tremendous greediness. I shudder a little when I think of all the violence I put through in Malte Laurids, how I landed with him back of everything in consistent despair, back of death in a way, so that nothing more was possible, not even dying. I believe no one has ever experienced more clearly how very much art goes against Nature; it is the most passionate inversion in the world, the road back from the infinite, on which all decent things come to meet one; now one sees them full size, their faces draw near, their movement gains detail—: yes, but who is one then that one *may* do it, that one should take this direction against them all, this eternal re-turning with which one deceives them, letting them believe that one has already arrived somewhere, at some end, and now has leisure to go back?

As for the landscape, it is much simpler here than in Lautschin, simple-minded almost, all kinds of sentiment and melancholy have got into the flowers, the blue cornflowers by the roadside want to look right into one's eyes like domestic animals, and the industrious apples want to be praised.

It is touching to see the three young orphaned children, the way they take their life, that must now be the whole of life, in hand, each in his way and yet in such charming considerateness and concord. I am by far the oldest in the house, I almost have trouble mastering the dignifiedness that is unfolding in me. Luckily there is so much superiority in the smallest and simplest of their ways, not to mention that which comes spontaneously even from the youngest. But shortly I want to read Kassner aloud to the children. Now I am reading Kierkegaard, it is magnificent, real magnificence, never has he moved me so.

A thousand greetings to you and yours, Princess, I often miss an hour of talk, a letter is no substitute at all.

[*3*]

To Countess Lili Kanitz-Menar

Schloss Janowič,
Selčan district, Bohemia
September 7, 1910

You shall not wait too long, just as I am I will at least thank you for your good and warm letter, which did not reach me here until three days ago. Our dear Malte has given you pleasure and has touched you deeply, yes, that he certainly was bound to do, that was the least he could do for you who kept believing in him and expected much of him. As for me, I draw a deep breath whenever I think that this book is in existence, indeed it had to exist, I was so indescribably committed to it, choice I had none. But now I feel a little like Raskolnikov after the deed, I don't know at all what is to come now, and I even shudder a little when I consider that I have written this book; by what force, I ask myself, by what right, I would almost like to ask.

I sat, as was my program, in Paris; I wanted to hold myself to my work, as every summer; it was not to be done, I had to give in, partly it was my health that demanded it, and then simply this: that Malte was a big, big division; it was a quite theoretical and pedantic idea simply to go on writing as if nothing had happened. After all, everything, so to speak, had happened. . . .

[*4*]

To Clara Rilke

77 rue de Varenne, Paris
November 18, 1910

. . . I thank you, the volumes of the Arabian Nights arrived very opportunely, everything was still hanging fire, only now is it as good as certain that I will be in Algiers the beginning of next week, rue Michelet, Hotel Saint-Georges. I have been invited to go along on a lovely trip that will take me through Tunis, perhaps on to Egypt, about that I will write as things develop. It is not entirely easy for me to go away from here, although Paris during this time has been by no means easy for me; it is indeed just by the difficult that one always recognizes it again and by the difficult that one is so strongly bound to it. And yet I feel distinctly that this time I must travel, just as far as possible. I like the thought that I am leaving my little apartment behind lying open, the books are there,—how will one return?

The Seine is rising, it is up to the armpits of the bridges, in the evening it is uncanny, this broad near-by water, now I can picture how the flood comes about, but it seems that again I am not to be in on the experience of it.

Much as I have before me, everything is in fact veiled from me by the death of Tolstoy in that little, unknown station; how much room to act there really is even in our time, how many paths to go away by, how this inner life did indeed keep breaking out again and again into the visible, passing directly into its legend. It is becoming more and more difficult to find the external action for what the soul does; Ibsen out of obstinacy carried it through within art, Tolstoy, ambitious where truth was concerned and namelessly alone, over and over again compelled life to be the degree-reading for the level of his soul. But the tremendous pressure under which this final event took place drove the fluid column of action far beyond the scale of conscience to where readings could no longer be taken; thus did he fulfill himself as a poet, *was* his own figure, which in its greatest sense, in the sense of its deepest urge and doom, he brought to its conclusion. I learned of his death yesterday morning through Rodin, who showed me the enclosed picture,—I think you know it. . . .

[5]

To Clara Rilke   Hôtel St.-Georges, Algiers
                                    November 26, 1910

. . . It is raining after the first very clear southern days, so I am writing quickly, but it can be only a few words: brightness and looking have made me very tired, besides almost nothing can be said; I foresee that it will be a long time before I shall be able to express myself about all this here, although it is absolutely familiar to me when I feel it around me. Algiers is in large part a French city, but a stretch of slope on which stand the old Turkish, Moorish and Arabian houses still has magnificent and innate continuity within itself and with sky and vista; existence there is out of the Arabian Nights, beggars and carriers go about as though in destinies, Allah is great, and no power but his power is in the air. My room faces east, I am awakened daily by the display with which the day prepares itself, suddenly after much splendor performed the sun leaps smooth and finished over the strong Atlas mountains. There in that direction lies Biskra whither we want to move on the beginning of next week . . . The climate is doing me good, and the sea is wonderfully southern in the big arc of this bay. . . .

[6]

To Clara Rilke   Tunisia Palace Hotel, Tunis
                                           December 17, 1910

. . . It almost seems I am already writing you this for Christmas Day, amid all the good wishes I have for the life of you two. Sometimes in the souks there comes one of those moments when one can imagine Christmas: the little niches are hung so full of gay objects, the fabrics are so lavish and surprising, the gold flashes out as promisingly as if one were to get it tomorrow as a gift, and then in the evening when a single lantern across from it all burns and moves, excited as it were by the presence of everything its light engages, then Arabian Nights pass over into all that ever was anticipation, wish, and suspense within one, and Christmas is not so unthinkable at all. But even in the morning I am astonished again and again at what the sun accomplishes as it reaches in through the tattered covering of the souks, how, falling here and there, it makes a green transparent, a red hot, a mauve give itself infinitely,—today one went about at an auction of gebbas and gandourahs as among a lot of precious stones, one went up to some such fabric and simply into it, into its clear green, right through its lilac, or simply on in a yellow that was still before one, without bottom, like a radiant clarity in the sky.—In the souk of the parfumeurs we already have a friend; when one shakes hands with him, it lasts for the whole day, and in the night one is awakened by the feeling that one's own fingers are wonderfully spiritualized. I asked for essence of geranium in his shop (which is often sold as rose water); my wanting that and not rose oil pleased him, he initiated me, and that is how our friendship came about. . . .

We plan, if we are not too tired, to attend midnight mass in a little church that was formerly a mosque. In any case the little girl's Christmas, which is yours, is mine, too, may it be full of joy and bright blessing upon Ruth's heart. A good festival for you both . . .

[7]

To Clara Rilke   Kairuan
                                        December 21, 1910

I have come over for a day into the "holy city" of Kairuan, after Mecca the great pilgrim center of Islam, which Sidi Okba, a comrade of the Prophet, erected in the great plains and which has risen up again and again out of its ruins about the enormous mosque in which hundreds of pillars from Carthage and all the Roman coastal colonies have come together to carry the dark cedar ceilings and support the white cupolas, so dazzling today as they stand against gray skies, breaking only here and there, out of which the rain is falling for which people have been crying these three days. Like a vision the flat white city lies there in its round-pinnacled ramparts, with nothing but plain and graves about it, as though besieged by its dead that lie everywhere before the walls and do not stir and are ever increasing.

One feels the simplicity and vitality of this religion in a wonderful way here, the Prophet is like yesterday, and the city is his like a kingdom . . .

[8]

To Clara Rilke S.S. Rameses the Great, Luxor
January 18, 1911

We are having three days in Luxor, today was the second, all of tomorrow still; but one ought to be here much longer, not be obliged to see just for the sake later of having seen a lot. On the eastern (Arabian) bank, against which we are lying, is the temple of Luxor with the high colonnade of budlike lotus columns, a half hour farther on that incomprehensible temple world of Karnak which I saw the very first evening and yesterday once more, in the moon just beginning to wane, saw, saw, saw,—dear Heaven, one summons up one's strength, looks with all the will to believe of two focused eyes—and still it begins above them, extends everywhere beyond them (only a god can work such a field of vision)—there stands a calyx column, solitary, surviving, and one does not encompass it, so out beyond one's life does it stand, only together with the night can one somehow take it in, perceiving it all of a piece with the stars, whence it becomes human for a second—human experience. And just think, that over there to the west above the two arms of the Nile and the corn lands, tower the Libyan Mountains, blossoming by the desert light; we rode today through the mighty valley in which the kings rest, each beneath the weight of a whole mountain, upon which the whole pressure of the sun lies too, as if it were beyond strength to suppress kings.

No, your experience here, when I think of your letters, was almost complete, I do not scorn it at all; imagine, at the recumbent Rameses in the palm grove at Sakkhara I already had the feeling I could turn back; now it has long since been too much, and one must study Arabic industriously and feel unhappy on donkeys, for the sake of the counterbalance. And you did see the Cairo Museum (nothing like the Rameses the Sixth with the fettered Libyan is anywhere in any of the temples—) . . .

[9]

To Prince Alexander von
Thurn und Taxis
Hotel Al Hayat, Heluan (Cairo)
February 28, 1911

. . . As for me, I can indeed say that much joy has passed through my eyes; I am so slow inwardly that I do not know what I am bringing with me and whether a kind of order and new life can be made of it. I know only that in these countries, which live, as it were, into themselves, one ought not to travel this way any more without a quite precise aim, I might almost say: without a very obvious excuse; one falls in with the do-nothings as against the natives; curiosity, which once, when few people traveled, was something delicate, almost expert, has become vulgar since it is no longer honest and no longer laborious. One is all the time fighting against a false situation and in the end deprives oneself of the right to look anywhere—; one would like blindly to take upon oneself and perform some native function or hardship for the sake of balance. To me it does seem that as regards the Orientals in particular only the former, solitary, painstaking traveler was possible; it is grotesque to confront this difficult, self-absorbed and toiling world as an onlooker unoccupied and sheltered . . .

[10]

To Princess Marie von Thurn
und Taxis-Hohenlohe
77 rue de Varenne, Paris
May 10, 1911

Alas, my dear Princess, my slowness is getting worse and worse, only now am I writing you. When I came here it was snowing, now the lilacs are almost over, the red and white thorn is peopled with blossoms, and tomorrow or day after tomorrow the blossoming cities and towers will stand in the full greenness of the chestnuts: how much Nature has done! And how much people do,— I don't know what they do, but for the most part they look busy or at least in love, they are on the go, I am sure they are accomplishing all sorts of things, they play their parts, they write letters, and with it all there is still time left over, stubborn time, which they set upon noisily as one would upon a clown, just to be rid of it. Everything catches up with me, time continually steals a march on me, I look at it from behind like a straggler, like a marauder; the devil, when will this stop?

Now do not think I am complaining or that Paris disappoints me. On the contrary, I find it just as full again and inwardly alive, just as one with the spring, of which it makes all that a beautiful woman can make of a dress she wears with pleasure and in a self-assured hour. If we could take a few excursions together here such as we did in Venice, you would show me much that I do not see for sheer redundance, and I would tell you things. Picture to yourself, Princess, that in addition the most important exhibitions are crowding upon one, that the most beautiful Ingres are being shown to one, glorious Rembrandts, pages with clear Persian illuminations; that out in Marly in his primitive garden Maillol is exhibiting his sculptures and that one cannot go out there without seeing countless woods in their youth beneath the skies inclining toward them and paths, on every one of which one would like to walk, they call so to one, so easy does it seem to advance on them, as if they really went and one had only to abandon oneself to them in order next moment to be far away, rustic, free. Tell me yourself, Princess, whether you should not be here? . . .

[11]

To Frau Lili Schalk   77 rue de Varenne, Paris
                                                                              May 14, 1911

You will not imagine that such great interruptions can tear open in a life, though you know how, for us, from the one solution, world, ability and inability keep precipitating separately, how with every emotion we have gone through both, accustoming ourselves to be open at the moment when the outside turned void, and being *closed* and bound when a season, a person, a god wanted to be lavish with us.—All this you know, with a glance we would agree on it, but I do not know whether, even if you were here, I could make clear to you why life for me has grown to such difficulty and dimness that I never wanted to write about myself. I shrank, before those who want to listen, from saying "I" and there was no word that brought with it more vagueness, and you would certainly have linked it with too large ideas, so that a letter would have slipped away in deducting, retracting and denying, without conveying even the suggestion of any qualifying interpretation.

Today, Sunday, I am rereading your letter of November 17 and see in the little bit of courage I feel to write you almost an indication that things will get better with me. I remember that on the day your letter arrived here, I set out on the long journey from which I only returned around Easter: word of it will have reached you; so I really was in Algiers, in Tunis, finally in Egypt, but it would have served me right if everywhere before the greatest external objects I had opened Saint Augustine to the passage that strikes home to Petrarch when, up there on Mont Ventoux, opening with curiosity the familiar little book, he finds nothing but the reproach of turning his eyes from himself to mountains, oceans and distances. So much a pretext was this journey, in which I let myself be taken along, and like a pretext that one has indulgently let pass, it also lies behind me, not really solid and maintainable; the multitude and often the prodigiousness of what was before my eyes, about me, beside me, existence against existence, impressed itself manifoldly upon me, but my taking some of it to myself as increase will perhaps be achieved only later, much later.

You write of Malte Laurids. That difficult, difficult book. Do you know that sometimes, as I was getting toward the end, it appeared to me so hard and so definitive a charge, that in it I seemed to be clutching all my tasks together and running them into me, like that single man who in hand-to-hand fighting takes on all the lances opposed to him, as far as he can reach, and in himself renders them harmless to all the rest? As soon as I tried in those days to look out beyond that work, I saw myself on the far side of it doing something quite different, never writing again. Now I have hesitated after all to try something else that I haven't learned, and have thereby come into a stagnancy where there is no current. Can you understand that? And tell me whether one of these is arrogant and which one: "to give up" work, to step aside as though something had already been accomplished, or, through all the aridity, to persist in it because all that it realized was indeed scarcely even the beginning of that to which one deemed oneself boundlessly committed?

I am writing, writing—, but do you really want suddenly to read all this? By means of it I make any third person and all rumor superfluous for a long time, and you see "where I stand". And so it is an advance at any rate, though by far no reunion. Will this year afford one? I hear of lots of people who are coming here or are here, and I myself am still wholly on the side of Paris and gaze at it in astonishment when it takes spring and deals with it as its own possession. Many things I would like to show you, tell you much.

[*12*]

To Princess Marie von Thurn
und Taxis-Hohenlohe   77 rue de Varenne, Paris
                                         May 16, 1911

By this mail, kindest Princess, I am sending you the certain sermon on Mary Magdalene and the Guérin Centaur; it is entirely selfish and forward of me to impose upon you in my German, before it has come into your hands in French, this vehement poem, which turns to the reader almost no surface but only fragments of its immense substance. But you see, I am so impressed at once again having anything at all that I cannot restrain myself from quickly communicating it to you, even though it is but a probably quite superfluous imitation.

I am taking counsel with myself a great deal as to why I am still not working, it should be time, this long drought is really reducing my soul little by little to famine. How does something like that come to pass? It is as if I had completely lost the ability to bring within reach the conditions that can help me; when I grasp at any, there are new aggravations and evasions, the days pass by, and with them who knows how much life. Shouldn't one invent some grotesque figure just in order finally to introduce the sentence: "He spent the last six or seven years fastening a coat button that kept coming undone"? . . .

I am prattling, Princess, don't listen, in reality I console myself that it is the bad conditions of my apartment, which takes on no body warmth and removes me too far from the Luxembourg and the whole quarter up there. As soon as I catch the air of those old streets and the happy quality from the incomparable garden I muster up all kinds of courage and feeling—, and if God wills, I shall dwell my way through to it again and amount to something after all.

Evenings I am reading in the letters of Eugénie de Guérin; it is moving, the way she kept up her life, that continued to be still and eventless, for her brother, so that for him, who also isolated himself in this remarkable city, this little fervent light should always burn, an eternal lamp before the dark image of his soul in which often nothing was recognizable. It is only too bad that provincial piety was so ready and present in her right from the beginning; I cannot comprehend religious natures who accept and follow God as given and sense him with their feeling without trying their hand at him creatively.

I think a great, great, great deal of Lautschin, of the woodland paths, of a certain spot in the park that I love very much. Only I am a little afraid we might one day meet a dried-up little centaur that has after all perfidiously and scantly survived Guérin's in permanent stuntedness. . . .

[13]

To Helene von Nostitz Grand Hotel Continental, Munich
September 14, 1911

A stream of business affairs, imagine, carried me away from Leipzig ahead of time and alas! far out of Auerbach's vicinity: your letter just reached me in Berlin, a few hours afterward I was traveling farther, and now I am quickly saving out this moment to thank you. The knowledge that I was almost expected at your house is dear and heart-warming to me, and even the possibility that under certain circumstances I could not be, is of so good and happy a nature that from part and counterpart I derive joy equally.

In Lautschin, shortly after my departure thence, a dear welcome grandchild also came into the summer world, and I had the feeling that this long season so assured in itself was quite particularly friendly and fitting as preparation and anticipation of that event.

We then drove in the auto from the heart of Bohemia to Leipzig, indeed on to Weimar, which I saw again still quite in the light of my former being-with-you; to be sure, I did not find it so unqualifiedly beautiful—preserved in its old essence rather than existing and quite worn out by the unyielding summer—, but, since feeling did not remain everything, I came all the more readily this time to all sorts of knowledge and insight, one or two figures seemed bright to me on their Goethe-facing side, in the Archive I read a magnificent letter of Bettina's and found that page on which Goethe in such a wonderful sudden flow wrote: *Everything proclaims Thee.* Besides this, I saw Tiefurt, the modest,—and saw Belvedere again and felt most directly in the Wittumspalais whatever echo of mutual hours of reading may still be dying away about Duchess Anna Amalia's big evening table. There a little experience befell me: as we entered the blue salon (next the ballroom) upstairs, I moved away from the group of people keeping together before a picture and had the surprise of seeing, from one of the draped, dimly shining windows, a big, beautiful, dark butterfly coming somehow significantly and expressly toward me (I instinctively turned round, no one had noticed it); it moved on slowly and complacently in the stillness, turned, lingered at a sunny spot in the air and sailed then, so very alone and adequate (heavy in its lightness as the glance of a dark eye), right through the open folding-door into the beautiful ballroom, after a time veered resolutely off there, vanished toward the left and, when we all moved around there in a while, was nowhere to be seen. All that transpired in so singularly detailed a way, passed in its bit of time so slowly, that it was as timeless as it was intimate, charming-serious, full of special tidings—, I wanted to tell you about it, perhaps Weimar is to be recognized in it and greets you in this way. . . .

I have just seen Hofmannsthal, in the old Pinakothek, in a room of indescribably beautiful Greco pictures, by the great and distinctive presence of which one was so fascinated that we rather promised to see each other again than actually saw each other. From here, in a few days, I must move on, perhaps by some little roundabout way, toward Paris, and only there will it develop how and whither, for staying does not seem very probable to me for the present, I still have much too much rusticity in me to start wintering in a city yet.

[*14*]

To Frau Elsa Bruckmann   Duino, Nabresina, Austrian Littoral
December 14, 1911

Since I have been here (7 weeks by the calendar), your name has been on my letter list, I am truly ashamed that you got ahead of me. In view of my negligence this will perhaps repeat itself sometimes, only you must not give in to the suspicion that I could have forgotten you. Absolutely not; you felt in the fall how much I liked being with you, and that settles it, also in spirit, also in thought.

I have a lovely picture of going over into a new year at your home, with you; with you one so often gets into the new, even in the middle of the year, so that currents would be summed up and we would glide, as through rapids, through the particular midnight that decides the matter. And really, I would need some such guarantee so as to drift into an actually *new* year; in the last ones I have been cheated, they were only remis à neuf when I began them, already on the second day bad spots showed, they were years cast off by Heaven knows what gentlemen, which our Lord, who is being frightfully economical with me now, deemed still wearable. Yes, but one couldn't parade in them.

So inclination, you see, is not lacking, and yet in all probability I shall have to try right here to clamber in the dark and all alone over the crest of the year, so to speak for disciplinary reasons. I shall not deserve it otherwise, that is; I have long wanted to be here alone, strictly alone, to go into my cocoon, to pull myself together, in short, to live by my heart and by nothing else. Now since day before yesterday I have really been all alone inside the old walls—outside, the sea, outside, the Karst, outside, the rain, perhaps tomorrow the storm—: now must appear what is within by way of counterweight to such great and fundamental things. So, if something quite unexpected does not come, it may be the right thing to stay, to hold out, to hold still with a kind of curiosity toward oneself, don't you think? That is how things stand, and if I stir now everything will shift again; and then hearts are labeled, like certain medicines: shake before taking; I have been continually shaken in these last years, but never taken, that is why it is better that I should quietly arrive at clarity and precipitation. . . .

[15]

To N. N.   (*temporarily*) Duino Castle near Nabresina,
                              Austrian Littoral
                              December 26, 1911

. . . Friend of your friend: you were not mistaken about it, this poetry, together with the few words about its author, could not but appeal to me, yes, somehow touch me—, why shouldn't

I say so. And yet I decline, absolutely decline to try influencing him in any way or even, as you express it, to be destiny for him. Don't you feel yourself that one must really wish nothing for him so much as that, for a long time yet, *nothing* may become destiny for him, that he may blindly invest his heart here and there and try it out and not know whether this is already the path or simply the heath still that is full of directions. You see, I wouldn't be able to name to him the place from whence he may continue. Perhaps this poetry is a scheme of his experiences, perhaps everything to come will be an ever new, ever differently arranged casting of these roles; perhaps with it too this particular plot has been conquered, so that everything to come will presuppose it and begin where it ends—I do not know. Who of us can know? Not even you, friend of your friend, are quite sure; but I surmise that if anyone can offer him the certainties, temporary and yet infinitely valid, without which he will not be able to get along—, it is you; have courage for him, and there will be much comfort and protection and thus life will go on.

Whether for him it will go on through art? What one writes at twenty-one is a cry,—does one think of a cry whether it ought to have been cried differently? The language is still so thin about one in these years, the cry pierces through and just takes along what is left clinging to it. The development will always be this, that one makes one's language fuller, thicker, firmer (heavier), and of course there is sense in that only for one who is sure that the cry too is growing in him ceaselessly, irresistibly, so that later, under the pressure of countless atmospheres, it will issue evenly from every pore of the almost impenetrable medium. . . .

Talent, you understand, scarcely has significance any more in our day, since a certain dexterity of expression has become general,—where is it not? Hence succeeding still means something only where the highest, utmost is achieved, and then one is again liable to think that just this unsurpassable something, once it appears in a person, is in itself successful.

And so there is no real ground for concern, only that we want never to remain behind our heart and never to be in advance of it:

that is probably needful. Thus we arrive at everything, each at what is his.

[*16*]

To Lou Andreas-Salomé   Duino Castle near Nabresina,
                                                        Austrian Littoral
                                                        December 28, 1911

Let me imagine that you are all but waiting for a letter from me, otherwise this big sheet is not justifiable at all, and I really cannot take a smaller one. There is a chance at this time that you are at home and have quiet, it was always so between the two Christmases—, so let me tell you about things for a few pages.

About you I heard through Gebsattel in the fall, but, you can imagine, he does not reflect complete pictures, he is like one of the mirrors doctors use for examinations; so nothing whole was to be learned from him, but I did understand that things are going well with you and that agrees with everything I know about you, independently of all tidings.

You see, I am still in a hurry to get to myself, I still presume that this theme can be of interest; would you like to go into it once more? Please, please, do, I will help you, as best I can, perhaps I'll be bad at it,—in that case there is a point of departure: Malte Laurids Brigge. I need no answers to my books, that you know,—but now I deeply need to know what impression this book made on you. Our good Ellen Key naturally confused me promptly with Malte and gave me up; yet no one but you, dear Lou, can distinguish and indicate whether and how much he resembles me. Whether he, who is of course in part made out of my dangers, goes under in it, in a sense to spare me the going under, or whether with these journals I have really got for fair into the current that is tearing me away and driving me across. Can you understand that after this book I have been left behind just like a survivor, helpless in my inmost soul, no longer to be used? The nearer I came to the end of writing it, the more strongly did I feel that it would be an indescribable division, a high watershed, as I kept telling myself; but now it turns out that all the water has flowed off toward the old side and I am going down into an aridity that will not change. And if it were merely that: but the other fellow, the one who went under, has somehow used me up, carried on the immense expenditure of his going under with the strength and materials of my life, there is nothing that was not in his hands, in his heart, he appropriated everything with the intensity of his despair; scarcely does a thing seem new to me before I discover the break in it, the rough place where he tore himself off. Perhaps this book had to be written as one sets a mine; perhaps I should have jumped way away from it the moment it was finished. But I suppose I still cling too much to possession and cannot achieve measureless poverty, much as that is probably my crucial task. My ambition was such that I put my entire capital into a lost cause, but on the other hand its values could become visible only in this loss, and that is why, I remember, Malte Laurids appeared to me for the longest time not so much as a going under, rather as a singularly dark ascension into a remote neglected part of heaven.

It is almost two years: dear Lou, you alone will be able to grasp how falsely and precariously I have spent them. I thought when they began I had a long, long patience; how often since then have I patched it, what all have I not shredded and tied on. I have gone through so much that was confusing, experiences like that of Rodin simply going wrong in his seventieth year, as though all his endless work had not been; as though something paltry, some sticky trifle, such as he had surely pushed out of his way by the dozen before, not leaving himself time really to get through with them, had lain in wait there and overwhelmed him easily and now day by day is making his old age into something grotesque and ridiculous—, what am I to make of that sort of experience? A moment of weariness, a few days of slackening sufficed then, and life rose up about him as unachieved as about a school boy and drove him, just as he was, into the nearest wretched snare. What am *I* to say, with the little bit of work out of which I keep falling completely, if *he* wasn't saved? Shall I wonder that life-sized life treats me downright scornfully in such interims, and what in all the world *is* this work if in it one cannot go through and learn everything, if one hangs around outside it allowing oneself to be shoved and pushed, grabbed and let go, becoming involved in happiness and wrong and never understanding anything.

Dear Lou, I am in a bad way when I wait for people, need people, look around for people: that only drives me still further into the more turbid and puts me in the wrong; they cannot know how little trouble, really, I take with them, and of what ruthlessness I am capable. So it is a bad sign that since Malte I have often hoped for someone who would be there for me; how does that happen? I had a ceaseless longing to bring my solitude under shelter with someone, to put it in someone's protection; you can imagine that in those conditions nothing made any progress. With a kind of shame I think of my best Paris time, that of the *New Poems*, when I expected nothing and no one and more and more the whole world streamed toward me merely as a task and I replied clearly and surely with pure work. Who would have told me then that so many relapses were before me! I waken every morning with a cold shoulder, there, where the hand should lay hold that shakes me. How is it possible that now, prepared and schooled for expression, I am left in fact without a vocation, superfluous? In the years when Ilya of Múrom sprang up, I sit myself down and wait, and my heart knows of no occupation for me. What will you say, Lou, when you read this? Did you foresee it? I remember a passage from your last letter, which I haven't here: "you are still going so far," you wrote. And if not,—what is to be done in order not to go bad in the standstill? What is to be done?

I am thinking less than before of a doctor. Psychoanalysis is too basic a help for me, it helps once and for all, it clears out, and to find myself cleared out one day would perhaps be even more hopeless than this disorder.

On the other hand I still busy myself from time to time with the idea of pursuing a few subjects consistently at a little country university.—You smile, you are familiar with that, yes, there is little that is new with me, and the worst of it is that certain of my plans and perhaps even my best and worst qualities have sense only with relation to a certain age and beyond that are simply absurd. Indeed it is almost too late even for the university, but you know what I mean by that; the terrible thing about art is that the further one gets in it, the more it commits one to the highest, almost impossible; here enters in spiritually what in another sense the woman in the Baudelaire poem means who in the great stillness of the full-moon night suddenly bursts out: que c'est un dur métier que d'être belle femme.

Here, Lou, is another of my confessions. Are the symptoms those of the long convalescence which my life is? Are they signs of a new sickness? I wish I could be with you once for a week, to hear and to tell. It has been so long. I get about so much, shouldn't it be possible to meet sometime?

Do you know that last winter I was in Algiers, Tunis and Egypt? Unfortunately under conditions so little suited to me that I lost my seat and bearing and finally followed along just like someone a runaway horse has thrown off and drags along up and down in the stirrup. That wasn't the right thing. But a little Orient was instilled into me anyway, on the Nile boat I even went in for Arabic, and the museum in Cairo perhaps made something of me after all, confused as I was on entering.

This year I am enjoying the hospitality of friends here (for the time being all alone) in this strong old castle that holds one a little like a prisoner; it cannot do otherwise with its immense walls. And at least the practical disorder in my affairs will benefit by my being taken care of here for a few months. Beyond that I know nothing and want to know nothing.

Goodbye, dear Lou, God knows, your being was so truly the door by which I first came into the open; now I keep coming from time to time and place myself straight against the doorpost on which we marked my growth in those days. Allow me this dear habit and love me.

Rainer.

[17]

To Lou Andreas-Salomé   Duino near Nabresina, Austrian Littoral
January 10, 1912

The elder Prince Taxis was here, I have been alone again only a few days, am now at last thanking you for your good letter. I have, you may believe me, read much between the words, I walked up and down in the garden with it as with something that one wants to learn by heart, what would I do without this voice: yours? I cannot tell you how intimate and comforting it was to me, I am the lone little ant that has lost its head, but you see the anthill and assure me it is intact and I will find my way into it again and make myself useful. And on top of everything came the surprise that you know this coast, so that your letter, as it were, applied not only to me but also to my surroundings, addressed itself to everything and was right for everything. You are right, it has probably always been like this with me, but, you see, I tire myself out with it; as someone who walks on crutches always rubs his coat through first under the armpits, so my one-sidedly worn nature will, I fear, one day have holes and yet at other places be like new. These last years it has often seemed to me as though many workers in art had got hold of themselves by outwitting and exploiting their own inadequacies of which they were aware, rather as they would have made use of a weakness recognized in someone else. I am too much on the side of my nature, I have never wanted anything of it that it did not dispense magnanimously and happily out of its innermost impulses, almost out beyond me. And by the other road the most that is accomplished is that one can always write; that I don't care about. What weighs upon me this time is not even so much the length of the pause perhaps, but rather a kind of dulling, a kind of growing old, if one should call it that, as though what is strongest in me had really been damaged somehow, were just a bit guilty, were atmosphere, do you understand: air instead of universal space. It may be that this continual inner distraction in which I live has in part physical causes, is a thinness of the blood; whenever I notice it, it still becomes a reproach to me for having let it get so far. No matter what is before me: I still get up every day with the doubt whether I shall succeed in doing it, and this distrust has become big from the actual experience that weeks, even months can go by in which I produce only with extreme effort five lines of a quite indifferent letter, which, when they are finally there, leave an aftertaste of incompetence such as a cripple might feel who can't even shake hands any more.

Shall I go on through all that nevertheless? Then if people chance to be present, they offer me the relief of being able to be more or less the person they take me for, without being too particular about my really existing. How often does it not happen that I step out of my room somehow like a chaos, and outside, someone being aware of me, find a poise that is actually his, and the next moment, to my amazement, am expressing well-formed things, while just before everything in my entire consciousness was utterly amorphous. To whom am I saying this, dear Lou, indeed it is almost through you that I know it is so, you see how little has changed,—and in this sense people will always be the false way for me, something that galvanizes my lifelessness, without remedying it. Alas, my dear, I do know so well that my earliest instinct was the definitive one, I don't want to do anything whatever against it, but as it is I have been placed among people and have felt real influences from them and have worked myself into them like one of them. I am not even mentioning that in a certain year when things weren't going on at all or rather couldn't begin anywhere (for there was simply nothing there yet), you came—: that can be only once, just as there is only one birth,—but I have other single memories in the human sphere to which I cling,— when one puts them into words, they are quite insignificant, as to content, and yet, will you believe me, in the long complicated solitude, often carried to the extreme, in which Malte Laurids was written, I felt perfectly certain that the strength by which I defrayed his cost stemmed to an important extent from certain evenings on Capri on which nothing happened except that I sat by two elderly women and a young girl and watched their needlework and sometimes at the end was given an apple peeled by one of them. There was no trace of destiny between us, it was never even investigated just how far *these* people were necessary in order that that should come into being which was born there; name it has none, but I experienced from it something almost of the mystical way of nourishment that is the Communion; while it was still going on, I knew that it was giving me strength and later, in the laborious solitude, I recognized these powers among all others; it was strange, they held out longest.

Dear Lou, when I wrote recently that I was almost hoping for people, I meant that since then I have not again experienced this and need it infinitely. Can't you imagine that there is some human being who is able to give this, spontaneously, unintentionally, and who would be content to irradiate mere presence and expect nothing? There are even people who do that for the sick where all care leads at best to health, while here it would begin as it were with the healthiest and reach God knows whither. It isn't in times like these bad ones that this need of mine developed; during the immense concentration which carried through the *New Poems*, it acquired contour and in a sense I finished the writing of the Brigge as though on condition that this would come true. I will demonstrate it to you by something quite concrete. Imagine that I think with the same anguish of trying again in the rue Cassette with a little furnished room, or of returning among my own furniture, which in recent years has turned completely into the scenery indicated for the last act of Malte Laurids. Ridiculous as it is, I undergo all these things like destinies, and that is why they have once been so fundamentally gone through and cannot be begun again. Do you understand that I picture a creature who would make the things exaggerated by me ordinary and guileless once more? Is there no such person? One might think I was experiencing what happened in the fable: that I had simply sung instead of building, and was left now, when it is getting cold, without shelter. But no, you see, what I am thinking of could not have been built in any case, it would be absolutely miraculous, and I would have no right to count on it had not everything decisive in my life been just as independent of my provision and in no wise possible to prepare and to lay foundations for. Perhaps everyone who hears of this will first ask with what I, for my part, intend to achieve such a relationship; there I must own that I really can respond with nothing, save perhaps with my own warmer and happier existence, as it may possibly have revealed itself to those women too that time in Capri. I believe in Naples once, before some ancient tombstone, it flashed through me that I should never touch people with gestures stronger than those there portrayed. And I really believe I am sometimes far enough along to express all the insistence of my heart without loss and fatality when I lay my hand lightly on a shoulder. Wouldn't that, Lou, wouldn't that be the only advance thinkable within that "restraint" of which you remind me?

It is three-thirty, I have scarcely eaten, I am spending almost all day writing to you, and yet it is so hard to make it understandable that my head is buzzing; I make hardly any progress, I keep wanting to begin again and say everything over once more,—but to what purpose, I do not want to convince you. Only you should know what I meant by "human beings": not a giving away of solitude; only, if that solitude weren't so suspended in air, if it came into good hands, would it entirely lose the accompanying tones of morbidity (that will sooner or later be inevitable anyhow), and I would finally achieve some sort of continuity within it instead of carrying it like a filched bone from bush to bush amid loud halloos.

There,—your old mole has shown you some digging again and thrown up a lot of dark earth right across a good road. Forgive me. To you I speak such inward things, like the people in the Old Testament, an entire scroll: for what stands there in the burning thornbush of your life is exactly what shall have power over me too.

Dear Lou, if it works, I shall probably stay here into the spring, although neither the house nor the climate really suits me; this continual shift between bora and sirocco is not good for my nerves, and I exhaust myself participating first in one and then in the other. Nevertheless when I add up the individual advantages of this refuge, it comes to a large sum and I must count myself fortunate in having it. In my present state any place would have been difficult for me, but not everywhere could I have gone so to the bottom of my condition as here. It is only too bad that Nature here offers me almost nothing, even the ocean leaves me indifferent; as if this stupid Austrian polyglotism took away even from the landscape its unified, unequivocal expression. I can hardly say how repugnant everything Austrian is to me. I long for Naples, or I would like to walk for hours in the snow through woods and afterwards drink delicious coffee with you. But it will be all right anyway . . .

[*18*]

To Countess
Manon zu Solms-Laubach   Duino Castle near Nabresina,
                                Austrian Littoral
                                January 12, 1912

. . . It is splendid that you have taken such strong and wide-spreading root in the fine tasks your dear little pupil ceaselessly offers you; from all you say of them emanates the vibration evenly transmitted to all sides by any deep pure activity, like the vibration of a bell rung for sheer joy. One just can't help becoming a little more cheerful and courageous for it; so much does all that is reliable and constant in life come together in experiences like that.

The work of the artist has many dangers and often does not let one make out so clearly in detail whether one is going ahead or being driven back by the pressure of the too great forces with which one has become involved. Then it is a matter of waiting and holding out, and this has always been very difficult for me because I have neglected everything outside of work, so that in such interims I lack everything, even the place where a crisis like that might be got over. Probably I have never watched more passionately than in the past year those who are engaged in something good, regular, that one is always "able to do", something more dependent upon understanding, thought, insight, experience—what you will—than upon those powerful tensions of inner living over which no one has control. They are not exaltations, surely not, or they could not effect something so indescribably real in the spiritual realm, but in their onrush and in their rebound they are of such extravagance that one might often think the heart cannot endure anything so extreme in both directions. In *your* reality there are certainly not inferior forces, but they are differently distributed, fortunately; I can scarcely conceive at all any more of a woman being able to pursue art without violating her nature; we are already a shade more removed, more estranged, more derived. Hence we manage it somehow. Only by a very wide detour probably can art proceed from Nature,—not without despair, I might say, not without original sin. Think of your mosses—: from that there keeps springing, if one lets them act on one, only joy, admiration, pure rapture, affirmation of life, a kind of emulation in existence—, but not art, not art . . .

[*19*]

To Emil Baron von Gebsattel　　　　Duino Castle near Nabresina,
　　　　　　　　　　　　　　　　　　　Austrian Littoral
　　　　　　　　　　　　　　　　　　　January 14, 1912

Dear friend, we haven't written each other at all since Munich, I know that isn't troubling you, but now for once I do want quickly to avail myself of the Sunday evening to ask about you and to communicate myself to you.

How have things gone since then? I would have many questions. Were you to reply with more, I could tell you that I have been here since the end of October, but only since quite recently alone, which after all was what was really intended. Over this new little while naturally I haven't yet managed to accomplish anything—, against the circumstances there is little to say; at most, that the climate, an incessant shifting between the extremes of sirocco and bora, is not exactly ideal for the inner steadiness I wish for myself. Hence not really entirely beneficial,—but on the other hand the advantages are so many that, if I manage at all well, I can still arrive at a kind of profit here. Just through the thorough solitude. The castle is an immense body without much soul: obsessed with the idea of its own firmness, it holds one by its inwardly directed gravitation like a prisoner; it is a rather austere dwelling. Along the steep cliffs, from the sea, an ever-green garden climbs up to it, otherwise any green is rare, we are in the Karst, and the hardened mountains forego the effeminacy of any vegetation.

So much for the externals. Of what is within me there is scarcely anything yet to say—, I long for work, sometimes I think for a moment it is longing for me too—, but we do not meet. The fact that I have no plans is agreeable to me rather than disquieting. The other day the furniture at last left the memorable, the tiresome, the strange house in the rue de Varenne and is waiting for my future in a garde-meubles . . . Marthe,—(of her I hear only indirectly through Madame W., who, it seems, is taking a more and more lively interest in her), Marthe is learning to cook and has a talent for it, in the evening she draws and has a grasp of that too such as one would scarcely believe; occasionally she goes with Madame W. to the theater, all that is turning with her into sheer life, finds untold readinesses in her nature—, it is becoming a miracle. But I am almost too much concerned about myself and self-absorbed,—it is clear that this quiet here must bring with it some kind of decision; among all that is going through my head, there is naturally analysis too. In that connection it occurs to me that we have never talked about whether you actually consider it appropriate in my case? It still seems to me that my work is really nothing but a self-treatment of the same sort, how else would I have hit upon work at all (already at the age of ten or twelve)? My wife, from whom incidentally I only rarely have short letters, thinks, if I am not mistaken, that a kind of cowardice is frightening me away from analysis, it would be in keeping (as she expresses it) with the "trusting", the "religious" side of my nature to undertake it,—but that is not right; my very religiosity, if one is to call it that, keeps me from this operation, from this great clearing out that life does not do,—from this correcting of the whole hitherto written page of life which I then imagine all rewritten in red as in a school notebook—a silly conception and surely quite false—, but that is how it looks to me.

In a letter of some time ago, shortly after my departure from Munich, my wife expressed much concerning me so precisely and correctly that I was moved by it: it is indeed true, much of me that was simply a bad habit, through which one occasionally reached as through bad air, is solidifying, is acquiring resistance and can soon have become a wall and shut me off,—I know all is not well with me, and you, dear friend, have also observed it,—but, believe me, I am still struck by nothing so much as by the incomprehensible, incredible wonderfulness of my existence, which from the very beginning was so impossibly disposed, and advanced nevertheless from salvation to salvation, as though always through the hardest stone; so that when I think of no longer writing, practically the only thing that upsets me is not to have recorded the utterly wonderful line of this life so strangely carried through. Alas, round about me I see dim destinies and hear talk of casualties and cannot help being amazed. Can you understand, my friend, that I am afraid of disturbing by any classification or survey, be it never so relieving, a much higher order whose right, after all that has happened, I would have to acknowledge, even if it were to destroy me?

You know enough of my life to turn to examples for what I mean. You are also acquainted, better than almost anyone else, with the way I have been lying here for two years, doing nothing but trying to get up, grasping now at one person, now at another, who happens along, and living on the time and the listening of those I cause to stand still before me. It is in the nature of this state to become a complete abnormality if it lasts for long, and I ask myself every day whether I am not bound at any cost to put an end to it somehow or other. And yet, you see, it was never I who made the end,—the new beginning took it incidentally, just as it was, out of my hands.

My dear friend, with all this I have now made myself amply present to you. Write sometime, tell me about things, and if you want to bring it up, let me read what you think of this creature with regard to analysis. When I go away from here, the next thing will have its turn,—won't it? I ask myself. You ask yourself sometime. Let us be prepared, and then let us let come what can, and we shall see.

[*20*]

To Lou Andreas-Salomé   Duino Castle near Nabresina,
                                                         Austrian Littoral
                                                         January 20, 1912

Don't be startled, Lou, that I am already here again: it will be only a little visit, if it doesn't suit you, put me aside until tomorrow, day after tomorrow—when you will.

Chance made me find your letter this morning and the enclosed from Gebsattel simultaneously on my writing table. I beg you, read it; here quickly the few data that will make it intelligible to you.

You understand that the thought of going through an analysis rises in me now and then; to be sure, what I know of Freud's writings is uncongenial to me and in places hair-raising; but the matter itself, which runs away with him, has its genuine and strong sides, and I can conceive of Gebsattel's using it with discretion and influence. Now as for me, I have already written you that, emotionally, I rather shun this getting cleared out and, with my nature, could hardly expect anything good of it. Something like a disinfected soul results from it, a monstrosity, alive, corrected in red like the page of a school notebook. And yet: dear Lou, as matters stand with me, I hardly have the right, out of mere feeling, to cast suspicion on a help that is right there and is holding itself in readiness. I knew more or less that Gebsattel was prepared to perform the whole excavation on me, but I had never actually asked him whether, so far as he knows me (and we had very detailed talks at a certain time in Paris and at, for me, a dim and wearisome period), the use of analysis seemed suitable for me. Hence the letter I sent him on the fifteenth of this month contained this question and at the same time a few of my scruples. The enclosed is his answer. It seems to me he is mistaken about some things; in any case it is time now, in view of his readiness, really to consider this expedient. The fact remains that from a purely physical standpoint I am quite unbearable to myself; certain bad habits, which I formerly always used to reach through as through bad air, are solidifying more and more, and I can conceive of their shutting me in someday like walls. The oversensitivity of my muscles, for example, is so great that a little gymnastics or an in any way exaggerated posture (as in shaving for instance) results at once in swelling, pains, etc., phenomena which are then followed by fears, interpretations, distresses of every sort as though they had just been waiting: I am ashamed to admit to what extent, often for weeks, this fateful circle dances about me in which one misery does the other every favor.

You know perhaps, dear Lou, that since sometime early in the year Gebsattel has had m[y] w[ife] under treatment,—with her it is a different matter, her work has never helped her, while mine, in a certain sense, was from the beginning a kind of self-treatment; though, in proportion as it has developed and become something independent, it is losing more and more of its therapeutic and considerate character and is making demands; a soul that has no alternative but to find its harmony in the immense exaggerations of art ought to be able to count on a body that does not ape it in any way and is precise and nowhere exaggerates itself. My physical being runs the risk of becoming the caricature of my spiritual being. Dear Lou, if it will not be too much for you, help me with a few words to think it over. (Under certain circumstances I would go to Munich, do a few things there at the University and at the same time attempt the analysis.) Your letter I will answer soon, thank you. You see how things go up and down with me and to and fro: what to do?

Rainer

[21]

To Annette Kolb   Duino Castle near Nabresina,
                                           Austrian Littoral
                                           January 23, 1912

Rarely am I so fortunate. Only in Paris does it occasionally happen that on the quai, with an accuracy unattainable by any sort of intention, I reach out my hand for the very book I happen to want—: so your essay comes to me with most wonderful timeliness—, I read it three times yesterday, accommodating myself more and more to it, and now fling myself upon this paper to thank you.

How often I have been on the point of pondering this very thing, as a subject it is so tremendously present, it is in the air, it issues from the pores of things—: mais moi, je ne pense guère au fond, j'avale mes pensées toutes entières sans en détailler le goût, je les ai dans mon sang avant d'en tirer le profit immédiat qui s'impose.

And then, I have no window on to people, definitively. They yield themselves to me only in so far as they themselves find words within me, and then in these recent years they have been communicating themselves to me almost solely through two figures upon which in general I base my inferences on mankind. What speaks to me of things human, immensely, with a calm of authority that makes my hearing spacious, is the phenomenon of those who have died young and, more absolutely still, more purely, more inexhaustibly: *the woman who loves.* In these two figures things human are mixed into my heart whether I will or no. They make their apearance in me both with the distinctness of the marionette (which is an exterior charged with convincing) and as finite types beyond which one cannot go, so that the natural history of their souls could be written.

Let us keep to the woman who loves,—by whom I do not so much mean St. Theresa and such magnificence as occurred along those lines,—she yields herself to my observation much more unequivocally, more purely—that is, undilutedly and (if I may express it thus) more directly—in the situation of Gaspara Stampa, the Lyonnaise Labé, certain Venetian courtesans and, above all, Marianna Alcoforado, that incomparable woman, in whose eight heavy letters woman's love is for the first time charted from point to point without display, without exaggeration or mitigation, as by the hand of a sibyl. And there, my God, we find that as a result of the unrestrainable logic of the feminine heart, this line, finished in the earthly sphere, completed, was not to be driven further unless one were able to prolong it toward the divine into the infinite. But there, in the example of that highly incidental Chamilly (whose foolish vanity Nature made use of to obtain the letters of the Portuguese Nun), with the sublime expression of the nun: "My love is no longer dependent on the way you treat me—" the man, as a beloved, was shed, discharged, *loved through*—if one may express it so considerately, loved through as a glove is worn through. And it is a wonder that the man held out so long since he took part in love only at his thinnest places. What a sad figure he cuts in the history of love: in it he has almost no strength save the superiority tradition attributes to him, and he carries even that with a carelessness that would be simply infuriating had not his absent-mindedness and absent-heartedness often had great occasions which partially justify him. But no one will change my conviction concerning what becomes evident through this extremest lover and her ignominious partner: that this relationship definitely brings to light how much all that was achieved, borne, accomplished on the one side, the woman's, contrasts with the man's absolute inadequacy in love. She receives, to to speak, to make it tritely clear, the diploma of ability to love, while he has an elementary grammar of this discipline in his pocket from which a few words have of necessity gone into him with which he occasionally forms sentences, beautiful and rapturous as the familiar sentences on the first pages of language primers.—The case of the Portuguese Nun is so wonderfully clear because she does not fling the currents of her emotion forward into the imaginary, but rather with unending strength leads this emotion of highest order back into herself: enduring it, nothing else. She grows old in the convent, very old, she becomes no saint, not even a good nun. It goes against her rare tact to apply to God what from the beginning was not meant for him and what the Count de Chamilly had been allowed to disdain. And yet it was almost impossible to stay the heroic onrush of this love just before the leap, and still through such vibration of her innermost being not become a saint. Had she, this creature beyond measure magnificent,—yielded for a moment, she would have plunged into God like a stone into the sea, and had it pleased God to attempt with her what he constantly does with the angels, throwing their whole radiance back into them—: I am sure, she would on the spot, as she stood there, in that sad convent,—have become an angel, within, in her deepest nature.

You call me back, but I haven't got so very far from your essay. You will see at once, we are in the midst of it. Woman has gone through, achieved, carried to the end something that is her own, most her own. Man who always had the excuse of being busy with more important things, and who besides (let us say it frankly) has by no means sufficiently prepared for love, has not since antiquity (the saints excepted) troubled himself at all with love. The troubadours knew precisely how little they could risk, and Dante, in whom the need became very great, got around love only by the prodigious arc of his gigantically evasive poem. Everything else is, in this sense, derivative and second hand. But you comprehend how, given this state of my secret mind, the view from your window could not but become remarkable and exciting to me. I take your word for what you see, and for the first time since you have so brilliantly set me going, I know what I really expect. You see, I am expecting man, the man of the "new grain", who is in process, for the present, of "going to pieces", after this for him very salutary interval to take upon himself, for the next few thousand years, his own development into the "lover", a long, a difficult, for him completely new development. As for the woman, dear Fräulein Kolb, the excellent, really unique situation of your window permits the assumption that probably, withdrawn into a beautiful, self-made contour, she will find the composure, without getting bored and without too much irony, to wait for and to receive this tardy lover. . . .

[*22*]

To Lou Andreas-Salomé   Duino Castle near Nabresina,
                                               Austrian Littoral
                                               January 24, 1912

Dear Lou,

Kind heart, you *speak* to me while you write, I am so at home in the reading of your letters that, despite the ink's blackness, I don't for a moment consider excluded the little stars you mentioned—; and what is more I am so prepared for what you say by my own feeling, that first, again and again strongest feeling, which you affirm, that I am not lacking in conviction. I acted upon it even before your telegram, thanking Gebsattel with a few lines for his letter full of friendly readiness and holding out the prospect of an early answer. And one of these days I shall write him, without too much haste.

I know now that analysis would have sense for me only if I were really serious about the strange reservation of *not writing any more,* which during the finishing of Malte I often dangled before my nose as a kind of relief. Then one might have one's devils exorcised, since in ordinary social life they really are only disturbing and painful, and should the angels by some chance leave as well, one would have to construe that too as a simplification and tell oneself that in the next, the new profession (which?) there would certainly be no use for them. But am I the man for such an experiment with all the consequences of that experiment? Or is it again just a crafty piece of creative activity, to imagine oneself from tomorrow on another person, as it were, not inside a task but in one's own skin now grown shabby? For a while it comforted me in a kind of general way that one could after all do something else at any moment, in case this that was before should be over. But yet, in a strict sense, long as the interval has lasted, nothing I could now take hold of has occurred to me except just the analysis, and that of course will only delay everything once more, present matters as well as whatever comes next. You must not laugh, but for weeks, toward the conclusion of the Brigge, I had the feeling I could still become a doctor afterwards, study and then [be] a doctor somewhere in the country.—

It is a shame, a shame we cannot meet one another now on a walk, I would tell you a great, great deal. But that will come sometime. In any case it is fine, glorious for me, that you know analysis so intimately and what is more have also seen Gebsattel (who indeed practices analysis only "for a while and in a few cases", as you say).

Your letter I shall read often.

Goodbye, I want this to go off today, and therefore am closing quickly. And *thanks*. (I hope I didn't break in on your work too violently?)

Rainer

P.S.   I have quickly copied, so that something more would come back to you with this hasty scribble, two poems from a quite new little "Life of Mary".

[23]

To Baron Emil von Gebsattel   Duino Castle near Nabresina,
Austrian Littoral
January 24, 1912

Dear, good friend,

Do not take this yet as my *very last* word—: not that I plan to back out of the decision once more, only in the endeavor to be quite precise in the face of your readiness that is so great and so important to me.—This is the point: I have been entirely alone here only since the sixth of January. Now I feel that this being alone, as yet not very long, is accomplishing all kinds of things in me, daily a little more. And all I would like is to retain the possibility (if it can wait that long) of being allowed to confirm to you after a few weeks, let us say the beginning of March, what

I am trying to write you today, or else of retracting it. And I may say at once that there is more likelihood of the former.

That is to say, by the most serious deliberations I have arrived at the result that I may not allow myself the expedient of analysis, unless I were really resolved, on the far side of it, to begin a new (possibly noncreative) life, a change which during the conclusion of the M.L.B. and often since in weary moods, I did sometimes promise myself as recompense, so to speak, for everything endured. But now I must admit to myself that I was never quite serious about such plans, that rather, behind such pretexts, I do feel myself infinitely strongly bound to the once begun, to all the joy and all the misery it entails, so that, strictly speaking, I can wish for no sort of change, no interference from without, no relief, except that inherent in enduring and in final achievement. Perhaps certain of my recently expressed scruples are much exaggerated; as far as I know myself, it seems to me certain that if one were to drive out my devils, my angels too would get a little (let us say), a very little fright and—you do feel it—that is exactly what I may not risk at any cost.

What I am going through is in reality no worse than what I have put up with many other times, and with it all my patience is now so much more mature and reliable than years ago. The length of the interval might in case of need be explained by the deep division which came through the gigantic working up of material in the Brigge. But even if this were just a small part of the interim, could it not nevertheless be that for my nature there is only *one* entirely right way: to hold out? I believe I shall be from one time to the next in the position of Sinbad the Sailor, who in the fatefulness of his distresses foreswore all travel and yet ever and again made ready and set forth one day, he knew not how. So that is how matters stand, my dear friend. Your good letter contributed much toward helping me to this kind of clarity, which isn't exactly brilliant, of course: but by it one can read and write and hold out, and it would be sheer curiosity and impertinence to require more right away . . .

Enough, dear friend.

Feel through all the restrictions that paper and ink entail the good lively gratitude with which I am, with many greetings

Your

Rilke

[*24*]

To Lou Andreas-Salomé   Duino Castle near Nabresina,
                                           Austrian Littoral
                                           February 7, 1912

Yes, dear Lou, Dai Bog zhizn! And what Christ manifested with so much consideration to Angela of Foligno will always be proved in the end: that he was daily so much readier to give than she was to receive. The bad thing is only that for me now, from a purely physical point of view, the receiving affects me almost like the not-being-able to receive. Alas, old calash that I am, my springs were so fine before, and now if the miracle happens to ride in me half an hour, I am amazed that it doesn't climb out: I bump and shake like the poorest telyega and in the process almost come apart myself.

Enough. For the third day now I have been padding about a little in the snow with the longingest bare feet; for two days indeed it has been thawing; but inadvertently such a quantity had fallen that, despite the sirocco, it still hasn't all dwindled away from the garden. (I must, I believe, sometime soon have a regular winter again, one with which to tussle.)

Today, to go back to your third letter ago, I wanted to tell you a little about Kassner. But it is difficult for me to leave the man himself out of consideration, indeed, I cannot do it at all. What I read of his before I knew him was "too difficult" for me; I have read him with real insight only since he lurks behind it for me, often directly in front of it even. Isolated, as he now is more and more, he has attached himself to me with strong confidence and considers me absolutely as his friend: wherein he is certainly not mistaken, he is really the only man with whom I can get anywhere,—perhaps better so: the only one to whom it occurs to make a little use of the feminine in me. I felt, unusually purely and directly, even when I saw him for the first time years ago in Vienna, the bright radiance of his nature which *shines*, which is an out-and-out light, a brightness in space. He has something which others, seen beside him, have not, he must have attained something that others do not attain. (For the rest, by descent and origin there is nothing Jewish about or in him,—you seem to take him for a Jew?—no.) He is certainly—which he too would admit—a spiritual child of Kierkegaard. Kierkegaard comes to an end in him and goes into the circle and on. I have an idea that what his "melancholy" was for Kierkegaard, Kassner's infirmity is for him. And as it was a kind of advantage for Kierkegaard always to have, instead of so many unpredictable hindrances, only this one immense, superhuman melancholy before which he ranged himself in ever new battle formations, so Kassner too somehow prevails by the fact that all oppositions coincide for him in *one* hindrance: that procures him a concentration and a tranquillity, nothing can, so to speak, attack him from behind. But this indescribable admiration for Kierkegaard may again be linked with the fact that Kierkegaard's adversary was more mystical, more inexhaustible, more dangerous, handed down in a way from the Beyond through his father, while that which he, Kassner, spiritually overcomes at every moment is even, in a divine sense, a merit. (Kierkegaard's melancholy is still an impediment even in heaven.) Do you know Kassner's earlier essay on *Indian Idealism?* I don't know if that isn't his best. If you like, I will have it sent you sometime by Bruckmann (where, if I am not mistaken, it was published). In the beautiful chapter (yes, the most beautiful in the book) about the chimeras, I might indeed be painted in down below very small and at least kneeling, as "little originator": that is, in Paris, in certain days when we were seeing each other often, I advised him—without knowing what he happened to be writing about— just to climb up once more to the chimeras on Notre Dame, said nothing further about them—; but that must have given the touch-off and been strangely opportune. Furthermore, I can imagine that what I felt in his books before I continually drew the man himself into them—is in reality akin to what you noted in reading. But to what is it due?—If you spoke with him, I believe you would hit upon it in half an hour, me he prejudices in favor of his own meaning, you would watch him quite delightedly and form your own opinion.

A few evenings ago I read the "Chamber Plays" of the aged Strindberg; they are frightful, frightful: it is appalling that old men should close thus, like the little twenty-three-year-old dauphine whose last words were: fi de la vie,—ne m'en parlez plus. The aged Michelangelo who writes in a sonnet: what is the good of having made so many dolls? (or something similar, I know only the Italian text, and it is hard to translate). But in Strindberg there must be strengths, the strength-masses of a landslide; to have *this* world, and nevertheless to be, to achieve, that is beyond all conception. For indeed he not only speaks of this despair to which everything gives rise, he *makes* something out of it, and he makes it magnificently, that one must grant him. (Have you read these plays? Chamber Plays, George Müller, Munich-Leipzig; especially the second, third and fourth plays!) . . .

But now proshchai, how long I have written! Thanks for your letter.

[25]

To N. N.   Duino Castle near Nabresina,
                                          Austrian Littoral
                                          February 8, 1912

Now it is my turn to thank you, not for Pierrot, for mercy's sake, *no*: that would be his ruin, Pierrot's ruin, the saddest story in the world. What are you thinking of, how would I cope with his boundless homesickness?! And then, besides the distress of helplessly looking on at it, I would also have that of its being quite specially difficult for me where dogs are concerned not to sacrifice myself: they come very close to my heart, these creatures that are utterly dependent upon us, that we have helped up to a soul for which there is no heaven. Probably, although I need my whole heart, it would end, end tragically with my breaking off first little bits from the edge of my heart (as dog biscuits), for Pierrot who would be crying for you and no longer understanding life; after some hesitation, I would give up my profession and live entirely for his consolation—; you see, that would be the result—a dreadful and at the same time hopeless one, for things would remain the same, existence would be on *your* side, nowhere else,—in a word, strength fails me to paint the picture further.

So not for Pierrot. But listen to what I am thanking you for, and tell me yourself whether one may be sparing of thanks there—for the Harz Journey in Winter; not the Brahms version (I know almost no music), but for the Goethe poem, which is pure splendor. Most learned girl, still growing in wisdom every day, what will you think of me when you read that I did not know until last evening these great verses of antique moderation (for else they would withdraw from us into excess). In your letter I found the one very beautiful passage quoted, that made me curious—, that is how I came upon them. Thank you.

I must tell you that only now for the first time, little by little and with all sorts of precautions, I am acquiring admiration for Goethe which, indeed as it comes to focus, is at once the greatest too, the most unqualified. Until a short while ago I knew only very little of his work, my need never turned instinctively to him, the great is both more accessible and more kindly disposed toward me at other high places—; but this Harz Journey I henceforth count among the strongest and purest, it is one of the most authentic poems: what harm could any time do it? To be sure, one may not turn to the commentary in which the aged Goethe returns the compliment of Herr "Dr. Kannegiesser, principal of the Grammar School of Prenzlau," that is annoying, it has no more to do with the self-sufficing verses than the scribbling of visitors on the stones of the Strassburg cathedral with the pre-eminent existence of that church.

But now I will quickly tell you further that I too had an encounter with Brahms, years and years ago, in Aussee. I was then just an ordinary boy, sixteen or seventeen perhaps, and was visiting a cousin there who was ill, which may explain the fact that one sat sulkily in the garden all the time and reciprocally eked out the boredom until it reached around the entire day. But I, as soon as they took their eyes off me, withdrew from this pious occupation and so too one afternoon tore out of the village, like something that had broken loose, into the Open, the Great, the Real, presumably without a hat, or at any rate, if there was one, it played no part. The going was rather stony up the slope, but I had taken such a flying start that I was as little aware of that as of any other resistance; I dashed ahead in such elemental fashion that my effort ceased to be something personal, to express it one would have had to say simply: *it* ran, as one says: it rains, it lightens. Both in fact were immediately impending. What convinced me of it most unexpectedly was a stout old gentleman coming comfortably down the slope, who had apparently been figuring out for some time the mildest way of managing our collision; to avert it entirely was, given the initial speed with which I had rushed out, and in view of the slow breadth of the man facing me, physically impossible. So it came about that, growling suddenly, he warded me off; he had reason enough to curse me, and as I looked up at him thoroughly frightened, I had the impression that he was very cross. But as our glances measured each other, for a while, this displeasure dissolved into a gentle buzzing that finally passed into a warning about a darkly gathered storm which he pointed out behind him: and really it was already driving threateningly from across the mountains.

Now it would be fine and proper if I had first apologized and then thanked him very much for the generous solicitude expended on me despite everything,—but, alas, my memory, to be quite truthful, passes on to me no such details. It is more probable that, stammering something or other confusedly, I dodged to the right and stormed on like one crazy, for only now it seemed to me boundlessly free and almost heroic to run into this upraised storm, while beside me the stones were already turning pale.—That is my story. A few days afterward they showed me the old gentleman in the town, on the promenade, and told me his name: Brahms. But I don't think he saw me (fortunately).

[*26*]

To Lou Andreas-Salomé   Duino Castle near Nabresina,
                                           Austrian Littoral
                                           February 19, 1912

. . . Recently I happened to be writing a few words to my grandmother (on the maternal side), who was beginning her eighty-second or eighty-third year; but what coarse material there; simply that it can't wear out, otherwise no mystery. I saw her in the summer in Prague for a moment: like ravening hunger, in children at table, there is in her a robust, an almost Flemish joy in being here,—one has to put it like that; she cannot stop. Life has attempted violent jokes on her, but, like clowns, she never understood anything but the bang,—and so it did her no harm. Even now, when my mother, who at times can scarcely walk, orders herself a carriage in Prague, she still manages to come down quickly and on foot, in the gayest mood, from her distant and poor suburban apartment, for the sheer physical joy of going along, no matter whither. To me she is alien in her joyful durability, the way even as a child everything in her then still rich and well-kept house was another world to me. (How unfamiliarly, I still remember, the soup spoons went into one's mouth at occasional family dinners.) For the rest, there must be in my mother's almost entirely used-up nature a few such firm threads that are still holding; it is scarcely comprehensible the way, with her existence all filled up with sufferings and devotions as well as with distractions, she retains a taste for life, is indeed just getting trustfully attached to it. If one could sometime arrive at a little peace and composure, it would also certainly be possible to understand, describe, possibly admire that and the whole unexplained phenomenon of her personality. But in my situation this too proves an uneasiness to me, as so often, seeing at this natural place a figure so vague, for which even now, in my more experienced heart, no sort of real feeling can be developed.

Dear Lou, yes, after the "enough" of recently there was ample progress in thoughts and conditions; then some comfort came in the course of the week from an unexpected quarter: looking up the way Goethe really took Venice, I suddenly read, among the most remarkable impressions, the whole Italian Journey, the Campaign in France, the Siege of Mainz, and would have had no objection to its going on that way. The ban against him was already broken in July when I came upon the youthful, charmingly emotional letters to "Gustgen" Stolberg; but then the "Journey in Italy" became out-and-out moving to me by reason of the seriousness, the caution, the labor with which a person spoiled by the happiness of producing, at the border of youth and in contact with things so long foregone, so in the right, attempts to win for himself new, more independent incentives to happiness. I sometimes sensed in the reading that this manifold learned appropriating was not without melancholy, not without a feeling of farewell, subsequently, perhaps, not without despair and that here in his way he went through the very thing I always missed in him. I am amazed at how everything comes in its own time and is not to be forced, but then is not to be held back either. For the rest I read Venetian history all day, sometime I will tell you to what end. Unfortunately here too I begin with the disgrace of having clear forgotten everything I read for it earlier, gone, not a trace. Now farewell. Greet the sandals for me, those good sandals,—they should not give up counting on me.

[27]

To N.N.   Duino Castle near Nabresina, Austrian Littoral
                        February 24, 1912

I know—, dear child, and that is the way I took it right away, as you recommend, after that doubt forgot that letter, I am just now tearing it up, but in my consciousness it never properly existed. I forgot it and looked forward to your next, and now that is here.

I have little time, books lie open all around me, my thoughts will shortly want to return to them—, but I want to thank you at once for so well and honestly going through what I somehow conjured up and for coming back now to communicate frankly with me. Surely we are not meant to set ourselves the difficult things; yes, be the child as which I at once addressed you and whom I asked to write me when she feels happy and moved to do so, because after all it would be utterly senseless not to give in to this joy. We don't know each other, but we have a lot of confidence in each other, that gives space enough to meet in a general way, yet precisely.

And now let me say something to you. As I did your friend recently when I answered a letter of his, it seems to me I must now warn you too, in another sense, against Malte Laurids Brigge. Do not get too involved with him, and above all never overlook the fact that his dejections transfer themselves as such to the reader *only* because the pure innocent power that breaks forth in them is accidentally (this is strictly speaking scarcely more than accident) introduced in the course of a downfall. That poor Malte is wrecked by it is his affair and need not trouble us further. Of importance is only that the too-great should not disdain to consort with us so familiarly; this is, as they would have said at a certain period, the moral of the book, the justification for its existence. These journals, in applying a measure to very far-developed sufferings, indicate to what height the bliss could mount that would be achievable with the fullness of these same powers.

Isn't it wonderful, firstly, to be assured that love can lead to such strength, that in the most real sense something is meant by it which entirely surpasses us, and that the heart has nevertheless the daring to venture on this thing-that-goes-beyond-us, this storm for which a whole creation would be needed? . . . why do you already want to think further, you, before whom life still lies? Whence do you want to know that this inclination of your heart toward devotion will not find great and noble incentives to prepare happiness and ascending? Why do you want to skip over everything and speak of an extreme from which your whole destiny separates you? And should things ever really go so far that your heart prevails, beyond every beloved object, who knows but that you will have the strength then to turn this situation in such a way that it would all the more become a splendor for you—?

And now I shall quickly tell you something quite different. Right after your big letter that time which informed me about Pierrot, a dog was introduced to me here that spent most of its time over at the farm buildings, so that I knew him only by sight. It turned out that his name is Peter, which after all has the same root and meaning as Pierrot; this, together with his good, solitary face, caused me to call him over frequently into the castle, and now he has been allowed to sit by me at my noonday meal all this time and to permit himself anything else that happens to strike his fancy. And all that in honor of you and Pierrot. I tell him, too, to whom he owes it. Farewell. (My books!)

[28]

To Alfred Walter von Heymel   Duino Castle near Nabresina,
Austrian Littoral
February 27, 1912

Dear Heymel,

Again and again and each time more energetically I feel reproach at not having written you yet,—even if it's only two pages this time, you shall at least have those; for to the old incentive (a report on the success of your lectures that certainly came to me at your behest) a new one has now been added which, since it came up, has been working on me: your translation of the Marlowe tragedy. I scarcely know Shakespeare, have scarcely any prospect of ever learning English, that whole enormous world will probably remain remote to me—: But up to now I probably owe to your Edward II the strongest sense of its strong existence;

that is how I expected Shakespeare to be, I see now, and was surprised, from the little I then read in Schlegel's translation, not to find him like that. Here, in this play of Marlowe's, is the taste of which I had a foretaste; I read it with a great readiness and was amazed to what moral authority the figure of the unhappy king grows; that is amorphous misery, misery in pieces, broken from a mountain range of misery, misfortune hard and sterile and sharp at every edge. As in the scaling of certain mountains, one arrives at the heights, one doesn't know how: the going doesn't seem steep, it is scarcely taxing, but suddenly one is over most of it. And the peak that stands out bare, desolate in the indifferent skies, nevertheless has destiny down below it, all that is habitable and confusible and shut away,—is in a great, cruel open region, in averted, self-absorbed world-space. This is immense, and one goes with it, before one is prepared for it, one hasn't the time to pull oneself together for it, it drives one along before it. I cannot judge, but I am sure that one could not achieve such emotion over it if you had not introduced the most important, most elemental forces of the original into the German: it must be a work that strengthened joy and zest in you while you were doing it; you must have felt alive and sure in it—: and so it is fine that it is here. My Froissart has been lying open since then, I wanted to go over the characters in him again, but haven't yet got round to it. . . .

[29]

To N.N.   Duino Castle near Nabresina, Austrian Littoral
                                        March 5, 1912

. . . Tasso deals not with love but with a lot of half things, it is a disaffected, ill-humored book; that which took place historically was, I believe, more by far, it certainly ought to be written over again quite differently. It is probably the wavering between outside and inside; as with Marianna a great advance broke through, so also in Tasso there breaks through a renewal of life values which was at first sad and dismaying. At that time there was perhaps beginning what we see so strangely consummated about us now: the retreat into the internal of a world abounding in the external. You will understand what I mean: inner experiences flourished in the sixteenth century to such magnificence outside in the visible world that they could be heightened no further. Love and desire, revenge and hate continually found immediate, brilliant realities that represented, portrayed and soon surpassed them. Someone loved,—his love *was* the beloved, and when she pensively tried on before her mirror a chain or earrings, this love of some person or other was *augmented* by that chain, that earring. And however much hatred someone accumulated within him, *it was an increase* if this hatred went into action and in the presence of a murder became tangible and tragic. For Raskolnikov the carrying-out is a disappointment—: and this reversal somehow took hold in Tasso and destroyed him. About this point his personality revolves. Just look, Petrarch could still be crowned with laurel on the Capitol,—had it come to the crowning of Tasso—it would have caused him nameless suffering—for already at that time there was no longer an external equivalent for fame . . .

That is a long road, I hope I can someday say all this better and definitively; if one understood this it would lighten many things, and one could henceforth spare oneself many festivities and commemorations in the certainty that this [externality] doesn't exist any more,—and after all it is not so poverty-stricken to imagine that the burning of Rome and the beautiful sea battle of Lepanto can only take place now *within* us. . . .

[*30*]

To Princess Marie von Thurn
*   und Taxis-Hohenlohe*   Palazzo Valmarana, San Vio [Venice]
                                            July 12, 1912

Strictly speaking, dear friend, I haven't a single quite clear need besides that of writing to you, and a little too of knowing your opinion of my present life; but it is indescribable what a ban against all activity is in the air and in one's limbs, a season for healthy infants—; as certain magicians get the idea of pulling endless ribbons out of their mouths, so from my eyelids closed to a crack I draw meter-long strips of daytime sleep; hardly is one finished before a new gray or lilac starts sliding forth, and I am entangled in all these slowly forming sleep-ribbons, so that I am living as in a snarl that only draws together more tightly at any attempt to escape.

This is happening oddly, my conscience is not getting better for it, and yet I don't want to cut right through everything and break out, but am just waiting along, letting it happen to me, and what comes takes on the habits and has the dimensions of dream.

There is a little key lying on my table (yes, it is really still lying there); it locks the strange, big hall in the Casino dei Spiriti on the Fondamente Nuove; whenever I wish myself thither, I can be there,—but what a lavishness, what extravagance, to wish.

Duse, my having been at her house, she at mine, that too is like a mirage in the air over-stimulated by clarity—you can imagine, we were like two characters coming on in an old mystery, spoke, as charged by a legend, each his gentle part. A meaning arose immediately from the whole and at once transcended us. We were like two basins one above the other forming a fountain and show-ing each other only how much was continually slipping from us. And yet we could scarcely be prevented from somehow agreeing on the magnificence of being so full, and perhaps at the same moment we thought too of the living, vertical ray that rose above us and fell (ever and again) and filled us so full.—Cowardly as I now am, I hardly dared look at her; it caused me a kind of pain to find her so broad and robust, that stoutly grown body, like a setting from which at some time the stone has already fallen. The fear of seeing a distortion, or simply something that is no longer there, is to blame for my remembering almost nothing but her mouth, that heavy mouth that looks as though only a fate unfeel-ing and not its own could still move it, as for certain swords the hero must come, the half-god, to raise them. And the smile indeed, surely one of the most famous ever smiled, a smile that needs no space, that retracts nothing, conceals nothing, is transparent as a song and yet so full of added being that one is tempted to stand up when it enters.

More staggering almost than the event itself was to me the fact that suddenly, without my lifting a finger, this meeting came about which for many years was almost my greatest wish. For some time now I have lost the precision necessary for wishing (wishing is target-shooting and I am under heavy fire before an invisible foe)—, but, as at several times in my life, I unconsciously took the quiet realization as proof that I am, despite everything, on my path, otherwise this village, so often sought out on the map, could not have come.

The experience with Rodin has made me very timid toward all changing, all diminishing, all failure—, for those unapparent fatalities, once one has recognized them, can be endured only so long as one is capable of expressing them with the same force with which God allows them. I am not very far off work, perhaps, but Heaven forbid that I should be called upon (right away at least) for insight into anything more painful than I was charged with in Malte Laurids. Then it will be just a howl among howls and not worth the effort.

Yesterday I wrote without premeditation in my notebook:
Alas, as we waited for help from mankind, angels
stepped over soundlessly, in a single stride,
over our prostrate hearts.

Here Moissi walked in on me, suddenly, coming from Duse, I knew she was already expecting him yesterday; he rushed, burst, broke in, at first I thought it was his tempo, an inner, absolute one,—but now, now I am almost afraid it is the tempo of Reinhardt enterprises: Heavens, what an *actor* he has become, I saw him shortly thereafter with Duse, we were standing by the window, she came by with her friend, Mme. Poletti (who is writing the Ariadne for her), we climbed into the gondola beside her and rode slowly toward the Lido. Duse was quite magnificent today, of a sadness such as cloud formations can have, one interprets it as sadness, but in reality it is nothing but immense space, not gay, not disconsolate,—great. Later we dropped Moissi off, but we remained together, I ate with them in their house on the Zattere, it was intimate, full of friendship, full of nearness, and again much meaning came out of the simplest things and passed into the great. Now it is late, with this I close a letter that would otherwise have continued quite, quite differently, but as it is, is more complete, for today we looked at each other really without fear, seriousness for seriousness, melancholy for melancholy: it seems we can do each other no harm. (And the world is so different from Moissi.)

This must suffice; we have telegraphed Placci he must come tomorrow; a thousand greetings to everyone, especially to the Prince and you, my dear friend, how often I think how you are in everything that befalls me, now again here,—how without you nothing would have come.—Your D.S.

[31]

To Princess Marie von Thurn
und Taxis-Hohenlohe   Palazzo Valmarana, San Vio, Venice
August 3, 1912

Alas, dearest friend, how badly the human affects me, what work, what toil, when I let myself in for it: instead of helping me, making me a little new and guileless, it stands me on the galley, I row, caulk, wash ballast, and yet (Heaven forgive me) haven't learned it at all. I am much at my great neighbor's, the table is set for me every evening, I can always come, and it is a matter of course that I will come. She is magnificent, expressing human things more greatly than any other individual; she does not try to make herself understandable, she begins her gesture with the being understood and proceeds from there. We go through our gestures, half repeat and repeat our lines, repent, retract, try again from the beginning; she says, shows, refuses to show herself, and right from the start it is all one, the whole, definitive of a higher order, as in the temple's pediment. What magnificence and what waste! No poet in all the world, and she is passing by. No one was ever in need of so much. So without a stage, without an instrument, she enlarges the raw material of everyday life; small things, quick, provisional happenings come to themselves in her hearing, transcend themselves,—would be frightened of themselves, could they see themselves there, would remain, stand still, no longer fade away. And she is left upholding, unmoving, unrelieved, overburdened,—because there are never spectators enough to take from her the fullness of her scene; every next moment she is like a vineyard that is already ripe again,—one would have to keep sending in thousands of laborers under the burden of the grapes.

But now here is this young friend, hard, ambitious, talented to a certain degree, but without flexibility even in her talents, learned because she takes to learning, determined, but only in what is determinable, more an energy than a necessity; the joy of taking on her plays has become for Duse an unretractable promise, a kind of duty, the firm, young character won't give an inch, and perhaps even she herself, Duse, doesn't dare let go what was after all the hope and the effort of these last years.

You have no idea how she has to drag all that along. I talk for hours with both of them, with the one as well as with the other, understand, ease things for the moment, come under the suspicion of being able to help, and yet haven't the right word, the decisive idea. Am still of the opinion that Mme. P. ought to go away now (whence recently my idea of Duino which I quickly wrote you), but Duse herself is pressing to leave and yet holds back, out of anxiety, I think, at being left alone. Voilà où nous sommes. Thank you for your good letter, thanks with all my heart.—Your D.S.

P.S. I shall perhaps send you through the publisher my White Princess, the scene I wrote thirteen years ago for Duse. We chanced to speak of it, she enjoys it, she would like best to have it translated at once, but how, by whom? Would you like to reread it and tell me what impression you have of it now with reference to D[use]? I would rather not touch it, it is an immature work in every sense, but she enjoys it for the moment, and every joy must be good.—Once more and a thousand times your D.S.

[32]

To N. N.   Palazzo Valmarana, San Vio, Venice
                             July 23, 1912

Dear child, you see I am writing at once, your letter just came, and great though the distress out of which it is written, there is good strength in it: the heavy lament is held up so high, far out of the confusion, a lament in the clear. Don't interpret, don't give things *more* significance than they themselves take; don't look at a sorrow from the outside, don't appraise it and give it a big name: the "great sorrow" . . . , you don't really know but that your heart has grown with it, that this great weariness is the growth of the heart,—patience, patience and do not judge in suffering, never judge; so long as it is upon one, one has no measure for it, one compares and exaggerates.

It was foolish of me not to have sent you the Journal of Eugénie de Guérin: the book had come, I needed it myself and gave it one day to someone who also needed it. And yet you needed it the most. But it is already ordered again, in a few days it will follow this letter. It will do you good, this book, Eugénie is the friend you need now, she has perseverance through the earthly and the heavenly, she makes no difference between one and the other, does not alter her voice: so one goes on in these pages and back and way to the end and way to the beginning and becomes familiar in the whole: for perseverance, which here is long sufferance, a little farther along is already eternity.

Take the cure easily, with the deliberate air with which one rows over a stretch of water once one has come to the point of having to cross. It will perhaps have its good side; keep watching, keep watching curiosity too, as if it were there only for the looking, then it loses its urgency and nearness, doesn't know what to do, becomes object-like. The time will pass, you will have observed much,—observe it like Nature, there is in everything a little remnant of world and innocence, and even in the most arrogant desire to help, helplessness is pure and moving. And nothing will hinder what you really need from coming then, the "complete repose", the "letting oneself go". Describe it to your father, he will understand it,—a wood, a clearing, a woodland meadow, a Nature accustomed in humanity: there I see you reading Eugénie de Guérin and arriving at courage and inner perspective, surely, surely,—there are a host of loyal appointments between you and life, you are young, full of good will,—everything will have its turn.

Farewell for today, many strong wishes are with you.

[33]

*To Princess Marie von Thurn
    und Taxis-Hohenlohe*   Palazzo Valmarana, San Vio, Venice
                                 August 3, 1912

Yes, it was really a little much, there came a moment when I was done, three, four days of being picked clean to a skeleton, as if ants had neatly brought all my inner structures to light,—but by that time the two had already separated and gone, each in a different direction. Duse, not knowing where to go, is on her way to a friend, Countess Sophie Drechsel in Tegernsee, Mme. P[oletti] is beginning a new life in Rome; now I have only to see to it that she understands I was merely the very last component of her past, for God forbid that she should include me in her future and go on building on me. Let her become what she must, I undertake no responsibility.

This much is certain. Duse has gone through a great deal with her and will need a while to recover from this life companion. Ah, dearest friend, that was a lot of grist to my oldest mill; how clean things are that one lives through in oneself, and how between individuals the well-meant, what once was delightful, turns bad, bad, spoiled, an abomination. How sad! Moreover one of them was really great and the other merely young, unfinished, turbulent, wrongly started perhaps, honest in her zeal, possibly unable to do otherwise—and then, between them the bad develops, out of what? like dust everywhere out of everything. I would give a lot if I could bring Duse to a happy thought, to the beginning of a hope, but I see I must be cautious; if one had strengths, but I have only a little piece of strength, big as the rosin for a fiddle bow, only just useful for stroking over once or twice before playing. . . .

[34]

To Anton Kippenberg   Duino Castle near Nabresina,
                                         Austrian Littoral
                                         October 2, 1912

. . . My still being here is connected with the relative extent of the plans which more and more outweighed every other prospect and now at last are so far along that I myself am beginning to believe in them and to act in line with them. I intend, that is, to spend this fall and as far as possible a part of the winter in Spain, as you will at once understand, not as a tourist who hurries, but I mean rather to settle down in Toledo and to live there. You know that Greco is one of the greatest events of my last two or three years; the need to deal with him more conscientiously looks almost like a vocation, like a duty implanted deep within;—but the impulse toward a sojourn in Spain extends far beyond that, back into those Roman days when, without knowing it, I began the *Malte Laurids,*—and over the course of the years since then, while one thing was fulfilled and another dropped out, this wish has remained so vigorous and lively to me that it is now almost the only one on which I can myself rely. Perhaps I exaggerate: but it does seem to me as if this journey would have for my progress a significance similar to that which the Russian one had formerly; as if it should bring with it the full power of much expression that has not yet been vouchsafed;—the still waiting state in which I find myself since the termination of my last big work may also contribute to my wanting to try my hand attentively at this new thing, in which, I suspect, the most diverse directions of my work will come together.

Added to this is an external incentive. Next year Toledo, I hear, is to be the scene of a big Greco exposition: not only would I like scrupulously to avoid this occasion, I fear that this hitherto still so uninterrupted earthly constellation, which is Toledo, will after this congestion be left changed, popularized, so that this is almost the last moment for surprising it in its remoteness.

Now it goes against me, dear friend, to give in to this important decision without knowing that I have your full agreement; you will not, I believe, withhold it from me . . .

[35]

To Princess Marie von Thurn
und Taxis-Hohenlohe   Toledo, on All Souls' Day 1912

Princess, for you the first word, let it be: hope; and if so soon again a wish may join in: may nothing else become clear to me for a long time, so that I can establish myself here in this, guilelessly and unrestricted.

What it is *like* here, that, dear friend, I shall never be able to say (it would be language of angels, their use of it among men), but *that* it is, that it *is*, you will just have to believe me. One can describe it to no one, it is full of law, yes, I understand at this moment the legend that when on the fourth day of creation God took the sun and set it, he established it right over Toledo: so very star-ish is the nature of this extraordinarily laid out estate so outward, so into space—, I have already got all around, have imprinted everything on my mind as though tomorrow I had to know it forever, the bridges, both bridges, this river and, shifted over beyond it, this open abundance of landscape, surveyable, like something that is still being worked on. And this joy in the first paths that one tries, this indescribably sure being-taken and being-led—, just imagine, I took Santo Tomé Street, then that of the Angel (Calle del Angel), and it brought me in front of the Church of San Juan de los Reyes on whose walls nothing but chains of prisoners or men freed hang down in rows and rest on ledges. P[asha] had told me in Munich he had meanwhile seen in Baedeker that there is a church like that with chains—, without remembering having seen it himself at the time. Now the first thing was to find it. And then to go on, nowhere was it incidental, and one almost wants, at such discovery, to look around as if to see just who is watching, whom one is pleasing by it, as children look around when they learn something.

It bothers me, if only I could strike it, the note; here for the first time I can conceive of going about and caring for the sick, daily walking through this city, one could turn in anywhere and unnoticed deliver oneself up there in the narrowness, so at the verge does this stand here, going outward one cannot get beyond it. But then again outside, scarcely a hundred steps before this unsurpassable city, it should be conceivable to meet a lion on one of the unconcealed paths and make him beholden to one by something quite unintentional in one's bearing. Between these two gestures more or less, life here may lie.—

My God, how many things have been dear to me because they were trying to be something of all this here, because a drop of this blood was in their hearts, and now it is to be the whole, can I bear it?

No more today, Princess. I arrived at ten o'clock yesterday, in Madrid (which I disliked almost as much as Trieste) going just from one station to the other, now it is about seven in the evening and the day between long as a day out of Genesis. My hotel is called Hotel de Castilla, passes for the best here and seems to be usable.

Many, many greetings to you and the Prince, where are you? How are you? The morning was very very cold, I was at first afraid at having come so late, but by day the sun fills out all there is of clearness. Enough, here justified weariness is closing over me and withdrawing me from you. Adieu, adieu.

[*36*]

To Princess Marie von Thurn
und Taxis-Hohenlohe   Hôtel de Castilla, Toledo, Spain
November 13, 1912

Dear friend, outdoors on my walks I write you the most beautiful letters, here, at home, I freeze and am a sorry peda͵ ˙ and put up with a hundred trivial and shameful things,—but be this only noted, Heaven forbid I should entertain you with it—, rather is it to be said (alas, there just isn't any expression for it), how much everything here goes on in the extraordinary, in the more-than-life-size, I simply cannot conceive how people to whom all this has not been intrusted so purely, so absolutely, so beyond all doubt, explain it to themselves—, I mean: what they take it for, where they place it, what they inwardly do with it. "A woman of Heaven and of the Earth," said the Jesuit Ribadaneira (with whose text we smoked up Dr. R. so that his eyes literally vanished) of the Virgin Mary; that could be applied to this city, "a city of Heaven and of the Earth", for it is really in both, it goes right through all existence; I tried recently to make this intelligible in one sentence to P. by saying that it is there in equal measure for the eyes of the dead, the living and the angels,—yes, here is an object that might be accessible to all three of those so widely different visions, over it, one feels, they could come together and have one and the same impression. This incomparable city is at pains to keep within its walls the arid, undiminished, unsubdued landscape, the mountain, the pure mountain, the mountain of vision,—monstrous the earth issues from it and directly before its gates becomes world, creation, mountain and ravine, Genesis. Again and again this region makes me think of a prophet, of one who rises from his meal, from hospitality, from being with others, and upon whom at once, on the very threshold of the house, prophesying comes, the immense seeing of ruthless visions—: such is the gesture of this Nature round about the city, yes even inside it, here and there, it looks up and doesn't recognize the city and has a vision.

And as for me in the midst of all this, I am still amazed at how deeply I was prepared for every detail,—somehow as I felt that in the Salone della Ragione in Padua everything which, outside, life and business and distress brings with it, appears in pictures—thus everything was there and made me accustomed, as though this vision were to be wholly given over to me. Just think that Cividale was still to come, as a promise of the Tajo, yes, that even at the very last someone or other was striving to tell me about a St. Christopher who is supposed to span the height of a whole church in the vicinity of Duino: while I now sit here every day in the cathedral beneath the gigantic Cristóbal which really does reach to where the vaulting begins.

Until yesterday the weather was of the clearest, and the pageant of the evenings proceeded in quiet spaciousness, only today the sky became complicated, right after midday it got to the point of raining, but a cold, taciturn wind interrupted the rain in the middle of a sentence, pushed the clouds upward and drove them into masses over the sun already inclining toward the west.—And after what I have got to see in the further course of things, I cannot help wishing (despite my physical demand on warmth) for many such episodes,—I have an inkling of what formations the atmosphere here must make use of in order to comport itself appropriately to the picture of the city: menacings rolled themselves up and spread out far away above the bright reliefs of other clouds that innocently held themselves against them, imaginary continents—, all that above the desolation of the landscape sombered by it, but in the depths of the abyss quite a cheerful bit of river (cheerful like Daniel in the lion's den), the great stride of the bridge and then, drawn wholly into the proceedings, the city, in every tone of gray and ocher against the east's open and yet quite inaccessible blue, ah, Princess, I think of the sunrise you once recorded so well from the window in Duino, and wish that much composure into my heart, for confronting such objects, quiet, attentive, as something existent, looking, not-concerned-about-itself . . .

Of Grecos I have seen many since then and several with quite unqualified admiration; but on the whole he can naturally be inwardly placed only somewhere quite else; hitherto, wherever one saw him, he signified all this, to one who is here he is at once submerged in all that is present, is merely like a beautiful buckle that gathers the great vision more tightly about things, un cabochon énorme enchassé dans ce terrible et sublime reliquaire.

Today your big letter, dear Princess, glorious, the way you translate, the way the Elegies have ebb and flow in you and through you for the first time really come under the influence of the constellations. Now I am distant enough, you see, it is not my neighborhood, no infection, but the spirit, about which no one can do anything. I am certain something conforming to law is taking shape there, just yield to it and don't let yourself become suspicious of it. Thanks for everything, for the copy of the remarkable pages of our Unknown, for the letter to Prince Ratibor; if I go to Madrid sometime, I will present it. Above all, thanks for all that you write, I see absolutely no newspapers here now, only once recently I applied my modestly growing Spanish in order to understand that the Bulgarian was allowed to become master in Constantinople,—and now you really indicate something of the sort, dear heaven, but that is counter to all history, that Constantinople, that Stamboul, that Byzantium should thus incidentally belong in with that Balkan disorder down there. (And I have never seen it.) . . .

Do you remember the glorious organs here in the cathedral? And like old arquebuses the trombone-stops stand forth from them; that and the grilles, the grilles: yes, if one had not come here, one would have said one's whole life long: "grilles, grilles", like a sheep, without thereby picturing to oneself anything real, but now one knows it, once and for all, and sees it in one's sleep. . . .

[37]

To N. N.   Hôtel de Castilla, Toledo (Spain)
November 17, 1912

You see, it is not my fault . . . if I am only now answering you,—or rather my fault only in so far as the porter in Venice hasn't my address yet and so your letter had to come by many stages. But it stood the trip, this morning I received it,—and if it hadn't come, I would have written you anyway one of these days, to provide the possibility of your good news (which I felt must be arriving soon) reaching me quite surely and directly . . .

What you call my "world", dear child,—that is at present not sufficient to nourish and sustain anyone; against just this one must take up counterweights in order to be in the whole. It may be that out of the fragments one little by little brings before one, some-time, in survey, something worldlike will be perceptible,—but it is still a good way to that, I am just now more than ever in the one-sided, lament has many times prevailed, but I know one may use the strings of lament so fully only when one is determined to play on them later, with their resources, the whole joy also which wells up behind everything that is difficult, painful, and endured and without which the voices are not complete—.

You will be surprised to find me here, an old wish has at last put itself through, and I saw on the very first day that there is a great deal here I have long needed. Only this today, many wishes, many greetings and confidence for everything.

[38]

To Princess Marie von Thurn
und Taxis-Hohenlohe   Ronda, December 17, 1912

I long for a letter from you, dear Princess, God knows where it is wandering about—and the last I wrote you seems quite vague in my memory; what was thoroughly alive in it was merely like warmed-up food from the one written only in thought in Cordoba, furthermore it bore no mark but that of my discontent with Seville, with myself, with myself and ten times with myself. Again there came a series of really irksome days, pains physically and the spirit so little attuned to endurance, if I had happened to have a "home", I would by all means have gone home, since for every journey, especially one through Spain, a certain equilibrium is required, the certainty of being able to rely on oneself, but for me the world collapses completely every moment, inside in my blood; and if then an entirely strange world stands all about outside, it is a strangeness beyond measure. I have it in mind, Princess, I must track down the cause of this malaise, discover the source whence evil keeps welling up; scarcely have I a little boat somewhere before this misery rises and overflows it and leaves it desolate behind. And I know that there a doctor can help, not I, if only he were the right one,—with me everything is too much of a piece for me to be able to suffer at some place and accomplish at another, really I am not at all addicted to suffering, a pain takes the world from me, that is why I am so completely unfitted to be a saint and haven't the slightest prospect of ever spreading abroad this good odor. (Instead you recognized and expressed it, that was inexhaustibly right.)

For the rest you must know, Princess, since Cordova I have been of an almost rabid anti-Christianity, I read the Koran; to me, in places, it takes on a voice that I am inside of, as it were, with all my strength, like the wind in an organ. Here one thinks one is in a Christian country; well, even here it is long since outlived, it was Christian as long as one had the courage to kill people a hundred paces before the city; thus the many unassuming stone crosses increased which read simply: here died so and so,—that was the local version of Christianity. Now there is a boundless indifference here, empty churches, forgotten churches, chapels dying of starvation,—really one should no longer sit down at this cleaned-up table and hand out as nourishment the finger bowls that are still standing about. The fruit is sucked dry, so now, to put it crudely, one just spits out the rinds. And then Protestants and American Christians keep making another infusion with these tea dregs that have steeped for two millenniums, Mohammed was in any case the next stage; like a river through a primeval mountain, he breaks his way through to the one God, with whom one can speak so magnificently every morning without the "Christ" telephone, into which people continually shout: Hello, who's there?—and no one answers.

Now just imagine, Princess, I am three hours from Gibraltar, five, when the weather is good, from Tangiers—, tempted like anything in this mood, to sail over sometime to the Moors; on the other hand, I am afraid a whitewash of light would then lay itself over dark, clay-red Spain.—For the present I am here in Ronda (since a week ago), I at once sent P. a few pictures, it seemed to me so very probable that the incomparable phenomenon of this city piled up on two steep rock-masses divided by the narrow, deep river gorge would confirm his dream picture; it is indescribable, surrounding the whole a spacious valley, busied with its expanses of meadow, its evergreen oaks and olive trees, and beyond again there rises out of it, as though well rested, the pure mountain range, mountain behind mountain, forming the stateliest distance. As for the city itself, in these conditions it cannot but be odd, rising and falling, here and there so open toward the abyss that not one window dares look that way,—little palaces behind crusts of yearly white, each with a portal set off by color, and under the balcony the coat of arms with crest slightly flattened, but in the shield distinct, detailed and full as a pomegranate.

Here would of course be the place to live and to reside quite Spanishly were it not for the season, were it not for my tiresome disinclination to let myself in for any but the most necessary hardships (innate and zealously assumed)—, to crown it all the devil prompted the English to build here a really excellent hotel, in which I am naturally living now, neutral, expensive and as this person and that would desire it, and still I am shameless enough to spread it abroad that I am traveling in Spain.

I tell you, Princess (no, no, you must believe me), things must become different with me, from the ground up, from the ground up, otherwise all the miracles in the world will be in vain. For here I see once more how much is lavished on me and just plain lost, the Blessed Angela had a similar experience—, quand tous les sages du monde—she says—et tous les saints du paradis m'accableraient de leurs consolations et de leurs promesses, et Dieu lui-même de ses dons, s'il ne me changeait pas moi-même, s'il ne commençait au fond de moi une nouvelle opération, au lieu de me faire du bien, les sages, les saints, et Dieu exaspéreraient au delà de toute expression mon désespoir, ma fureur, ma tristesse, ma douleur, et mon aveuglement. This I marked a year ago in the book, for I understood it with all my heart and, I cannot help it, it has since become only the more valid.

Today, when I saw these mountains, these slopes, opened up in the purest air as if one were to sing from them, I had to tell myself to what joy that would have incited me even three years ago, how it would have transformed me into just sheer joy—, now it is as if my heart had moved miles away, I see many things that start off and go in its direction—, but I do not learn of their arriving. Alas, I am not quite over expecting the "nouvelle opération" from some human intervention, and yet to what end, since it is my fate, passing the human by as it were, to arrive at the ultimate, at the rim of the earth, as recently in Cordova where an ugly little bitch, to the highest degree prematernal, came to me; she was not a remarkable animal, and certainly she was full of accidental young ones about which no fuss will have been made; but since we were all alone, she came over to me, hard as it was for her, and raised her eyes enlarged by care and fervor and sought my glance,—and in hers was truly everything that goes beyond the individual, whither I don't know, into the future or into the incomprehensible; the situation resolved itself in her getting a piece of sugar from my coffee, but incidentally, oh so incidentally, we read mass together so to say, the action was nothing in itself but giving and accepting, but the meaning and the seriousness and our whole understanding was boundless. That after all can happen only on earth, it is good at all events to have gone through here willingly, even though uncertainly, even though guiltily, even though not at all heroically,—one will at last be wonderfully prepared for divine conditions.

How the tiniest bird voice outside affects and concerns me, dear heaven, would that it were spring and I were approaching Nature somewhere with all my senses,——I have discovered for myself such a singular valley, a kind of hunting park of the Marquis de Salvatierra, scarcely laid out at all, only so rearranged that rabbits don't quite know their way any more,—something out of a dream or out of the "Elective Affinities"; I take long, long walks—, but still recognize myself most truly in the fateful coincidence of the first excursion in each city,—even in Seville, where nothing else went right, I began, God knows how, with the Old Men's Home of the Caritad; it was morning, in the long, cheerful halls the old men were sitting around the brazier or simply standing about finished like toys, two lay in bed resting from life as though they didn't at all need the extravagance of dying for that purpose; but on the other nicely made beds, everywhere at the same spot on each of the flowered bedcovers, lay two of the enormous, pale Spanish loaves of white bread, peaceful in their evident superfluity, pure recompense and no longer to be eaten in the sweat of the brow.

Here the church of San Francisco, outside in the southern suburb, was the first thing I discovered, I shall tell you about it another time; anyhow it is time for me to close and say Merry Christmas, I shall think many thoughts in your direction—, newspapers I haven't seen, but let us hope you have no more war misgivings; from the Prince's kind, good letter, which reached me by the first mail that caught up with me in Ronda, I see that he has hope and that no one really sees what good a war would do.

Princess, your letter! That is what I call coming in the nick of time. I shall go right on writing without reading or discussing the poems now (I must first get hold of the German text in my memory in order to be able to compare), for I saw that with the little delay in Seville your lines really took *six* days, and, festive or not, I still have the ambition that this may be with you for Christmas. It is frightful that the danger of war is still not out of the air, politics usually makes a point of being swift, it is a bad joke when it gets as slow as God.

As for Seville, to the last we did not get together, not at all, although the Sevillians take the festival of Mary very personally and a whole octave of ceremonies was impending, in the beginning of which I was just able to participate. The cathedral was so fundamentally repugnant to me, even hostile, nowhere does it become serious, there is something vague, evasive about these ambitiously upward-built spires, a spirit of out-trumping that would like to out-trump even God and, as it were, manage to take him from above. And the infamous organ made the air so sweet with its pampered voice that the colossal pillars felt quite weak, it was a matter of indifference to one, this softening of stone, a conjuring trick, however far it might go.

Have you been seeing books, Princess? In the evening some-times (I have such congestion in my eyes that I cannot read much) I read Don Quixote in German translation and find it rather childish; from an artistic point of view this book has no limits at all, except perhaps those that a witty, ingenious disguise would have in reality—, and they are frivolously far overstepped. But Christmas: Christmas greetings to you, to the Prince, to the Mzell family with all my heart. Do you know that exactly on the night of Christmas it will be full moon: how that will go with your white world in its silver dress. Everything that is affectionate and grateful—Your D.S.

[39]

To Lou Andreas-Salomé Hotel Reina Victoria, Ronda, Spain
December 19, 1912

Gently, without stir, it is getting toward Christmas, here too,— let me write to you. Once more I am a burden on my own heart, with all the weight and with the heaviness of I know not what things—. The last you heard of me was through Gebsattel, but I doubt whether he conveyed to you the right idea; the peculiar refraction that is effected in him is always interesting because it leads to new points of intersection, which then also at once be-come polar, attract and repel, that is, dispose—, as a metaphor this is every time of perfect truth, but as mere news not exactly useful.

It is so natural that I should now look back to a year ago, when I also began to write to you, and it does honestly seem to me that I haven't moved since, except for going around in a circle—, God knows . . . The good, generous asylums, such as Duino was and immediately thereafter Venice, haven't helped me along very far; also these so specially configured surroundings require so much adaptation each time, they have their existence in too varied alien conditions, and when at last one has got to the point of belonging to them, the only thing accomplished is the lie that one belongs. Until into the autumn I was in Venice, upheld by kind friendly relationships, yet in reality staying from day to day, from week to week, because I didn't know where to go; finally out of perplexity, out of instinct, out of impulses dragged along through years the decision took shape to go on this journey through Spain, actually just for a stay in Toledo, and on arriving there, breathlessly exposed to the really infinitely anticipated which yet infinitely surpassed all anticipation,—I believe myself already almost torn out of my dullness and on the way to a broader participation in what validly exists,—there are no words with which I could tell you how beyond everything this city stood before me in the midst of its untamed landscape, through and through the next thing, that which a moment before would not yet have been bearable, at once chastening and consoling, like Moses when he came from the mountain with horns of light—, and yet again, little by little, recalling everything in my life that was ever necessary, strong, pure, and reliable. But from the very fact that I did not stay (I was there four weeks), that the cold, that my old pains, the congestion in forehead and eyes, that this and that discomfort persisted beside so great and to me so eloquent a presence, occupied and distracted me, you can see that I was not up to what was perhaps intended to effect "la nouvelle opération"—, I went southward, I stood marveling in Cordova, I had time to perceive that Seville was not for me, something drew me to Ronda—, and here I now am and in these no less incredible surroundings am mainly expecting only a better distribution of my tormenting blood through the influence of the high pure air that everywhere comes wafting over, from the mountains pitched all around, into the city which for its part is steeply held aloft.

When I wake up in the morning, there lies before my open window in pure space, well rested, the mountain range; how on earth do I manage not to have that move me within, even four or five years ago a sunrise on the crossing from Capri toward Naples could transform me from head to foot into sheer joy, into quite new joy that had not yet existed, that arose all along me and was added to everything like a spring one has found; and now I sit here and gaze and gaze until my eyes hurt, and show it to myself and recite it to myself, as though I were supposed to learn it by heart, and still haven't got it and am so truly one with whom it doesn't agree.

Dear Lou, tell me, how does it come about that I spoil everything—, now it seems to me sometimes as if I were using too much violence toward impressions (which I do in practice on so many occasions), I stay too long before them, I press them into my face and yet they, by nature, already *are* impressions, aren't they, even if one very quietly lets them be for a while; au lieu de me pénétrer, les impressions me percent.

I take long, long walks outdoors here, for a few hours occasionally the sun is such that one can rest beside an evergreen oak, then a little bird voice favors me, or the roaring from the deep river gorge makes superfluous everything that has been and everything that can be. But in walking I ponder so many things,—from the first of January on a studio in Paris will belong to me; I foresaw that, however this journey turns out, the most important thing for me will be immediately afterwards to get to an independent place of my own, therein I was certainly right. And whether Paris, which has taken so much of my strength, is still necessary, will do me any good, time will have to tell. I know one mustn't leave a plaster on all one's life because it once did good, also I would rather not go back to Paris if possible before the worst of winter is over.

I must tell you, Lou, I have a feeling that what would help me would be an environment similar to that I had with you in Schmargendorf, long walks in the wood, going barefoot and letting my beard grow day and night, having a lamp in the evening, a warm room, and the moon, as often as suits it, and the stars, when they are there, and otherwise sitting and hearing the rain or the storm, as though it were God himself. When you get around to it, dear Lou, think about it and take note of whether you see a place where that could be done. I sometimes imagine the Black Forest, the region of Triberg, Rippoldsau, then again I think of Sweden, as it would be at Ellen Key's for example (but I would rather not be "at" anyone's)—or near her by a lake in the woods or near a little university city in Germany; for to have books, preferably a person too with whom one could learn something, would naturally suit me. Do you know whether it is true that the Books of Moses in the original text are something completely different from what both the Greek and Latin translations contain? I have read remarkable books by that curious Fabre d'Olivet (beginning of the 19th century) to whom this discovery gave the incentive for reconstructing a whole Hebrew grammar (the way altogether his whole life was consumed in preliminary work for a gigantic, never begun main project—); here I am reading the Koran and am amazed, amazed—, and again feel a desire for Arabic. Could I carry that on with your husband, if by any chance Göttingen for example should come under consideration—I am talking at random, you see, and to that there are no limits. . . .

[40]

To Lou Andreas-Salomé   Ronda, January 6, 1913

"Actually he had long been free, and if something kept him from dying, it was perhaps only the circumstance that he had already once overlooked death somewhere, so that he did not have to go on toward it, like the others, but back to it. His destiny was already outside him, there in the convinced things with which children play, and in them it perished. Or it was rescued in the upward glance of an unknown woman passing, at least it put its trust there at its own risk. But even dogs ran past with it, uneasy and looking back to see whether he wouldn't take it away from them again. But when he came before the almond tree in its blossom, he was startled nevertheless to find it so completely yonder, wholly gone over, wholly occupied there, wholly away from him; and he himself not precisely enough confronting it and too dimmed even to reflect this his own being. Had he become a saint, he would have derived a serene freedom from this condition, the infinitely irrevocable joy of poverty: for thus perhaps did Saint Francis lie consumed, and had been enjoyed, and the whole world was a pleasant savor of his being. He however had not peeled himself clean, he had torn himself out of himself and given away bits of peel as well, often too had held himself to an imagined mouth (as children do before dolls) smacking his lips, and the morsel was left lying. So now he looked like refuse and was in the way,— however much sweetness might have grown in him."

This I wrote this morning in my notebook, you will perceive whom it concerns. Yesterday came your good letter. Yes, the two elegies are here—, but I'll be able to tell you by word of mouth how small and how sharply broken off a piece they form of what was then put in my power. Circumstances and strengths as at the time when the *Book of Hours* began—: what all wouldn't have been brought to light. *If only we see each other, dear Lou,* that is now my great hope, my support, my everything as always. I often tell myself that only through you am I linked with the human, in *you* it is turned toward me, senses me, *breathes on me;* everywhere else I come out behind its back and cannot make myself knowable to it.

Greet the Beer-Hofmanns warmly for me (and Kassner) and comfort me in your heart,—oh you.

[41]

To Anton Kippenberg Hotel Reina Victoria, Ronda, Spain
January 7, 1913

. . . I have behind me a few very bad weeks; nevertheless I have remained here, for air, lodging and diet could nowhere be more pleasant. My indispositions are not due to the climate, are only a new chapter in this singular overcoming or renewal which my entire nature, I must believe, is having to accomplish in these years; my most hopeful insight is more or less this, that in the physical as in the spiritual, the same thing has been going on since the "Malte", a digging-up process in the entire soil of my being whereby the uppermost gets to the very bottom: times, when it would be most propitious to have no consciousness what-soever; for the continual revolution of such processes cannot there express itself otherwise than as torment and a being exposed. The appearance of the Elegies last year has drawn me a little into the confidence of that which, unutterably slowly, under pretext of such great devastation, may be ordering itself, and in the worst days I do still keep finding a remnant of patience, not patience with myself (that is long since used up), but patience toward God, if one can put it that way, a quiet resolute desire for his standard of measurement.

It is indescribably much, dear friend, that you, on the grounds of I know not what trust, are in these difficult enigmatic years putting me in a position to be patient in this sense, to require nothing of my nature, so that it can pursue, where I myself do not disturb it, its inner and averted activities in all their disguises. If I am destined to reach the next phase of my existence, I shall be, thanks to this protection, more sound and more complete in it than I ever was. As concerns the present journey, it actually has difficulty in distributing itself over inner conditions so disturbed and uneven, nevertheless I am not for a moment in doubt that it is the very thing to do the most urgent service to these changes, in that it draws certain regions, lying there as of old, into the realm of these movements. . . .

[42]

To Annette Kolb　　　　　　　Hotel Reina Victoria, Ronda, Spain
　　　　　　　　　　　　　　　　January 9, 1913

You should know, dear Fräulein Kolb, that the December number of the *Rundschau* did not reach me—, just last evening I received another—, but now I can assure you, by no means quickly enough for my need, how beautiful, how consummate, how masterly the close of the *Exemplar* is. If I were not at this confounded distance, I would send into your house all the flowers I happen to see, just to do something that equals my joy and emotion, for words are too remote and critical here, such things should remain in suspension and in suspension communicate themselves.

You have accomplished something remarkable there, one can well say, achieved it cleanly and without residue; that which you intended is there, indeed, the crucial point is that along with it is realized what we can neither know nor will nor intend, that melancholy and blissful More about which we can do nothing, grace, or however one might call it, something homeless between God and ourselves which, without asking just where it is, finds repose with him or with us.

Something I suspected right from the beginning, there is a discovery in this book, one effected not with instruments and calculations, one for which the moment had simply come to the great attentiveness of your heart, had fallen due, not to be ignored, as Tycho Brahe just could not help, one evening on the way home, seeing the new star in Cassiopeia. Nothing had preceded it but his long, inquisitive gazing, secretly fostered through nights, into the fulness of the constellation, whose throng had thereby unconsciously fallen into such order that the new star entered as though someone with a light walked into his tidied room.

In matters human I can never help thinking right on to the saint (in whom for the first time everything becomes comprehensible and necessary to me), but I am able to understand through Mariclée that (as people have occasionally assured me) the saint is no longer in the same measure exemplary and illuminating to us, as at certain periods he was in the highest degree; that it interests us rather to trace what effect this expenditure has on God when, instead of collecting himself there, he unnoticeably distributes himself in the relationships of the here and now, a more inconspicuous but no less great task. In their intensity, devotion, fervent absoluteness those two months of Mariclée's existence are a saint's life; when the book comes and I have my books once more around me somewhere, I will place it in this neighborhood: close by the Portuguese Nun and Angela da Foligno.

I would almost like to entreat you not intentionally to become further initiated and involved in the literary, in the métier, car ce beau livre, ce n'est pas de la littérature, c'est un état de grace tout simplement—: cela ne vous suffit-il pas? Of myself another time, Spain is incomparable, but I could wish for it another season and state of health. . . .

[43]

*To Princess Marie von Thurn
und Taxis-Hohenlohe*   Paris, Good Friday, March 21, 1913

Your letter was an elixir of life, your beautiful letter (and thanks for all its news), but everything works slowly on me now, I shall reread it often; for the present, à quelques exceptions près, I am going about really depressed, somehow amazed that the new beginning, new as it is, fits so exactly on to the old end on which a year and a half of absence has settled merely like a little patina.

What, now what would have to happen to me, to make me feel it? Duino, Venice, Toledo that gripped my heart so violently, all that is past now, like any interruption, like a bit of deep sleep in the open. God knows: is it due to the vehemence with which Paris takes me in again, takes possession of me, sucks me into itself, into the midst of its existence; though sad, though bewildered, though not to be envied, outside in walking I occasionally feel a smile on my face, a reflection of this wide and open air, just like one of the houses shimmering at the end of the street, brightly, brightly, notwithstanding perhaps that the saddest thing is happening in it. What reality in this city, I marvel again and again at how pain stands there, misery, horror, each like a bush, blossoming. And every stone in the pavement is more familiar to one than a pillow anywhere else, is a stone utterly and entirely, hard to the touch, but yet as though descended from the stone that Jacob pushed under his head. La mort du pauvre qui expire, la tête sur une de ces pierres, est peut-être douce quand-même.

You ask about Marthe: I have seen her only twice, the first time however for a whole night. It was mi-carême, two days after my arrival, I went out to Sceaux, Frau W. was away, so I went into the park and knocked at the studio of the Russian. He himself appeared at the door, a little, blond, Christlike peasant, surrounded by the vague immensities of his already darkening studio; we didn't know each other, I said my name, a pure smile fought its way through his face, he called my name breathlessly upward as a bird does his soul, a high curtain to the right was clutched from within and impatiently thrown open, Marthe rushed out, forward inclined like a deer, a golden headband about her temples, in a quaint, Tanagresque garment—, but quite swallowed up in the bigness of her own eyes—. It turned out that she wanted to go in to Paris, to dance; all day she had done nothing but wash and comb and dress herself, and always, as she told me, with the presentiment that it was not for the ball—for much more. The night was sad, I took her to the Bullier, we missed the last train to Sceaux, my rooms were not in order, so till morning we loafed about in the streets and in inhospitable cabarets, in barbarous surroundings (my maladroitness in knowing nothing better!). She had insisted on going barefoot in her sandals in order to be properly Grecian: that gave her something improbable, touching (something as of a beggar-girl in Heaven); at the Bullier and on the street where, enveloped and draped in her tunic, she stepped with strangely little steps over the confetti lying there and whirling like colored snow, they looked at her surprised, embarrassed, * I would even say with a kind of timid respect. So different was she from all this world of obstinate and cheap amusement. Among all those more or less scabrous girls she looked like a little dying maiden who will be a saint a few years after her death. They took her for a little woman, they scarcely dared speak to her, she seemed to have fallen from a very high nest that she will never find again. She was not much troubled at dancing so little, she needed only to talk and to eat endlessly. She was hungry, she ate with difficulty and effort, with despair, like a ghost that is materializing. And at the same time she wanted to leave that world and enter completely into my eyes and into my ears; she bent over me like a little girl on a lake, desirous of finding her image there even at the risk of drowning in it. She spoke much of her life, of her so provisional life, so incomprehensible, and that no event causes to advance. She lives with this Russian like a sister, she says, immensely relieved not to love him, for "the woman who loved him he would drag about by the hair". He is a savage, a Mordvin, a Siberian, good and terrible, who makes the people he loves decidedly unhappy. The Mordvin language, his own language, possesses only a few words for the most elementary objects; speaking rather little Russian, he has created for himself, since he had to leave his country for political reasons, a mixture of his idiom and Italian (having lived a few years in Milan), an imaginary language with which Marthe seems very well acquainted. His vast studio, a part of which serves as sleeping quarters, is in such disorder that one would doubtless call it a landscape if it happened to be out of doors. One sleeps on pallets among piles of things strewn there and forgotten.—Marthe, very proudly, showed me hyacinth bulbs that have begun to sprout among the covers in the innocent warmth of her poor feet. For the moment, the Russian has a few amateurs who are interested in his work (I remember having seen a Christ on the Cross, gigantic, expressing, with that musical disquiet the Slavs introduce into sculpture, the final agony),—he has some money, but his kindness and his negligence cause the pennies to disappear with the rapidity of running water,—days and nights, they use them without any organization whatever, they sleep from time to time, they eat rarely, only he smokes all the time since he has lived abroad in exile,—from nostalgia. Marthe, while profiting by this irregularity that must seem ideal to her, nevertheless perceives that it is difficult to walk in the mire of liberty. I think she suffers a great deal, that she is using herself up, also she told me she no longer wants to accompany the Russian if he goes to Italy now as he proposes. She sees no existence for herself, for the moment she goes about on the back of this other life like the little heron of Egypt that lives on the backs of cows. Having worked since she was four, doing all the little tasks that fall between the chinks of professions, she sees no further work to broach and all roads seem closed to her by the heavy shadow of the "boss" which one has to pass through with closed eyes if one wants to arrive at profitable and lasting jobs.*

And I, you understand, Princess, know nothing to advise, can just simply let it go along and from time to time go there; I am neither the man of experience who can with composure be helpful, nor yet the lover overtaken by the inspiration of his heart. I am not a lover at all, it moves me only from without, perhaps because no one has ever shaken me utterly, perhaps because I do not love my mother. Very poor I stand there before this rich little creature, in whom a character less cautious and not quite so imperiled (as I have been for a while) could have found endless delight and unfoldment. All love is exertion for me, something achieved, surmenage, only in relation to God have I any ease, for to love God means to enter, to walk, to stand, to rest, and to be everywhere in the love of God.

Marthe has been here for five minutes, she knocked softly as though this writing about her had attracted her; she was sick, had been lying somewhere at one of her sisters', since at Erzia's no one gives her anything to eat; she has quite lost her voice, prétend que "le sang lui était monté à la gorge". I have the impression that she was pretty sick. I have put in her hands Claudel's "L'Annonce faite à Marie"; she is reading, quite far off, as always when after a long time she gets to a book. She must read a while longer before I take her with me to lunch, for I must quickly tell you further: that Monday I lunched with my good and great Verhaeren and with Romain Rolland—I accepted (by way of exception) because

Verhaeren is already leaving—, well, Romain Rolland made such a sympathetic and humanly significant impression on me, that I strongly urged him to visit you sometime in Duino. He is just now going to Italy again, to Rome, but to work, wants to see no one, it seems, so it will not be this time, unless Placci (who also happens to be in Rome and who naturally knows R.R.) stages a visit. One must not expect an artist, but even without being told his name one would be strongly and particularly struck, wherever one met him, by this man who looks up so clearly out of a courageously achieved sincerity. I had the impression of sitting opposite a tireless reader, whose glance, every time his scholar's eyes became exhausted and worn out in his books, God, by some special favor, freshly painted with the purest blue of his childhood; we took to each other with some warmth and curiosity; Verhaeren was magnificent, it was a by no means superfluous lunching, you would have enjoyed it.

Now I must close. Rodin is sick at the moment, otherwise better, and the frightful Mme. de C. is no longer around; unfortunately the end came about for quite a miserable reason, I had hoped it would come more from within and would be more convincing and more real for him. This fantastic Paris, everywhere in the house the opinion persists that this American woman had operated with some Indian poison with which she spiced Rodin's milk! Now with God's help, she's over.

Farewell, Princess, remember me cordially to the Prince, to P., etc. Today and yesterday I am hearing old Italian music by the singers in St. Gervais. Vittoria, Palestrina, Ingegneri . . .

[*44*]

To Princess Marie von Thurn
und Taxis-Hohenlohe   17 rue Campagne-Première, Paris
                                              April 17, 1913

. . . I am thanking you at once for your good eight pages which, as one read them, became even fuller; after this I seem to myself excellently informed about all of Europe, only of the danger of war between France and Germany, with which my femme de ménage runs the broom through my rooms every morning, you make no mention in your bulletin: so I assume things don't look as bad on that score as ordinary people here imagine for the spice of it.

No, as regards Jean-Christophe, I shan't protest any more. (So you have read it all, including volume ten!?) I am near the close of the fourth, and the further I get, the more patience and clemency I have with this small and badly printed paper,—ce n'est pas de l'essence de rose, certainement, mais c'est une tisane qui a eu le temps d'infuser et qui, si on la dégoutte avec lenteur et abandon, arrive parfois à vous rappeler la douce intimité de la petite fleur bienheureuse. The various females turn up quite spontaneously and sturdily, and each time there are a few rich moments before the character makes itself at home in the genre setting. The episode headed Sabine comes within a hair of being a great work of art (Volume III, L'Adolescent, page 71; as it is, it has the unqualified and arresting attraction of certain portraits. (See gallery at Brescia where I would have preferred to stay all the time before the one old lady with the dog, which hung high above a door.) Meanwhile I have returned Romain Rolland's visit; was at his house recently in the evening for a long hour, in the little work room, au quatrième, with the view over three old monastery gardens. There is an air of crampedness about his place, a little spinsterish (I exaggerate, but a shade in that direction) and discreetly quiet. We spoke actually like people who have known each other a long time, without first trying ourselves out on one another with every possible broken surface. Got to discussing music; on his piano lie a series of little black notebooks, filled, as he showed me, with his own neat, almost Japanesely light notation; he set up one of them in front of him and played me a piece of ancient music, an epitaph, full of mourning that finds its compensation in the great. Then a spring melody, taken from a Gregorian mass, just as brief, just as monodic, knowing no exaggeration, but reducing something really infinite to a proportion that is calmed and in itself complete (and therein still quite in the

Greek tradition). Judge for yourself, R.R. noticed how it moved me, sent me next day the copy (which I enclose here and which I shall ask back at your convenience). It will also interest the Prince, you will try it with him perhaps. Give him all my love. By the way, did he ever get the "Salve" I had sent to him from Ronda? I believe he was in Petersburg just then. He should not write me, by heaven, but if he has it, I shall enjoy hearing his opinion of it sometime when we meet again. It seems more barbaric to me than the fragment from the mass of St. Margarita of Cortona. . . .

[45]

To Lou Andreas-Salomé Insel-Verlag, Leipzig
July 22, 1913

(Right after the departure from Göttingen. Lou:)
At moments I feel as though, with everything that you know and are, I were slowly beginning a new life, I can repeat nothing to myself and cannot communicate at all how thoroughly in order everything is, but I feel it going around in my blood day and night, lovingly.

If only I could still make it good or at least just quietly let things take their own good course. If, instead of all the external aspects of the time, which mislead me, I could keep in view this inner world of serene crystals which are not disturbed by anything accidental, in which only the pure revolving of constellations turns inward to lovingly centered activity.

To look off and gently let one's glance have its way where one is facing certainties. . . .

[46]

To Ellen Delp Ostseebad Heiligendamm
Thursday morning (August 14, 1913)

Lou's daughter, Ellen of the morning,
Isn't it quite natural now once more to confuse you with the

sun which has shone exceeding generously into these shoes? (I'm doing it again, without thinking.)

But it is almost disgraceful, lazy, to get up at seven and to find before the door how much bright time there has already been for doing purest day-work.

Concerning the cherryblossom-flower, I picked one recently in the Bollhägen marsh (of the little woodland before Heiligen-damm), contemplating it all day, taking it with me: so astonishing to me was its way of being white out of sheer meadow-green, white with green blood in its heart—; my guess is a little swamp anemone, led thereto by the anemone-ish leaf down on the stem, which is attached curiously low, and yet already knew down there that higher up it would come to this little creature, for which it probably forms a shield or even merely a broadened conduit for the too much moisture of the meadows, the thoughts of which are here distracted for a while, so that the flower above can meanwhile come to its white, which required a trace of dry-ness.

The roses are beautiful, beautiful, rich and, as they stand there so, glorify one's own heart immeasurably.

Rainer

[47]

To Eva Cassirer
Hotel Marienbad, Munich
September 17, 1913

Even before I read it, my dear, I rejoiced in the ampleness of your letter; how could you think you would tire me with it. That I am replying only with a little is due to the unrest of present cir-cumstances—, in all periods when I have to give myself out at-tentively and accurately in the spoken word, as here again too, written expression leaves me, so that even where there might be time for writing, I could scarcely manage a real letter. But I am grateful to you for talking to me somewhat of your inner cir-cumstances, I cannot read them, dear friend, without the feeling that the Tolstoy letters I am sending you today will absorb you most aptly. As far as people are able to inform one another about the ebb and flow of their life feeling, it has happened in this correspondence, the boundaries of help are marked out and look very narrow in comparison with the whole of our existence,—and yet, within these limits what greatness of desire to love. This correspondence is one of the most sincere and hence purest testimonies of inner intercourse with others and with oneself, the figure of Tolstoy emerges from these pages more direct, more moving than I ever realized; what the personal contact with him conveyed, his not being able to do otherwise, his being right behind all error, all this, which moved me so utterly that time, streams over to one from these pages, not overheated, just with the natural warmth of a man toilingly and joyfully alive; let it act on you, I am sure it will release the dispositions in you for which you are waiting and which after much previous accomplishment are closer perhaps and more tangibly at hand than you are able to estimate.

You are right about Werfel; though solitary, he nevertheless creates out of what is common to humanity, rather than out of Nature; but it often strikes one the more deeply, the way he gets at the elemental, at the almost inorganically ruthless, steps out of the room immediately into the all and endures it; occasionally I marvel at him; then again I admire him with all insight into the achieved, with the wonderful freedom of the artist who after all can find repose only there where he sees another successfully accomplishing the ultimate. The Carrion Way I had just read in the Rundschau,—it has magnificent spots, perhaps it lacks a final concentration, I would have been tempted to give something similar in four stanzas. . . .

[48]

To Lou Andreas-Salomé   17 rue Campagne-Première, Paris
                                     October 21 [1913]

I cannot be entirely unhappy with all the understandings into which, so far out above us, so deep behind us, you have given me insight—, but I am so, just as much as I can be, very heartily. You have shown me that I am still somehow the same, even the same in a more fortified way, that actually none of my old possibilities are laid waste or lost, perhaps they are really all there, only that for a while I don't know how to use them.

Paris this time was just as I had promised it to myself: difficult. And I seem to myself like a photographic plate which is exposed too long, in that I still lie open to what is here, this powerful influence. My room was full of last June, waiting, threatening to make me work off in living everything I had then begun. From fright I went right off Sunday to Rouen. A whole cathedral is necessary to drown me out. Provincial France always has something soothing for me, there are so many old houses there in which I mentally play at being at home as I pass by, and then when I look at them, they really are mostly for rent.

Will you believe me that the glance of a woman coming along a quiet street in Rouen so affected me that I could see almost nothing afterward, could not collect myself for anything? But then gradually the magnificent cathedral was nevertheless there, the legends of its densely filled windows where earthly happening becomes transparent and one sees the blood of its colors.

I believe I can stay in Paris only if I imagine myself to have come here quite without responsibility for a few days, taking things casually, as they come: in my neighborhood some very young people have opened a theater that proposes to do old and new things in a clean and honorable way, so I can carry on the Hellerau métier; if only I succeed in remaining as hidden as possible, so that I may get used to myself again, in the fine old sense: content. A little reading, resting, looking out,—I would be satisfied with everything were it only wholly mine again, without flowing out into longing. I am frightened when I think how I have been living away from myself, as though always standing at a telescope, ascribing to each woman who came a bliss that was certainly never to be found in any of them: my bliss, the bliss, once upon a time, of my loneliest hours. I can't help thinking so much of the poem

from the New Poems which, I believe, is called "The Stranger",—
how well I knew what it comes down to:

"To let all this go ever undesiring,"

and I who only went on desiring—. To begin again. Indeed, even
with a school notebook it helped then to open a new page; this one
here, Paris, is now really full of the most humiliating mistakes,
red on top of red, and where one remained absent of its own accord before or changed its mind, there stands the final correction
across a spot erased almost completely through, on the thin skin
of a hole.

Dear Lou, somehow you have indeed helped me infinitely, the
rest is now there for me and for the angel, if only we hold together: he and I, and you from afar. . . .

[49]

To Frau Helene von Nostitz   Paris, 17 rue Campagne-Première
                                            November 4, 1913

. . . I cannot help thinking continually of Duse, whether
money couldn't possibly still be quickly got together in Germany,
where anything can be put through now, for a *Duse-Theater?*
Still, still, I say to myself almost daily, if it were possible, even
today, even tomorrow, and for how much longer; perhaps a real
call, the news that here is a theater which, just as it is, belongs to
you for six months,—would suffice to intensify in her all the
strengths that are still there—: is she then, who had such a beginning, before whom, even when they carried her to her baptism,
the guard presented arms, is she then to go under thus in mist
and smoke? It leaves me no rest that she is lifting her hand somewhere now, somewhere now perhaps is exposing her grieving face
to someone on whom it is lost,—is smiling on some animal a smile
we ought all to see; *that there at some unrecognizable place essence of tragedy is constantly pouring out of a vessel that is really
only upset and not yet shattered.* How full of trifling all these

theaters are compared to the task, to the mission laden with which this woman goes. Do speak sometime to Geheimrat Martersteig. Tell him how I found her last year in the weeks in Venice, strong nevertheless, again and again strong, willing to perform the play, the Ariadne of her friend Poletti, this play that had grown up under her eyes, on every word of which, even while it was coming into being, she tested her speech, whether it rang in her—: would he think it entirely out of the question for someone to undertake, to venture, while there is yet time, to propose to Duse: Come, play this "Ariadne"?

The less other commitments to a bigger or longer season were tied up with such a proposal, the more possibility would seem to me to exist that Madame Duse, once in the theater again, would feel moved to do other plays, that one might suggest to her for instance the plan to play the Virgin Mary in the "Passion" of the Gréban brothers (about 1450) . . . I can never forget the way she spoke of going across the stage once more, "tranquille, mais bien armée", as she said and I understood: *departing across the stage:* as the sun after all can dip under only in the west, so she can go away only across the boards: shouldn't this be procured for her at a time when means and possibilities are so much more readily and flexibly available to this person and that? . . .

[50]

To Reinhard Johannes Sorge
Paris
December second, [1913]

Today I am sending you my promised prose book and the Life Of Mary; the poems ("Emmaus" and "Journey to Hell") came into being last spring and so far have drawn after them nothing of kindred nature.

I am also sending back to you your copy of the "Song of Love"; one surmises the pure splendor, but *what* does a casual translation like that allow one really to perceive? Moreover, as research has long since established, *no* love song by St. Francis exists. A poem of that sort belongs to Jacopone da Todi, to that great minne-poet of our dear Lady Poverty. For a long time it was ascribed to Francis, it begins:

> Amore, Amore che si m'hai ferito
> Altro che Amore non posso gridare;
> Amore, Amore, teco so unito
> Altro non posso che te abbraciare.

Unfortunately I have no edition of Jacapone here to go on quoting. But you do feel the massiveness of the stanzas here in contrast to the hollow translation: this beginning would run more or less:

> Liebe, Liebe, wie konntest du mich verwunden,
> Nichts kann ich schreien, als die Liebe heissen;
> Liebe, Liebe, mit dir bin ich verbunden,
> Nichts könnend, als dich in die Arme reissen.

The copy you took from the Manz edition gives a piece of work, bungled in any case, drawn up from various hymns and poems of that (but also of a later) period, and I cannot conceive of its having satisfied you. I will not conceal from you that in the point of view of the believer I see a danger to the accuracy of feeling which has otherwise been of such decisively great concern to us. When I consider that I might today become a practicing Catholic, where is the church that would not offend me with the paltriness of its pictures and representations; it would have to be a little tumble-down chapel, such as I found in Spain which no modern hand arranges or touches any more. In St. Francis' time, to be sure, this was the soil on which art put forth its tenderest and freest blossoms. To come into contact with the church today means to become indulgent toward incompetence, toward the sweet phrase, toward the whole immense expressionlessness of its pictures, prayers and sermons. Bossuet could still express something tremendous within the church; and the really intense emotion aroused by the figures of Christianity was able endlessly to evoke in hearts new greatness and evidence for new hymns: but, I cannot help it, such exaltation and such fullness would not fall back into the boundaries of the church, but would always descend far above all that is human.

Perhaps I am mistaken; I wrote this in case indulgence on your part toward bad, approximate, inadequate expression (merely because it might be "Catholic") should actually exist. This would have made me anxious, not for your heart, but for the witness it was artistically determined to bear.

[51]

To Princess Marie von Thurn
und Taxis-Hohenlohe   Paris, December 27, 1913

This will sound curious, but nevertheless I am crying out: *don't* come, Princess, don't come, and that is not jealousy of the Lady del Giocondo that makes me cry out so (I don't want to see her at all)—; but I have taken a vow not to look at anyone, not to open my mouth, except inwardly—; if you came, I would either have to adhere to this imposed condition, which would be absurd—or if I did abandon it, I am afraid, Princess, that I would travel right off again or would speak to other people too once I allowed myself a single lovely, lovely exception. I am in a cocoon, dear friend, there is a floating as of gossamer in my room, enveloping me with everything I am spinning out by day and by night, so that already I am no longer recognizable. Wait, please, please, for the next butterfly; you saw in the fall in Berlin how sad and revolting the caterpillar was, a horror. If in the end no butterfly comes out,—all right too, then I shall stay put in this fuzz and quietly dream by myself of the grandiose Mourning Cloak I once had some prospect of becoming. If I don't take flight, someone else will, the Lord wants only that there be flying; whoever happens to see to it, in that he has only a quite passing interest.

Laugh at me, Princess, or scold me. Do both, I am an exasperating bird, here I sit on my perch, all molted and shabby, my feathers are flying into my own bill, and this shameless bill is crying to you: Don't come, don't come,—as a New Year's greeting. Naturally there is a bit of vanity involved too, that you should see me thus. . . .

Dear Princess, here is one of those newspaper pages with a repulsive illustration,—it is the only one I have seen in the Schrenck-Notzing case, and, truly, it is indeed nauseating enough. The book I haven't ordered, the bookseller sent me notice of it upon its publication, I thought it over—, but for me all that really isn't the right thing. (You yourself can imagine what the right thing is.) I will gladly answer to any spirit; if it has the expanse and the need to break into my life, then it will also have something sensible to say of which neither of us need be ashamed; but to scatter this spirit-sugar, so that God knows what spirit-rabble cast off and tabooed over there may slink up and, just like the savages dragged here from Africa, trick us with rites and mysteries that belong to no world at all, that is unsavory and clouds up this world and the next with its dregs. You feel that this is not to disparage the "Unknown"; she had expanse, and even if I never hear from her again, yet she will remain to me something undefined somewhere and in communication with everything in us that stays undefined. But not even with *her* would I like to make the slightest attempt to attract her,—does not immeasurably much that is immaterial flow continually into our spirits; what prevents her from letting herself be carried along into my innermost soul, what from entering this high room in the evening under pretext of some noise? Isn't even this curiously lifelike portrait of a woman hanging here, portraying I know not whom, out of whose blackish background, that by day is dull and spoiled, ever new darkness seems to come along at night, feeding and deepening the high chamber?—No, despite the crystal gazer's solemn assertions, I do not like this métier and shall take care not to lead my meager waters into those dubious channels, perhaps to have them idle themselves completely away into a swamp and play bubbles and will o' the wisps in the bad air.

But you, Princess, are invulnerable, for you *know* something of these things, are not dependent upon your feelings and do not let yourself be fooled by any spirit, because you also know spirits from within and can judge how much more helpless and limited one may be that tries to work on us from without. I can well imagine it would be strange for you if you and the Prince sought out Schrenck who, formerly, at least, must have been a not insignificant figure. Although the slightest experience of one's own, once one does want to experiment, would help infinitely more, I should think, than what goes in for such motley sensationalism at so irritated a spot.

Is Kassner with you now? Do give him all my cordial affection.

I see no one, it has frozen, there has been glare ice, it rains, it drips,—that is the winter here, always three days of each. I have had quite enough of Paris, it is a place of damnation, that I have always known, but formerly the pains of the damned were expounded to me by an angel; now I am supposed to explain them to myself, I find no very laudable interpretation and am in danger of subsequently making mesquin to myself what was once greatly conceived. If God has insight, he will soon allow me to find a few rooms in the country where I can rave quite in my own way and where the Elegies may howl out of me at the moon from all sides, however they please. With that would belong the possibility of taking long solitary walks and exactly the person, the sisterly person!!! (alas, alas) who would look after the house and have no love at all or so much that she asks nothing but to be there functioning and protecting at the border of the invisible. Here the substance of my wishes for 1914, 15, 16, 17 and so forth.

But for you, dear Princess, for the Prince, I have a special corner of my heart in readiness that is very full, may Heaven preside over whatever wishes are there.

Entirely

your D.S.

[52]

To Thankmar
Baron von Münchhausen　　　17 rue Campagne-Première, Paris
December 27 [1913]

See, I wanted to cut the leaves of the poetry volume for you, so that it would come to you rather more personally, more browsed in; but the weeks pass, and other things have been giving me no respite. But since you knew D., it will be warmed for you even this way by personality, his: Deubel's.

Am I mistaken in thinking that in the introduction, which I read, the stress falls on the wrong place? Or, if his life is really to be read with these accents, I miss a harmony sounding through it which, as all the conjugations are over, ought to be felt in its now final life-infinitive.

I wonder, in view of such impressions, whether, whatever the misery among us, the line of the poètes maudits didn't end with Pauvre Lélian; for in the end, in this most singular of callings, bénédiction preponderates, it simply prevails, that everyone must concede. Hence there arises something arbitrarily distorted, no longer true (to our eyes), when one wants reproachfully to expose misère (cette misère revêche qui s'entête) and at the same time to make it into a constructive element of a poet's existence. We simply *don't know* what need destroys in a heart, what it erects. Constructive it is in no case, at most the scaffolding that is hung with rags, behind which the final stones may at times arrange themselves and deliberate. But then one must also allow it to be pulled down quietly, when it is no longer absolutely necessary, instead of giving importance to planks and boards, together with the placards and posters which little by little have taken over the place. In the right is only he who leaves the door open for heur and malheur, so that each can come, but also go, as it must. To accustom misery to oneself, daily to give it the sugar from one's coffee, so that finally it is lying under every table and won't leave, is to inculcate in this phantom a training contrary to its ruttish nature. As a poet one should not make even détresse one's beloved, but should transfer all affliction and bliss into one's work, and one's external life must be stamped with one's refusal to undergo either of them elsewhere.—Something like that is what occurred to me in reading the introduction, I scarcely got to the poems, they will probably speak for what I mean, at least most of them. . . .

[53]

To Eva Cassirer   17 rue Campagne-Première, Paris XIVe
                                      January 2, 1914

Yes, Tolstoy's correspondence with Countess Alexandrine Tolstaia has been for me the point of departure for much inner preoccupation and agitation; now I have seen from your good letter, dear friend, that it is acting in you too, be content with that to which it stimulates you; it seems to me you need not wish any more at all (how much comes up, testing and recognizing itself by this reading).

As for those letters, it is wonderful in itself that two human beings are able to maintain themselves over a period of almost fifty years in real divergence, continually reshaping and renewing in the spaces of their distance apart the constellation of their relationship, so that, beyond all reversals and upsets, they yet remain to each other, if not comprehensible, at least accessible through unconfused love and moving through a hundred facets of the heart. In her introduction Countess Alexandrine tries to *understand* and every so often has to admit that she cannot do so: that gives the impression of pettiness, but is only a light coating on the deeper truth of that relationship which, like all human relationships, proceeds in the unjudgeable and reaches into the realm of opinion almost solely with that which expels. An aunt of Tolstoy's, on whose estate I stayed for a time, spoke quite similarly of him—, for his "well-meaning" relatives he had sides which did him harm and by which they felt hurt and menaced as by personal atacks.

You are quite right that here in these words two who are "just" often contend with one another; Tolstoy indeed did everything to be such a "just man", and it was the "saint" in him, as well as the poet, that retrenched. To me, in this sense, the just man would appear to be one who, on the way to saintliness, suddenly takes notice of his time, takes it seriously, resolves to check it as in itself unjust, one, in short, who applies to the immediate the resources that are probably meant to lose themselves functioning out into the infinite: a task which fell to the Gospels too and which always, where it is due, will be full of hardship: for where the divine settles directly on the petrifactions and calcifications of human life, how could it be other than hard, a basic steel hardened in white heat, driven in by the sure hammer of truth. If, as I under-stand it, the just man is this saint who has almost prematurely exhausted himself on the temporal, Tolstoy could pass as a particularly clear example of such a phenomenon—and yet: when one met him (I saw him very quietly in 1899 in Moscow, the next year on an unforgettable spring day on his estate—), when one met him—: I doubt whether I am able sufficiently to assure you how preponderantly the other then emanated from his being, the pure, the angelic rightness that gives no heed to the time and shines right through and out beyond it, overtaking it once and for all. The very thing you find in a high degree in Dostoievsky, in whom it also increased so that finally he might contemplate even the time (in his "Diary of a Writer"), because he did not interfere in order to stop it, did not stand in its path to persuade it, but rather in-terpreted it as an extremely temporary image for the infinite happening, the scene of which, for a while by God's measure, has been left blank in our inner existence (a divine decree intending to develop it at the darkest place). But I see from your question about Prince Myshkin that you do not know Dostoievsky's perhaps most beautiful book, *The Idiot:* so it may be a little additional Christmas greeting from me to you, it will place in your heart a wonderful figure in which, once one has it, much of thought, that would otherwise be lost in one, precipitates and remains; in such a manner that with the figure of the Prince there is given one of those receptacles, of which great art has produced a few, cups in which the soul's purest rain keeps gathering, fruits that ripen in us to such sweetness that we must believe in the mildness of our innermost climate.

Kassner, I surmise, is neither the "saint" nor the "just man", but rather one who has insight into both, equipped therefore at certain moments with a superiority that cannot entirely avoid the appear-ance of presumption; for it does not dawn on us right away that anyone might "have insight" into the saint. But the human mind may naturally do this too. Kassner, for moments, is able to view the saint from the place from which, I will not say God,—but a god would see him, and so he is in a position to see through him. He will be able to give us the most fabulous conclusions on the inner origin of the saint, on the nature of the anomaly that he is; he will betray him; which would be irresponsible in an age when the saint was still visibly projecting his influence into the visible world; now he has deserted his being's previous organization, it lies there uninhabited, one may set foot in it and look about amid the most astonishing architecture, in which for centuries the human heart has tried its bearing power and audacity. The existence of the saint among us has not been abolished; however, he will have to found new colonies for his spirit, or, if he does not want to make up his mind to this, it may be that the time of wandering has come for him once more, which will unfold for him (whom fame so little becomes) countless possibilities for a penetrant conspicuousness. . . .

[*54*]

To Frau Helene von Nostitz   17 rue Campagne Première,
                                                              Paris XIV°
                                                    January 23, 1914

Thank you, yes, for *both* letters, which came safely into my hands, each with many friendly good things.

On February 4th then my thoughts will go in your direction; about coming, alas: I now know definitely I must not stir from here; however little may for the present outwardly result from it, in my innermost it is sure to bring about something, this obstinate retirement; at last my room is again beginning to be completely filled out of myself, at last I am again on the way to being able to imagine nothing that could be more inexhaustible, greater, more spontaneously-blissful than my solitude, and notice only now how very indifferent and alien it had become to me in the last bewilderedly truant years, how I suddenly expected everything from people and nothing more from it, this solitude which after all, since the boundlessly frightful pains of childhood, had given me all that was greatest, all that was always *too great*.

So I shall not stir, though I might wish and wish more and more intensely that the rooms were quite elsewhere, in the country, that the place were no longer Paris; every going out depresses me and is inimical to me; God knows, I have lived up this city and must shortly look about for a ruralness that will allow one to live apart and wander beneath big skies; easy it will not be, since all countries are possible and none probable, also I would then need someone to devote herself to me, cook for me, understand me and yet make no demands, in short an inconceivable creature that God will certainly not have made, and should he even now bring her quickly forth, she would first have to grow and thrive, and while that goes on it will become too late.

It struck me as particularly sweet that in both letters you mention Malte and even want to have read from it the passages concerning Charles the Bold. This book is beginning to be wonderful to me again, I could write about it as about that of a stranger, for all that is beautiful in it I have a big heart; how much had to happen for it to be there one day, my boundless childhood, so much will of course never accumulate again, even if one were to have decades more to achieve under the most unspeakable sufferings and most incomprehensible blisses.

Duse, I read in the "Figaro" of her illness in Viareggio, convalescence beginning under the care of Isadora Duncan; for writing her I lack the inner security, one would have to stand there like an archangel, in order to incline toward her pain with an untroubled smile—. That nothing could be done I foresaw, I spoke about it here with Verhaeren recently—. Even with Reinhardt nothing could have been attempted, certainly not; he was the very one who did not want to take hold seriously that time when Duse herself had written to him. It would seem to me he is another person now, caught in other plans, intentions and purposes, carried along by the breadth of his undertakings, no longer independent. Comme tout change, "viene meno" et on ne sait pas quand on diminue . . . . C'est toujours cela qui m'effraie le plus. . . .

[55]

To Helene von Nostitz　　　　　17 rue Campagne-Première, Paris
January 27, 1914

. . . As I telegraphed you, Gide, whom I saw yesterday, knew of a newspaper report which was immediately afterward retracted. Besides that, I saw at an acquaintance's a letter of R[odin]'s written on the 21st, in which he told them that he felt "malade un peu" and would remain a few days in his room (there was no talk of going to bed).

I experienced, even now again, a real compulsion to go straightway to Meudon, and you mustn't think that any petty touchiness is keeping me from it; a feeling like that I would easily overcome, if I were able to entertain it at all toward Rodin. But that in itself really unimportant incident of last spring seems to me, when I think back, like a place at which the actually existing sickness of our present relationship clearly emerged, so that one could see how no real benefit was to be gained from it at present. Our intercourse was in fact unhappy and unfruitful, at least measured by that powerful necessity out of which it had formerly arisen and out of which it seemed always to shoot up into new healthy sprouts. This too is one of the curious limitations within human approaches, that it seems denied us, or at least surpasses our strength, one day to experience half, conditional, lesser things with someone with whom we have known how to get on in the greatest.

To this is added a kind of cowardice or perhaps merely caution: since I am now maintaining myself on so narrow a rim of calm and on it trying, sleep-walking rather than walking, to reach a place in my inner being on which I might quietly settle down to all kinds of confident achievement, every diversion into the external is fateful for me: fateful to see again places like Meudon, or even just the rue de Varenne, which I cannot glimpse without everything in me, disintegrated by sharp memories, assuming another structure, stopping, stiffening and, if at all, only slowly taking shape again in other forms.

Where feeling determines, one should not raise such misgivings, but I have behind me so many years that are lost or at least have almost eluded me, that I am now ruthlessly living toward a certain inner ownership and feel equal to drawing into my obstinate isolation *only* what I can immediately resolve and turn to use and nourishment for myself.

Beyond this I hope that after all there is no cause at present for real concern; haven't you tried writing a word to R. himself, perhaps you will receive the most reliable reassurance by a line from his own hand.

The cold which had the mastery here for two weeks seems since yesterday to have broken, perhaps this too will be to the good.

I was at Gide's yesterday, though I don't go out otherwise and don't see anyone, because I translated his "Retour de l'enfant prodigue" some time ago and needed a few bits of information on passages doubtful to me. The translation is to represent Gide in the Insel-Bücherei, that work is beautiful and characteristic of him (long a favorite of mine).

[56]

To Hedwig von Boddien   17 rue Campagne-Première, Paris XVIᵉ
February 23, 1914

. . . For about two months a book has been out (a French one) which I won't positively say will bring into absolute accord all those who take part in an evening's reading: on the contrary, it seems to me just designed to be understood and felt in the most varying ways, yes, so manifoldly that almost all the spectral colors of judgment could be present, in which case the final pure sunlight of mutual undestanding could be charmingly recomposed at the close. Marcel Proust's "Swann" is actually no book for *reading aloud* either; two passages prohibit that straightway, quite incidental ones it is true, which take up only a few pages,—but even if one skipped them, I don't know whether, with the indescribable wealth of ideas, spiritual analogies and intimate joys, someone reading aloud would be able to broaden himself sufficiently to keep all that present side by side (and not just in sequence). I like to imagine that life at Wendthof passes spaciously so that your summer friends, one after the other, would find the leisure quietly to go over Proust's book,—and that only *then* would the memorable evenings begin in which one person or another would read aloud what especially struck home to him out of the inexhaustible pages and would hold it out in a specific way to the general opinion: I am convinced that not alone would there result a many-sided and entertaining consideration of Du côté de chez Swann, but also to many a one his own childhood would appear out of half-oblivion, and one would pass from tale to tale far into the summer night, but also far into the mutually true, rich and alive. . . .

[57]

To Princess Marie von Thurn
und Taxis-Hohenlohe
Hotel Subasio, Assisi
May 18, 1914

Here, dear Princess, comes with the utmost tardiness, a report on my last ten days; to tell anything sooner, the least bit, was beyond my resources, every atom in me was made of a heavy, dull dumbness,—so too nothing came of the good refuge in the mezzanino; for I would have had to see the Valmaranas and through them this person and that, to feign an alive exterior, to speak, to act sympathetically,—all of which was quite beyond my strength. So, as the heavy, numb object that I was, I made myself travel here right away Friday, have been here in this good loveliness since Saturday morning before last, but, God forgive me, so closed and averse to every possible benefit that between me and these companionable surroundings no commerce and no joy takes place. Il faut que je me remette, que je me retrouve, ce sera long et je ne crois pas que cela passera ici.

No, sometimes when I look out through a little hole in the wall of my apathy into the real, just for a moment,—I am amazed at how far I now am from the "poverello" que nous importe le bon coeur de cette petite bourgade d'Ombrie, Saint Francis, that is a lot, but it no longer encompasses us; poverty is one thing, tangible as a stone and just as hard, but since then money has become incorporeal, far transcending tangible possession, a vibrant, all-pervasive element, almost independent of the possessor, an atmosphere to which there is no longer any contrast. Now it is a question of finding the new poverty for this new "wealth", all that having withdrawn far into the invisible; one can of course always outwardly imitate being poor, but real poverty must be born again anew inside in the soul and will perhaps not be Franciscan at all. —All this does still move us here, and ten years ago, with the imaginative joy of youth, I would have attuned myself to it,— now, to agree here even for a moment, is pure imitation of feeling and in the deepest sense sterile. Alas, if this still lived from its own flame and were not only kept up from heart to heart laboriously, how different would be the intensity in the intimate lower church, in which the Giottos maintain an inexhaustible nearness to that saint's life. How ashamed and excluded and utterly out of place the mere spectator, the observer, ought to feel there,—whereas it works excellently to go about simply assuming an artistic point of view,—one is remarkably little affected in this grottoed darkness, —that *I* am not might easily lie with me, but even so I see only inquisitive people about me, and even if I didn't shudder at them, I would not ascribe to expressions like "lovely" and "charming" any high degree of inner warmth. . . .

[58]

To Reinhard Johannes Sorge   Paris, June 4, 1914

. . . The concern I expressed once before now seems to me too almost superfluous; if you know you are quite capable of carrying out every movement and portrayal of your heart within the adopted and passionately acknowledged enclosure, if even ultimate words and last cries still have room within the compass you call the church, it is natural that you should find unrestricted in it all the mobility for which your being is designed. Even at our first meeting I did not conceal from you that my case is different; in the purely spiritual realm, if one conceives it very broadly, the church may be an immeasurable compass, the greatest earthly one, which, along an almost invisible track, passes over into the eternal—; but where someone (such as I) is committed to a making visible of the spiritual, then art must clearly strike him as by far the greater life periphery (as the one that leads him farthest into the infinite): for otherwise he could not allow himself to follow its laws and forms into those works that have originated outside the air of Christian faith and are even now, here and there, originating in purest validity. That within the Christian church ways to God of most blissful ascent and of deepest achievement can be trodden, we have the prodigious evidence of the saints' lives and besides them many a strong and sincere enduring, perhaps in our immediate neighborhood. But this conviction and experience does not exclude in me the certainty that the most powerful relationships to God, where there is need and urge for them, can develop in the extra-Christian spirit too, in any struggling human being, as all Nature, after all, where it is allowed to have its way, passes over inexhaustibly to God. . . .

[59]

To Lou Andreas-Salomé   17 rue Campagne-Première, Paris
June 8, 1914

Here I am once again, after a long, broad and heavy time, a time with which once more a kind of future is past, not strongly and reverently lived out, but tormented to death, till it succumbed (in which no one will so easily imitate me). If sometimes in recent years I might make excuses for myself on the grounds that certain attempts to get a more human and natural footing in life itself miscarried for the reason that the people involved did not understand me, had inflicted on me, one after the other, violence, wrong and harm, thus causing me bewilderment,—I am now left after these months of suffering with quite a different verdict: having to see this time that no one can help me, no one; were he to come with the most warranted, most spontaneous heart, and proving himself clear to the stars and enduring me however difficult and stiff I make myself, and holding the pure, the unerring direction to me, though I were to break the ray of his love ten times with the cloudiness and density of my underwater world—: I would still (that I now know) find a means of exposing him in the whole fullness of his ever-welling help, of imprisoning him in a region airless and loveless, so that his aid, unusable, would grow overripe in him and wilted and horribly atrophied.

Dear Lou, for a month I have been alone again and this is my first attempt to come to my senses—; you see what state they are in. One will perhaps have learned many things from it,—so far, indeed, I notice only this: that once again I was not equal to a pure and joyous task in which life stepped over to me once more, innocent, forgiving, as if it had had no bad experiences with me. Now it is clear that this time too I flunked the test and will not be promoted and will be left sitting for another year in the same pain-class and daily will have the words written for me, all over again, on the blackboard, the same ones whose blurred vowel sounds I thought I had already mastered to the ground.

What finally turned out so completely to my misery began with many, many letters, easy, beautiful ones that came rushing from my heart; I can scarcely remember even having written any like them. (That was the time of the exuberant "S", you will recall.) In these letters (I realized more and more) a spontaneous liveliness sprang up, as if I had hit upon a new full welling-up of my most intimate being which now, released in inexhaustible communication, poured itself over the blithest declivity, while I, writing day after day, felt at once its happy flow and the enigmatic repose that seemed most naturally prepared for it in a receptive person. To keep this communication pure and transparent and at the same time to feel or think nothing that would be excluded from it: this all at once, without my knowing how, became the measure and law of my activity,—and if ever a deeply troubled person can become pure, I became so in those letters. The everyday and my relationship to it became to me in an indescribable fashion sacred and responsible,—and thence a strong confidence seized me, as if now at last the way out of the lazy being-dragged-along in the always fateful had been found. How much, from then on, I was in the process of changing I could also note from the fact that even what was past, when I happened to tell about it, surprised me by the manner in which it emerged; if, for example, periods were concerned of which previously too I had often spoken, the accent fell on formerly unheeded or scarcely known places,—and each one, innocent as a landscape, as it were, took on a pure visibility, was there, enriched me, belonged to me—, so that for the first time I seemed to become the owner of my life, not by interpretive appropriation, exploitation and understanding of what had been, but simply by that new truthfulness itself which flowed through even my memories.

June 9, 1914

I am sending you, dear Lou, this sheet of yesterday: you understand that what I described there is long past and lost to me; three unachieved months of reality have laid something like a strong, cold glass over it, beneath which it becomes unpossessable as in a museum's showcase. The glass reflects, and I see in it nothing but my face, the old, the last, before last—, which you know so well.

And now?—After a useless attempt at being in Italy, I returned here (two weeks ago today), intending somehow to busy myself up to the ears; but I am still so dull and benumbed that I cannot do much more than sleep. Had I a friend I would ask him to work with me every day for a few hours, at no matter what. And when at intervals I think with the heaviest heart of the future, I most readily imagine rather a kind of work that is disciplined from without and is removed as far as possible from productivity. For I no longer doubt that I am sick, and my sickness has gained a lot of ground and is also lodged in that which heretofore I called my work, so that for the present there is no refuge there.

I am slowly reading in your Bergson and can follow from time to time; am reading Stefan George's strange new book (*The Star of the Covenant*),—passed an afternoon recently with Maeterlinck's essay on the Elberfeld horses. (Have you read it? *Neue Rundschau*, June number.) In this connection it occurs to me, in Duino, where I was also for a while, another experiment was made with spiritualistic writing, through the same person,—and the result this time too was extremely remarkable. After several manifestations in foreign languages—Arabic, Greek,—the same being seemed to re-establish itself, and indeed with such vehemence in its return that the medium could finally manage it no longer and went about for three days with pains in the arm. . . .

[60]

To Lou Andreas-Salomé

[Paris, June 20, 1914]

Lou, dear, here is a curious poem, written this morning, which I am sending you at once because I spontaneously called it "Turning", because it depicts *the* turning which probably must come if I am to live, and you will understand it as it is meant.

Your letter in response to the dolls I sensed in advance, surmising that one would come and with something comforting, with a somehow ordering impression. And so it was. Yes, I understand exactly what you discern there, even the last sentence, which "words" do not achieve, even that last sentence about the doll's becoming one with the physical and its most horrible fatalities.

But isn't it frightful that one should have unsuspectingly written down something like that, dealing under the guise of a doll memory with what is most intimately one's own, and then quickly laid aside one's pen in order once more to live out the weirdness limitlessly, indeed as never before; until every morning one was parched with the tow with which one's hide was stuffed, through and through, right up into one's mouth?

Your

Rainer

Turning

"The road from inwardness to greatness goes through sacrifice." Kassner

Long he was victorious in gazing.
Stars fell to their knees
under his wrestling glance.
Or he gazed kneeling,
and the fragrance of his earnestness
wearied a something divine
so that it smiled at him, sleeping.

Towers he gazed at so
that they were afraid:
building them up again, suddenly, upward, all in one stroke!
But, how often, the landscape
overburdened by day
lay at rest in his silent perceiving, at evening.

Animals trustfully stepped
into his open glance, grazing,
and captive lions
stared in as into inconceivable freedom;
birds flew straight through him,
the open of soul. Flowers
gazed back into him
big, as into children.

And the rumor that there was one gazing
moved those less visible,
more doubtfully visible,
moved the women.

Gazing how long?
For how long already with fervor foregoing,
imploring in the depth of his glance?

When he sat, waiting, abroad; the inn's
diffuse, averted room
morosely around him, and in the avoided mirror

again the room
and later from his tormenting bed
again:

debate was held in the air,
debate impalpable
upon his sensible heart,
through the painfully shattered body
his nonetheless sensible heart,
debate and the judgment:
that it did not have love.

(And forbade him further ordainment.)

For gazing, see, has a boundary.
And the more gazed-upon world
desires to prosper in love.

Work of sight is done,
now do heart-work
on the pictures within you, those captives; for you
overcame them: but now do not know them.
Behold, inner man, your inner maiden,
this, won from
a thousand natures, this
creature, now only won,
never yet loved.

(June 20)

[61]

To Thankmar
Baron von Münchhausen   Assumption of the Virgin, 1914
[Hotel Marienbad, Munich, August 15]

Your mother could have done nothing kinder than to send me
the envelope, in which I now hastily enclose this greeting, with a
couple of verses from the early days of this appalling August.

. . . I had already learned of the fine chance for you to take part as an officer in the activity of this world-year; nobody has it harder than the man who remains behind inactive: will he be at all able to grasp the new time to come afterward, that will be so different?—

Now your unsettled plans have been taken off your shoulders by a settled common destiny—I can imagine that this is an unforgettable joy, thus all at once to be involved in One power and One emotion, especially after the many-minded times that have long since confused and wearied all of us.

[*62*]

To Anna
  Baroness von Münchhausen   Ascension of the Virgin, 1914
                                                Hotel Marienbad, Munich
                                                    [August 15]

Who: who would have thought it! And now one thinks nothing but this, and everything former has become as it were immemorial, separated from one through abysses and heights of no longer feelable feeling. . . .

The high heart of all those who are out there must sustain us over the still water of not-knowing and not-grasping which sometimes threatens to engulf even me.

[*63*]

To Anna
  Baroness von Münchhausen   Pension Landhaus Schönblick,
                                        Irschenhausen—Post Ebenhausen,
                                                Isartalbahn, Bavaria
                                                  August 29, 1914

. . . If I could only send him something soon again from a more uplifted heart; he is riding forth there so bold and gloriously-young, really it is wonderful, this ancient knight's destiny upon a young man of today, unawares.

Gradually I am beginning to find my having stayed behind in the rear of so much break-up bewildering and vexatious: in the first days my spirit went along with the general current, could in its own way join in; then, as one unspeakably isolated, I remembered myself, my old heart as it had been hitherto (which I cannot give up), and now I am having a very hard time finding, by myself, across this span, the valid and if possible somehow fruitful attitude toward the monstrous generality. Happy those that are in it, carried away by it, drowned out by it.

Until now I have, in spite of circumstances, lived according to my plans; was in Munich to confer with and be treated by my doctor, came out here Monday on his advice; but this is now the most unendurable of all, to side with unsuspecting Nature and take care of one's self. While I am trying it, an impatience and a discontent are growing in my breast which I shall not long be able to stand. Probably I shall go back to Munich after all and then to Bohemia to my friends there: to see if I can't make myself somewhat useful from there and leave "convalescing" and "getting strong" for later, until we (when?) are across the terrible mountain-range in the unforseeable future which no one can picture to himself.

The Hölderlin volume is a comfort now; wonderful, that these poems live and reach to one's heart through all the tangle of apprehension. I read the *Hyperion* too with keenest participation: how much it sounds like what is happening to us, and yet from the start goes far beyond it, forming pure clouds above the war and above love. . . .

[*64*]

To Lou Andreas-Salomé   Landhaus Schönblick, Irschenhausen
September 9, 1914

How often, dear Lou, in this monstrous August, have I known that there was just one place where one might really survive it: with you, in your garden; for if one can imagine two people to whom this unsuspected time brings exactly the same suffering, the same daily horror, we are they—how could we help it?

Thus I felt your telegram and understood it more deeply than I can say, but still I don't at all know how to answer its questions right away,—so little have I yet considered what one might go on to do of one's own initiative. Since this fortnight out here in the country I have really been hesitating, from the very beginning, only between two decisions: going back to the city, or, if it is really a matter of recuperating, taking the cure at Ebenhausen, where at least baths, sunbaths, etc., would be at my disposal. Just staying in the country is, this year particularly, a half-hearted business, since one lacks the simplicity of mind to be with Nature; her influence, her quiet penetrating presence is outweighed from the start through the mere thought of the nameless human doom that is happening irresistibly day and night. I would almost have gone back to Munich; but then Clara wrote that she wanted in any case to come back with Ruth for the opening of school, which would be around the end of this week—and so I hesitate, for she hasn't much money and if I am to help her I can most easily do it from here, where I need little for myself and each week exactly the same. My arrangements with Insel-Verlag, which looked so comforting, are not exactly canceled, but, as Kippenberg told me in the end, they hold only "when possible". That of course is already a good deal, for how much has not become simply *im*possible. Freiburg, for example: a gleam of probability finally fell upon the plan, when we were considering everything in Leipzig, that I should attempt certain studies there in the Schwarzwald air, not too far from Paris, near Colmar and other lovely places. I would like, even now, to choose my next abode with these intentions in mind—which incidentally, imagine it, greatly surprised and pleased Stauffenberg, who in the back of his mind wanted and planned something very similar for me. The good man had prepared himself for me as honestly and fully as it is possible to do through my books and from his own most sympathetic attitude,— so that what we said seemed merely the continuation of all the inner intercourse with me which had long been natural to him. Against this background it was not easy, in the continually disturbed present, to find the composure for our talks, but the time he always found, whole hours, even when work in the hospital was piling up around him on all sides; then he would come to me or we would quickly arrange for a walk together.—The result? He kept trying to get to the region in which he believes he has particular authority, and we did walk across it now and again, only that all digging and hoeing and real work there remained out of the question. With terror I sometimes felt a sort of spiritual nausea which he was trying to bring on; it would be awful to throw up one's childhood like that in fragments, awful for a person who is not committed to resolving the unconquered part of it within himself but exists quite particularly for the purpose of using it up in converted form, in discoveries and feelings, in things, in animals—in what not?—if need be, in monstrosities.—At one of his thorough examinations Stauffenberg discovered an old pulmonary lesion, harmless and unimportant in its way, and from then on there was at least something definite to warrant his dealing strictly physically with me, which made things easier for both of us. . . .

Dear Lou, this is about how things stand with me. Write me about yourself, what you may be thinking. Herewith a few pages written in August, chiming in with the universal theme. How one's *own* looks in with it, what it will become because of it, I am but slowly understanding—I keep thinking, as with approval, of those who have died in these last years, and that they no longer had to grasp all this from here.—Write me; meanwhile I shall see better what is to be done.

[65]

To Thankmar
  Baron von Münchhausen   Pension Landhaus Schönblick
                                   Irschenhausen—Post Ebenhausen
                                   September 17, 1914

. . . Your dear mother writes me that you never got [my letter]. I have been considering whether I would copy the poems for you again, and cannot bring myself to do it; for they date from those very first August days. (Where are they?) Then we all threw ourselves into that suddenly set-up and opened universal heart; now—wherever each separate one of us may be—we have probably to survive and endure the contrary: the rebound from the universal heart into our surrendered, deserted, unutterably own heart. I am filled and shaken by the thought, my dear fellow, how much alike all our positions may be,—yours, restlessly riding out there, and ours, restless, here. For what is apparent external security when there is all this life and death extremity in one's innermost being?

I have as yet seen no one who understands, save Lou, in whose letter day before yesterday were a few lines of divining insight, by which I am now trying to go on, alas, to feel my way.

My dear boy, we shall survive it! And then it will be one power more in us, and our heart shall have grown more mighty through it and all that we can feel more holy and more pure and more obligating.

[66]

*To Prince Alexander von
Thurn und Taxis*
temporarily Pension Pfanner,
2 Finkenstrasse, Munich
October 4, 1914

The mournful news that has reached me, only now, by roundabout ways, awakens in me the most melancholy chords of response and an immediate need to be with you and really sharing. Believe me, in these lines I am utterly so. In my feeling there is often something of the truth and beauty of a son's submission toward you and the Princess, that you know: thence I can understand what you are now going through and can measure it by the reverence of which your relationship to the old lady who is now dead gave me a feeling so in the highest sense noble and ideal.

To me certain evening hours of that summer three years ago, when the Princess favored me with many a lively tale and expressly elaborated reminiscence, stand in my memory as something lasting, and it made the strongest impression on me to find the legends of a long life so purely and definitely preserved in an austere mind.

Now her quiet going falls in a time that drowns out everything; perhaps a sort of consolation may involuntarily proceed from the fact that in these days of monstrously accelerated dying the sorrowful natural event comes about in a way that is by nature milder.

How much my thoughts have been at Lautschin in these months and are now particularly so; to write the Princess was one of my strongest impulses—but one hears onself living so little, as though one stood day and night beside the most booming waterfall; those out there are in the great sweep of rushing events—a person like me, who is only standing beside it, waits, keeps silent, hoping that in the end a word, a feeling, an insight, may ripen in his soul that might be useful at the moment when the exhausted war collapses into itself, leaving the immense spaces it takes up to emptiness, stillness, a future that is to be begun anew. . . . When? . . .

[67]

To Alfred von Heymel   Pension Pfanner, 2 Finkenstrasse
Munich, October 12, 1914

. . . Today I read your letters . . . and read them aloud. How often in August, when this movement with its unforeseeable end arose, did I think of you as one of those for whom this had to come, so that he might make full use of himself and get about everywhere in his own heart; how very right I was in this opinion appears almost overwhelmingly from your hearty and happy letters, my dear friend; a frame of mind that embraces heaven and earth speaks out of them—God grant us all sometime to be of such a heart. Perhaps these changing destinies are leading us also, each individual one of us that is left behind, to make most unheard-of demands upon ourselves; perhaps they are preparing us too for a new presence of mind and presence of heart—this much everyone feels, that life is cut to allow for growth and that one may vigorously put on weight before one fills it out entirely.

[68]

To Frau Helene von Nostitz Pension Pfanner, 2 Finkenstrasse
Munich, October 21, 1914

When was it (I often ask myself) that I had Johannes Kalck-reuth show me your house—I still see its quiet street and the way it showed its face so simply out of the garden—when was it? A few days later fate broke out of the impenetrable world, this world-noise which overnight drowned out one's thinking back, and on beyond which no one is yet able to think. Not even now when so much dreadful accomplishment and progress has been going on on all sides. Who might say what is really happening to us now and what sort of people those who survive this year will later turn out to be. To me it is an unspeakable suffering and for weeks I have been understanding and envying those who died before it, that they have no longer had to experience it from here; for somewhere in space there will surely be places from which this monstrosity still appears natural, as one of the rhythmic convulsions of the universe which is assured in its existence, even where we go under. And indeed we are going under, into the midst of it, into the most existent—here one must look upon the fullness of destruction and suddenly know something of death. Perhaps this is what is meant by the terrible war, perhaps this experiment is going on before some unsuspected observer; if it is conceivable that there are unconfused eyes, the seeing, experienced eyes of the investigator who is examining this like a hardest sort of stone, and confirming the existence of a further degree of hardness of life under this up-boiling death.

[69]

To Karl and Elisabeth von der Heydt Pension Pfanner
2 Finkenstrasse
Munich, November 6, 1914

. . . You ask after me with affectionate concern. So I will just quickly relate that, without presentiment, I left Paris on the 20th of July; for two months, as I thought, leaving all my possessions behind me in customary fashion. These I have long since and freely abandoned to fate, as it is absolutely not for me to take possession literally. Two or three things, it is true—the daguerreotype of my father, an old picture of Christ that I have had standing before me since boyhood, and certain letters and particular irreplaceable books among all my several hundred—still follow me from afar and wave farewell, and I wave to them . . . But that will pass and, as one simply has to learn, the individual absolutely does not matter, even if I do not see the common bonds either that might matter; it probably does not matter at all anyway, but instead fate is right and behind fate the all-surviving stars. Everything visible has simply been cast once again into the boiling abysses, to be melted down. The past remains behind, the future hesitates, the present is without foundation; but hearts, ought they not to possess the power of soaring and maintain themselves among the great clouds? In the first days of August the phenomenon of the war, of the war-god, gripped me (in the Insel War-Almanac you will find a few poems that came out of this experience); now the war has long since become invisible to me, a spirit of tribulation, no longer a god but the unleashing of a god over the peoples. Nor is more to be achieved now, than the soul's endurance, and misery and evil are perhaps no more present than before, only more graspable, more active, more apparent. For the misery in which mankind has daily lived since the beginning is really not to be increased through any circumstances. But increases of insight there surely are into the unspeakable misery of being man and perhaps all this is leading to them; so much decline, as though new ascents sought—distance and space for their running off.

. . . I hope we shall see each other soon in days when we can breathe again; perhaps we are all learners, and if we hold through there will afterward be heart-holidays as never before.

[70]

To Clara Rilke   Hotel Englischer Hof, Frankfort a.M.,
                                                November 18, 1914

And last evening I heard a singularly moving story from an officer of Hussars, who was among the first to be wounded before Longwy—it does matter after all to hear real voices—and the *Cornet* is touchingly interwoven with it all—the Hussar officer, not knowing who I was, asked me whether I knew this ballad . . . ?! And then what recognition, that it should have been I myself who wrote it.

[71]

To Anton Kippenberg   6 Bendlerstrasse, Berlin W 10
                                                January 4, 1915

. . . The new year was no perceptible division at all for me either; since after all the year of war in which we are living continues and cancels all other calendars, far into the season. I spent the night in solitude with many an inner settling of accounts and finally, by the light of my Christmas-tree, which I had lit once more, read the Psalms, one of the few books in which one can bring every bit of oneself under shelter, however distraught and disordered and bothered one may be. . . .

[72]

To Frau Hanna Wolff   Munich, January 29, 1915

. . . I would have been so glad to see you . . . but: I must consistently and strictly sequester myself, after a month and a half of Berlin have brought me much strain and confusion; physically exhausted and unprecise in mind I came back here to be silent, to keep myself absolutely hidden, nothing else. My sequestration is still too new to bear an exception so soon, so it is safer for me to decline and go to bed, following my rule, at 8:30.

The uncertainty out there, this flickering world in which one

can place no object, no word even, without its casting most un-
quiet shadows, quite unconditionally obliges me to draw myself
in; perhaps thus one may arrive at some further inward place,
where one has never oneself been, and from there out be stable.
. . . Who would have thought, when in the beginning of August
we strolled from the Englischer Garten through the excited city,
that for so many months the anomaly then beginning would still
be unresolved over us and in the right. In the right for how long—
and so much that is wrong! . . .

[73]

To Anna Baroness von Münchhausen   2 IV Finkenstrasse, Munich
February 4, 1915

. . . More and more, the longer this anomaly in our life continues, I am losing the inner connection with my nature, and this
condition leads to a silentness inwardly and outwardly, to an
insensibility, of which I daily complain and which I still cannot
overcome. So I am silent toward you too. But when news of you
comes, like the card recently and now your good letter, I feel
it in all my apathy as one of the signs by which one survives . . .

Of the music to the Cornet, which is by a young Herr von
Pászthory, my friend Frau von Hattingberg (who is also performing it with Kurt Stieler, in Leipzig) once gave me an idea
here; it contains lovely and purely animated moments, although
to me it takes some things too sentimentally; but what I would
have against it, if it came to that, is not against the music, but
against the juxtaposition of music and word that is intrinsic to
the melodramatic form (which to me is not an art form). Perhaps a strong speaker can establish the momentary accord: that
will now be seen. I regard this combination as a loose and provisional one and consented to the Leipzig trial only for the reason
that Frau Hattingberg had the liveliest faith in Pászthory's music
and because an influence on many people was to be expected from
it: (on the many, here concerned, where the individual succumbs
or is active or silent in the commonest direction). It would give

me pleasure, in case you really want to go to Leipzig, to learn what *your* impression was . . .

[74]

To Ludwig von Ficker   Pension Landhaus Schönblick
                                          Irschenhausen bei Ebenhausen (Isartal)
                                          February 8, 1915

I would have written you long ago, did not the weight of the time lie upon the slightest communication and expression, so that I cannot write a word without disproportionate effort: from this I would not shy off if I did not have to fear that such striving against intangible and unsurveyable obstacles cancels and outweighs, as it were, the very content of what is written; since after all there is present no inner single-minded impulse which would force the laboriously achieved exercise into a clean expression, the mere ability to write being phenomenon enough.

So I kept silence. But I am grateful to you for yourself breaking silence in order to remind me of my promised contribution to the "Brenner". I could send you something at once from among my papers, a few verses; meantime as I still have ten days' grace, or at least a week's, I will let it depend on whether some poem or other may not come into being, a new one, for now,—even though it be no more than the noise with which a piece of silence breaks off from the great dumb mass inside me . . .

[75]

To Thankmar
Baron von Münchhausen   2/IV Finkenstrasse, Munich
                                     March 6, 1915

. . . The Cornet was being performed in Leipzig with music . . . I could not positively advise [your mother] to go, for this reciting to music is a running-along of one art beside the other as though it depended on which won: and only one does actually win. . . . So, my dear boy, I quite unexpectedly find myself

Drawing by Emil Orlik

Rilke with Max Reinhardt and the Gerhard Hauptmanns at a rehearsal of Hauptmann's, Berlin, 1917

Facsimile of a fragment of the Tenth Elegy

among the authors of this exceptional year, my voice of fifteen years ago speaks into the attentive ear of the people who have been frightened for months—mine? The voice of that one distant night of my youth in which I wrote the Cornet, stimulated to it by clouds passing in strange flight high across the moon. . . .

But from the fact that Christopher Rilke is thus being turned to account today you may notice again and again how dumb we have grown here. I am sure everyone is so at heart; even if a few must hear themselves and pluck their strings with this thought and that, there is no one who can draw sounds from the air that sweeps through him, not even to lament,—it is a silence of halted, interrupted hearts. I am certain no one loves in these days; however much one or another heart may achieve, it acts out of some sort of universal stores of human kindness, warmth, willingness and devotion, it does not give what is its own, but behind every act primeval store-rooms of human need are opened up; even you out there act and struggle out of such strengths as were hoarded up in some sort of barns of involuntary fellowship. It seems to me as though the heart in each of us were only passing things on, confined to gazing in astonishment at the store that is going through its hands.

What we are doing here, so far as reading still counts as doing (for who could achieve a contemplative mood?), is to read Hölderlin (over and over), I for my part Strindberg, Montaigne, Flaubert, the Bible. . . . There are some new Werfel poems, one tries them and yet is elsewhere and cannot get back into the tone of day before yesterday. . . .

[76]

To Princess Marie von Thurn
und Taxis-Hohenlohe   2 IV Finkenstrasse, Munich
March 18, 1915

. . . For the time being, of course, I have to stay in Munich
. . . God help me. Shall probably have to await enlistment here

too, in case it is true (as I read recently in the Corriere della Sera) that Austria is calling men up to 42. There would be little sense in making plans before one knows how the die will fall.

I would have much to tell you. A few lectures to which a man otherwise quite a recluse has been persuaded, singularly excited and absorbed the little circle that assembled for them. I could not help thinking a great deal of you, wished you there—, just imagine a person, starting from an intuitive insight into old imperial Rome, undertaking to give an explanation of the world which presented the dead as those who really exist, the kingdom of the dead as a unique, fabulous existence, but our little span of life as a kind of anomaly: all this supported by a boundless erudition and of such a cataract of inner conviction and exaltation that the meaning of immemorial myths seemed to come rushing, released, into this channel of speech, bearing on a great current the sense and the stubbornness of this strange eccentric—. I heard only the last of the three lectures and thus received in a sense only the conclusion of his ideas, but was nevertheless induced, full of surmise, toward a whole that seemed set up with remarkable completeness in this mind averted from us. But I see I cannot give you a proper picture; I spent a few hours with this person, don't know whether it is possible to see him again,—in any case, since I cannot ask further and go into it more closely, I feel myself attracted to and separated from his lines of thought much as I do with the "Unknown". . . .

[77]

*To Princess Marie von Thurn
und Taxis-Hohenlohe*   2/IV Finkenstrasse, Munich
June 10, 1915

I have not seen a newspaper for a week or ten days—yesterday one was brought me in which were the names Monfalcone, Sagrado, Duino; I do not know how far the demolition reported there will prove true. But everything that is called destruction is possible now of course—so to speak taken for granted from the start, probably. It is with these names that for the first time since the war a single event has struck me so directly to the heart.

Dear, dear friend, if only I had written all the Elegies at Duino, if only they were unutterably more beautiful than they are—. (All this that is irretrievable!) What weight, what obligation now falls on things that survive a little more. . . .

[78]

To Thankmar
  Baron von Münchhausen　　　　temporarily (most provisionally)
　　　　　　　　　　　　　　　　　　32/III Widenmayerstrasse
　　　　　　　　　　　　　　　　　　June 28, 1915

. . . For such a good thing as meeting again must [in these times] have a sweetness one would never otherwise ascribe to it; the appalling calamity creates a new scale of sensation; since it reaches so deep down, does it also rise higher, is it *more* too, what we feel? Or do we simply read life's degrees in Fahrenheit instead of the usual Réaumur?

People like us, my dear friend, who have remained so entirely non-combatant have much time for doubting: probably, to ourselves, all people like us say misery is always there and all distress even to the most extreme. The whole of distress is always in use among men, all there is of it, a constant, as there is also a constant of happiness; only the distribution varies. Anyone who may not have known there was so much distress would now have his turn to be shocked. But who, truly alive, has not known that? Wonderfully manifest indeed is the endurance, the acceptance, the carrying through of so much distress on every side, on everyone's part. Greatness comes to light, steadfastness, strength, a standing-up-to-life quand-même—, but in such behavior how much is bitter constraint, is desperation, is (already already) habit? And that such greatness appears and holds good, can that in any way at all diminish the pain over the fact that such confusion, such not-knowing-which-way-to-turn, the whole sad man-made complication of this provoked fate, that exactly this incurably bad condition of things was necessary to force out evidences of whole-hearted courage, devotion and bigness? While we, the arts, the theater, called nothing forth in these very same people, caused nothing to rise and flower, were unable to transform anyone. What is our métier but purely and largely and freely to set forth opportunities for change,—did we do this so badly, so half-way, so little convinced and convincing? That has been the question, that has been the suffering for almost a year, and the problem is to do it more forcefully, more unrelentingly. How?!

Dear Thankmar, that's how things look with me, inwardly. Outwardly I am preparing to go to the country, if I can find a little cottage (for me alone) such as I am looking for; meanwhile sitting here in the apartment of friends (who have gone to the country) with the finest Picasso (the "Saltimbanques"), in which there is so much Paris that, for moments, I forget.

[79]

To Princess Marie von Thurn
und Taxis-Hohenlohe (% Koenig) 32/III Widenmayerstrasse
Munich, July 9, 1915

. . . Thank God, I said, thought, felt at the news about Duino and still dared not answer Thank God aloud to you, for so long as havoc is in the world, who may breathe freely, who may consider anything safe, spared, rescued? In personal matters as well as in general it is a giving up, an offering of all possession, at what cost? At what cost; if only there were not that question, who would not cast off everything that was his and himself into the bargain, if he but understood, if he but guessed, that, sheerly surviving, a thing needs such underpinnings in order to rise up further?—We, some of us, have long been feeling continuities that have nothing in common with the course of history; even over the present vicissitude the furthest past and the furthest future will come to an understanding, but we, constrained between yesterday and tomorrow, shall we ever again simply, quietly, serenely take part in the swing of great affairs? Or remain frightened below with the stamp of a period on our shoulders, co-knowers of unforgettable details, co-responsible for the big as for the merely fearful, used up by this endurance and performance and persistence—; and shall we not then later, forever, as we are learning to do now, defer all understanding, hold what is human to be inextricable, history to be a primeval forest to the soil of which we never reach because it lies, layer on layer, unendingly, upon tumbled stuff, an apparition on the back of destruction—?

Are you reading, and what? I have been busy with Hermann Keyserling, also with Strindberg, the Strindberg of the truly incredible "Ghost Sonata" (very movingly performed here), the most important thing in the theater besides Georg Büchner's *Wozzek,* which the Hoftheater . . . generously came out with. A monstrous affair, written more than eighty years ago . . . nothing but the fate of a common soldier (around 1848) who stabs his faithless sweetheart, but powerfully setting forth how, around the most trivial existence, for which even the uniform of a common infantryman seems too wide and too much emphasized, how even around the recruit Wozzek all the greatness of existence stands, how he cannot prevent, now here, now there, before, behind, beside his dull soul, horizons from being torn open onto violence, immensity, the infinite; an incomparable play, the way this misused person in his stable-jacket stands in universal space, malgré lui, in the infinite relationship of the stars. That is theater, that is what theater could be like . . .

[80]

To Helene von Nostitz   (% Koenig) 32 Widenmayerstrasse
Munich, July 12, 1915

Yesterday, Sunday, came your letter. I should have answered it that same evening, but before I can persuade my pen—writing now means somehow prevailing over oneself, for what to write when everything one touches is unspeakable, unrecognizable, when nothing belongs to one, no feeling, no hope; when an enormous provision, gotten I know not where, of suffering,

despair, sacrifice and misery is used up in large amounts, as though
everybody were somewhere in the whole mass, and the single
person nowhere; nowhere any longer is the measure of the individual heart applicable which used to be the unit of the earth
and the heavens and all expanses and abysses. What used the cry
of a drowning man to mean—even if it was the village idiot, who
with a suddenly sharper cry reached out of the water, everybody
flew to the scene and was on his side and against his sinking, and
the swiftest risked his life for him. How immemorial everything
has become, Heiligendamm, times, like childhood itself, so remote
and innocent—who will ever feel them again!? You say that "one
now feels Beethoven and the stars more deeply and more over-
poweringly"; that is perhaps because (as you write) a personal
sorrow has come to you out of the continuously common lot—
perhaps that helps. It is not so with me; for me all that, all that is
biggest and most stirring, remains attached to the *other* world,
the earlier, the former world, in which I had long been a sufferer,
but never a numb person, never an emptied-out person, never a
person shouted at who does not understand. The longer it lasts,—
the disturbing thing is not the fact of this war, but that it is being
used and exploited in a business-ridden, a nothing but human
world, that the god himself, once someone has flung it into that
world, cannot call it back, because people cling to it greedily,
with all the weight of their heavy conscience. Man-work, as
everything has been man-work in the last decades, bad work,
work for profit, save for a few painful voices and pictures, save
for a few warning figures, a few zealous individuals who clung
to their own hearts, which stood against the stream. Rodin, how
often, as always, repeated words of disapprobation, mistrust for
the course of things; it was even too much for me that he always
did it with the same expressions. I took it for weariness and yet it
was judgment. And Cézanne, the old man, when one told him
of what was going on, and he could break out in the quiet streets
of Aix and shriek at his companion: "Le monde, c'est terrible
. . ." As of a prophet one thinks of him, and longs for one who
will cry and howl like that—but they all went away beforehand,

those old men who would have had the power to weep now before the peoples. . . .

To Elsa Bruckmann   % Koenig, 32/III Widenmayerstrasse
                                       Munich, July 19, 1915

Since our understanding on the telephone, I have been discovering more and more thoroughly that I aroused your kind enthusiasm with the most irresponsible precipitancy—: we must give up the reading we had planned or at least postpone it over the summer; I am really in no condition now to undertake it. I wrote you, as the impulse came up, at a time when I chanced to be reading the "Book of Hours", but this very impulse, as spontaneous as it was unforeseen, is not easily transposed and gathered together for a particular evening, at least not as I see things at present. What I was appealing to with that recent reading was the multitude *in me* and it is before this and no other whatsoever that I shall have to conduct and to acquit myself. Of this I have only gradually become aware in the last few days, and by way of the realization that I could read scarcely a third of the "Book of Hours" before an invited public without letting myself in for a few preliminary explanations about the inner occasion for this reading. Considering *how* this introduction would have to be shaped up, I set in motion such a mass of carefully saved, hitherto unlooked-at ideas and feelings, that I saw at once the ordering of a few words would make necessary a prodigious reordering and rearranging in myself, a process so laborious and multifarious that I could only dare to undertake it independently of any date or purpose. But even assuming it were carried out, under pressure, within this week and that I could cast some of its results into my address, then this in turn would become something else than a mere explanation of the "Book of Hours"; it would, even if it did not presume to touch upon present conditions, nevertheless bring up such implicit contradictions to them, one after another, that it would have small chance of not being offensive to the censor; to speak out in terms trimmed to suit the censor would be painful to me, while on the other hand it would, of course, hardly become me to let things come to the point of inveighing against such a situation. Because even proceeding from my innermost and to me most immediate convictions, still I know I am entirely unauthorized to give out such impulses otherwise than enclosed in the hardest production, where, God willing, they are then removed from every censorship in the world and are of such ungraspable influence that no hand can halt their working. Until then—until I have got so far—I am (it is clear to me again) assigned to that resolute silence which for many months has been my business, my most special business. It was more than a velleity which allowed me to disturb you, it was a strong wish to take part with others and in their fate at least momentarily, but on looking at it more closely I have to take wishes of this sort as not exactly mine. Forgive me, then I shall not come to the war-relief tomorrow . . .

[*82*]

To Regina Ullmann   Wednesday [1915?]

The proofs of the "Field Sermon" I sent on just this morning, so difficult was it for me to part with them. I had sanctioned all your improvements and carried them out in ink, suppressing only a few exclamation marks. You are too generous with them, there just aren't that many. It is requisite to the firmness of a style that it be sober in this respect, even in its drunkenness. Heaven forbid, no no, that there would have been anything to change in the "Field Sermon". Never has it seemed so beautiful to me! It still is, I can't help it, your most beautiful, your divine work, that in which you were simply obedient, most deeply serving, docile toward God, and silently led through by the angel. What purity in the dialogues, what purity behind them! A contour as of mountains toward the east in the evening, as of hills that are meditating.

Yesterday two different things went through my head: whether you do not urgently need the *country* again, whether you oughtn't to live in the country altogether in order to produce that sort of thing?, that is so very much yours! (This is already the third exclamation mark on this page, but, please, I am really exclaiming.) One must see cows by day, in order to arrive at repose and recumbency like that in word-layers, cows, and people who do not, if one touches them, fall apart into a heap of words (like us in the city), but who are as it were the cake-mold of a single, always identical word that is baked in them on Sunday. (And otherwise are silent—.) This—, and then I wondered how it happens that you never before hit upon the scenic form so very suited to you? I think it is so entirely suited to you because it may reject all that is confusing or shift it in among the accessories and may purely set forth in the words, the spoken words, the entire content of the character. Not action has driven this material into the dialogic sections, but the wish rather to pour out figures than to describe them, to place their inner content before the light, as happens when one decants dark bottles into open glasses. There stands each drink, and the strength, spirit and clarity of each becomes apparent.

Shouldn't this form still be for you one of the most immediate, most tractable? Goodbye and: good fluting! . . .

[*83*]

To Princess Marie von Thurn
und Taxis-Hohenlohe   % Koenig, 32/III Widenmayerstrasse
                                        Munich, August 2, 1915

How should I not constantly with all my heart be with you, when participation in what you suffer and hope is so thoroughly natural to me. I do not understand the present hell, but how you bear it and go through with it I do understand. There are few constants in human affairs, and how many have changed, have become incomprehensible—have taken on the color of a time that could not itself say whether it has a color, a time that I believe is going on at some still undiscovered point of the spectrum, in an ultra-red that goes beyond our senses. . . .

Munich is getting empty, I imagine it has just about its usual summer appearance. I have outwardly the most even days, but inwardly it's an abyss, one is living on the edge, and below there lie, perhaps in pieces, who knows, the things of one's former life. Was it that? I say to myself a hundred times, was it that, which in these last years has been lying upon us as a monstrous pressure, this frightful future that now constitutes our cruel present? I have to think of how I one day said to Marthe: Marthe, il n'y aura devant moi que des désastres, des terreurs, d'angoisses indicibles; c'est avec vous que finissent les bontés de ma vie—, it came out of me just like that, as though in the midst of a calm the impact of a storm had torn it out of me. I pricked up my ears as I heard myself say it, I was thinking only of my own curiously collapsing destiny and did not guess that the world as a whole would be bringing forth destruction. And Marthe made an unforgettable gesture of taking-me-under-protection. Now for the first time do I realize, it was just like that that those two powerful old men went around, Tolstoy and Cézanne, and uttered warnings and threats, like prophets of an ancient covenant that is soon to be broken—and they did not want to live to see that break. Whatever comes, the worst of it is that a certain innocence of life in which after all we grew up, will never exist for any of us again. The years ahead of us, many as they are—what will they be but a descent, with trembling knees, from this mountain of pain, up which we are still being dragged ever farther. . . .

You are reading Balzac, I have always stuck to Flaubert, read a wonderfully fresh early version of the Education Sentimentale which has scarcely anything in common with the later novel: for the latter is highly deliberative, spontaneous sentiment occurs in it only as in rich savory translation. And then Strindberg. They are giving the Dance of Death here, after the incredible Ghost Sonata, and these dramas have almost reconciled me to the theater, which for years has given me nothing. At first it seems so hopelessly obstinate to present humanity's disconsolation as its absolute condition, but when someone like this has power over even the most disconsolate, there hovers above the whole, unspoken, a concept of illimitable human greatness. And a desperate love. . . .

[84]

. . . Your letters belong for me among the very very few things that signify a continuity between what has been and what is to be. I hold onto them, so to speak, in crossing over—if I only knew whither. My not having written comes from this very reserve and reluctance of my nature, from which I can wrest nothing, unless it be a misgiving or a complaint, and why should I want to come to you with such things! Even to come in joy over the so far good condition of Duino has no sense—for . . . sense will come back into our rejoicing and hoping and suffering when we once more have to do with more comprehensible, more human matters. Ah, Princess, a few years earlier and I might have been able to bring up in my heart, then not yet so downfallen, visions that would have withstood even such a time, a Book of Hours state of mind that would have had the power to treat the simply incomprehensible like *that* which in its essence transcends all understanding; for what do I seek more than the one point, that of the Old Testament, at which the terrible coincides with the greatest, and to show it up now—, that would have been like the lifting of a monstrance over all those who, stumbling and falling, again and again get up. For even though no one cares to admit it openly, consolations would be needed, the great inexhaustible consolations, the possibilities of which I have often felt at the bottom of my heart, almost frightened to be containing them, the boundless, in so limited a vessel. It is certain that the divinest consolation is contained in humanity itself—we would not be able to do much with the consolation of a god; only that our eye would have to be a trace more seeing, our ear more receptive, the taste of a fruit would have to penetrate us more completely, we would have to endure more odor, and in touching and being touched be more aware and less forgetful—: in order promptly to absorb out of our immediate experiences consolations that would be more

convincing, more preponderant, more true than all the suffering
that can ever shake us to our very depths. Not in the sense of the
"Unknown", probably, but in a still much freer, less detached
sense do we live, belonging within the most tremendous tides;
I often have to turn, asking what force is perhaps now passing
there behind me to its work, each to its work, and the way of so
many leads through the center of our heart (qui n'est pas une
auberge, mais un fameux carrefour quand-même—). Dear Princess, how have I not misused this heart of mine, that it now gives
no witness of our consolableness! I have so often in these last
years spoken complainingly to you of this heart, revilingly, de-
grading it among the least—, but still always too kindly, still always too hopefully. Could I say of it that it overflows with bitterness, that it is numb with pain; but no,—as though its contents
were simply balled into formless lumps, thus do I carry it about.
There is a way out, to call this sick, and some days too I am nothing
but that, sick, that is a small matter, and I imagine that the good
Stauffenberg might have been able to change that; for it was to
that end after all that I came here. A year ago,—this year! You
can see, beloved Princess, today I am not to be borne with, I wish
we were sitting in your boudoir in Duino or up in the retreat in
the chapel, where I read aloud to you out of my pocket notebook, for to groan orally does still show consideration, but to
groan on paper is cowardly, I know—and yet . . .

Princess, I have been puzzling in silence like all the world over
the common future, that of all of us, although I am committed
to fewer assumptions than any man in the street, for history is
dark to me; also I suspect that it is not history at all that one might
know and draw conclusions from, but an odd selection from the
fortuitous and the systematic, in which man recognizes himself
because the continual confusion of the two is his most familiar
emotion. But now it is so suddenly, overtakingly autumn, here at
least. I see from unaccustomed windows the tree-covered banks
of the Isar turning yellow, and the yellows, under the cold rain,
are not increasing gradually but next-to-last tones are almost
there, then will come the falling of the leaves. These rainy nights

and this winter at the threshold—, and the widespread need suddenly contracts into my very own, into helplessness before my own tomorrow and day-after-tomorrow,—whither, whither? One Munich year is over, I have not done much with it. On the contrary, I seem to myself to have retrogressed in every respect, how shall I now do better? My inner world is so inhospitable that I simply cannot undertake to lead you about in it, yes it is probably obstructed and impassable,—restons dehors. My whole cognizance is limited to the highly negative realization that I should no longer stay in Munich, the people here make too many demands on one, one has to *be finished* or pass oneself off as such,— et moi, si j'ai encore quelque avenir, ce sera en recommençant humblement que j'y parviendrai; for whatever in my books may count as (to a certain extent) finished, that too is over for me, since five years ago, since Malte Laurids closed himself to behind me, I stand here as a beginner, as one, to be sure, who is not beginning. So to begin—but how?! . . .

My situation has become in a way still more real through my learning, day before yesterday, that I really have lost all my Paris belongings, that is, practically everything I possessed: the entire contents of my apartment was auctioned off in April! You know that I do not take this hard, I had long been inclined to regard everything that had collected around me during those twelve years in Paris as M. L. Brigge's estate, and perhaps with all these things that know what I know and books and the few heirlooms, the obsession of this figure, which I was sincerely determined to dismiss finally from my mind, has been taken from me. And yet, dear friend, to you I may confess it, since that news from Paris I have been going around with a curious feeling, rather like one who has stumbled, got up again unhurt, and yet somehow cannot rid himself of the suspicion that a belated pain may suddenly break out in his insides and make him cry aloud. By and large I had long ago given up everything and practiced testing my renunciation by my consciousness of the few objects that meant the most to me—, it worked; but now I see that they were nevertheless still there; since I know that everything is gone a singular fear has been stirring in me, as though it were conceivable that one might suddenly be gripped by the recollection of one of those lost objects that is absolutely indispensable, a little piece of paper, perhaps, a picture, a letter in one of the hundred packets of letters, or whatever—as though something insignificant but dear could have got lost that was linked to the center of one's life by a light fine thread that is now broken. . . . Ah, Princess, how singular, how unpredictable all experience is; I am only writing this down because it surprises me and makes me feel something I would never have invented in this way or attributed to anybody. Now I am of course detached enough to assume that this singular feeling can be quickly overcome; perhaps it is already so inasmuch as I am taking account of it here. Also it would probably never have arisen if my belongings had been really wiped out, for with annihilation we are indeed most tangibly related and at one, but this having lost one's own things, most characteristically one's own at that, to people, to strangers, has something extraordinarily reproachful about it. I cannot imagine at all what happens to a box full of letters and papers in such a case—?

Dear Princess, my heart has emptied itself out again, voyez quel débris—, perhaps I shall go to a small university, perhaps to Berlin, perhaps to Janowitz . . . it is so hard to make up one's mind, because of course I know it is a matter of winning an *inner* abiding place, only that an impressionable person like me continually assumes that the *right* outer condition could help up the inner. Je suis un enfant qui ne voudrait autour que des enfances toujours plus adultes—

[85]

To Fräulein A. Baumgarten   32/III Widenmayerstrasse, Munich
August 22, 1915

Since great spaces of time are usual between us, it will not disturb you if I answer your letter of April 26 so late. My lateness is not to be interpreted, is it, as though I felt any the less this sign of your long-continuing interest; on the contrary. With it something good has happened to me and how highly the good is now valued we need hardly, in the present circumstances, protest to each other.

You will, if you remember the young man you once met, be able to imagine that the homeless and in many ways aging person he has become cannot manage to find his bearings in a world almost entirely canceled, crumbled, tearing itself to pieces! The contemplation he ought to arrive at is so deep, so thorough, he would have to come so far through all his childhood back to himself again, everything that he had been would have to be present in him, indeed he would have to be allowed in an unheard-of sense to take possession of his entire heart in order not to notice the losses, in order to have in himself *the* center that once again is world-center and not just any place inside of a hundred restrictions. With certain prisoners known to history things went so that in the days of complete external privation they strove for and won, in the depths of their being, both themselves and the most inexhaustible freedom—if that could be done now; but then again, being shut off from one's environment is not prison enough to win such great contemplation in; even for him who has no part in that environment, it is too imminently fateful, too uncertain and restless, too much shot through with pain and hope, too full of premonition, too agitated and too unhappy. And while one admits it is all this, one is almost tempted to complain that it is not enough so. How much hushing-up in the cities, how much dissipation of the worst sort, what hypocrisy in living on undisfigured, supported by gain-greedy literature and pitiable theater and flattered by the irritating press, which surely is much at fault for this war and even more at fault for duplicity and lying and falsification making this monstrous event into a sickness, where it might have been allowed to be a pure frenzy. But news reported overhastily, falsely, in a spirit of hate and without the least responsibility—, surely the wicked lie has for the past year often been the cause of actual happenings, lies by the hundred have put facts by the thousand into the world, and now the grandeur, the sacrifice, the resolution, that is continually happening, is tied in to the welter of misery and untruth, swallowed up by the "enterprise" of this war, which must bring gain—fame? Oh no, all these conceptions have grown meaningless in newspaper use,—the world has fallen into the hands of men.

What has got into me that I write you all this, perhaps into calm summer days! Probably my holding forth to you once in the mail coach was just as inconsiderate, only that then I had my extreme youth as an excuse, whereas now the whole outburst is dependent on the consideration you will perhaps grant to one who is more than ever alone. . . .

[*86*]

To Ellen Delp   32/III Widenmayerstrasse, [Munich]
                                       Sunday [October 10, 1915]

. . . I must leave these rooms tomorrow, as the owner is returning from the country, and with them the glorious big Picasso beside which I have been living for almost four months now. Four months—what times are passing and how? For me with always more dismal insight into the in-sanity and non-sense into which everything is incorrigibly pressing on, using man's energy and man's existence, which were there for what is beyond all naming, as names for something abitrary and imposed and overdone. What a helplessness this will make afterwards, when all the accepted orthodox concepts are taken off the pedestals upon which they have been exhibited, and the bewildered survivors will want to attach themselves again to the abandoned laws of innermost being. Can no one, then, check and prevent it? Why are there not a few, three, five, ten, who stand together and cry in the public squares: Enough! and who will be shot down and will at least have given their lives that it should be enough, while those out there are now succumbing only so that the frightful thing shall go on and on and there shall be no taking account of destruction. Why is there not *one* who cannot endure it any more, *will* not endure it any more; did he but cry out for one night in the midst of the untrue, flag-hung city, cry out and not let himself be

pacified, who might therefore call him liar? How many are holding this cry back with difficulty,—or no? If I am mistaken and
there are not many who could cry like that, then I do not understand human beings and am not one myself and have nothing in
common with them.

Forgive me, Ellen, but I have felt like this for nearly a year,
I storm it out against you because you are a girl and looking
towards high things and moreover in your inmost feelings full of
equilibrium after your rides through the radiance of autumn into
its new opennesses . . . So you will be able to stand it all right
if one's bitterest heart overflows. . . .

[87]

To Ellen Delp   11 Keferstrasse, Munich
                                   October 27, 1915

Were you, Ellen, happy Ellen, not so secure in having gone
through and come through the almost impenetrable present, I
would have to reproach myself for having brought up again, in
my recent letter, the vast impending doom in all its strength and
persistence. But it has not done you any harm, I feel, since
"through the thick of it" (as you say) you have come on to open
ground again, in the deep surviving world of Nature, with which
your whole being is in harmony.

Was this way possible for me as well? I also am pushing on, but
I linger all too much on my way through, Nature behind things
does not draw me enough, "tree, beast and season", all that no
longer has the immediate magic for me which at times, like a sheer
decree to be happy, could still prevail over my heart, however
much entangled. "Working after Nature" has in such a high degree made that which *is* into a *task* for me, that only very rarely
now, as by mistake, does a thing speak to me, granting and giving
without demanding that I reproduce it equivalently and significantly in myself. The Spanish landscape (the last I experienced to the utmost)—Toledo—drove this attitude of mine
to its extreme: since there the external thing itself—tower, hill,

bridge—already possessed the incredible, unsurpassable intensity of the inner equivalents through which one might have been able to represent it. External world and vision everywhere co-incided as it were in the object; in each a whole inner world was displayed, as though an angel who embraces space were blind and gazing into himself. This world, seen no longer with the eyes of men, but in the angel, is perhaps my real task—at least all my earlier experiments would come together in it; but to begin that task, Ellen, how protected and resolved one would have to be!

[88]

To L. H.   Villa Alberti, 11 Keferstrasse
                                              Munich, November 8, 1915

Your letter, L. H., may be taken up from so many angles, almost every sentence calls for ten letters—not that one need answer everything in it that is question (and what in it is not question?), no, but of course these are all the questions that have always been covered up again with more questions or (at best) showed more transparent under the influence of other self-illuminating questions—; they are the great question-dynasties—who then has ever answered?

What is expressed in the suffering that is written into Malte Laurids Brigge (forgive me if I mention this book again when we have just discussed it) is really only *this*, with every means and always anew and by every manifestation this, *This:* how is it possible to live when after all the elements of this life are utterly incomprehensible to us? If we are continually inadequate in love, uncertain in decision and impotent in the face of death, how is it possible to exist? In this book, achieved under the deepest obligation, I did not manage to express all of my astonishment over the fact that men have had for thousands of years to deal with life (not to mention God), and yet towards these first most immediate problems—strictly speaking, these only problems (for what else have we to do, today still and for how long to come?)—they remain such helpless novices, so between fright and subterfuge, so miserable. Isn't that incomprehensible? My astonishment over this fact, whenever I yield to it, drives me first into the greatest dismay and then into a sort of horror, but behind the horror again there is something else and again something else, something so intensive that I cannot tell by the feeling whether it is white-hot or icy. I tried once before, years ago, to write about Malte, to someone who had been frightened by the book, that I myself sometimes thought of it as a hollow form, a negative mold, all the grooves and indentations of which are agony, disconsolations and most painful insights, but the casting from which, were it possible to make one (as with a bronze the positive figure one would get out of it), would perhaps be happiness, assent,—most perfect and most certain bliss. Who knows, I ask myself, whether we do not always approach the gods so to speak from behind, separated from their sublimely radiant face through nothing but themselves, quite near to the expression we yearn for, only just standing behind it—but what does that mean save that our countenance and the divine face are looking out in the same direction, are at one; and this being so, how are we to approach the god from the space that lies in front of him?

Does it perplex you, my saying God and gods and for the sake of completeness haunting you with these dogmatic terms (as with a ghost), thinking that they must immediately mean something to you? But assume the metaphysical. Let us agree that since his earliest beginnings man has shaped gods in whom here and there were contained only the dead and threatening and destructive and frightful, violence, anger, superpersonal stupor, tied up as it were into a tight knot of malice: the alien, if you like, but, already to some extent implied in this alien, the admission that one was aware of it, endured it, yes, acknowledged it for the sake of a sure, secret relationship and connection: [for] *we were these too*, only that so far we have not known what to do with this side of our experience; they were too big, too dangerous, too many-sided, they grew beyond us to an exaggerated significance; it was not possible, in addition to the many demands of existence, set up for use and performance, always to treat with these unmanageable and ungraspable states; and so one agreed to put them outside now and then.—But since they were excess—the strongest, indeed the *too* strong, the powerful, indeed the violent, the incomprehensible, often the monstrous—how should they not, brought together in one place, exercise influence, effect, force, superiority? And, remember, from the outside now. Could one not treat the history of God as a part, never before broached, of the human mind, a part always postponed, saved up, and at last let slip, for which there was once a time of decision and calm, and which—there where it had been pushed aside—gradually grew into a tension against which the impulse of the individual, ever again scattered and pettily wounded of heart, hardly counts any more.

And so you see, it was the same with death. Experienced, and yet in its reality not to be experienced, knowing better than we all the time and yet never rightly admitted by us, hurting and from the start outstripping the meaning of life; it too, so that it should not continually interrupt us in the search for this meaning, was dismissed, pushed out; death, which is probably so near us that we cannot at all determine the distance between it and the life-center within us without its becoming something external, daily held further from us, lurking somewhere in the void in order to attack this one and that according to its evil choice—; more and more death became suspected of being the contradiction, the opponent, the invisible antagonism in the air, that which shrivels up our joys, the dangerous glass of our happiness, out of which we may be spilled at any instant.

God and death were now outside, were the *other*, the *one* being our life that now, at the cost of this elimination, seemed to become human, friendly, possible, achievable, in a firm sense ours. But since in this life-course for beginners, as it were, this preparatory class in life, the things to be classified and understood were still innumerable, and really strict distinctions could not be made between problems solved and problems only temporarily passed over, there resulted, even in this restricted form, no straight and reliable progress; instead one just lived along, as it came, on real profits and wrong additions, and in the total result there was

bound in the end to reappear as fundamental error that very condition upon the assumption of which this whole experiment in
existence was set up; that is, while from every accepted meaning
God and death seemed to have been subtracted (as something not
here-and-now, but later, elsewhere and different), the smaller
cycle of the merely here-and-now revolved faster and faster, the
so-called progress happened in a world self-preoccupied and forgetful that, however it might exert itself, it was beaten from the
start by death and God. Now this might still have made a kind
of sense had we been able to keep God and death at a distance,
as mere ideas in the realm of mind; but Nature knew nothing of
this removal we had somehow accomplished—if a tree blossoms,
death blossoms in it as well as life, and the field is full of death,
which from its reclining face sends out a rich expression of life,
and the beasts go patiently from one [to the] other—and everywhere about us death is still at home and he watches us out of the
cracks in things, and a rusty nail, sticking up somewhere out of a
plank, does nothing day and night but rejoice over death.

And love too, which mixes the ciphers between people to introduce a game of near and far in which we always line up only to
a certain distance, as though the universe were full and space nowhere save in us;—love too takes no heed of our divisions, but
sweeps us, trembling as we are, into an endless consciousness of the
whole. Lovers do not live out of the detached here-and-now; as
though no division had ever been undertaken, they enter into the
enormous possessions of their heart, of them one may say that
God becomes real to them and that death does not harm them:
for being full of life, they are full of death.

But of the experiencing of life we need not speak here; it is a
secret, not one that locks itself away, not one that demands to be
hidden; it is the secret that is sure of itself, that stands open like
a temple, whose entrances glory in being entrances, singing between gigantic pillars that they are the portals.

But (and with this, Fräulein H., I come back to your letter
again) how do we manage to be properly prepared for that experiencing of life which at some time or other, in human relations,

in our work, in suffering, seizes upon us and for which we must not be casual because it is itself never an accident, but exact, so exact that we can only meet in inverse correspondence; you have discovered various ways of learning for yourself, and one feels that you have gone about it attentively and reflectively. So even the shocks of which you write have shaken you down more firmly and have not overwhelmed you—I would like to support you all I can in your preoccupation with death, both from the biological approach (recommending Wilhelm Fliess and his very remarkable investigations: I shall send you a little book of his shortly) and in calling to your attention a few important people who have reflected more cleanly, calmly and grandly about death. One first of all: Tolstoy.

There is a story of his called the Death of Ivan Ilych; the evening your letter came, as a matter of fact, I felt a strong urge to read those extraordinary pages again,—I did so, and, thinking of you, I almost read them aloud to you. . . . Can you get hold of it? I wish you might get hold of a lot of Tolstoy, the two volumes "Steps of Life", the Cossacks, Polikushka, the Linen-Measurer, Three Deaths: his enormous experience of Nature (I hardly know anyone who so passionately devoted himself to studying Nature) made him astonishingly able to think from a sense of the whole and to write out of a feeling for life which was so permeated with the finest particles of death, that death seemed to be contained everywhere in it as an odd spice in the strong flavor of life—, but for that very reason this man could be so deeply, so frantically frightened when he discovered that somewhere there was pure death, that bottle full of death or that hideous cup with the handle broken off and the senseless inscription "Faith, love, hope", out of which one was compelled to drink bitterness of undiluted death. This man observed in himself and in others many kinds of fear of death, for through his natural composure it was given him to be the observer even of his own fear, and his relationship to death will to the last have been a fear permeated with grandeur, a fugue of fear, as it were, a gigantic structure, a tower of fear with corridors and flights of stairs and railless projections and sheer edges on all sides—only that the force with which he experienced and admitted the very extravagance of his own fear may—who knows—at the last moment have changed over into unapproachable reality, was suddenly this tower's sure foundation, landscape and sky and the wind and a flight of birds around it— . . .

[*89*]

To Princess Marie von Thurn
und Taxis-Hohenlohe

11 Keferstrasse, Munich
November 26, 1915

No, there has been no letter before your good long one of the 10th; it did atone for a certain amount of silence, it was long, though in view of the need of you it might have been much longer. How much memory it stirred in me, how many questions; I often feel now as though everything one had formerly experienced should be lived out in one even more fully, as though, in impatience for the next and again the next or in covetousness toward oneself, one had never made full use of it and, while one helped oneself, still left most of it in the dish. When you say Saonara, what a flood of memories: things upon which no emphasis formerly fell now all at once come to themselves—in me, for example, a morning hour early on the second day, in the little salon next the billiard-room, no one had yet come down, I was reading a hymn of a poeta ignoto (I have just opened to it at the first turn in my little pocket note-book—still the same one as in those days, so little gets entered now—), was reading and full of composure and serene in mind; the park outside—everything was in unison with me, one of those hours, not made at all but as it were saved up, as though things drew close together and made room, a space untouched as the inside of a rose, an angelic space in which one keeps still; I forgot this moment at the time, it was in no way determining for the whole day, but here it stands in me now in a strength and survival of its own, as though it had been of a higher grade of being. I know of two or three such moments in recent years (once, beautiful beyond anything, in Córdoba, I told you about it), it seems to me that they suffice to fill my inner world with a clear—an even radiance, they are just like lamps in it, quiet lamps—, and the more I ponder them in memory and in attentively feeling them through again, the more these experiences, contentless in a present sense, seem to me to belong in a higher experience-unity. But what a beginner I am in them: for what definitive changes in one's life should issue from a single such experience.

Oh yes, I remember the drive to Saonara too (Marthe's letter is among the things now lost), all our lovely drives in those days—what an innocence of living, as though all that had been a great childhood, compared to the evil present.

Since I have been here in this quieter, more remote house, I have remembered many things, have inwardly lived back through and beyond much, and then work was very near, indeed it was actually here, two or three things I might read you. But now: news!: I am between two examinations, imagine it, and the first has resulted in my being ordered to Turnau on January 4th. Now of course my physical capacity, especially with the approach of winter, is so minimal and precarious that possibly the next examination will correct this first result again. Nothing remains but to wait. That I wish God might leave me to my work as long as possible, especially now that I have just had the taste of it on my lips again, no one will hold against me who knows *how* I stand toward that work and who realizes that in it I am a power and a glory and outside of it not even a little force. So God help us to our proper use. . . .

[*90*]

To Anton Kippenberg   11 Keferstrasse, Munich
                         .   February 15, 1916

. . . To add a brief account of personal matters: [In Vienna] from December 13th on, I finally achieved, shortly before enlistment, not having to go to Turnau (even that was very hard to achieve!). Called up on the 4th [of January], I joined in almost three weeks' duty and training in barracks; my physical inability to go on fortunately coincided with a new summons to the War Archives; thither I was ordered the end of January. My situation there (office hours from nine to three) is now outwardly better and more comfortable, but probably untenable if I do not succeed in being transferred to purely mechanical copy or registration work; for the fiction-service at which these gentlemen have been practicing for a year and a half is utterly impossible for me. I cannot describe it, it is very paltry and ambiguous in nature and the stoppage of all intellectual functions (as was the case in barracks) seems enviable alongside this crooked and irresponsible misuse of writing activity. The gentlemen themselves call it "hairdressing the hero"; for a long time they shuddered at the thought, but now they have overcome their objections and turn it out with a flick of the wrist. There will certainly be lots of difficulties,—for the moment, they do not know what to do with me and are keeping me in that incalculable idleness which belongs to the most intense military experiences. The being spent and weary, as it came over me in the period in barracks, has understandably enough not been removed by the new position; at three I get out of the office, eat, go home by trolley-car (i.e., Parkhotel, Hopfner, Hietzing, Vienna XIII) and yet am not in a condition to give the little remainder of the day its own stamp and its own meaning. For that I am too full of rolling stones from the mountains of strangeness that have fallen over me. I taste, if I try myself for a moment, nothing but patience, patience in which nothing is dissolved, pure, colorless patience. . . .

You ask about my work. Almost—no, certainly—the most provoking thing is that a fortnight before the muster here, in which my lot was drawn, I was in a rapid ascent of work, a fore-storm of work, some curious single poems, the Elegies, everything mounted and flowed, and the stores of Michelangelo increased from day to day in a manner indescribably surpassing myself. Never before have I written down such strong and accurate and clean translations. I already thought the freest prospects were ahead, when the gray army cloth fell before my clarified vision. . . .

[*91*]

To Hugo von Hofmannsthal   Hopfner's Park Hotel, Hietzing
Vienna XIII, March 28, 1916

You cannot know (or do you feel it?) how I reproached myself—that same afternoon—for having been so talkative about a lot of my own affairs, old ones in part, wholly worth forgetting—, this having let myself go really calls for a special apology. But I have so often in the last months wished for a talk with you and imagined, in feeling, that no one could understand my position better than you yourself—so that my tongue at last just ran away with me and I couldn't stop it.

Not to continue this outpouring, on the contrary to relieve you of the last afterthought concerning it, I will just tell you what happened yesterday. The most important seems to me that Lieut.-Colonel V. sent for me, asked about my situation and finally instructed me to have the Munich Headquarters release sent to the War Archives. It would have been called in already had they known exactly where to ask for it. Once the document was there, he would see what could be done with it, and he hopes in this way to get me entirely free. So from this side everything possible will surely be done. This interest of my superiors is extraordinary and it goes without saying that I no longer complain of remaining idle here either, since it is only an expression of this same tendency to eliminate me from the whole apparatus until I am fully discharged.

So I beg you, my dear Hofmannsthal, not to worry about me, also not to tell anyone of my complaint, for now that this extremely well-intentioned effort is impending I must of course admit that my position is bearable, no worse than any time of waiting. I am still not yielding to too great confidence, to be sure—who knows how far the Munich decree is still alive—but if the War Archives administration's plan doesn't succeed, one may be sure nobody's would have.

Troublesome as I may have made myself the other day, to *me* the hours with you were extraordinarily delightful and at a distance so pleasantly linked with those first ones years ago. It was all most enjoyable and of your Picasso I think with amazement. . . .

[92]

To Countess Aline Dietrichstein   11 Keferstrasse, Munich
                                          All Souls Day [November 1] 1916

. . . It was just this that contact with Mogens and Frau Fönss and other works of Jacobsen's aroused in me nineteen years ago, this amazement you describe, this amazed delight in finding such things felt and given form, and an almost incredulous expectation of similar and of quite different products of imagination in which the world was shown and understood as richer and more akin than one had yet suspected. This is being young: this fundamental trust in the loveliest surprises, this delight of daily discovery. Just keep me well posted on the way your thoughts run so that from time to time I can really contribute a little, recommending or introducing the right thing to you at the right time.

The question whether art is to be experienced as a great forgetting or as a greater insight is perhaps only apparently to be answered in one sense or the other; one could imagine both might be correct, in that a certain abandonment reaching to the point of forgetfulness could constitute the first step to new insights, as though the shift were to a higher plane of life, where a riper, larger awareness, a seeing with rested, fresh eyes, then begins. To *remain* in forgetfulness would of course be entirely wrong. I believe that many people often give nothing but a comfortable abandon to those arts that strongly overwhelm (music for example), indeed it is this, I fear, that most people really understand by the "enjoyment" of art, a laziness at the expense of those abundancies that are effective in the work of art: here begins the comical misunderstanding of the worthy citizen who promptly settles down where he sees more has been achieved than he understands. In the end it will be a matter of intellectual conscience how far one may succumb to an artistic impression or, standing in it, must keep one's eyes open. Music could often bring me mere "forgetfulness", but the more receptive I have become to pictures, sculpture and books, often by long processes, the better prepared have I become for music too, the less is it able to put me entirely under water and delude me with a transformation in which, the music over, I should after all not be able to keep my bearings. . . .

[93]

To Imma Baroness von Ehrenfels

Villa Alberti,
11 Keferstrasse, Munich
February 20, 1917

Since the shocking certainty has been with us, I have daily felt the urge to write you, and daily denied myself; for how inadequate must every word of communication be to you. Today I have at last wrung from my own inner muteness a few lines to Frau von Hellingrath, and now to you I want to add at least the assurance that I think of you and through being so deeply stricken am placed as close to you as you may be willing to permit a person whom you have not often seen.

I knew enough of Norbert and had so much affection and veneration for him, that from my relation to him I can well appreciate your position. It is both harder and more creative than that of his mother and sister. Where these two may rest under the burden of sorrow in long remembrance of things past and realized, of you, from whom things promised and to come seem withdrawn, a limitless poise is demanded: but for this very reason you alone are able to develop into a purely spiritual experience that for which sorrow is no sufficient name, in order creatively to enter into, as a very great, immeasurable inheritance, that which but now was future.

It lies in the nature of every finally perfect love that sooner or later it may no longer reach the loved one save in the infinite. May your youth and the deep spiritual community with Norbert help you to see in your destiny not really a revocation but only this extreme, this greatest—, this exhaustless task.

The only thing for which I have words, Baroness Imma, is to beg you, for the sake of the memory I hold dear, to let me keep some touch with you throughout the years.

[94]

To Anton Kippenberg   11 Keferstrasse, Munich
April 15, 1917

. . . About myself I would rather not report until conditions are better. I have unfortunately been justified during these difficult months in my fear that the Vienna interruption would not be so easily overcome. With the fatal resemblance of its circumstances to that most difficult stratum of life at the military school it has, as I am only now properly realizing, inflicted on me something like what a tree would have to undergo that found itself upside down for a while, with its crown buried below in the bad and stubborn soil out of which, a tree's age ago, it had with the most unspeakable effort grown up to the light. To which must be added that this crown just at the instant of being buried stood full of new sap, ready to blossom and bear as it had not been for a long time . . . Now fortunately one knows the almost unlimited endurance and renewal of Nature, but one also knows that she works slowly and protractedly—. So I am proceeding but very slowly along the course of the translations, and the attempts to continue my own very particular work, interrupted by the enlistment, have simply moved into daily experience a torturesome inability to work. Those broken surfaces have gone hard and cold and the warmth of simple joy is lacking to melt them, and how could the so much greater condition for the happiness of producing something new help being all the more unattainable to the mind dispossessed!

How I wish for you, dear friend, an easy return to what is yours. Even what is mine, though it now seems that I was not kept from it all this long time, will be able to count on me again only in a healing world. But then it will be a new, determined, clean beginning for all of us. . . .

P.S. At Hofmannsthal's lecture last week I had a chance to shake Hans Carossa's hand; he was here on a short leave after a long time. Kassner, who sends greetings, I see nearly every week.

[95]

To Elisabeth Taubmann   11 Keferstrasse, Munich
                                        May 18, 1917

. . . How long I have left you without an answer. By this I clearly see the degree of my numbness and apathy. The present time with all its hindrances and its activity gone to the most frightful ruin is like lead poured around me—, I cannot move, not outwardly and not far inwardly. And should there still be some life in my inmost being, I am too blunt and too untransparent to feel and recognize myself in it. . . .

After our meetings in Paris I completely absorbed only Cézanne's work; later paintings, with the exception of a few Henri Rousseaus, did not claim my full attention, on the one hand because Cézanne still seemed to me the biggest and most modern, then also because long journeys had, as is their way, filled me with pictures and demands which, without the misfortune of the war, I would have developed and worked up within myself. Only in the "exile" in which I live here did I begin, more out of désoeuvrement than receptivity, to look about me again, and here I began to get a feeling for Picasso (as certain pictures chanced to come through here, and other important ones are privately owned in Munich). Among the Germans it was Franz Marc, who fell in the war, that interested me particularly; sculptors none—and if you ask me how I feel about these artists, I am really embarrassed to give an answer that would be useful and to the point; for how much else forces itself upon our eyes that purports to be art and often in fact carries a certain strength and conviction. Directions and individuals, of yesterday and today—no, I could not say how many of them are in the right, within the law—I do not know. I must assume that our experiences are shifting always further into the invisible, into the bacillary and microscopic: and thus it is possible to understand the absurd violence with which painting, like the stage, comes to display its magnified and wrenched-out objects. What violence here too, how little Nature, how little peace.

Ah, I would counsel you, Frau Elisawetta, to work heart and soul from the stores of life, out of the savings of only subjects you yourself have experienced without trying to orient yourself too much with regard to other contemporaries, at most in connection with a few reliable experiences with the really great. Too bad you did not stick to painting. . . . But now you are a sculptor. And at the same time hold livable life in your sure hands. Do let me sometimes watch and listen, even should I prove unfit as an adviser, cut off as I now am from everything.

[96]

To Anton Kippenberg   Villa Alberti, 11 Keferstrasse, Munich
July 5, 1917

. . . The days at the Chiemsee did me good physically, though they also proved to me again that no natural benefit of any kind can now effectively penetrate one's inner being. What could counterbalance there the perpetual weight of the time? You yourself will often have thought with concern how heavily it presses on my own mind and spirit and distorts all that I inwardly possess. If I turn up my most fruitful memories—I hardly know one that is not as though scratched out and canceled. What is the use of anything that makes sense, if, contrary to all sense, a universal bewilderment was prepared for us?

One thing more, dear friend. Don't be disappointed if I do not send you an Elegy for the Almanac. These poems must be allowed to remain my inner possession until the whole group is in visible form and we publish it in one. Making it known any earlier would, believe me, be unfair to this work, and what is worse, would diminish my own inner tension toward it . . .

[97]

To Countess Aline Dietrichstein   11 Keferstrasse, Munich
July 9, 1917

. . . As I was partly supervising, partly doing the packing of my books collected here, three volumes came into my hands which I am sending on to you by the same mail, because it seemed more proper to me that someone should read aloud to you from them in your days of convalescence than that they should repose here for no one's pleasure, piled up inside a packing-case with hundreds of other books. It is Adalbert Stifter's extensive novel "Nachsommer", one of the most unhurried, even and even-tempered books in the world, and hence one capable of emanating extraordinarily much purity and mildness of life. I think it would be good if you were to listen for many hours to these pages, as long as you must "have time", for this book has time too, it has the measured pace, so to speak, of eternal life, as if the world were without pressure and haste and menace. (If it were!) Many connoisseurs and admirers of Stifter consider this novel his most important work; of this opinion too was Herr von Kühlmann (the present German ambassador in Constantinople), who sent me "Nachsommer" to Paris a few years ago (as you see from the inscription); he discovered this old-fashioned edition for me, therefore I cannot give it away, but I give it into your care for as long as you want to keep it; for a *very long time please*. And don't send it back, I will fetch it sometime at your home in Vienna. A new edition of "Nachsommer", if I am not mistaken, has not followed up to now; it is congenial too to read Stifter in these editions which are not beautiful but are contemporaneous with him.

Phot. Monad

Rilke with Paul Valéry in the garden at Anthy.

Rilke's Grave in Raron

Good hours! (It wants to be read aloud slowly by a quiet, reconciled person.) . . .

[*98*]

To Elisabeth Taubmann   Hotel Esplanade, Berlin
July 19, 1917

Your letters are tied up, together with all correspondence worth saving, in a trunk of letters which I packed along with our other trunks and boxes (who knows now for how long). . . . Just think, we might have seen each other again here for a brief moment! I don't know whether I should think of it or whether the mere imagining of it does not already conjure up too much that is irretrievable, for how could we see each other without Paris at least within reach? The painful longing would perhaps be stronger than all actuality, and I should get in addition an unbearable yearning for myself, for my heart of those days, so sensitive, so creative, and for an instant so moved toward you and so tender toward you, Lisawetta. Tender with an infinite understanding of life, with all Nature and the world, as my heart in those days absorbed them out of everything—tender, tender for the sake of the spot on which you stood, your *inner* spot, which somehow lay in shadow and on which you stood waiting, obstinate and gentle at the same time, like a child on its inexplicable favorite spot. Could it ever be like that again—? What have we since become? The years, alas, have cramped my spirit badly and made me much less susceptible to people—and then came the war and did this and that to hamper me, lock me in, confute me.

And you too have long been another—your hand must have become more accurate and sure, your personality itself, dominating the gait and behavior of such strong and willful animals, must have grown less yielding, grown more masterly and determined, quite confirmed indeed by tests of daring, resoluteness, presence of mind, which for years you were able to give yourself.

If you were only able to be in your artistic output all this and the other earlier things too, for in art there really is room for all

contrasts in inner make-up, only in art; I now understand better
what you have to suffer from "technique", but remember how it
was in riding, after all, what techinque meant there; was it, in
actual use, something so separate, so distinct in itself; was it not
rather the right impulse clearly understood, sheer action and
counter-action? So it must be in painting too; one should, in the
application, hardly be conscious any more of the method as such;
practicing is one thing, executing another; probably in riding, too,
one who does not lack the spirit of riding has the right hand and
the right position when often he could not possibly have acquired
them as yet; one has to rely on that, at least where it is a question
of "having to". . . .

[99]

To Countess Mary Gneisenau   Gut Böckel bei Bieren,
                                                Kreis Herford, Westphalia
                                                August 9, 1917

. . . I am startled by the contents of your letter; in recent
years whenever I thought of you, I saw you in the center of a
circle animated by you and in turn understanding and confirming you, busy, full of interests and wishes the greater part of
which remained not unregarded—in short, in a state which, if
I avoid calling it "happy", appears to me the more surely pleasant
and agreeable. . . . And now you disavow all this through the
admission that you have been "suffering". "For years", as you
say, from a feeling of "dying off", of "becoming a stranger to
yourself and empty". Here I should answer admission with admission, for I know just *that* so painfully well, and am only too
often in the position of marveling how everything used to be
lively and remarkable to me and how I now stand here in the
world so indifferent and hard to move (since when?)—, yes:
but neither should we forget in what a world. These states of
rigidity may easily be transformations, inner alterations, to be
followed by renewed existence and awareness of ourselves when
the alteration has taken place—perhaps it already has, that is

possible—; but what is something thus completed to do when it finds no environment, nothing but downfalls and collapses? Might you not justly attribute a large part of your condition to the time, which is impossible and full to the brim with doom, mistakes, ill-will and confusion? I am myself just realizing how much, with all my aloofness, my feeling and what I produced were based on the silent assumption that they were going on in an evenly regulated, evenly striving world: today's air and attitude of mind contradicts and confutes me in the inmost recesses of my mind, even far into my memories—how much that is beautiful and big, how much that I have felt and thought, opens up, when I try to recall it, like a page crossed and criss-crossed out. It will be similar with you, dear Countess; what you call "emptiness" is simply everything that has become invalid, been retracted: for you too have assumed a human world, in which you loved and felt, different from this one which now sullenly and angrily admits to all the opposites of kindness, joy and an open future.

The people around you are "hostile", you write; dear me, what people? The populace? And yet it is so easy now to be on good terms with them, since one wants less than ever to be counted among the "upper ones"; rather, in suffering one stands lower than the lowest, poorer, more restricted than they, afflicted with if possible still more penetrating injustice. Or are they people you yourself have called to you? Then away with them. What shall I quickly advise you to read? Bettina: read the correspondence with a child again. And of present-day books, Gustav Sack's "Ein verbummelter Student" (Fischer), and write me again. . . .

[*100*]

To Dr. Wolf Przygode   Gut Böckel bei Bieren,
                                          Kreis Herford, Westphalia
                                          September 14, 1917

You have occasion to think me forgetful, but still you would do me an injustice with any such reproach. I have not neglected my promise; besides the slowness imposed on me by the impediments of the time, it was only my extreme solicitude about making a really appropriate choice that so greatly delayed me. But now here are five poems which I believe I may lay before you with a better-satisfied conscience. If their inner connection seems to you very vague, I beg you to consider that they were supposed in a measure to show the distant boundary-marks of my more recent lyric output, and this would naturally produce a merely peripheral relationship. The order in which you will find the poems enclosed is the one most favorable to this view; they are all unpublished with exception of the last; this "Journey to Hell" appeared in the Insel Almanac in 1914. To me it is altogether the most important of the five contributions, as it is in this one that my lyric work up to now will be recognized at its highest (although it was written in 1913, in Spain). . . .

[101]

*To Marietta Baroness von
    Nordeck zur Rabenau*
        Gut Böckel bei Bieren,
        Kreis Herford, Westphalia
        September 19, 1917

. . . For the moment I am bad at answering, for the terrible, incomprehensible world-conditions . . . have caused me to grow inwardly numb so that almost only by violence can I force myself to say anything. But when I think how much salvation and relief will be implanted in my spirit the moment the great healing process of this wounded world can be begun, then I believe that not only shall I be allowed to give myself once again more vigorously and happily, but also I foresee a point of time at which, in an irrestrainable reaction of dispossessed humanity, all things and all people will again strive toward us and concur with us, more strongly, more passionately, more unconditionally, than was the case in those so remarkably tense years before 1914. . . . I sometimes think that every day the war still lasts increases the obligation of humanity toward a great better-intentioned common future, for what could be more productive of obligation than the suffering augmented beyond all measure, which must after all join millions of people in all countries more closely together. Ah, then it will be possible to speak again, and every word of love or of art will find a new acoustic, a more open air and a wider space—, I grant you that *only* at the price of this prospect do I care to live on; without it everything that happens must remain like a mountain lying over us.

You wish me courage,—over and over again I have had to conquer infinite hopelessnesses, but now one may hope indeed to be near those decisions through which the spirit will be restored to its own most particular influence. How much it will have to make good and to re-establish everywhere. . . .

[*102*]

To Clara Rilke   Hotel Esplanade, Berlin W.
                                     November 4, 1917

. . . Daily I have more the impression that on account of all that is happening now we are not moving from the spot, and yet the spot is so cruel that really everybody must be agreed to leave it at any price. "Victories", however great and successful, lead not a step further, and in one's inner world one cannot make up one's mind to any real changes, everything is appearance and play, always and everywhere the old and the fateful are still betrayed at work, the new forces, insofar as there may be any, impatient, painful, nowhere manage to make use of themselves. In Kühlmann I continue to have confidence, he is certainly the only more far-seeing person among the "ruling", it is much that he has reached this place, it is always a hope; but even he will hardly be able to do the decisive thing. I am of the opinion that many changes are still ahead before the next development really comes, we must be prepared for much time, misery and darkness; no wonder, for the changes which alone lead on would have to reach to the roots of present conditions; only through one of the biggest and most profound renewals that it has ever been through, will the world be able to rescue and uphold itself. A vague feeling of wanting to see and hear still a little more, has again kept me here another whole week and may perhaps keep me part of next too; it has been worth while inasmuch as Count [Paul] K[eyserlingk], whom it was in many respects important for me to see, is here at last. I hope to see something of him and promise myself to make the most of it, for he is almost the only one of my acquaintances who knew and experienced our former life (I mean Paris and the whole glorious open world) and is now actively engaged in the present, so that I think I can somehow measure and understand my own attitude by his. Unfortunately I am compelled to go out a lot evenings, which I dislike, but I take it a little as a duty and it will have to go on these few days more. Thankmar, who is here again, stands loyally by in everything like an adjutant; [his mother] says very sweetly of him that he "confers" me on the people he occasionally takes me to, herself for example, "like an order". Von der Heydt often has me to lunch. . . . Uexküll was staying with him for a few days and in spite of his "pan-German" attitude I felt very friendly with him.

. . . You are quite right, whoever now makes himself bigger, freer and more human in his own existence, is doing his part toward peace,—as yet it must be worked at *in an inward direction*, not until a few have it all big and ready within them can it let itself be brought into the world. To lay a peace egg won't help as nobody wants to hatch it; one must be able to bring forth a lively young peace out of oneself—unfortunately that means still more than nine months' gestation and under conditions of the most uneasy and dangerous pregnancy.

. . . I am lunching at von der Heydt's, with the Kaiser's Wing-Adjutant von Moltke, who has just come from Constantinople, so shall lack neither nourishment nor "news" (alas, alas!).

[103]

To Clara Rilke   Hotel Esplanade, Bellevuestrasse Berlin W
                              November 19, 1917

I was about to write you a little birthday letter yesterday when I got the news of Rodin's death, and then all my thoughts, you may imagine, were switched in that direction and rearranged. My wishes now stand before that background, which you and I still immeasurably share—like me you will be steeped in memories and sorrow and, with Paris and all we have lost in it, will have to go through this now so final loss. I do not know what Rodin's death would have meant to me in normal circumstances—perhaps something after all reconcilable—; for the present, I am dominated by perplexity that something so close should come to pass without standing out at all sharply defined against the chaos of the time, that behind the unnatural and terrible wall of the war these clearly known figures sink away from one, somewhere— Verhaeren, Rodin, those great wise friends—their death becomes indistinct and indiscernible . . . , I only feel that they will not be there any more when the horrible vapor clears away, and will not be able to stand by those who will have to raise the world up again and nurse it. Yesterday and today I received a few deeply moved letters about Rodin—if I could only still properly believe in the power of human emotion, in the midst of this predominating inhumanity.

But now the heartiest wishes, dear Clara. Have a good birthday as a new landed proprietress; may you, together with the growth of a life that is awaiting its peaceful time, set yourself up a dear little house on your home soil. I do hope Grandmother has seen to providing the materials for about the right (white flour) sort of birthday cake. I can't send anything of the sort from here, only occasionally in a private house is one surprised by such desserts. . . .

[*104*]

Forgetful toward you I have never been, bad enough that I have carried procrastination to extremes. The copies were to reach you for Christmas, early in the new year at latest—that was my intention and was to be my pleasure quite as much as yours; and when I now try to find what has caused my backwardness, I see no important reason save that retardation which permeates my whole life now.

The consciousness of the present world, as it repeatedly takes shape in my inner being, shatters all my relationships. It must— since so many endure the most impossible—it must probably be weakness that all I long for is the end of this terrible helpless man-made business, and beyond that, before everything is lost, a broadly general, well-disposed beginning. In *that* alone will my heart participate again. Until then I belong among those who are confuted, overcome by the utterly chaotic contradiction, and have nothing to hold on to save here and there the most rebellious words. Of what avail that they are the most human!

In your good letter, as though you wanted to anticipate my confession of loneliness, you speak of the connection of the poet with his whole living generation. Alas, dear friend, in this I think with the youngest, that we, all of us, who yielded to the current of sustained loftier words, have not made this very connection sufficiently secure. Perhaps it is indeed only to be effected in Tolstoy's sense, which then, to be sure, brings with it a renuncia-tion of the most sublime impulses to artistic performance.

My letter, dear Herr von der Marwitz, cannot do you much good—as you see. I hope the poems still can, as they did on that evening we had together, which I also warmly remember. I have written them in a little book, to be handy for you, and I will ask for it back again if something comes to me that could give you pleasure out there. There is little prospect of that! I haven't even opened up Claudel yet with real attention: my unconquerably reticent state of mind makes receiving and giving equally difficult for me. . . .

[*105*]

To Lou Andreas-Salomé
  [*two unsent fragments*]   Hotel Continental, Munich
                                                February 20, 1918

Like a sleepwalker I went into Jaffe's a few days ago and straight to your little book, though it was lying among many and, modestly, with the title downwards. Since then I have read the "Three Letters" again and again and like that time in Paris, they are important and pertinent to me, as if I could still at any moment instate in myself all three age levels and on each of them, regardless of the rest of my life, be receptive. At any rate, more plainly than before, I desire this time to see you treat the same contents for my present age and for every further one; for the making-oneself-small, however directly it may give the subject, does also do it sensible injury: in that it cannot make the coming to know death count sufficiently beside the experience of love. From this point of view the remark about the plant fruit and its twofold (white and black) birth especially impressed me this time. Were you the first thus to observe this process?

. . . That a host of creatures which spring from seeds exposed outside have *that* relationship with the maternal body, that wide, excitable free thing,—how at home they must feel in it all their lives long, indeed they do nothing but leap for joy in their mother's womb, like little John; for indeed this same space received and bore them, they never get out of its security at all.

Until in the bird everything becomes a little more apprehensive and more cautious. His nest is already a little maternal womb made secure for him by Nature, which he only covers instead of wholly containing it. And suddenly, as if it were no longer safe enough outside, the wonderful maturing flees wholly into the darkness of the creature and emerges only at a later turn into the world, taking it only as a second world and never again to become

quite weaned from the conditions of the earlier, more fervent one.
(Rivalry between Mother and World . . .)

[*106*]

To Bernhard von der Marwitz   Hotel Continental, Munich
March 9, 1918

At how many times in my life I would have been able to reply
in full measure to a letter of the cordiality of yours. To let you
take even the smallest part in my life now would mean plunging
you into a poverty so great that I have not sufficient means to
describe it. What might, under the violent and extraordinary conditions of your present life, make you desirous of getting letters,
is surely only the assurance which flows from them that intellectual and spiritual continuity has not been given up in this land
of ours. And it is just *that* for which I cannot produce the least
evidence. On the contrary, where I am concerned, all general
circumstances and the most difficult personal ones have worked
together to interrupt all flow in me and to separate me from the
nourishment that otherwise, even in the worst days, rose up to me
imperceptibly from unerring roots. The more I felt this fatality,
the more I began to look about in the disastrous events of the
time, but this very orientation made me more and more miserable.
For where for us here is the visible in this desperate world?
Doesn't one think one should, laden with the years-long consciousness of whatever of evil is fulfilling itself therein, finally
come to some place where people are on their knees and crying
out—, this I should understand, I should throw myself down
among them and might then have *my* outcry too under the shelter
of theirs. Taking part in the visitation means here in our country
reading the newspapers—stuffing oneself with the ambiguous
sham-happening they are daily piling up, and being able at last
to think of pain and worry only in the transposition which they
impose upon everything. Fearful as the war is in itself, it seems to
me still more dreadful that the pressure of it has nowhere contributed to bringing man out more distinctly, to forcing him—

the individual or the mass—face to face with God, as great tribulations in earlier times had the power to do. On the plane meanwhile cultivated, on which the newspapers are able to give a conscienceless verbal cross-section of all that happens (a scrimmage in which what is beyond us and conjectured stands beside the factual, what is most commercial beside the most incalculable): on this plane an incessant equalizing of all tensions is created and humanity becomes accustomed continually to accept a world of news in place of realities which no one has time or is minded any more to let grow large and heavy within them.

I never was and *cannot* any longer become a newspaper reader. . . .

[*107*]

To Anton Kippenberg   34/IV Ainmillerstrasse, Munich
                                     July 3, 1918

. . . So far as my own activity is concerned, the disturbances have gone too deep for me to be able to go securely ahead. You write that the world-picture, the external as well as the internal, has altered from the ground up. What *I* am aware of, my dear friend, is still only the disastrous breaking off of a former world, in which I in my own way took part the more intensely as for me it led over into the most open future. The longer the confused interruption lasts, the more I see that my task lies in carrying on the past with absolute constancy of purpose and in inexhaustible remembering; though the conditions out of which I grew may have come to an end, I believe I have understood their mandate so timelessly that I can look upon it even now as inviolable and final.

I see, if I am not mistaken, some small external progress in the setting up of a new household of my own. Your wife saw just the after-growth of possessions standing around me; since then this has warmed up a little with use, even though it makes me realize daily, of course, that it cannot mean a settling down in Munich but just a very transportable world of protection which I hope soon to transfer out of the worry and bustle of life here into more settled surroundings.

[*108*]

To Hertha Koenig   34/IV Ainmillerstrasse, Munich
July 25, 1918

Am I too late to find you still at Böckel? . . .

To figure in your thoughts and your concern cannot be other than continually beneficial to me. I am touched that you have the upper rooms in mind for me, but almost frightened that now they too, through the Providence of lucky discoveries, are to be more beautiful than originally foreseen; for I distrust myself lest I continually fall short of the favorable circumstances people create for me. All these weeks such a burden of unhappiness and worry has lain upon me, I had fallen into such lowlands of my spirit that the going was simply impossible. Happily, this was due in part to physical conditions, if I did not at least know that, the wretchedness of such an abandonment would be limitless.

Do not let me report further about it, today is the first better day, as regards the weather too moreover, for after everyone had called for rain it came, but not a summery, nourishing one,—an autumn rain with all the disadvantages of cold and penetrating-ness.

My state of mind permitted me that much better to gauge how young you are, Frau Hertha, and how assuring even the most oppressive appears from which you have to suffer. You are again and again placed before the most completely new beginnings in everything and are then each time in the position of a happy season, which from one day to the next unfolds for itself the most manifold things. You have indescribably unbroached strengths and impulses, zest, sight, readiness and a maturity that has flourished in all secrecy and has come to its determining moment under the shelter of long shynesses that had almost become definitive. That you still sometimes behave as if those embarrassments were there, act with a running start, and so must make on possible observers a disproportionate, inaccurate effect, overshooting the immediate (—for your "boisterousness" is always a kind of running start of purest seriousness and a somewhat vague leap out beyond the mark): how small and how innocent is this temporary disadvantage in the face of such healthy and serene resolutenesses. Even Kassner—be sure of that—in case you are not mistaken about his impression, will have to correct it, just man that he is in his great depths! And it is magnificently provided that you have to make all these transformations not only in a *spiritual* sphere, that it all has to be tested out and inflected through possession, in the highly tangible form of your property and the people bound up with it. For in the spiritual such simple and reliable proofs would never have been given as have been supplied you by people and things—, were Tolstoy still alive I would sometime have told him about your life, about the woman who through her possessions, through the deep, genuine, unshaken, even reverent taking possession of all that she stood beside in shyness and waiting poverty—about the woman who arrived at freedom through her possessions: for that is how I think of your road and see it climbing up to free places of widest view and independence. There are indeed few who *experience, live through* their property, and without yours you would have remained a person without precedent. As it is, you can underlay each of your many advances with some thing and bring to rest and adjustment in a material world the tremendous fluctuation of spiritual realities. Your possessions are a course of instruction in contemplation for your soul: one cannot, it seems to me, possess in a more childlike and humble way than you do.

I have long felt the impulse sometime to express these realizations, your letter has now brought something of them to precipitation, in time I hope to write it all down better, perhaps only for myself for the sake of the reckoning that is such an obligation to me in all experience. Take this little as—say—an hour with Stauffenberg; who knows how far his pervasive influence is co-active in my finding these expressions. In any case, do not fear any overestimating in this conception; it perhaps anticipates many a turning, but that one of your directions seems charted out in it, a spontaneous joy and approbation of your nature will tell you. . . .

[*109*]

To Joachim von Winterfeldt-Menkin 34/IV Ainmillerstrasse,
Munich
September 16, 1918

Again and again since your letter came, my dear Herr von Winterfeldt, I have taken up my pen and tried and have no command of the words the moment calls for. Which are they? Have we not long since dispensed all those adapted to the various demands of grief? Anything there might still be to say we would have to break off with a piece of our heart—, it lies beyond exaggeration, beyond any extreme ever possible to words, and the excess of mourning for the dead that threatens to break out presupposes, in order still to be kept within bounds at all, an infinite extension of soul in us which again cannot have developed in such a tangled and chaotic time.

What shall I say: I know, I feel, you have lost a young friend, the best, the biggest, the incomparable thing that in essence these two words can stand for. Among the thousands of young men who have sacrificed their own, specially intended lives in the impenetrable destiny of the war, Bernard von der Marwitz will remain, to those who knew him, one of the most unforgotten. The memorial you are gathering for him in your heart will have more than personal significance. For the "being young" and the "being friend" of this young man of fine culture and large capacity for emotion was a more than personal manifestation, was in a certain sense standard for that German youth which, without the interruption of such fearful disturbances, would have assured our future in a wide-open spiritual world. The continued and inextricable wrong of the war has called up more and more young people of contradictory mind, who think to deduce the future more cleanly out of the negation of the past. In Marwitz, on the contrary, tradition functioned together with a perfect readiness for intellectually responsible freedom: if a future is to come out of German youth, it must be an attitude very closely related to his that would be determinative for it. So the thought of his survival, it seems to me, is linked with those most intimate hopes that we have yet to direct toward life which is altogether to be rescued.

I cannot at the moment, dear Herr von Winterfeldt, do more to comfort you than admit with entire conviction the great and unique worth of your friend.

How indescribably, furthermore, I hold myself a loser you may understand from the circumstance that one of Marwitz's magnificent letters (written the 9th of August) has not only occupied me continually all these weeks, but (to be truthful) contained for me a human appeal such as has not fallen to my lot from any association for a long time. After that letter (the answering of which I incomprehensibly, tired and frustrated as I am, put off to a more favorable hour—) I was certain of having in young Bernhard von der Marwitz a friend, a *close* friend, and I regarded this relationship as a possession not yet entered upon, the future productivity of which seemed to me the more precious in that men have seldom sought my intimacy. Thus the number of my hopes, with which I have been left in the lurch, is at least as great as the quantity of your orphaned and uncontinuable memories: may this maintain a sort of lasting understanding between us, my dear Herr von Winterfeldt.

Had you not expressed the wish to let me have a look (advisory) into the writings your friend has left, I should have come out with it as a request: in the feeling that this reciprocal, almost unexercised friendship would entitle me, with gentle affection still, to retrieve intimacy I had in a way neglected.

And now to add a real request. If there was anyone in his immediate family (it seems to me he spoke particularly of a sister) with whom he had a really close understanding, I feel I would like to write that person a few words of sympathy and sorrow, perhaps even a certain assurance of devotion such as would be comprehensible in one left behind with a quite unexpended affection.

If you know such a person and advise my writing the letter, I beg you to give me the name and address.

When we meet again, as I now the more sincerely wish we may, I shall be unable to repress many questions about his last days, as indeed I shall always be grateful to you for everything through which you connect me with his memory, which I love and honor.

[*110*]

To Marie von Bunsen   34/IV Ainmillerstrasse, Munich
                                          September 22, 1918

. . . The summer went, yes passed away over my head, nor did it bring the good hours out of which I hoped to write you more fully or perhaps more happily. For complaining and miserable words, wrung from an arid state, are indescribably in the wrong before you who possess the secret of preserving for yourself vistas in no matter how distorted a world, of finding in no matter how spoiled a one the good flavor of nourishing existence, and who are above all in a position still to conceive of history in that nobly traditional sense before which even the present, be it the most irresponsible and impenetrable, will sometime have to elucidate itself as proportional continuity.

Your new letter is again full of proofs of your lively and unswervable determination: how you can still love the work of men; how you trace the confirmed and insubvertible order in it and, where palaces might make one reflect, recognize in the simplest farmhouse the achievement and solution of harmonious satisfactions from which spiritual fellowship, from which comfort emanates! How coldly, coldly, in comparison did I journey through Ansbach the other day. Saw, remembered, tried to admire: but through the present malicious confusion I have come to be so suspicious of everything human, even far into the past. I can hardly stand before beautiful old things without being frightened at their forlornness,—how lost they have become though they still continue to exist, in the midst of cautious people looking all about them, who beside some beautiful generous, prodigal thing have set up something not by any chance useful even—no: a shameless sign of their exploitation, their non-reality, their nothingness! Doesn't one seem, I said to myself, to be moving in a world through whose greedy fingers its best inheritances have already been slipping for decades: for it is perhaps something almost imperceptible that gives all heritage its significance; the zero groove that fades on the measuring rod, and the whole scale loses its genius, its rise and fall, its longing and tension and polarity. Is it not so? Would not a something have to vanish, to fall away, out of the proportion of doorframes and windows, out of the sequence of stairs, out of the winding of grilles, before a time like this hopeless one of ours was possible? . . .

I long for people through whom the past in its large lines continues to be connected with us, related to us; for how much the future, particularly now—the bolder and more daring one imagines it—is nevertheless still going to depend on whether it falls in with the direction of the deepest traditions and moves and is projected out of them (and not out of negation). The war robbed me of two young friends in August and September, precious ones, whom in the interests of that future we had so hoped for I infinitely deplore, a young Keyserlingk and that fine true young Marwitz from Friedersdorf, whom you may also have known. I was growing very fond of him . . . Losses, losses . . . if only each loss were a full pledge and relentless in demanding of us a life more serious, more responsible and more sensitive to mysteries!

[*111*]

To Countess
Aline Dietrichstein
                              34/IV Ainmillerstrasse,
                                           Munich
                                    October 9, 1918

. . . I do not want to complain again (and certainly not at this moment) of my indescribably benumbed and inhibited state of mind; but this it is with which the time has stricken me—as it has thwarted and interrupted everyone in some way—and through just this condition of inwardly turning to ice, which makes my heart almost inaccessible to me, I am continually shut out from everything: from friends, from Nature, and (most baffling of all) from the happiness and the fullness of my own work. You, my dear Countess, did not know me when this oppression was not yet upon me, when I lived in an open world and more than any-one else (I may well say) was borne along by the currents that carried the great inspirations of a common humanity across all lands and skies. When I now imagine that the day might come again when I could use my natural self, made for gazing and marveling, for acquiescing, for infinite worship, then I rejoice in this future for your sake too. You shall (this too I promised myself that day on the balcony, in the face of the rising thunder-storm), you, Countess Aline, shall always be among the few people who may claim a direct share in my being happy and clear, in my growing powers, as something that belongs to you as naturally as the sun of an open-hearted day, as the feel of a free wind, as a view over the clear valleys of the serene and har-monious landscape.

All these years I have not asked myself (it would have been imprudent to do so) how much, with all the affliction, confusion and disfigurement of the world, I still believe in the great, in the consummate, widely inexhaustible possibilities of life; may your wedding-day be an occasion for me to test myself. And so I con-fess to you, dear Countess, that I hold life to be a thing of the most inviolable preciousness, and that the entangling of so much doom and horror, the prostituting of such countless destinies, everything that in these last years has been unconquerably growing for us into a still augmenting terror, cannot dissuade me of the fullness and goodness and congeniality of existence. There would be no sense in coming to you with wishes did not the one conviction *precede* all wishes, that out of subversion and destruction the goods of life spring clean and unspoiled and most deeply desir-able; but that I (although myself sad, dejected and bound to a heart I can scarcely unravel) can hold this conviction—may this give my wishes the greatest and truest validity. And if on the one hand I thus vouch for the wonderful provisions of life, on the other I am inwardly convinced that you of all people will know how to value what it bestows at its most fundamental worth.

The happiness and confidence of a courageous love fills your richly-endowed heart. Amid superficiality and chance you unerringly recognized your destined companion and humbled yourself before the law that is related to those laws by which the stars move. And already this natural honesty and sincerity of yours has rewarded you, in that at one stroke not only was he who loved you loved, but the whole world turned a different face to you and was yours. And so on your beautiful wedding-day celebrate the doing right and the being right of your heart!— Celebrate it confidently, even though external confusions and tribulations still surround everything that is personal and of one's inner world. The moment for an awakening and a turning no longer seems quite out of reach and the happy new beginning and progress of your own life will perhaps soon be borne along by a current of universal awakening and good will. . . .

[*112*]

To Clara Rilke   34/IV Ainmillerstrasse, Munich
                                    November 7, 1918

Your letter (of October 28th) with its great free breath blew in ahead of the events. We here in the city have now to go instead through all the ups and downs and the many newspapers, the hundred repugnant rumors—and at every hesitation in the strife of that which finally has come, one's heart stops as though this future, still going on foot through the crowd, might stumble or turn back again.

I was so busy watching and listening, and above all hoping, that I overlooked how long it must have been since I had written you both. Now, in face of your telegram, I reproach myself for having made you uneasy by this silence: there was no reason whatever for that.

. . . In the last few days Munich has given up some of its
emptiness and quiet, the tensions of the moment are noticeable
here too, even though between Bavarian temperaments they don't
act in an exactly spiritually elevating manner. Everywhere gatherings in the beer-halls, almost every evening, everywhere speakers,
among whom Professor Jaffé is of the first prominence, and
where the halls aren't big enough, gatherings of thousands out
of doors. I too was among thousands Monday evening in the Hotel
Wagner; Professor Max Weber of Heidelberg, national economist, who is regarded as one of the best minds and as a good
speaker, spoke, after him in the discussion the anarchistically
overstrained Mühsam, and then students, men who had been four
years at the front,—all so simple and frank and of-the-people.
And although they sat around the beer-tables and between the
tables so that the waitresses only ate their way through the human
structure like wood-worms,—it wasn't at all stifling, not even for
breathing; the fumes of beer and smoke and people did not affect
one uncomfortably, one hardly noticed them, so important was it
and so above all immediately clear that the things could be said
whose turn has come at last, and that the simplest and most valuable of these things, in so far as they were to some extent made
easily accessible, were grasped by the enormous multitude with
a heavy massive approval. Suddenly a pale young worker stood
up, spoke quite simply: "Did you, or you, or you, any of you,"
he said, "make the armistice offer? and yet *we* ought to do that,
not those gentlemen up there; if we take possession of a radio
station and speak, we common people to the common people yonder, there will be peace at once." I can't repeat it half so well as
he expressed it; suddenly, when he had said that, a difficulty as-
sailed him, and with a moving gesture towards Weber, Quidde
and the other professors who stood by him on the platform, he
continued: "Here, these professor gentlemen know French, they
will help us to say it right, the way we mean it . . ." Such moments are wonderful, and how we have had to do without them in
this very Germany where only invective found words, or sub-

mission, which in its way was after all but a sharing in power of those who submitted. . . .

Enclosed is a not uncomfortable letter from Grandmama Phia; it speaks for the Czechoslovaks that she feels comparatively calm and protected in the new state . . .

P.S. Friday morning early.

We have a remarkable night behind us. A soldiers', peasants' and workers' council has now been set up here too, with Kurt Eisner as first president. The whole first page of the *Münchener Neueste* is taken up by a decree he has issued, through which the Bavarian Republic explains that peace and security are assured the inhabitants. The night's enterprise was preceded by a gathering on the Theresienwiese attended by a hundred and twenty thousand people. Now it only remains to be hoped that this unusual insurrection will engender sense in people's heads and not go on beyond to fatal intoxication. So far everything seems quiet and one cannot but grant that the time is right when it tries to take big steps.

[*113*]

To Dr. Burschell   34/IV Ainmillerstrasse, Munich
                              November 11, 1918

With this morning's mail the expected letter from the Bernese Legation has at last arrived; I must now get myself ready to travel, possibly earlier than I assumed yesterday. With the increased work this puts on me I cannot think of preparing a talk to the students and so beg you not to instigate anything of the sort for the present.

If my trip should *still* not come off, I would seek an opportunity for talking over this plan with you again.

The morning paper, which brings the reassurance that most businesses are functioning and in order, speaks for the fact that the hour now belongs not so much to words as to quiet confirmation through work.

[114]

To Margarete Hethey   34/IV Ainmillerstrasse, Munich
                                         December 2, 1918

You were not mistaken when you assumed that Herr von Kaufmann's proposals would very much appeal to me: in fact I actually read the interesting pages with the readiest wish that some such establishing of contact might be possible; my past would in that case indicate France for me, and even a fortnight ago an attempt to establish relations with Paris would have seemed not entirely hopeless. Since then, through third parties, I have unfortunately been informed of such a definitely and conclusively irreconcilable attitude that I cannot but fear only time, if not indeed *much* time, can bring about a gradual amelioration.

In spite of this I would, since of course I remain in many ways dependent on foreign countries, be very grateful for a chance to confer along these lines with you and through your kindness with Herr von Kaufmann; perhaps something could be arranged for the end of the week (Saturday?)? My time is pretty well taken up until then, and as a number of appointments usually exhaust my powers of absorption, I never dare undertake more than *one* matter of an afternoon. . . .

[115]

To the Presidency of the North
Austrian Government, Vienna

The undersigned respectfully begs to call attention to the following:

When in May of this year he learned through the newspapers that an honor had been most graciously bestowed upon him, he immediately decided to decline it; for it has always been his intention never to accept any decoration that might be designated to him. At that time informed friends called his attention to the fact that since he was still in the army he had no right to exercise such a refusal.

The official notification of the bestowal of this honor, as well as the order itself, have only now reached the undersigned, at a moment when he is free to act according to his conviction: may he therefore be permitted to return the order together with all the accompanying papers to the office which conferred it.

It would certainly be unfair to attribute this action of the undersigned to any lack of respect; he declines simply in order to remain personally inconspicuous, as his work as an artist unconditionally obliges him to do.

R. M. Rilke

Munich, December 17, 1918

[*116*]

To Dorothea Baroness von Ledebur   34/IV Ainmillerstrasse,
Munich
December 19, 1918

. . . Your news, though it comes from a house plunged in the deepest mourning, kindly reassures me of your own immediate welfare; quite particularly I can feel with you that the return of Baron Ledebur will at last permit a real life together again! How long it may last no one will dare to say in his own case, for whereas before during these last cruel years one had two conceptions— war and peace—everything has now fallen apart in a confusion of anonymous fragments which the individual finds himself unable to piece together.

I confess that I was able to feel a certain quick and happy confidence in the overturn itself, for ever since I can remember, I have wished humanity nothing more urgently than that it might some time or other be empowered to turn up an entirely new page of the future, on to which the whole wrong sum of the unfortunate past need not be carried over. The revolution seemed to me a moment so endowed. But it was taken up and carried out by such a casual and profoundly uninspired minority—the spirit did not try to enter and force its way in until afterwards, and even this was spirit only in name and had no youth and no convincing fire in its nature. Perhaps revolutions are possible only in very full-blooded moments, in any case not after a four-year bloodletting. Because we have never seen peace as a whole, but are only picking up the thousand fragments into which, falling from all our hands, it broke, we have each one of us missed the deep breath of relief that seemed to have been promised us. After the indescribable exertions and trials of the war, a moment of security and rest would have been the last thing one could forgo; one does not see how the enormous exertion that is continually needed can now follow upon the intense exertions of the military campaigns. Moreover I understand by revolution the conquering of abuses for the benefit of the deepest tradition, and from this point of view I look upon today and tomorrow, as you may imagine, with the greatest concern. Nevertheless let us, each in our own little spot, plant a fervent hope. My inclination is now more than ever to do what I really *can*, quite against the call of the time which would like to seduce everyone away from his real ability into a political dilettantism.

[*117*]

To Anni Mewes   34/IV Ainmillerstrasse, Munich
                                    December 19, 1918

No, there is no question of any more agreeable news from here; under the pretext of a great overturn the old lack of principle works on and gives itself airs under the red flag. It is terrible to say it: but all this is just as little *true* as the summonses that exhorted to the war; neither this nor those were made by the spirit. . . .

My little confidence in a new clean beginning (for which, to be sure, even the most natural forces are now lacking) is indeed not altogether gone, but still I must nurse it like a highly fragile little plant, in which process I can observe too how cold and sunless my inner climate has become.

People, who have of course also gathered here now in large numbers, have only frightened me on the whole; individuals,

where they spoke out, were often close and moving to me—
especially people coming back from the field, cheated of almost
every token of homecoming!

And yet, yet: how hopeful the individual is again and again,
how real, how well-intentioned, how rich,—then when one sees
the doleful confused multitude, one does not understand how he
loses himself in it so tracelessly, as it were.

. . . If I look forward to the holidays it is because I hope to
settle down more solitarily than most days during these last weeks;
if you were here you would have to spend a long evening with me;
I should not take it as company but as a dear natural sounding
in harmony with me. And surely whichever of us were the sad-
der would be the more consoling.

[*118*]

To Elisabeth Baroness Schenck
  zu Schweinsberg   34/IV Ainmillerstrasse, Munich
                                              January 5, 1919

If I were to say what binds me to people in the most touching
way, it is these tokens of steadfastness that are sometimes, richly
as they are undeservedly, given to one: the happy perenniality of
a memory that apparently without any care still goes on and
survives in the manifold and distracting (alas, in the so indiscrim-
inate) congestion of life and, in the midst of loss, brings a subtle
sure permanence to mind in him who a moment ago was still bewildered by a surface of transiency. How one's thoughts collect
at such moments of being remembered as you, charming Caprese
of long ago, were able to prepare for me in a few lines, a few pictures! Alas, I too need to remain connected with that past; the
longer the exceptional period of the war lasted, the denser and
more impenetrable it grew, the more did I take pains not to be
separated by it from all that had been, the more did I insist on
keeping what was happy, open, guileless in my past, indeed, on
nourishing and continuing myself, across the terrible interruption,
out of this very past. Practically my only achievement in these

dreadfully annihilated years was to believe in what once in the past was mine, in Capri, in Rome, in Paris, in Russia, in Egypt and Tunis—in all the marvelous sheer happenings of my life, to which a different future seemed to belong. Tell me yourself, how else should I have survived, I especially, to whom the onset and course of all that has happened since 1914 could mean nothing after all but revocation and insanity? But I do not really know whether I have survived. My inner self has shut itself up more and more. As though to protect itself, it has become inaccessible even to me, and so I do not know now whether in my heart's core there is still the strength to venture upon world-relationships and realize them, or whether only a tombstone of my former spirit has quietly remained there. I still do not know, and have not been able (for how long) to give myself the slightest proof of inner activity; the intersection point of my forces has lost its starriness, has fallen out of the great constellations that used to shelter and support it in spiritual space.

And with us it is not at all to be taken for granted that we survive years of unproductiveness, of hindrance—years that somehow leave one out of use. With women it is different. Do you know the letters of Caroline Schlegel-Schelling, two volumes—shall I send them to you? They should become a reinforcement for you in moments when you yourself incline to doubt the fruitfulness and meaning of your own life just because for a few years perhaps it may not lend itself to any entirely gratifying use. Today as formerly, Elisabeth von Schenk, I believe *wholly* in your riches: if you cannot make full use of them now, that cannot lessen them and ought not to lower their value in your own mind. . . .

[*119*]

To Emil Lettré   34/IV Ainmillerstrasse, Munich
                                        January 5, 1919

Do not think me forgetful: your cuff-links are at my wrists, and were they not, there would still be inner proofs enough of my obligations to you. The *Insel Yearbook* which goes to you here-with (with four of my contributions) I had taken to the post office at the end of December, but I had to bring it back home again, as well as all my letters, the registration windows being hopelessly crowded for an hour ahead. Hence the unpunctuality! I wish for you what I wish ever more determinedly and ever more desperately for myself: work—possibility, strength and joy for *work!* May this difficult, and confused, and yet less burdened year grant us *that!*

I still have not been to Switzerland. I have just put off the trip again. Beside all the longing to get out and refresh my gaze, dulled by the local scene, in a more open one, I keep feeling the obliga-tion to see that my establishment and my apartment in Munich should first have been of some use. The quarters in which you know I have been since March, have not yet properly benefited me: instead of protecting me they have, I don't know how, at-tracted more and more restlessness to me! My inner instability is probably responsible for that; it makes me more susceptible to people and chance happenings, to every sort of distraction, than I have been for years.

To communicate in writing about what the time has conjured up over us has little meaning: revolution to me would mean a simple setting-aright of man and the work he gladly would and could do. Every program that does not set *this* aim as its end seems to me just as hopeless as that of any of the former governments and people in power . . .

[*120*]

To Countess Stauffenberg   34/IV Ainmillerstrasse, Munich
                                                                January 23, 1919

Since the end of last year I have been meaning to send you the *Insel Almanac:* it goes to you so late that it no longer has its own excuse of arriving at the beginning of the year. I would hardly have dared recall myself to you in such an impromptu fashion, had not the selection of my contributions to this calendar been essentially determined by the sad event, now almost a year old, through which I may consider myself associated with you.

The Comtesse de Noailles's lovely poem, my two little experiments, but especially the diary-page which I have published under the title "An Experience"—all these, each in its own way, contain approaches to the border-sensations of existence and all strive toward that divinable balance I once found incomparably represented in a fragment of ancient music. Romain Rolland, who played it for me, had found it in a Gregorian mass. As I heard it and heard it again, I had the impression of two scale-pans that, gently ceasing to fluctuate, came to rest opposite each other. I described my sensation to Rolland and only then did he confess that this was an ancient grave-inscription, a musical grave-inscription: the most striking confirmation of which certainly was that it could be grasped and understood through such an image.

What I have called "An Experience" happened to me exactly like that in the garden at Duino (near Trieste), now shot to bits and in ruins; one year after this remarkable incident, while in Spain, I tried to put down the facts with the utmost possible penetration and accuracy, in which process the realm of the sayable did not really seem to suffice. I know I have fallen short—, perhaps I have not even made myself understood. Experiments of such a far-advanced kind may nevertheless lay claim to some indulgence.

If in the universal turbidity and bewilderment of human affairs, and now particularly of public life, I still see one task set clearly detached before me, it is this: to confirm confidence toward death out of the deepest delights and glories of life: to make death, who never was a stranger, more distinct and palpable again as the silent knowing participant in everything alive. . . .

[121]

To Countess Stauffenberg 34/IV Ainmillerstrasse, Munich
February 5, 1919

. . . For two weeks I have been reading the poems in [Verhaeren's] "Flammes hautes" and reading them aloud, and in the midst of it I sometimes think it is *his* energy that drives my voice into these lines and compels me to make known and spread abroad how unswerving, how invincible at that very time (for the book was actually finished, just as it is, in July 1914) was his faith in mankind and in the certainty of that future which, as he believed, would arise—as the tall flame—from human unity, from brotherly agreement! If ever anyone prevailed over himself to apply all confidence struggling, streaming, rushing upward to God, every demand and every infinite need—in a word, everything that is called faith—; if anyone ever applied all this horizontally, to mankind and *only* to mankind—at the risk of being left incredibly alone—: this great poet gave such proof of heroic faith in mankind with his whole heart, grown up with God and Nature, as every page in the "Flammes hautes" consummately testifies.

As during the whole interruption of life by the war—for me so profoundly frustrating—one's deepest obligation seemed to be to give up nothing of what mankind had previously gained and acknowledged after honest search, so it is now my passion to fit life, which is eager to go on and better-intentioned now than ever, to the violent ruptures of that fateful month of August, and from among the many pregnant voices of those days to transmit and to glorify the powerful and true voice of my great friend!

Read . . . the poem "Au passant d'un soir": I read it as a legacy, because it gives me back Verhaeren in the intensity of one of his moments and at the same time most lastingly.

[*122*]

To Countess Stauffenberg   34/IV Ainmillerstrasse, Munich
February 15, 1919

. . . Who knows whether *we* have not the hardest part of confusion and danger to overcome, and whether the next generation may not grow up into a world that is at once spontaneously of the future: for the watershed of the war, horribly high as it was, must after all make possible a flowing off into the farthest and the new; and I tell myself that in the essential nature of upheavals like the one we are at present going through, there must also be at work a most profound rightness, a resolve of humanity as a whole: which indeed, when it gathers itself together, however clumsily, is always impelled again into the realm of divine powers, as a thing blind, but in all its good intentions blessed!

[*123*]

To Countess M.   34/IV Ainmillerstrasse [Munich]
Wednesday

Do you think your youngest . . . already too grown up and proud to take interest and pleasure in the Freyhold books? If so, I think she will conquer her objections once more when she sees her brothers and sisters and, as I foresee, you yourself gladly occupied with them: surely they are the most delightful picture-books there are, and how few people know them!

To understand the malicious agitation about Rodin in Paris one has to know how strong opposition was in the Chamber when the suggestion was introduced that the Hôtel de Biron be given over permanently to his works as the Musée Rodin: in return the city of Paris was to inherit all these works, but the good citizens were always worrying whether they were really getting enough counter-value by this arrangement; many contested the matter even at the time and sought to reduce as far as possible the value of Rodin's bequest, which the experts had estimated at nearly

three million [francs]; now this is the consequence of their efforts! This master, whose first step into the public eye was
marked by the accusation that he had made the statue of the Âge
d'airain by means of casts from life,—is subjected even *after* his
death to the persecuting rancune that will not admit his enormous
capability. A singularly persistent fate.

It would have been quite possible for forgeries, especially il-
legitimately reproduced bronzes, to get in among his works (I
recall that of his smaller bronzes hardly one ever came back from
an exhibition without tell-tale traces of having been misused in
secret reproductions), but that a *substantial* part of his work is
not by him must naturally remain a malicious inimical statement.
The marbles were carried out to a certain refinement of surface
from Rodin's clay models by M. Lebossé and other praticiens, but
still undoubtedly always brought to the last finish by himself; of
course certain of these assistants had in the course of years become "his hand" to such a degree that it would also be conceivable that there might be marbles in circulation which he did
not even have to touch any more: these were nevertheless per-
fected entirely under his own supervision, and if he put his name
to them he would have done so with the same sense of responsibility in which the masters of great art-periods acknowledged so and
so many works that came, filled with their own most characteristic
spirit, out of their immediate studio circle. That Rodin did not
attack the marble in the block but each time had his clay model
transferred into the stone, was a well-known fact he himself never
concealed; and even his most powerful antagonists could hardly
succeed in representing such a procedure as falsification, since
there is probably hardly a sculptor today who would be capable
of doing differently. (On the whole again a sad sign of the spirit
of the times which without more ado believes another, even the
greatest, capable of what it would permit itself.)

The Isenheim visit—may I beg for still further postponement?;
this spring air overcomes me with a sheerly unconquerable fatigue;
but even so I am doing my daily stint, even if creepingly so to

speak, which for the moment consists in translations from the Italian. So hour after hour goes by until, as early as nine o'clock, I resign myself to well-earned rest.

[*124*]

To Baroness Heyl zu Herrnsheim   34/IV Ainmillerstrasse, Munich
March 1, 1919

. . . As for me, there predominates in me, with all my worry, a broad confidence that looks out over and beyond this utmost urgency, a feeling I never knew toward the phenomenon of the war. Only now have ideals really become clear—the most human and most irresistible ideals—and we should not be misled by the fact that the multitude stands up for them so ponderously and awkwardly and helplessly; it knows no better. And on the other hand we should not be misled by the fact that those who do not yet want to raise the question of the maturity of this multitude for its rights, try to secure themselves by all the antiquated means of opposition; did there not flow between the parties the lying flood of the press, out of which the most deceptive vapor clouds constantly arise, perhaps an understanding would be comparatively foreseeable.

The war could be nothing other than an ending; it was an extreme, following its own inner anomalousness, a breaking off of humanity from itself. Only a new beginning of existence could set in after it. In this beginning we now are, and it is of course the first condition of the future that it cannot be easy: how could it be?

A hard, hard beginning. Nothing new for me; I have felt, ever since I can remember, like a beginner.

[125]

To Elisabeth von der Heydt   34/IV Ainmillerstrasse, Munich
March 20, 1919

. . . Just quickly a word about Ruth. For two months now she has been, so to speak, a farmhand; that was *her* way of taking the revolution; she longed to work and only the most practical would satisfy her. On the 15th of January she started in, just when it was coldest, moved into a little maid's room to the north, without a stove, began her day's work in all seriousness at 6 o'clock, and sank dead tired into her coarse checkered peasant's bed at half past eight. Dead tired and happy beyond words. Never have I had gayer letters from her. When I approached her after a few weeks with another proposal, she thought it over and then turned it down: for, she wrote, it was just *this* that satisfied her—to be doing something not like school work any more but wholly real, belonging in life-sized life; being *necessary* in this little spot was giving her an indescribable, pure joy,—and as there were not exactly too many happy people just now, she was the more determined to keep her happiness.—Can one experience that more delightfully?

I naturally hope it will take its course: but then this intermezzo will have been a better training than any imaginable school, and as it had such intensity of joy and life it will acquire the significance of those great things that happen to us, which one cannot provide for oneself and no one can provide for anyone else. . . .

[126]

To Anton Kippenberg   34/IV Ainmillerstrasse, Munich
May 22, 1919

. . . The embargo on mail, externally long since lifted, still continues in me; for who would not rather remain silent about the experiences we had here in April, and particularly about those other infringements and interferences that have been going on since the first of May. "Poison" and "antidote"; but the right deeper therapeutics is nowhere being used, sore though the moment confesses itself to be.

From a purely domestic, housekeeping point of view we have not had to suffer much, thanks to Rosa's foresight, but one's spirit has been damaged. Since my lingering cold I have not gained much in health either, my body longs for helpful change and everything suspended and watchful in me is indescribably ready to think that it is right. So I grasped the friendly hand, offered me again yesterday in a telegram from Switzerland, with an affirmative answer. It now seems possible to get in through the Hottingen reading circle, perhaps the permission will follow in a few days. . . .

At present I doubt whether later, on my return, I shall keep my Munich quarters; one hears and sees nothing but departures; many of the most permanent residents are giving up their houses, here and there great moving vans spend the night before their gates; for most people believe that from now on innocent Munich may continue to be a bad and uneasy spot, and that, worse luck, not because of the temperament, but because of the sluggishness of the mass now that it has been set in motion. Who knows, dear friend, but I may choose Leipzig for next fall and winter; I turn over the idea often . . .

[*127*]

To Countess Aline Dietrichstein   Soglio (Bergell, Graubünden)
Switzerland
August 6, 1919

You wrote me on the 14th of June—three days earlier I had gone to Switzerland, an undertaking long hoped for, finally realized when I hardly thought of it any more, and which I am now in the midst of. Well, you can imagine that I needed to get away from Munich: really and actually one did not have to suffer too much, the newspapers, in their way, exaggerated a lot—, but emotionally it was an indescribable and, worst of all, in the end a futile tension in every direction. For behind so much upset, racket and malicious crowding there was after all *no* will to real change and renewal, to share and to take part in which one would have been only too ready. The intellectual would of course have to be from the start an opponent and disavower of revolutions; he of all people knows how slowly all changes of lasting significance are accomplished, how inconspicuous they are and, through their very slowness, almost imperceptible, and how Nature, in her constructive zeal, hardly anywhere lets intellectual forces come to the fore. And yet on the other hand it is the same intellectual who, by reason of his insight, grows impatient when he sees in what miscarried and muddled conditions human things are content and persist: indeed, we are all continually experiencing the fact that this and that—almost everything—needs changing (and that at the root): life, this infinitely rich, infinitely generous life, that is permitted to be cruel only by very reason of its inexhaustibility: life itself—in how many instances it simply cannot make itself effective any more, pushed aside as it is by a lot of secondary institutions, grown lazy by their continuance,—who would not often wish for a great storm that would tear down everything obstructive and infirm, to make room for the again creative infinitely young, infinitely benevolent forces. There is no doubt that many such clean and forceful impulses collaborated in the birth of the revolution: for the only thinkable counterweight to the dreadful war would have been if a new state of mind on humanity's part, prepared to be different, had here and there arisen and penetrated various parts of the shocked and bewildered world. For a moment one hoped. But the preponderance of material aspirations and inferior, if not indeed evil and vengeful impulses, almost in its first hours destroyed the cleaner future of this forward drive, joyful at first, but later desperate and finally totally senseless—in the whirlpools of which many innocent persons went under and almost all *those* who thought to carry ahead a vision of humanity, impatient indeed, but noble. Strictly speaking, the unswerving intellectual could side with neither party in this chaotically confused struggle which the poison of the stagnated war—turned back as it was into the country—further and further provoked; neither with those who drove ruthlessly ahead nor with those who met the often criminal outbreaks of this insanity with old and no less unjust and inhuman means: the future lay with neither, and to *it* the intellectual is after all allied and sworn, not in the sense of the revolutionary, who would presume to create from one day to the next a humanity freed (what is freedom?) and happy (what is happiness?), but in that other patient understanding that he is preparing in people's hearts those subtle, secret, tremulous transformations out of which alone will proceed the agreements and unities of a more clarified future. If now, my dear Countess, you will measure against these thoughts of mine the sad and from day to day more hopeless events that have taken place since November, and take into account also with how little foresight and reflection, how witlessly they have been combatted—, then you will understand how much I am likely to have suffered. Not so much under privation and uncertainty as under this very disappointment and worry that reaches out beyond one's own life and its realizations. But finally I did have to think once more about this life too, mine, and the tasks that have, after all, been set it, and before which it has stood for five years hampered and paralyzed, without collecting itself for its own inmost function. And so from day to day the wish grew for some thorough external change, such as has always had most acute influence on me—for a journey into some foreign country not directly affected by the war, for its landscapes, cities, streams, bridges, woodlands: since what I have suffered most in losing during these painful last years has been just this very contact of mine with Nature, usually so close. I could no longer succeed in making it. The human being of this war, and every one of his contemporaries, I myself, seemed to me so far removed from the world of Nature—, it seemed to me arbitrary and untrue to have recourse to a tree, a field, the clemency of evening, for what did the tree, the field, the evening landscape know of this hapless, devastating, killing human being? It is true that neither have these things fundamentally any share in one kindly disposed, constructive, blessed, but still there is an inexpressible connection between a person peacefully working, creating, and Nature busying herself in holy and thorough fashion.

. . . so here too (for my consciousness) a rift had become apparent, to which I was the more sensitive since that secret unison, that being in tune with the natural, as I know better all the time, somehow belongs to the premises of my productiveness, even of my daily life itself. If man would only cease to invoke the cruelty in Nature to excuse his own! He forgets how infinitely innocently even the most terrible happens in Nature; she does not watch it happen—she hasn't the perspective for that; she *is* wholly in the most dreadful, even her fruitfulness is in it, her generosity—it is, if one must put it that way, nothing other than an expression of her fullness. Her consciousness consists in her completeness; because she contains *everything,* she contains the cruel too;—but man, who will never be able to encompass everything, is never sure, where he chooses the terrible—let us say murder—of already containing the opposite of this abyss, and so his choice, in the very moment of making him an exception, condemns him to be an isolated, one-sided creature who is no longer connected with the whole. The good, the straightly determined, capable man would not be able to exclude evil, fatality, suffering, harm, death from those interrelationships; but where one of them struck him or he became the cause of it, there would he stand exactly as one afflicted amid Nature, or, afflicting against his will, he would be like the devastating brook, swelled with those tumbling freshets whose influx into itself it is not able to shut out. . . .

But now you ask about me in connection with Switzerland. Indeed, it is not so easy to travel after five years of immobility! At first it looked as though I didn't know how any more. . . . I felt the need to take advantage of my "freedom" and see the country, which in other years, it is true, I always regarded as merely a country of transit, in a sort of mistrust of its too famous, too obvious, too pretentious "beauty." Mountains are just naturally difficult for me to grasp,—I was able to see the Pyrenees, the

Atlas Mountains in North Africa belong to my grandest recollections, and when I read about the Caucasus in Tolstoy I had the indescribable fever of its immensity. But these Swiss mountains? They seem to me something of an obstacle anyhow, there are so appallingly many of them. Their shapes cancel each other; that somewhere a contour runs out clean against the sky, I can indeed establish with satisfaction,—but I lack, how shall I express it, the image, the inner sensible parallel to it which alone makes the impression into an experience. First I had a little to do with the cities: Geneva . . . then Bern: and that was very very lovely. An old, enduring city, still quite unspoiled in many parts, with all the characteristics of a dependable and active citizenry, even to quite a high self-assurance expressing itself in like-minded houses that toward the street bear themselves with a certain reserve above their arcades, but toward the Aar in their pretty garden fronts are of more communicative and open mind. Luckily I had Bernese friends there with fine old inherited houses of this sort, and that removed at one stroke the hotel atmosphere for me and helped me very much to experience the nature of the country, even where, as now once more displaced among strangers, I have to find myself to rights again from their level. About Zurich, that politically turbid city, there is hardly anything to say—, it made me very anxious to get out of the cities: country and, if possible, southern skies over it—that was in my mind's eye—, and that has now come to fulfillment for a while here, in a special manner. A map of Switzerland will easily show you the situation of Bergell, the haste of this valley to reach Italy; above the valley, halfway up the mountain, lies this little gneiss-tile-covered nest, on the declivity a church (unfortunately Protestant and therefore empty), quite narrow streets; I am living in the very midst of it, in the old ancestral house of the Salis (Soglio line), even among their old furniture, and into the bargain the palazzo has a French terrace-garden with the old stone balustrades, traditionally cut box-hedges and between them a profusion of the gayest summer flowers. But I must tell you another time of the chestnut woods that extend down the slopes, toward the Italian side, in grandiose beauty.

P.S. next morning: If only I had a certain book here: I would have liked to send it to you right away, in response to your inquiry about books; at the moment it is not to be had in Switzerland either, as the second edition was quickly sold out. I am now placing an order with the publisher to send it along to you in my name when it appears again, for the Austrian book business may be still slower now than it was anyway in the old days.—The book in question is Count Hermann Keyserling's "Travel Diary of a Philosopher". A trip around the world by this excellent writer, which ended shortly before the war, is reflected in these everywhere fruitful notebooks, which, though they move in a wholly intellectual sphere, are still thoroughly effective for all they sense and see, the book of a man of the world in the rarest and most aristocratic sense, oriented in all directions, greatly assenting and approving, and at the same time mobile, accurate and of the most perfect tact of feeling and conviction. Some six hundred pages, grand for reading aloud to each other in the garden or before the fire! . . .

[*128*]

To Countess M.   Soglio (Bergell, Graubünden)
                                              August 13, 1919

. . . Need I tell you that [my thanks] are heartfelt and a little homesick? For a moment, when you referred to it, I heard the stillness at R. and in it realized how well off I would have been there with you all. I picture this to myself actually and palpably, not in my mind but somewhere in my heart's range of vision—and life seems really to be crowding and wasting itself on me in offering both these things for *one* summer, Switzerland and R.,—quand-même, la vie toute dépourvue qu'elle semble, a encore d'étonnantes générosités—! My letter, the one of August 4, will meantime have described to you where I am living—and now to be sure the prospect of this summer bringing me to you has closed in. Even here it will have been much much too short for me! That is due in part to my slowness, which is not to be exaggerated. I must be allowed to begin a life anywhere and give myself up to imagining that at this place or that, if it is to become even to some extent favorable and friendly to me, infinite pasts have gone on, which with one branch at least seek to grow toward me and into me, as though they were my own or those of my family. It was like that even before the war, in Spain, in so acute a way that I left with reluctance after six months,—and it is like that here now in this very special mountain nest. . . . Old houses, old things can acquire the most compelling power over me, the smell of old cupboards and drawers is so familial to the nostrils. But I told you what a lot of this sort of thing is around me here—I described the wood- and stucco-work and my four-poster, didn't I? and the old garden in whose trimmed box-frames all the wild bloom of summer renews and obtrudes itself. But at that time I had not yet encountered the most seductive of all: just think what was yet to reveal itself: an old room full of books, not usually accessible to guests, the old Salis library still preserved here in its entirety! An old-fashioned room, quiet, facing the garden (which now shines and buzzes in through the little open windows), over the mantel a huge coat-of-arms of the Salis willow, before it an old spinet, in the middle a solid square seventeenth-century table, opposite that a high and mighty easy-chair, Louis-Quatorze, with the old embroidered upholstery; at one of the three windows a real iron chest (the gigantic, much-bearded key lies on top of it)—and for the rest? Books, books, books. Rows of them and cupboards full. Books of the seventeenth century, even many pigskin volumes, large and small, of the sixteenth (among them some Aldus and Elzevir); the memoir-literature of the eighteenth in enchanting leather bindings, a complete Linnaeus and naturally many volumes relating to Switzerland and the Confederacy, also the poets: Albrecht von Haller, whom I read in the day time . . . and Salis-Seewis (in the 1800 edition)—where else should one read him!—whom I reserve for the evening hours in case one of them should prove of a slightly more sentimental mood. Then I read him aloud, the forgotten one, in this room of books, and I am touched at the way he comes to voice, not exactly great, but still in the loveliest, purest lines, so pathetic and nightengalish, as befits that time and the garden, surviving out there, more surviving than the poet once inspired by eternity. So now you understand that I am doomed. How could I resist this room, in which I still make discoveries every day—, and then the garden calls me, and then the chestnut woods come to mind: there is no getting through and no finishing. But you will understand. The moment is so delightful, this Venusberg encircling me—in which a tangled rosebush is the Venus and books shine out like the alluring ore inside the mountain—has me in its power, I do not want to plan beyond it let alone even think of the winter, for which I can imagine neither place nor mode of life. I am not really thinking of Munich at all for that purpose—, but whither? Whither?

[129]

To Elisabeth von Schmidt-Pauli   Soglio (Bergell, Graubünden)
August 14, 1919

That mountain of joys, Sister Elisabeth, from which you run breathlessly down into my expectation, always wide open for you —that mountain of joys is evidently higher than anything I have before me here,—its summit is suffused enduringly with the divine, and so I rejoice to know you full of blessings and full of inner tasks! May you succeed in much, and succeed *imperiously*, in the same spirit in which it has been laid upon you. All work on the present world is in vain that compromises with it; the absolutely-different must be presented to it, and even though this is at home in another sphere, one must move it down and into this world, implant it and naturalize it, even against the world's will. Now you know this just as well as I, only one should repeat over and over to oneself that compromising has no sense at this turning-point. Not between man and man, and not in general

and absolutely not within one's own discussions with oneself.
. . . Switzerland [is] certainly no country for me; it strikes me like one of those painted or modeled nudes intended to make apparent all the "beauties" of many women in a single figure; that is, if I mistake not, the aesthetic of Switzerland—for us an abominable one; which is also why her artists so quickly turn pedagogical, for where examples of every type are present together, what remains but to point to them, to consider them picture-books and to educate through them. Bern, which is one of the most beautiful cities, first helped as a focal point to give me an idea of the old life-permeating force of these states; Swiss history, in which the forces of Nature (not the outward forms of these interior countries) have proceeded along a straight line, is unified and easy to survey, is beautiful; this variety, contradictory and running to intensest exaggerations, could only grow into an entity in man, and the Swiss, however differently the separate cantons may have developed him, carries the consciousness of all his federated landscapes in a singularly prepared and fruitful spot in an otherwise not easily penetrated mind. . . .

All through this letter I have avoided speaking of impressions. Even were this landscape less eclectic, I would be unable to take any in. Spain was the last "impression". Since then my nature has been worked from inside (travail repoussé), so strongly and steadily that it cannot be "impressed" any more. From all this you may understand what I am hoping from the winter. The beginning of that retirement granted somehow at last, for which I would now fully have the conscience, however much one ought on the other hand to be there for other people. Indeed I should then properly be there, infinitely more positive and able to hold out!

[*130*]

To Anni Mewes   Soglio (Bergell, Graubünden)
                                              Switzerland
                                      September 12, 1919

. . . It seems to me I have already known the Vogeler pamphlet you send, in a somewhat different, obviously earlier form; in those days it did not yet bear the title "The Silver Steeds", but was called Expressionism of Love, one being as incomprehensible as the other. The incentive I can well understand, who would not have it?—who would not wish for the making-good, the making-different, the sincerest and most widely-shared resolve toward humanity? But this resolve has not been taken, either in Russia or elsewhere, and it probably couldn't be taken because no god stands behind it who would urge it forward. What clothes itself with the pretext of this new brotherhood is really still the war, the destructive element let loose and far from quieted: grown meaningless years ago, this desperation holds up a slogan over its head, shouts "Brotherhood", and yet itself contradicts it at every instant; for it is still the subsidence of war, the after-storm of those years, the revenge of misused and ravaged powers that now, since they have become ungovernable, think themselves busy in a larger service and yet are only overturning, as though a train leaping its tracks were a picture of freedom. Vogeler is anything but consistent, he is easy to refute, and I am sure conditions round about him refute him every day. Yet I, who have for so many years been privileged to be his friend, am moved by this outbreak of his calm and really shy nature: what shocks, what crashes, what earthquakes must have gone on in this man so variously and daintily entangled in his reveries, that he felt the need thus to cry out and use his influence? This sentence grips me repeatedly: "A condition never known to man is in process of becoming: peace." In this declaration the sincerity of the former Heinrich Vogeler is increased by something infinite: by an actual having-suffered, by a having-been-in-hell and thereafter hoping—indeed, it is out of an immense reality of emotional experience that these words go forth, as though spoken by one resurrected, who is no longer to be misled, even though he comes out of a sepulchral moment and arises staggering into a chaos. All these voices can hardly help. The expressionist, that inner-man become explosive, who pours the lava of his boiling mood over all things, to insist that the chance form in which the crust hardens is the new, the coming, the valid outline of existence, is simply a desperate man and one may let the honest ones among them go ahead and blow off steam. Perhaps through these striking and importunate manifestations (which become utterly repulsive only in their commercial utilization) men's eyes will be diverted from the delicate growth of that which really, little by little, will show itself as the future. It is so understandable that people have become impatient,—and yet, what is more needed now than patience; wounds require time and do not heal by having flags planted in them. In some other way must the world enter into a stable consciousness, and perhaps that by which it first finds itself again will be something quite inconspicuous, in any case something inexpressible! To me the least thing seems building-up, which each individual attempts in his own place, the carpenter simply planing again, the smith hammering again, the merchant again reckoning and reflecting: *these* are the progressives, these are the pure revolutionaries, the more they strive, the more quietly and busily and lovingly they work, each in his place. . . .

[*131*]

To Gertrud Ouckama Knoop   Soglio (Bergell, Graubünden)
                                                                     Switzerland
                                                        September 12, 1919

. . . Picture to yourself that being "abroad" was almost a strain at first. One didn't quite know how any more, one spent half days (or was it only I?) in front of the perfumers' reading the names of Houbigant, Roger and Gallet and Pinaud; yes, for a little moment that was what freedom meant,—who would have thought that possible? The pastry shops did not impress me nearly as much and so far I haven't yet bought any chocolate, but soaps fascinated me, I was really defenseless against one of those clean overfilled showwindows in Zurich's Bahnhofstrasse. By such roundabout ways, however ridiculous they may have been, I arrived slowly at the rest: at the French bookshops and art-galleries, at the bustle of the streets and traffic, even, with some effort, at Nature. Too bad that in Switzerland Nature seems to me to occur only in exaggerations; what demands these lakes and mountains make, how there is always something too much about them, they have been broken of the habit of simple moments. The admiration of our grand- and great-grand-parents seems to have collaborated on these regions; they came traveling along out of their own countries where there was, so to speak, "nothing" and here there was "everything", in de-luxe editions. Good heavens: a drawing-room-table Nature, a Nature with ups and downs, full of excess, full of duplication, full of underlined objects. A mountain? save us, a dozen on every side, one behind the other. A lake: certainly, but then at once a magnificent lake, of the best quality, with reflections of purest water, with a gallery of reflections and the good Lord, as custodian, explaining them one after the other—when he doesn't happen to be busy as stage-director turning the searchlights of evening's red glow toward the mountains, whence all day the snow hangs down into the summer, so that one may have all the "beauties" so nicely together. For winter of course has its own beauty, and so the most perfect thing is not to be deprived of it while feeling secure among the warmed enjoyments of the opposite . . . I can't help it, I reach this assorted Nature most easily with my irony, yes, and I remember the lovely times when, traveling through here, I used to draw to the curtains of the compartment, whereupon the rest of the travelers in the corridors greedily devoured my share of view with theirs—I am sure there was none left over.

Now you are saying: how ungrateful this fellow has become at every turn, wantonly ungrateful! He is ungrateful toward Munich, which after all did provide him in such insuperable times with a not unfriendly refuge, and now he is ungrateful even about his new enviable freedom, which he mocks instead of humbly recuperating through it. No, it really isn't as bad as that with me: I even believe I am beginning to understand Switzerland, in her singular penetrativeness and hereditary unity. This I owe Bern, where the most hospitable weeks were prepared for me, and whence these lands that Nature has built out of boundaries and obstacles become distinct in a remarkable clarity and transparency. Switzerland's history is full of natural force; the people, wherever they came together here as a mass, had something of the consistency and hardness of the mountains and their impetuous will has in the most decisive moments been a continuation of that irresistibility with which her torrents arrive in the valleys. And to what an exact and well-formed self-assurance this experienced and proven force has developed in the expressive cities: how unanimous Bern stands there, every house above its fretted stone arcades, which draw in even the traffic under their protection too, so that outside there remain only the markets and the wonderfully picturesque fountains that make even the water into a good citizen! One readily decides to explain the Swiss himself as a part of this security: that is the easiest way of understanding his outline and his structure, the ground material of which seems indeed to have been kneaded from the most homogeneous mass and cut from the whole: so that in each individual the nation is present (what we miss so at home, where we always have to do with the obtuse or even the amorphous, or else are confronted by the individual as an exception). Singular, by the way: psychoanalysis takes on the most pervasive forms here: almost all these perfectly clean and angular young people get analyzed—, now think that out for yourself: one of those sterilized Swiss, in whom all corners are swept and scoured—, what sort of an inner life can take place in his mind, which is germ-free and shadowlessly lighted like an operating room! . . . I have been here six weeks; only, how slow! really to come to my senses, sojourn and season would have to be granted me indefinitely. And in the end I still ask: Munich? What does it promise? How will the winter be? (which will surely have to become my winter too). . . .

[132]

To Countess M.   Begnins sur Gland (Vaud)
                                    September 26, 1919

Soglio is far behind me now. . . . I am writing you from Begnins, a village above Nyon, where there is a pension installed in a
little château with which I had a cursory acquaintance, and where
I am today to meet a young girl from Paris. I am curiously excited:
Marthe, whom I found in the last stage of destitution when she
was seventeen, was my protégée, a working girl, but of that spontaneous geniality of heart and mind that is probably to be found
only among French girls. What surprises, what indescribable,
yes, overflowing happiness she gave me in certain years through
her wide-awake understanding of the greatest and most perfect,
which surpassed my own. I do not know if any human being has
ever similarly shown me what a spirit can spontaneously unfold
into if one gives it a little room to live in, a little quiet, a little bit
of good climate. It will be almost a return to Paris for me, the
meeting with this creature who knows about me with the deepest
conviction; through her—even if it is only a few days I can spend
with her—I shall soonest be able once more to heal on to the
ruptured surface of my former life; Marthe's hands will hold the
fractured end and the new beginning tenderly against each other.

. . . When I think it over, I would say you are entirely right,
Munich had long since become only depressing for me, and when
I think of the return to Germany—, it would be a relief to return
elsewhere. . . . I almost wish you would give up the city . . . ,
for the winter will be in many ways more tolerable and more
natural in the country, from all they say and fear. . . .

Leaving Soglio was not easy. Many inner workings were
thereby interrupted. And what began as joy—finding the little
library so suitable and so made for me—had to pass away in melancholy: some day to have such a room for a long, long time, and
all the solitude of a house and garden with it—God provide it for
me. *This* only and nothing else. . . .

[*133*]

To Anton Kippenberg   Hôtel Baur au Lac, Zurich
December 2, 1919

. . . Since the 27th of October (the day of my first Zurich reading; I read there twice) I have been on a regular tour: St. Gall, Lucerne, Basel, Bern, Winterthur followed one upon the other, in all seven evenings. All good, some surprising for everyone concerned. I hit upon a curious procedure which proved most persuasive to the Swiss, who are stolid, often arid, and hard to penetrate. I did not simply read poems but began with a general introduction which was about the same everywhere I went,— whereas I led off the second part of the evening with an absolutely impromptu causerie, flexibly adapted to the particular place, which led back over various subjects (. . . in Winterthur finally, where excellent pictures had been assembled, I centered my observations around Cézanne) to my work and, quite imperceptibly, prepared and explained it in such a way that even very personal and "difficult" poems were then unusually well received. I did not even hesitate occasionally to set up little platforms of understanding before the individual poems too; all this in a lively, spontaneous way, letting the moment suggest what was appropriate. With Italian or French translations I first read the text of the original, which was quite the right thing for the Swiss, who are mostly polylingual. I probably owe it to this simple idea that, as they tell me, even Geneva papers and especially the Gazette de Lausanne commented favorably on my readings: I myself read, as is my custom, no press opinions . . .

I made many and valuable friends: in Basel particularly one of the finest and most admired houses (of the patrician Burckhardts) was and still is open to me as more than a guest—a friend. But do not, dear friend, expect a financial return; the societies that engaged me are in part newly founded and poor, in part abstrusely avaricious; living was expensive everywhere, and the stopping-places so far apart that I had pretty well used up the fee for one lecture by the next; by roundabout ways there will certainly be some income, for the booksellers, whom I also see, are quite dizzy with the sale of my books.

. . . The next number [of the *Inselschiff*] will meanwhile contain nothing of mine, for December is here, the issue is probably already completed,—and for me these weeks were too restless to write anything down; they also required continuous, uninterrupted outgiving; not through the lectures alone, but because they brought people to me everywhere, and I took it seriously, trying not to appear parsimonious, so far as genuine giving was expected. . . .

[134]

To Anton Kippenberg   Pension Villa Muralto, Locarno, (Tessin)
December 29, 1919

. . . Order and protection! Dear friends, when will that be granted me for my greater tasks, and where?! For once in my life a year removed from all chance intrusion and intercourse, in the quiet of the country, steady, regular, in an immediate environment that is congenial at all times. I can assure you that with each day I know better what I need, but the conditions grow continually more precise and in the end are not to be bargained with. Look at Soglio! You felt right away, before I told you, what a head start it gave me from one day to the next. And there it was just the room and a garden path; so much was lacking—solitude, the right care—and yet . . . ! . . .

A still (to my shame) unanswered letter from Dr. Hünich suggested that I might offer the *Inselschiff* that general introduction by means of which I thought I ought to help establish a rapport with my readings; but all that my papers contained were a few large-written catchwords: and what held them together under the inspiration of the moment that called them forth has vanished again, and I should be glad to have paid the price of its transitoriness. For what pleases me is just this: that so far it has appeared only as the spoken word, as such possessing the whole tension that is so essentially different from the stored energy of the written word.

I must also, dear friend, still keep you waiting for the article on the Aksakov Chronicle. Up at Soglio I could have written it (had the summer there only been three times as long!). Now I would rather not tackle it until I have leafed through my old Russian Aksakov again. Then the warmth of so many old memories would enter into the work too.

And the "Bibliotheca Mundi"—but, dear friend, what would we not have to take up and discuss. The tower room becomes urgent. And I believe that only there will the monstrous "interval" be ended which we, from that purely contemplative spot, saw dawn with all its fatalities. If I could only move in there soon for a few days' confident companionship! That is one of my wishes, just as it is one of yours—we are agreed; and agreed in so many ways, dear loyal friend, that we may wish each other many things. For that is of course the assumption upon which, mutually wishing, one is neither mistaken nor deceived. We may take that risk . . .

[*135*]

To Prince Schönburg   Pension Villa Muralto, Locarno, Tessin
                                      January 12, 1920

. . . I hoped, when I left Soglio and the old Salis palace, to find somewhere a quiet old garden pavilion with old furniture, in which I might live more or less in retirement. After the upset and ruthless interferences and interruptions of these last years I need nothing so much as the quiet of a daily equable inner reflection, something of the sort I was once allowed to find for months in poor destroyed Duino; if that is a disgrace—well, then I just am ashamed to be so entirely dependent on externals. I can't change it, I know I shall not be able to take up my work in full measure until some such refuge comes to my assistance; contact with people has now, more than ever, something confusing about it, in which a lot of situations are discussed that no one has a clear conception of, so that one remains reduced to repetitions and phrases, —and my work was always so much inspired by being alone, that I must for its sake, quite positively and not just out of shyness of people, wish for quiet, especially where there is still so much impediment and fright to make good inwardly. And my wishing for *old* things about me, that is not aesthetic affectation and being fussy either; what humaneness have *they* not brought me (how often have I experienced it!) in the very times when all intercourse had been given up: how much they tell, how much destiny passes from them to one who since childhood has held with *things*. That I have done since away back with eagerness and absorption.

But a refuge of this sort, with this preliminary condition of most rigorous solitude, is hard to find—, and I am indeed aware, one may not *seek* it: it must remain to the dispensation of chance to bring along such a privilege. . . .

What you say of the region of Fribourg made me prick up my ears. . . . If you would sometime, my dear Prince, think of mentioning the places that struck you as so very quiet and secluded, I would at any rate enter them in my notebook; but I shall also entirely understand if you keep them to yourself, for doesn't one already abolish a third of the secludedness of a region when one reveals it to someone? . . .

How homeless we all are! Dr. Kassner, who is sitting in Oberstdorf for the present and published a very important book just before Christmas, laments to me about the destruction of Austria too; even staying on his brother's estate in Moravia has become quite different, he writes, since Vienna is no longer what it was. Where shall one go? In Germany particularly people like us will feel themselves strangers—I know how little I was in my element in Munich. . . .

[*136*]

To Dorothea Baroness von Ledebur   Pension Villa Muralto,
Locarno (Tessin) Switzerland
January 15, 1920

. . . It began to snow heavily here on the 23rd so that the probability of Christmas, which had just before been very slight, rose to that degree of incomparable expectancy that is characteristic of this festival. How many lonely recollections I have had for years now of this evening, which I was very often obliged to spend in hotel rooms, in Tunis one year, in southern Spain once, in little hotels in Paris, then later in my apartment there, and now here in a Tessin pension,—and always, often at the last moment and malgré moi, it became Christmas, often just because the wood in the stove crackled and one had to interpret that so furtively-festively, whether one wanted to or not. What power this insistent festival has, I believe we have it in our blood, like something elemental, like ebb and flow, like the seasons, like the constellations—, and it is the influence of a star too, at that.

. . . It would hardly be wise for you to move to Austria when everyone there, aside from want and distress, is being made to feel homelessness. Austria's walls have fallen in and now the wind blows over her as over the scene of a conflagration, and all her things lie there exposed, laid bare, and have that improbable disproportioned look that household goods take on when they land in the open! Even I, though I have never really made the most of being an Austrian subject, feel this shelterlessness with singular intensity and the Whither? stands before me with so large a "W" (Woe) and so gigantic a questionmark that it is not for a moment to be overlooked. A little cowardly, I have, as you see, not yet dared trust myself back across the frontier, although Switzerland is not without restrictions and since those summer weeks in the old house at Soglio I have not found any other place that was protective and beneficial for me. But then I am uncommonly demanding. It grows always clearer to me *what* I would need in order to conquer the tremendous, cruel interruption in

me and really to hold my future work so closely to those painful, broken surfaces of 1914 that it would heal on there: this
would need at least six months of the most protected solitude,
congenial conditions of the most equable and healthy sort—in a
word, extraordinarily much. And *no* people all that time, not
one,—not out of defensiveness and shyness of people, but just
simply so that my inner reflection might be complete, without
break or tear—, only work, every day, and the influence of
Nature and, as in Soglio, a few old things in my immediate surrounding which can replace all intercourse through their ample
knowledge of that sorrow and joy that are just simply human,
without really being personal. For *that* I long and for that I am
waiting as one—well, as one waits for a miracle. So many little
country churches, quite deserted on weekdays, lie here among
the hill-vineyards, rural settlements in which a Saint George or
Laurence lives carefree on the capital of the being-believed-in
which the piety of so many generations has accumulated for him;
I sit in one, now here, now there, and sometimes the tears come
into my eyes for sheer joy over the pure serene silence in these
churches; *such* silence, it seems to me, I must be allowed to have
around me for a year, to become aware of myself again and of that
little spring of renewal in the middle of me which is the secret
of every life and which was for so long drowned out and cloudy.

In what region will you be newly settling? Munich is not at
all congenial to me, and moreover I now hold it against the place
that I was there in the war, as the convalescent loathes the room
that is associated with a long illness. . . .

[137]

To Leopold von Schlözer   Pension Villa Muralto,
                                             Locarno (Tessin)
                                             January 21, 1920

. . . these linkings-up-again on all sides—Switzerland has
granted me many, also some really remarkable connections with
Capri and Rome days—are so far the only symptoms of the

healing I so badly needed. For me, so far as myself is concerned, nothing remains but to hold myself so long and so closely to my sudden anguished ruptures of 1914 that I heal to them; in those days I began (from 1912 on) my big, perhaps biggest and most decisive works; the war reduced the sheltered place where I began them to a heap of ruins over countless soldiers' graves: the old castle of Duino (near Trieste) where I could do such grand days and nights of work. All that is gone, and with it Paris, to me so indispensable—and yet I do not want to, I *cannot* give it up, nothing, none of it. Within the last five years there has not been a single point I can hold on at, not one, the precipice has been so steep for me that I cannot root at its edge; also there is over it neither air nor Nature nor sky, nothing but a dense mist of doom. . . . During almost all the war years I was, par hasard plutôt, waiting in Munich, always thinking it *must* come to an end, not understanding, not understanding, not understanding! *Not to understand:* yes, that was my entire occupation in these years, I can assure you it was not simple! For me the open world was the only possible one, I knew no other: what did I not owe Russia—it made me what I am, from there the inner me went forth, all my instinct's homeland, all my inner origin is *there!* What do I not owe Paris, and will never cease to be grateful to it for. And the other countries! I can, I could take nothing back, not an instant, in no direction reject or hate or despise. The exceptionalness of the general situation has dictated to all an exceptionless attitude: no *one* nation may be particularly considered to have gone beyond the bounds, for this rashness has its basis in the helpless lostness of all. Who is helping? On all sides only exploiters of the turbid, nowhere a helper, nowhere a leader, nowhere a great superior individual. There may indeed have been such periods before, full of destructions, but were they equally formless? With no figure to draw all this around itself and expand it away from itself—*this* way tensions and counter-tensions are set up without a central point that first makes them into constellations, into orders, at least orders of destruction. My part in all this is only suffering. Suffering with and suffering beforehand and suffering after. Soon I won't be able to stand it any more. Please, do not believe the preacher about the "bestiality" of the French in the Rhine-provinces—we must stop making anyone out bad—it is the confusion that now here, now there, creates excesses and turbulences, it is no one's fault. C'est le monde qui est malade, et le reste c'est de la souffrance! Since June I have been in Switzerland now here, now there, without a place. Shall wait another two months on Swiss soil, then back—but whither? Even though I never made the most of being an Austrian subject, still I am now aware of the homelessness of the Austrian. I have done no work. My heart had stopped like a clock, the pendulum had somewhere bumped against the hand of misery and stood still. . . .

[*138*]

To Dory von der Mühll   [Guthaus Schönenberg bei Pratteln
                                                in Basel-Land]
                                    Easter Sunday [April 4] 1920

. . . I am struggling daily with all sorts of distress and chiefly with the influences of a quite unbearable fatigue; and I haven't even got so far as to find out to what extent the fatal effect of this condition has its root in the body or whether it just overpowers the body as it were out of an exhausted spirit. I know myself well enough to know that indispositions of this sort take their time, and much as one's will may work against them, it is in the end through checks on patience that they are best paid off.

It really is perfectly wonderful that in these weeks no one is demanding anything special of me; the living room and its long even days give me all freedom for that seemingly unimportant activity that withdraws itself into one's inmost recesses. To judge by the pleasure I take in reading, I still think something must be stirring in me under so much laziness; for the moment, reading takes the place of almost all exercise and when it begins to tire me, the view from my window does more than the needful. . . .

The Sunday choral below also has set in, as it was bound to; how much it already belongs for me to the mood and quite particularly to the stillness of Sundays here.

Since we have a real postman a great deal of correspondence has come for me again,—alas, none of it answered yet, every outward gesture costs me so much effort now. . . .

[*139*]

To Countess M.   Palazzo Valmarana à San Vio, Venice
June 25, 1920

. . . This charm of the Venetian mezzanini: nowhere can low rooms be so large, so spacious, so harmonious in their proportions (for all spaciousness, as in life—also the inner—is in the last analysis a question of proportion), as though out of abundance they had imposed upon themselves the limitation of being low. And the Princess, who has since childhood continued to belong to Venice, has decorated this pied-à-terre with special sympathy and feeling. I myself in 1913, at the time of my long stay here, had contributed a few little things, as occasion chanced,—a few pieces of glass, a little Italian library in uniform dix-huitième bindings, even the desk at which I am writing you. It was like a dream to touch these forgotten things again; I noticed then how great my inner renunciation in general had been: I had to take back, to recall a gesture of renunciation in myself, in order to admit again the existence of these things. Strange, it is all as it was, and as I sit here I could without more ado come to terms with my surroundings, with the noises and with the air itself, upon the date being 1914; even the Countess Valmarana upstairs (who at once received me naturally in continuation of the old friendship) involuntarily speaks of l'année passée every time she thinks of my last stay in the mezzanino. So if I hoped to find everything unchanged this wish has, I must admit, been fulfilled with that precision with which the fairies sometimes astonish mortals, in that they fulfill more than was humanly foreseeable. In fairy tales the wish is always something hasty, rash—so was mine: for I did not suppose that I would find myself too so entirely unchanged toward all these things. My life, stopped and disconnected deep inside by conditions, must have undergone a real petrification (I wanted it that way, it was my only means of surviving the general, invasive disfigurement!), but now it is indeed hard to be seven years further along, older, more worn, without those proofs of consecutive inner transformations that in the last analysis constitute being alive. Perhaps I am mistaken about the degree to which I have stayed the same—and yet I am different somehow, it remains to be seen how. Since I have been alone here now I live always on the verge of repetition, everything does finally manage to make itself present, but coupled with too close a cousinage with the old days! In spite of this, how happy I am to have broken out of Switzerland, which, more and more, I really can take only for a waiting-room on the four walls of which a few Swiss views have been hung up. . . .

This letter, dear Countess, was left intentionally, I wanted to go on writing a little more, but now for three days we have been provided with so dissolving a heat that I shall not get far; I notice that I feel the enervation arising from it more strongly than years ago; a sea bath on the Lido would be the right thing, but the vaporetti have been striking for a week, one would be grateful to them for their absence if only the gondolas had not at the same time become prohibitive. Most Venetian families, my housemates the Valmaranas as well, have given up theirs; and so all excursions that cannot be made right within the calli are rendered extraordinarily difficult. I would have had yet another destination, the garden of old Mrs. Eaden over there on the Giudecca, the last survivor of the once so charming Giudecca Gardens: high trees, only a few at the border, but a garden intérieur of grapevine walks, little stone-framed pools, turf parterres, pomegranate bushes on which the blossoms blaze up, and in the fluctuation of the vine-leaves' shifting shadow the towering mallow stalks; hedges and an old wall in whose niches stand weather-beaten stone figures, conclude this serenity that delights in itself, and beyond them there lies stretched before the whole toward the lagoon, a simple strip of lawn, which one feels, stepping out through one of the little gates, to be singularly empty and serious, already belonging more to the ocean than to the garden, leaving room for the ocean-space that sweeps in over the simple brick parapet, renewing itself perpetually out of the infinite. I have always admired the great tact, which the dix-huitième still is, and which saw to it that the joyous turbulence of the garden was not shoved forward right to the waters of the fore-ocean; nothing is more impressive than this strip of inter-world, as if in it one were supposed to disaccustom oneself to multiplicity and prepare for an Eternal that is simple. How Duse, who always loved this garden very much, must have recognized herself when, from its filledness in which one is hidden and beguiled away, she strode out a thousand times into the open where one is all at once isolated, solitary on a meadow strip, forsaken—: sheer figure! At certain moments of the year this fore-land, which has no path, only greensward so that one's step always remains soundless, can be like a beach for those who have said farewell—never have I seen the feeling of farewell so utterly transposed into phenomena of space—, now, in the growing summer, a kind of alleviation enters even there, the lagoon dazzles and involuntarily one turns back toward the garden and remains in the consciousness of its uninterrupted happiness. The beautiful old trees of the background build up into the translucent sky and above them, pale in pink and gray, wall and cupola of the Redentore!—I know, dear Countess, that that is no description; just like a face, a look, a soul, the Giardino Eaden can only be experienced, not told—, indeed isn't that really so of all Venice, one takes in here not as with vessels and hands, but as with mirrors, one "grasps" nothing, one is only drawn into the intimacy of its evanescence. Filled with pictures all day, one could bring forth proof for no single one of them, Venice must be "believed"; when I first saw it, in 1897, it was as the guest of an American! So it wasn't there at all, and for some reality nevertheless to come into this nothing, a very potent poisonous fly stung me, so that I had to orient myself to some extent round about its sting!

I shall not stay much longer this time, am indeed considering whether I should not go in three or four days. As in Switzerland, here too I am merely hiding from the decision, which I am the more obliged to make as on the Schönenberg, since my hosts have moved out there, I shall not find any working atmosphere. Whither?! . . .

[140]

To Anton Kippenberg   Palazzo Valmarana à San Vio, Venice
                                         July 1, 1920

. . . Dear friend, I seem to be very much divided: I long so to be out in the world, among the images I was accustomed to receive from it, in foreign-speaking regions where no one knows me and where language, my own language, again flashes out in steady relief as the material of my work. On the other hand, the waiting-time quality of my Swiss sojourn has grown ever clearer to me, and I see that from this spring-board I shall for the present get no further into the open, but must go "back"—, if only the objective were more definite and more natural, I should not have let myself in for so many delays. Incidentally it has not even been possible to return to Munich—: news did not reach me until I got here that the energetic influence of a friend . . . has obtained a residence permit for me. But meanwhile I have sublet my apartment, so I can only use it as an accommodation; nor would I like anything better than to leave a place which for me will long remain part of the conditions of the war years, which was never really of use to me, and which at the end also provided plenty of other causes for dislike.

I do not quite see myself actually taking refuge at the Fürstenbergs'; the thought of being under obligation to new and entirely unknown people rather oppresses me, just as I shall always fear every expenditure of energy that must be wasted in adjusting myself to something not precisely suitable. But the place I would need—in strict accord with my conscience, not out of fastidiousness—is it to be found in the present crowded Germany? . . .

[*141*]

To Princess Marie von Thurn
und Taxis-Hohenlohe　　Schönenberg bei Pratteln, Basel-Land
July 23, 1920

. . . Oddly enough this time, my stay in Venice began with a high point—our meeting again, which I found so extraordinarily good and was so completely grateful for from day to day,—but after your departure, after I had to experience and to connect up with only my own life there, every variation was lacking, not a trace of more or less,—a complete uniformity, like the warmth itself of all those weeks in which there was scarcely a fluctuation; and no finish to it because all proportion was lacking—like an always even ribbon running through one's senses . . . Only for this reason was it so hard to go away, for this singular continuity, somnolent as it was, and yet not without invitation to dreaming, could be given up at any point and still did not have to be. It was one of those external conditions that merge without delimitation into a state of mind which they only attract rather than produce,—perhaps I went too far in supposing this even flow must finally diminish or increase, and a moment must come that would introduce a before and after into something so undifferentiable. Nothing of the sort. Only later, when sometime it will be possible to take account of one's reflections, shall I be able to see *what* this time in Venice after your departure could really have been. As yet I only observe that life cannot be joined on to the broken surfaces of pre-war days in the way I had thought—, after all everything is changed, and the sort of traveling for "pleasure", to be taken simply and always rather leisurely—in short traveling of the "cultured" traveler will once and for all have run its course. It will "go empty" in future, which of course will not prevent many from continuing it without taking account of the desuetude of their undertaking. I believe that all aesthetic observation that is not immediate accomplishment will be impossible from now on,—basically impossible, for example, to "admire pictures" in a church, or not unless, open through sorrow or exaltation, one is again swept away before this one or frightened and blessed by that. You would not believe at all, Princess, how different, *how different* the world is become, the point is to understand that. Whoever thinks he can live from now on as he was "accustomed" to live, will find himself continually facing the sheerest repetition, the bare once-again and its whole desperate unfruitfulness.

The biography of Dostoievski, written by his daughter and translated into German from the French manuscript, was awaiting me here. I will have the book sent you tomorrow. . . . Even in the short introduction, Mlle. Dostoievskaia, living on among her father's Slavophile associations, gives what would be the most wonderful and forward-looking interpretation of conditions in Russia today:—the Russian muzhik, the inexhaustibly surviving and constructive element of Russia, is, in her belief, already at work, is creating big and deep contacts toward the East and is using Bolshevism only "as a scarecrow" to keep off the Westerners and their dogmatic and disturbing interference. Even if it does not yet look so today, I am sure Liubov Dostoievski is only telling ahead of time, through her father's eyes, what is bound sooner or later to have its turn, else the whole world must stand still. Among its next movements, however, this will be the grandest and the most just. . . .

[*142*]

To Oswald von Kutschera   Zurich, en route
August 3, evening [1920]
(Address. Schönenberg bei Pratteln, Basel-Land)

. . . I communicated with no one [from Venice]. So incredible did the ground seem to me on which I was living, that I feared it might vanish from under me as soon as I should mention its name, and so little was accomplished with the mere being there. Paris, the last and actual breaking-point before the turbulent years, I might perhaps, if I could get there, really fasten and grow on to: Venice was not an altogether natural spot in the body of my old life, and every time I wanted to test and experience the continuation of what had been earlier, it turned out something else by a hair's breadth: mere repetition, intentional and in itself unfruitful. That is, I didn't really experience it, but was always passing very close to it and only the finding of one's friends unchanged, well-wishing and affectionate all over again, prevented the entering in of the iteration that constantly threatened out of things and situations. Perhaps one had also lost much of one's readiness and alacrity in meeting with lively and spontaneous comprehension what offered itself at times. One is so slow in confiding and the new has made itself in every way so questionable to us that we almost prefer recognition of something earlier to being surprised, though such recognition, where instant readiness fails it, is petrified and then simply enters into our consciousness after a slight hesitation merely as repetition.

How difficult anyway to find oneself to rights again!

I see . . . that your illness still gives you a good many troublesome days and keeps you from activity and work you want to do, which puts your patience to a long test. But, my dear boy, I say to myself at the same time, hasn't it its good side, since it has to be, the spending of *this* particular period in a certain disconnectedness; wherever you might now be taking an active part, you would weary of the helplessness and groundlessness gaping under every province—, all the many letters I get give forth a unanimous lament, because for all intellectually striving persons, the foundation is lacking, the confidence in their being protected and necessary and therewith also the final conclusive desire to consider themselves necessary. . . . Surely a world so sore and everywhere uneasy can give the independently working individual no guarantees; it makes him dependent without for that reason being able to define the degree and the nature of this dependence. . . .

[*143*]

To Helene Burckhardt-Schatzmann   Geneva, August 16, 1920

. . . today for the first time I have got around to linking up with our afternoon before the "Peintres Genevois": I have come from the museum, and had the pleasure of confirming the at least pictorial genuineness of the Liotard beard . . . at all events "la barbe de Liotard" could remain a by-word for something in which, despite all greatness and evidence, one still cannot quite believe. For the rest, I was already in the museum Friday, but did not get to the pictures, detained below in the Salle Amélie Piot and the Salle Louis Ormond by something of outstanding and irresistible concern to me: by the rich lace collections, which gave me the loveliest surprises and in which a few pieces—one just has to say it that way—really moved me. What a miracle of devotion! When I then, at the very end in a vitrine of the Ormond Room, discovered antique ornaments as well (necklaces of the fifth century B.C., of Greek origin) and beside them a few extraordinarily beautiful pieces of eighteenth-century Lucern gold-work, then every prospect of reaching the upper floors was over. Laces and ornaments, just because they are mostly treated merely as decorative achievements, always hold me in a special way—, I am lured into discovering in them the work of art per se, that is, the complete transformation and enchantment of their producer consummated and transfigured in the work. Why shouldn't one regard laces in this way, which have always been a life in themselves, a renunciation and in exchange for just that joy and permanence and exhaustlessness. And *old* jewelry in particular too can be thus conceived, it is not merely a decorative shaping, it is a translation of what one's own existence could be into the life of stones and of gold: from then on it is a matter of *their* pride, *their* strength, *their* lavishness—no longer of the peculiarities and fortunes of the craftsman who understands them. Even today I began with the lower rooms and was in danger of forgetting myself there; also of what the gallery provides I looked up only those things for which I was a little prepared by that afternoon, the pictures of Agasse, Liotard and Saint-Ours—(of the last do you remember a delicate little picture portraying Simone Simard?)

[*144*]

*To Princess Marie von Thurn
und Taxis-Hohenlohe*
Geneva, August 19, 1920
Regular address still:
Schönenberg bei Pratteln, (Basel-Land)

I am enormously reckless—in Geneva a fortnight and cannot
tear myself away. Four—four days I had allowed myself for
leavetaking, but there is always an excuse for yielding, and always a tendency on my part to give in. It is not Geneva alone, it
is everything here that recalls Paris and almost makes it real: the
playing gray light in which bright clothes and the planes of a
face take on the same sweet haziness that makes many a time of
year in Paris so fatally attractive. This must actually be true,
Geneva was so lovely, the open lake with the lateen sails, the
quays and along the shores the great Genevan "campagnes" with
their magnificent trees. I don't quite know why, I feel I ought to
be so indescribably open to it all, as though it were to be the last
for a long time; for the return seems to me, God help me, a
somber picture, much as I try to save out the little house and
Lautschin in general from the rest of the dismal background. . . .
It is a tour de force for God to keep his hand so long over my
little house,—surely he has already let it go and some worthy man
is living in it with whom I cannot stand comparison. I am prepared to have trifled away this lovely prospect, and, j'en conviens,
I deserve nothing else. What does Kassner say to my not coming? . . .

I see Pitoieff almost every day. You know, the Russian who
has set up the wonderful theater here, whose experiment and
success I am so keen about. For the first time I recognize the
"work" of the actor as exactly as central, independent and big as,
in another realm of art, Rodin's work was in its magnificence and
utter independence; and one always experiences the same happiness in seeing how an ability thoroughly realized at one point takes
the whole world in an unexpected manner into its possession and
from that center out renders it inexhaustible. Yesterday we went

through a very fine play, and one ought to see Pitoïeff—with what vision he penetrates an author's scenery and words: he emphasizes something, and suddenly the imaginary bench from which he has just risen, the wall from which he moves away, simply leap from his eyes. *That is theater*, I have never known anything like it. If I could arrange it I would work near Pitoïeff for a year, attend all his rehearsals—, genius is after all the only thing that really grips us and matters to us; how much one is ready to forgive the world if only at some one spot a single unswerving determination of this sort is happily at work. By and large, in the outside world the bungling of recent years continues—, I hope you are not too much aware of it. The children will have come home meanwhile . . . and everything will surely go well according to program—only my numbers have had to be canceled until further notice. All the more do I want news, Princess, *please* news, so that at least in spirit and endeavor I can count myself included. . . .

[*145*]

To Hans von der Mühll   Geneva
                                                October 12, 1920

You will hardly, I imagine, have recovered from the astonishment you may have felt at my notification (for it really couldn't be called a letter) concerning the sudden prospect of Paris (a sort of key-hole prospect for the present, like that through the door-lock of the Villa de Malte in Rome of the cupola of St. Peter's), before another of my surprises came to hand: that telegram from Sierre. How beautiful this Valais really is. The impressions of Sion and Sierre have at one stroke made my Swiss recollections, already so various, more complete by much, as always happens whenever I get to the Rhone—: its banks smile at me with a wonderful friendliness—as though this stream more than any other had the power to make its own the lands that it refreshes: Vaucluse, Avignon, the Île de Bartelasse and this uncanny Jonction here: all of them are related by marriage and

akin through the spirit of this river—and now at last, in the
generous valleys of the Valais, what room it has to spread out and
be itself in every curve. I have seen not one among the beautiful
valleys of Switzerland that was more spacious: the Valais is a plain
a long way from the mountains; and these are themselves no more
than a background, conveying no effect of weight and with
slopes so hazy that at times they seem imaginary, like the mountains pictured in a reflection. And most spacious in perspective
too are the gradations of the hills in the foreground with the
accent and inflection of their progressively upward-climbing vil-
lages. . . . Sion was surprising in every way: we had the right
day for it—and I understood from step to step this choice of Hofmannsthal's, and how in the great picture book of Switzerland
he likes to turn up this page above all others.

. . . I will be with you Saturday at the latest . . . though this
time, to be sure, only until the moment I am permitted to leave
the country, and this, so as not to be in Paris too late, I shall do
everything I can to hasten: for this your support and Frau von
der Mühll's will be much in demand,—who knows how much.
Will it be possible for me to board the Paris train early next week!?

[*146*]

To Countess M.   Hôtel Foyot, rue de Tournon, Paris
                          October 27, 1920

You will not, I believe, be nearly astonished enough, my dear
Countess, when you read this address—? You have always believed me capable of progress of this sort, the most extensive! But
just look, just look!: what shall I say, everything is absolutely,
absolutely all right; for the first time since the dreadful years I
am feeling the continuity of my existence again, which I had been
ready to renounce; for even Switzerland only prolonged the interruptions (more mildly, more pleasantly, under cover, if you
will—), but here, here: la même plénitude de vie, le même inten-
sité, la même justesse même dans le mal—: by and large everything

has remained independent of political stewings and doings and is pressing, stirring, glowing, shimmering: October days: you know them.

I fit at all the broken spots, yes, and now I hardly feel it any more. If I could remain here, I should have my life tomorrow, all its dangers, all its blessings: my entire life: ma vie, depuis toujours mienne— —But, the exchange prevents that: it will have been only four or five days,—but even so it is right with me and I like it: I now *know* again, my consciousness has given over its constraints, the standing-still-in-one-spot has stopped, I am again revolving in my consciousness. *One* hour here, the first, would have sufficed for that. And after all I have had hundreds, days, nights—and every step was an arrival. . . .

In haste: for outside is the Luxembourg, shimmering: so how can I hold out any longer at my desk? . . .

[147]

To Princess Marie von Thurn
und Taxis-Hohenlohe
Schloss Berg am Irchel,
Canton Zurich (Switzerland)
November 19, 1920

De grâce: if I am not yet entirely lost to you (I slip through fingers like . . . "desert sand") and you have not yet thoroughly denounced me for failing to come, then lose yourself awhile in this little picture: even if I don't really deserve it. For now the dice, which pointed with all their spots toward you, have been picked up once more and thrown anew—and the result, I am continuing to stay in hospitable Switzerland and, as you can almost see by this [card], Schloss Berg on the Irchel . . . is to be my abode for the next months, perhaps for the winter. Under conditions somewhat resembling those in Duino: that was what settled it for me. I live alone in the solid, centuries-old stone house, alone with a housekeeper who cares for me as silently as I silently let myself be cared for; a deserted park opening on the quiet landscape, no railway station in the neighborhood and for the present, furthermore, a lot of roads closed on account of foot-and-mouth disease—donc, retraite absolue.

It happened so suddenly, without my doing the least thing about it, simply offered itself, I could not resist. More particularly as the choice was put to me at a remarkable moment. I came—you will not guess from where—dear Princess—I came from Paris, where I had just as unexpectedly spent six days, indescribable autumn days, glorious ones,—and it was . . . to an extent that far exceeded all expectation—*my* Paris, the Paris of former days I would like to say: the eternal Paris. Anyone now visiting chiefly the rive droite, dependent on personal connections and altogether on society and conversation, would certainly have to admit many sad and disfiguring changes. But I have the singular good fortune to live through *things,* and so far as any influence came to me from them and from the intensive air, it was the old, indescribable one, the same to which almost twenty years ago I owed my best and most resolute frame of mind. I cannot say (but you will guess!) with what emotion I enjoyed these contacts, how I held myself against a hundred intimate broken surfaces, the healing on to which remained but a matter of self-abandonment. And that, believe me! I did not lack. Only now have I the hope again of carrying on, really continuing my work, and I came back with a real impatience for it—, then Schloss Berg offered itself. And instead of handing myself over and delivering myself up to a long journey, to the tasks that would have awaited me in Munich, and so and so many unforeseen things that I would have had to attend to *before* Lautschin, I drove blindly from Geneva hither and closed my old oaken doors. Now I have been here a week, and the experiment speaks for my staying on. Dear Princess: absolution. More: your blessing on it! . . .

[*148*]

To R.S., who in sending in manuscripts, called special attention to
his having gone blind.   Schloss Berg am Irchel,
                                   Canton Zurich, Switzerland
                                   November 22, 1920

Your letter of October 16th went a long way round to reach
me; so my delay is not quite so great as it might seem.

Now as to my answer, it is more concerned with your letter
than with the work you enclosed. My conscience does not allow
me to express "judgment", since I know how much I lack the
movable yardsticks for appraising the more or less in artistic
endeavors; I have no link with the manifestations of art other than
that of admiration, and so I am in every way made, while I live, to
be pupil to the greatest and their acknowledger, rather than finding myself able to act as adviser to those who have not yet truly
found their way into the essential nature of their tasks. For these
I may only wish that they hold joyfully to the road of longest
learning, until there comes to them that deep and hidden self-
assuredness which—without their having to ask anyone about
it—pure necessity, that is, irrepressibility and thoroughness
of their work secures to them. To hold our innermost conscience
alert, which with every fully formed experience tells us whether
it is thus, as it now stands, altogether to be answered for in its
truthfulness and integrity: *that* is the foundation of every artistic
production, which ought to be laid even there where an inspiration kept in suspense can, so to speak, do without the ground.

Great decisive misfortune, such as has been your lot, is singularly enticing to those winged inspirations that like to settle down
wherever a privation has become greater than any possession we
can imagine. You could not help simply setting this consummate
misfortune, when you noticed how attractive it is to the invisible and spiritual, in the center of your rearranged consciousness; it remains, rightly, the unshiftable point from which all distances and movements of your experience and your mind are to
be measured. But now that this arrangement has once been hit

upon, your quiet practice should be directed toward enduring this central misfortune more and more without any special name, and this would manifest itself in your artistic efforts somewhat in this way: that nowhere any more would it be possible to recognize in them *what* limitless restriction is the occasion for your laying claim in the earnest entreaty of your work to limitless compensation. Art can proceed only from a purely anonymous center. But for your life too (whatever else it may be destined to bring forth) this endeavor seems to me decisive; *it* would be the real kernel of your resignation. While you bore your misfortune as a nameless and then at last unnamable suffering, you would be preparing for it the freedom of being at certain moments not misfortune alone but: dispensation (—who can see that far—): privilege. Unequivocal destinies of that sort have their god and are thereby forever distinguished from those variously complicative fates whose privations are not deep enough and not closely enough joined to serve as negative mold for the casting of such a greatly responsible form.

[*149*]

To Countess M.   Schloss Berg am Irchel,
                                    Canton Zurich, Switzerland
                                    November 25, 1920

. . . How has this come about? It has come about by a miracle.—There's no other way of accounting for it. How shall I hasten to impart to you the incomprehensible thing that has befallen me? Imagine, the same privilege that allowed me to go to Paris has, so to speak, had a second act in that, at the moment of my return, the remote little old Schlösschen Berg was offered me (to me, all alone!) as an abode for the winter. You can see it fairly well on the enclosed card: a solid old house of hewn stone, dating back in its last form to the seventeenth century, with a set-back gable roof seen from the side,—in the front a somewhat neglected park, in which high trimmed beech alleys mark out right and left the unbordered pièce d'eau, in the center of which, day and night, like a playing tree (un arbre de luxe) the fountain-figure stands slim. (And this, with its continually modulated cascade, is indeed the measure of all sounds, seldom can anything be heard above it!) Looking in the direction opposite from that given by the card, out of one of the windows (mine are those on the ground floor) into the garden, one sees it in the background, beyond the wide-set alley of old chestnuts, running on into the landscape, into meadows which, in gentlest ascent, reach up to the foot of the Irchel, that wooded hill which gives way, as it were, closing the picture without perceptibly shutting it in.— My rooms are fine, large, full of sympathetic old things—big tile stoves, in addition to the fireplace, provide the heating—and whenever the sun is out it shines radiantly in at all my windows. A quiet sensible housekeeper looks after me, exactly as I need to be looked after, and doesn't seem to show any particular surprise at my being silent and reserved (for so I must be in order to get at work!)— —I've been telling a fairy tale, have I not? Well, what do you say to my being the center of that tale, unexpectedly? Am I really happy? No, my heart beats with worry over whether I shall be able to wrest from these conditions, to the last degree favorable and congenial, *that* which they now at last really allow and which I (after all the distractions and disturbances of the last years) must urgently, unrelentingly expect of myself. Now there's no excuse! Shall I be able to do it? Shall I be strong, clean, fruitful, productive?: the having seen Paris again, which was so healing, obliges me to be, and here this obligation is now really so clearly and unambiguously set up round about me—, if I fail this time, here, at Schloss Berg—then there is no help for me. The first thing a stranger walking in here would say is: How one must be able to work here! Shall I be able to do it? My fear (my cowardice, if you want to call it that) is just as great as my joy,—but that joy is really immense.

From a place like this . . . I can measure doubly well how sad it must be for you to give up your Carinthian estate: it is true, an indescribable amount of life goes into a piece of permanent property one has built up, and this cannot be pulled out when one gets into the position of giving the place away. Here the Escher portraits, such as have remained in the château, still predominate over everything that the Zieglers, despite four children grown up here, have been able to impose upon the surroundings!

The mourning border on your letter I explained to myself at once, even before I read it—, in the sense of that great near loss that had unfortunately lain not outside the realm of a certain expectation. It is true, one must, particularly under the present bottomless conditions, muster a sort of reconciliation with the going of those who would not have been able to endure such great changes without continual amazement and suffering. I myself could scarcely get possession of myself or get at my work if I had to notice too much of the helplessnesses that everywhere don't want to admit they are that, but in the form of false certainties, would like to overpower the world.

Had I wanted and been able to "profit" by the exchange in Switzerland I would perhaps have become strong enough to acquire your Carinthian estate—I say that jokingly, of course—but still with the thought in the back of my mind that perhaps the original home of the family, which I have never learned to know, would be the country where a comparatively homelike striking of roots (should I ever get to it) would come to me not unnaturally.

For the spring I am thinking of Paris anyway—to continue the life there would seem to me the most perfectly straightforward thing that could happen to me. But, in any case, as I remain dependent on Insel-Verlag as concerns my income, it is not exactly to be foreseen how the disastrous German exchange is to serve me in the realization of this plan.

No—I was not longer in Paris, six days. It was so perfect that duration played no role. My heart, my mind, my passionate remembrance of what had there been achieved and fought for were so magnificently and surely satisfied in the very first hour, that when that was over I might have left without any real deprivation. I long ago accustomed myself to take given things according to their intensity, without, so far as that is humanly achievable, worrying about duration; that is perhaps the best and discreetest way of expecting *everything* from them—even duration. If one begins with *that* demand, one spoils and falsifies every experience, indeed, one hinders it in its own inmost inventiveness and fruitfulness. Something that is really not to be got by entreaty, can never be but an *extra* gift,—and I was just thinking that often in life things seem to depend only on the longest patience! . . . That I ever should have grumbled!

[*150*]

To Major-General von Sedlakowitz   Schloss Berg am Irchel,
Canton Zurich, Switzerland
December 9, 1920

Your letter and its duplicate were forwarded to me by the Insel-Verlag as soon as I was again to be reached at a more permanent address, after several months on the move.

Had I acted on the feeling aroused by your remote recollection, I must have thanked you at once—, and you thought it a little strange too, as the repetition of your letter shows, not to get any answer from me.

Meanwhile the emotion that agitated me was so complex that I had to let a few weeks pass, comprehending it, as it were, if my thanks were not to be superficial and, in a certain sense, embarrassed,—which would in no way have satisfied your sincere wish to renew acquaintance.

A voice that appeals to those most distant years (it is the only such voice that ever sought to find me!) was bound at first—you will pardon the directness of my expression—to be incredible. I would not, I believe, have been able to realize my life—that which I may now, without taking it in the whole, go ahead and call so— had I not, for decades, denied and suppressed all recollection of those five years of my military training; what, indeed, have I not done for the sake of that suppression! There were times when the slightest influence out of that rejected past would have disintegrated that new and fruitful consciousness of my own that I was struggling for—, and when sometimes it inwardly obtruded itself, I had to lift myself out over it, as over something belonging to a most alien, a quite unrecognizable life.—But later too, when I found myself more surrounded and protected in a life increasingly my own, that affliction of my childhood, long and violent and far beyond my age at the time, seemed incomprehensible to me—, and I was able to understand its impenetrable fatality just as little as the miracle that finally—perhaps at the last moment—came to free me from the abyss of undeserved misery.

If you, Sir, find exaggerated the embitterment without which even today still I cannot so much as enumerate those facts of my early life,—I beg you to consider for a moment that when I left the military college, I stood as one exhausted, physically and spiritually misused, retarded, at sixteen, before my life's enormous tasks, defrauded of the most spontaneous part of my energy and at the same time of that preparation, never again retrievable, which would have built me clean steps for an ascent that, weakened and damaged, I had now to begin before the steepest walls of my future.

You hear me state all this and you will ask, how then was it conceivable to retrieve these indescribable things I had missed and head into the paths along which my original instincts could still drive me ahead, weary as I was: this question it probably was which made you doubt for so long my identity with the "pupil René Rilke". I cannot tell how such a thing could have happened either. Life is very singularly made to surprise us (where it does not utterly appall us). Of course I looked around for help in those years of dismay; much as I remained apart—for my contemporaries were in a normal and incomparably clearer position and did not come into consideration as companions for me—I was not spared the drawing of comparisons and the realizing ever anew what entirely different preliminaries I might have expected for my talent. That did not help me. But it is present to me even now, how, in my moroseness, I found a kind of help in those five evil and anxious years of my childhood having been so *utterly cruel*, without a single mitigation.

Dear Sir, do not think me unjust: I imagine I have achieved a certain degree of fairness and I wish for nothing more than some day to be allowed to recognize even in the boundless suffering of those years those brighter spots in which—because there was no longer any other way—some kindness befell me as if by chance. For the workings of Nature penetrate far into the unnatural, and an attempt at striking a balance might occasionally take place even there.—But how slight that was measured against the daily despair of a ten-, a twelve-, a fourteen-year-old boy.

So—for individual later moments of my youth—I had to be granted the support of including that which happened so long ago in the feeling of one single terrible damnation, out of which I was cast up merely as out of a sea that is stirred to its depths with destructive intent and is not even concerned whether it leaves here and there upon its devastated shore a live thing or a dead.

When in more reflective years (for how late I arrived at a state where I could read calmly, not just to make up for lost time, but purely receptively!) Dostoievski's Memoirs of a Death-house first came into my hands, it seemed to me that since my tenth year I had been admitted into all the terrors and despairs of the convict prison! Please take all the pathos out of this statement. It means to express nothing but a simple recognition of an inner state the external causes of which—I will admit at once—were different enough from the surroundings of Siberian convicts. But Dostoievski, when he endured the unendurable, was a young man, a grown man; to the mind of a child the prison walls of St. Pölten could, if he used the measure of his helplessly abandoned heart, take on pretty much the same dimensions.

Twenty years ago it was, I spent some time in Russia. An insight, prepared only in a very general way by the reading of Dostoievski's works, developed, in that country where I felt so at home, into a most penetrating clarity; it is hard to formulate. Something like this, perhaps: The Russian showed me in so many examples how even a servitude and affliction continually overpowering all forces of resistance need not necessarily bring about the destruction of the soul. There is here, at least for the Slavic soul, a degree of subjection that deserves to be called so consummate that, even under the most ponderous and burdensome oppression, it provides the soul with something like a secret playroom, a fourth dimension of its existence, in which, however crushing conditions become, a new, endless and truly independent freedom begins for it.

Was it presumptuous of me to imagine that I had, instinctively, achieved a similar complete submission and resignation in those earliest years, when that block of an impenetrable misery had been rolled over the tenderest first shoots of my nature? I had, it seems to me, some right (with an altered standard naturally) to assume something of the sort, since indeed of any *other* endurance of disproportionate, over-lifesize wrong there is nowhere any indication.

So I hope you realize that even a long time ago I undertook to enter upon a certain reconciliation with my older destinies. As they had not destroyed me they must at some time have been laid upon the scales of my life as additional weights—, and the counterweights that were destined to bring the other side into balance could be made up only of the purest performance, to which, too, I found myself determined after those days of mine in Russia.

If thus I no longer suppressed altogether the old days in military school, I still could admit them only in the large and in general, somewhere behind me. For an examination or even a reconstruction of details my energies, otherwise busy in any case and working toward the future, would never have sufficed.

So that when you speak to me of some particular recollection, as happens in your letter, I should have difficulty in unexpectedly describing such memories, never having cultivated them.

The irony you manifested for my writings must have been a highly justified and educational one,—even that fragment from the later letter of 1892 (!) shows indeed how very right one would have been even then in strictly and severely trimming the ragged and crinkled edges of my expression!

That you incidentally kept that letter among your papers and were even able to find it again, fills me, my dear teacher, with a peculiar emotion, which I may hide the less as nowhere in these brusque remarks have I yet thanked you for your new sympathetic communication. It is done at this point, believe me, without any reservation.

Must I, in conclusion, reproach myself for having gone into so much detail and above all to such a length? Should I have taken the renewal of acquaintance in your kind letter more "unconcernedly"?—No; I believe that for me there was only the choice, either to remain silent or really to let you take part in the emotion which the only voice that has ever come across to me from thence was bound to arouse in me.

If you, Sir, can take this unusual answer in a sense as just as it is forbearing, then you will also feel that I cannot close in any other way than with the expression of sincere wishes for your welfare. How should I not see a special privilege in your remembrance ever having afforded me the pleasure of expressing them!

[*151*]

To Phia Rilke   Schloss Berg am Irchel, Canton Zürich, Switzerland
December 17, 1920

My dear Mama,

Once more at our blessed hour, most loving remembrance of Christmas days of longest ago, and the wish that now, after such bad times, there may be granted you celebrations each year more quiet, more peaceful, and finally too in a little home of your very own again!

Now that this has been expressed, really everything has been expressed, for now it is a matter not of *reading,* but of *going-into-oneself* and, in one's own heart, for the year's holiest hour of celebration, preparing the manger, so that therein, this hour, and in it the Savior, may with all fervor be born into the world again!

What I wish for you, dear Mama, is that on this evening of consecration, the remembrance of all distress, even the consciousness of the immediate worry and insecurity of existence may be

quite checked and in a sense dissolved in the innermost knowledge of that grace, for which indeed no time is too dense with
calamity and no anxiety so sealed that in *its own* time—which is
not ours!—it could not enter and penetrate what seems insur-
mountable with its mild victory. There is no moment in the long
year when one would be able to call so vividly into one's soul its
ever possible appearance and then omnipresence, as this winter
night, autonomous through the centuries, which, through the incomparable coming of that child who transformed all creatures,
all at once outweighed and surpassed in value the sum of all other
earthly rights. Though the easy summer, when existence seems
considerably more bearable and more effortless, when we do not
have to guard ourselves against such direct antagonism from the
air and from serenely absorbed Nature—, though the happier
summer may pamper us with consolations,—what are they all beside the immeasurable comfort-treasures of this outwardly unassuming, even poor night that suddenly stands open toward the
inside, like an all-embracing and warming heart, and which with
beats of its own bell-toned center really does reply to our hearkening into the innermost cell.

All annunciations of previous times did not suffice to herald
this night, all hymns that have been sung in its praise did not come
near the stillness and eagerness in which shepherds and kings knelt
down—, just as we too, none of us, has ever been able, while this
miracle-night was befalling him, to indicate the measure of his
experience.

It is so truly the mystery of the kneeling, of the deeply kneeling
man: his being greater, by his spiritual nature, than he who stands!
which is celebrated in this night. He who kneels, who gives himself wholly to kneeling, loses indeed the measure of his surroundings, even looking up he would no longer be able to say what is
great and what is small. But although in his bent posture he has
scarcely the height of a child, yet he, this kneeling man, is not to be
called small. With him the scale is shifted, for in following the
peculiar weight and strength in his knees and assuming the position
that corresponds to them, he already belongs to that world in

which height is—depth,—and if even height remains un-
measurable to our gaze and our instruments: who could measure
the depth? . . .

But this is the night of radiant depth unfolded—: for you, dear
Mama, may it be hallowed and blessed. Amen.—René

[*152*]

To Carl Burckhardt   Schloss Berg am Irchel,
                                         Canton Zurich, Switzerland
                                         December 21, 1920

. . . It came to the point where my life at Berg—I may safely
refer to it by so inclusive a word, for right away it was of a peculiar
validity and realization—where this life at once took on the dimensions of work—, whereby my letter-pen, so to say, fell under the
supervision of its stricter sister dedicated to production and only
now and then obtains a little freedom to let itself go for a few easy
pages.

For the same reason—because everything here was at once so
conducive that from the second or third moment the most serious
things became unpostponable and the deeper work of inward absorption set in (for the true and uninterruptible taking up of
which no house has been solid and remote enough for me during
these last years)—I did not go to Basel either, after all. To the
friendly understanding of your sister and the ever active kindness
of your mother I owe the sending over of my things; and with the
arrival of these trunks, boxes and baskets my existence here has
been complete; entirely shut off and remote as it was from the start,
the sudden snowfall has as it were moved house and park still
further off, and should even that not suffice, the regulations that
have been issued on account of foot-and-mouth disease see to it that
the strictly closed roads not only make any coming here to me,
but also my going out, practically impossible. My inner confusion,
into which so much disturbance had penetrated during the world-
disasters, needs such a shutting-off for a while—exaggerated, if
you will—to set itself in order; I must really be able to be sure that

for a long time nothing—save what may come from Nature or be engendered through incommensurable activities inside oneself—that *nothing* comes up, if I am to get through at all with everything that fills my mind to overflowing; not because it would be too much, but because I would not have the strength to put it by in obedient and significant form. So I best sum up my present condition when I say that it answers to all my inclinations; what might somehow be disturbing about it would at most be this, that the wonderful congeniality of it lays upon me the extreme obligation to produce; but as of course I want nothing but that—this bringing to completion at last of interrupted and imperiled tasks —, we will manage (so far as human strength suffices) to come to terms on this point too.

What a blessing that I had those days in Paris beforehand! Without this connection with my earlier existence (with all my difficult years of learning), through which alone my full consciousness was once more set in order and, so to speak, the great cycle of my spiritual breathing was opened again, the retirement at Berg would not have been half so well prepared and provisioned. This time one good thing was added to another and indeed one would not have had enough with only one, after such long association with unkind, malicious, uncongenial and sad things! . . .

You remember the forty drawings of my little (twelve-year-old) friend Balthasar Klossowski, whose destiny was decided one day, on the stroke of twelve, in the green room of the Ritterhof. The publisher is actually getting them into the bookstores toward spring. And I have begun my work here by sketching out the promised "Preface", which, just as it lies before me—full of mistakes, I fear—nevertheless pleases me because I wrote it down very rapidly, in one good session, and can assure you I did not translate it in an antechamber of my mind, but, franchement et heureusement, *thought it in French*. Despite that, this little personal infatuation with an unexpectedly easy success would not justify my forcing this essay upon you (in a copy made for you). Although these pages deal with "Mitsou" the tomcat and will be used as an introduction to the book of that name, yet I also see in them (in reading you will understand why)—since knowing of the death of my friend "Prince"—a kind of little memorial I was unwittingly allowed to put up a few days before he ran into the guns of the guards in the Biningen preserve. I know how this closely attached friend, with his unrestrainable heart, sharing your thoughts and feelings, had a part in many of your recollections, and how much the news of his going must have moved you,— as though one of those understandings were now taken away which, because they do not act "helpful" at all, are more helpful and thoroughgoing than the most give-and-take conversations; and into which life, always discreet, does after all, perhaps, transfer the purest compensations we are allowed to experience outside ourselves.

What a good companion Prince was to me, you know. Odd how he, who seemed to know that life and death are equally difficult—only so can I ever express what his sigh, that single one on that rainy night in May, seemed to impart to me—was driven into an accessible death, at that singular parting of the ways beyond which growing old would have set him against one of the two, made him unjust toward life and sullen toward death.

So quite particularly in *his,* Prince's, honor, did I intend for you the little piece in the accompanying copy; accept it with the indulgence with which alone such an incidental thing should be taken, and yet also in that larger sense about which, I believe, we agree. . . .

P.S. I am searching for Hofmannsthal's Beethoven lecture, having realized at once how *very fine* it must have been.

[153]

To Inga Junghanns   Schloss Berg am Irchel,
                                      Canton Zurich, Switzerland
                                      January 5, 1921

. . . Yes, how curiously things do happen in life; were there not a bit of arrogance somewhere in it, one would indeed like very much to stand outside, confronting everything, that is, everything that *occurs*, so as surely not to lose anything—; one would then still remain fixed, perhaps for the first time really so, in the actual center of life, where everything comes together and has no name;—but then again, the names have bewitched us—the titles, the pretense of life—because the whole is too infinite, and we recover by calling it for a while by the name of *one* love, much as it is just this impassioned restriction that puts us in the wrong, makes us guilty, kills us . . .

[*154*]

To Joachim von Winterfeldt-Menkin   Schloss Berg am Irchel,
                                        Canton Zurich
                                        February 2, 1921

. . . I did not know Seckendorff, and . . . it is really not my custom to write about the plastic arts. Rodin's case is for me wholly unique. Rodin was, as I might say, my teacher; the example of his powerful work influenced me through many years of learning, and from the friendly association of so many occasions it was possible finally for a series of notes to precipitate out. Even in the next case, when a painter's work—that of Cézanne—had the greatest influence on me, I renounced any written statement of my experience, as nothing seems to me less reliable than literary analysis of painting or plastic production. The present condition of the arts on the one hand and on the other the uncommon agility and readiness of the word, obligate one to the greatest economy and caution in expression; even the most responsible writer is today more than ever in danger of exaggerating or at least of prematurely appraising works of art that in any way concern him, since it has not been possible to alter and adjust the divisions of the measuring-scale in such detail as would correspond to the modifications and variety in the flood of art production. My part toward all this is the modest one of keeping silent and this resolve of mine has for years been too much a matter of principle for me not to stick to it even if Seckendorff's works had been familiar and significant to me. . . .

[155]

To Francisca Stoecklin

Schloss Berg am Irchel,
Canton Zurich
March 8, 1921 (Tuesday)

I had taken your letter along yesterday on the post road to Flaach and was reading it again as I walked; as I finished and looked up, my glance involuntarily took in, on the right, in the garden before a farmhouse, a little creature some five years of age. The little girl, scarce looked-at, dropped everything and came hurrying toward me, over her slanting round shoulder an open umbrella (which because of its weight had slid so far back that it made a complete background for her little person),—over to the road, her tiny right hand ready to offer, even from afar, open, so open that the palm was almost convex—, and when it then actually succeeded, when the offer of this generous, eager, very earthy and dirty little hand had been, with quickly hid astonishment, accepted by me, the little girl experienced such deep contentment and her little face radiated so much fulfillment and joy that her whole expression no longer had any relation to the degree of giving that might have been ours at that moment.

What was it? A mistake of the little person who took me for an acquaintance, perhaps for the vicar of Flaach? (for in general, friendly as children may be in greeting one orally, I have never yet seen one of them take upon itself the charges of such a welcome). Even if this élan was not meant for me, enough to make one happy was still left over, and this it bestowed on me notwithstanding. But now I have a better explanation for it (and for your sake I am telling you the sweet incident). My gaze, as it left your letter, must have been so friendly, so happy, so clarified with universal friendship, that the world now suddenly facing it knew no other way to fill it out than with this pure spontaneous occurrence.

This is my impartial little story. . . .

[156]

To Countess M.   Schloss Berg am Irchel, Canton Zurich, Switzerland
March 10, 1921

I wanted to write you long, long ago! Now almost two months
have passed since the date of your letter—, but I was living under
such great pressure that any communication would have been as if
distorted. I want to say right away that *that* did not happen to me
of which you so perspicaciously warned me—a forcing, an urging,
impatient either-or toward work—, no, *not that*. You wrote so
comfortingly and trustingly: "Your work, your art comes when *it*
will"—yes, and it is that way—, but then around New Year's,
it was there, *it was there*—, and at the same moment circumstances
arose to meet me, urgent, difficult ones—, that needed all of me
and to which I had to concede the right on the spot to tear me
forth and away from all that was just about to begin—and for
which circumstances here were incomparably favorable and prepared. A fatality: in effect exactly like that time in Munich when
I was just beginning to reflect and pull myself together,—and
I was called up; of course it was no calling up this time, but something just as relentless, against which no protest could be of avail.
Everyone, in the last analysis, experiences only *one* conflict in
life, which only disguises itself differently all the time and shows
up somewhere else—, mine is, to make life and work agree in a
purest sense; where the infinite incommensurable work of the
artist is concerned, the two directions are opposed. Many have
helped themselves by taking life lightly, surreptitiously snatching
from it, so to speak, what they did nevertheless need, or transforming its values into intoxications the murky exaltation of which
they then swiftly flung over into art; others had no way out save
the turning away from life, asceticism, and *this* means is of course
cleaner and truer by far than that other greedy cheating of life
for the benefit of art. But for me this does not come into consideration either. Since in the last analysis my productivity springs
from the most direct admiration of life, from the daily inexhaust-

ible marveling at it (how else would I have come to produce?), so I would see a lie in that too, in rejecting at any time the streaming of it towards me; every such renunciation, however much one's art may potentially gain from it, must finally come to expression in that art as hardness, and have its revenge: for who would be entirely open and acquiescent in such a sensitive domain, if he had a mistrustful, constraining and timid attitude toward life!— So one learns, alas how slowly; life works its way over a lot of "first principles"—*to what purpose* do we master it a little in the end?

Rodin often reflected upon this in his old age. Sometimes, at five in the morning, I would find him standing in the garden, sunk in contemplation of the cliffs of Sèvres and St. Cloud that slowly rose out of the wonderful autumn mist of the Seine as though they were now coming, perfectly correctly formed, into being—, there he would stand, the old man, and consider: "*To what purpose* have I mastered it now, this marveling, the knowing how much a morning like this is . . . ?" And a year later he understood not even this, *was not master of it after all*, had not been master of it after all, for an influence, a destiny, far below his level, had shrouded him and surrounded him with the most dismal confusions, out of which no glory declared itself!—

Dear Countess, I only wanted to give you the reasons for my silence—where have I got to? . . .

[*157*]

To Countess
Maria Viktoria Attems   Schloss Berg am Irchel,
                                           Canton Zurich, Switzerland
                                           March 12, 1921

. . . In view of the kind interest I discern in your note, it almost comes hard for me to admit the attitude or prejudice which, to be honest, I must nevertheless confess to in face of your inquiry.

I do not know to *which* of my works your artistic ideas have reference,—but fundamentally it holds for *all* that I am, alas! quite sincerely averse to any accompaniment—musical as well as illustrative—to my works. It is after all my aim to fill with my own creative output the whole artistic space that offers itself to an idea in my mind. I hate to believe (assuming my creation to be successful in a highest sense) that there can be any room left over for another art, which would itself then be interpretative and complementary. I find illustration quite particularly annoying because it dictates certain definite restrictions to the free play of the imagination (of the reader): that the reader should, however, keep his whole special freedom in his reception of an artistically really well-developed work—(one might of course approve of illustration for some slighter, purely entertaining category)—this seems to me to be of the essence of that work's effect. So that I cannot imagine the individual arts being nearly separated enough; which exaggerated attitude, as I hasten to admit, perhaps has its most sensitive reason in the fact that I myself, with a strong leaning toward expression in painting, had in my youth to decide for one art to escape distraction—and so this decision happened with a certain impassioned exclusivity. Moreover, in my experience every artist while he is producing must, for the sake of intensity, regard *his* means of expression as, so to speak, the *only* ones; for otherwise he might easily come to the conclusion that this or that bit of world was not expressible at all by *his* means, and would finally fall into the innermost space *between* the individual arts, which goodness knows gapes wide enough and which only the vital tensity of the great masters of the Rennaissance was really able to bridge over. *We* are faced with the task of each clearly deciding for *one*, his own, form of expression; and to this creative activity, enclosed in *one* province, all coming-to-the-rescue on the part of other arts becomes weakening and dangerous. . . .

[158]

To Erwein Baron von Aretin
Schloss Berg am Irchel,
Canton Zurich, Switzerland
last day of March, 1921

Let me, since memory allows me, dwell a while in thought of your father. . . . I can imagine, dear friend, that to the old gentleman the end will not be too hard—easier than to you the thought of losing him, even though you have seen him suffer so long—. For that generation, strong and active in such vastly different hopes and expectations, the turning away from things as they are today is something final—, it is almost that for us too, since even that least ability still to understand is missing, by which one practiced principally in looking into his inner world might still remain connected with something more universal.—Do not for that reason, therefore, regret the uneventful rural remoteness of your existence,—it offers, perhaps, just as it is, the most favorable conditions for a silent and, in its way, steady connection; be it ever so inactive and without marked ups and downs, it is still confirmed, believed me,—by deepest Nature. Productivity indeed, even the most fertile, only serves to create a certain inner constant, and perhaps art amounts to so much only because certain of its purest creations give a guarantee for the achievement of a more reliable inner attitude—(et encore!). Particularly in our time, when the majority are driven to artistic (or pseudo-artistic) activity by ambition, one cannot insist nearly enough upon this last, this only fundamental in the evalution of art, which is so deep and hidden that the most inconspicuous service in its behalf should all the more be regarded as equal to that most conspicuous and illustrious service (i. e., of real production).

Indeed, "my" Paris is not the political one! Those characteristics through which, in the days of my most intense learning, it became in an unsurpassed sense a world to me, probably never had much influence on the behavior of its politicians, but neither, fortunately, could they be destroyed by the mistakes of those politicians. Furthermore, what now appears as the extremest blindest chauvinism and has indeed the effect of such, still does not altogether correspond to that "pan-Germanest Berlin" and the dread that it arouses. The Frenchman has too long been accustomed to consider himself incomparable suddenly to compare himself; his overestimation has so infinitely much memory and tradition that it becomes perfectly delighted with itself, while his every presumption (just like Keyserling's so often) becomes charming and innocent. Certain temperaments, too, are so apt to see the foreign in the light of something inimical and bad—something irreconcilably "different"; and what, for the Frenchman, has not been simply "different" through all time! I am always reminded how utterly impossible it was to impress on Rodin a foreign, Austrian or Scandinavian name; one might pronounce it for him as often and as accurately as one could—, *he heard it differently*, and like the French ear the Frenchman's other senses are altogether unalterable. How many frightful mistakes may have their reason in this limitation. Also the new insight into the real German life could have been successful only in a single very transient moment in recent years; as it did not happen then, the mistakes of the observer on the other side were bound immediately to grow bigger and grosser again, for already the possibility of discerning what the German entity wants to become was diminished—one will obscured the other—, and the Frenchman, as a beginner in looking out and beyond, promptly failed to follow and withdrew into the security of his prejudices which to him were incomparably more palpable and dependable. Even we have no vision capable of grasping and reconciling that whole—mixed rather than chemically combined—as which a nation appears that is at once so shaken and so unawake—: the bearer of this vision would have to be that very statesman whose absence, in face of the need that is demanding him, is almost incomprehensible!

But where have I got to, on the sixth page of this letter, merely making *my* Paris, that I once left and now know to be unharmed in its glory, a little more conjecturable to you. It happens to be the only place in the world where, out of temperament and unsupervised impulses, such a cross-section of all the directions and tensions of human life could develop,—one of those hidden foci of that ellipse "life" whose other focus is probably but a mirror-image of a place fixed far above us.

Dear friend, I will *nevertheless* go the ten kilometers over to Neuburg and back, at long intervals, to tell you still further about all this: for now I *know* my *whole* self again, and no part of it more than that scared momentary cutout with highly uncertain edges, to which I was confined during the war. . . .

[159]

To Erwein Baron von Aretin
Schloss Berg am Irchel,
Canton Zurich, Switzerland
May 1, 1921

. . . I am sure you are fully resigned in feeling and under the influence of the pure serene order that indeed cannot but be mute and indifferent toward our limitation.

Your mother will find in her faith that deepest consolation that has its source in the very center of sorrow; I only hope you may all feel able to make her having to stay behind gentle and reconcilable.

For the rest it is our grief's strange prerogative that *there,* where it does not appear confused by the contradiction that in individual cases we think a life seems incomplete, interrupted, broken off—, it is allowed to be all learning, all work, purest, most perfect awareness. And nowhere does it more largely manifest itself in this singular challenge to us than in the loss of our father in his old age: which, in a way, obligates us to collect ourselves anew, indeed to a first self-reliance of our inner capacities.

So long as our father is living, we are naturally as though modeled in relief upon him (hence too the tragedy of the conflicts); this blow it is that first makes us into the full round, free, alas, standing free on all sides . . . (our mother, of course, courageous creature, from the beginning set us as far out as possible—). . . .

[160]

*To Rolf Baron von
    Ungern-Sternberg*   Le Prieuré d'Etoy, Canton de Vaud,
                                                   Switzerland
                                                   June 26, 1921

. . . I cannot very well wish myself, for a long time to come, any other occupation than my own and special one, and with it those most quiet, regular conditions that favor it. Schloss Berg was a privilege of this sort,—but although there was six months of it, the period granted was after all still too short to allow me to complete what I had so spaciously begun; also my inward sensibility to fright has grown so great in recent years that any termination set in advance, the until-that-time, would almost be enough to hamper me.

That I am without a secure living-place is entirely *my* fault; perhaps, had my family kept their land in the countries in which they had from time immemorial been at home, I might have been able to evolve for myself from that inherited spot as a starting point a useful consciousness of home. The city in which I grew up offered no proper soil for that; in its air I could neither breathe nor plow. So it inevitably happened that I chose places to live in, in the measure in which they answered, that is, I involuntarily feigned a lineage for myself *there* where the visible in its outer form somehow more closely approached my instinctive need of expression . . . So long as the world was open and the choice of such a composite homeland unlimited, out of everything thus acquired, something like a floating and yet sufficiently sustaining place actually built itself up, as it were *above* countries. . . .

[161]

To Princess Marie von Thurn
und Taxis-Hohenlohe
Hotel Château Bellevue,
Sierre (Valais),
July 25, 1921

It is getting toward the end of July, and I am not with you. Don't prepare any room for me yet, but also don't pronounce the death sentence yet on my coming: in August perhaps.

In these last weeks I have often come very near announcing my visit, and a peculiar current came into my rather sluggish spirit whenever I wanted to do so; but what holds me on the other hand is this wonderful Valais: I was imprudent enough to travel down here, to Sierre and Sion; I have told you what a singular charm these regions exercised over me when I first saw them last year at the time of the vintage: the circumstance that in the physiognomy of the landscape here Spain and Provence so strangely interact struck me immediately even then: for both landscapes spoke to me in the last years before the war more strongly and decisively than anything else; and now to find their voices united in an outspread mountain valley of Switzerland! And this echo, this family likeness is no imagination. Just recently I read in a brief treatise on the plant life of the Wallis that certain flowers appear here which are otherwise found only in Provence and Spain; it is the same with the butterflies: thus does the spirit of a great river (and to me the Rhone has always been one of the most wonderful) bear endowments and kinships through the countries. Its valley here is so wide and so grandly filled out with little heights within the frame of the big border mountains that the eye is continually provided with a play of the most delightful changes, a chess game with hills, as it were. As if even hills were still being shifted and distributed—so like Creation in its effect is the rhythm in the arrangement, with every point of view astonishingly new, of what one beholds—, and the old houses and castles move the more delightfully in these optical games since for the most part they again have the slope of a vineyard, the wood, the woodland meadow or the gray rock as background, as incorporate in it as pictures in a tapestry; for the most indescribable (almost rainless) sky takes part from far above in these perspectives and animates them with so spiritual an atmosphere that the special way things stand to each other seems, quite as in Spain, to exhibit at certain hours that tension which we think to perceive between the stars of a constellation.

But now to the particulars of my being detained: when I departed from Etoy about three weeks ago (with my visitor), we were offered the prospect (we did not want to stay long in the hotel) of a little house here which on sight proved impractical; we looked at some others in the neighborhood, the time passed—, until suddenly an object of the greatest temptation appeared. This old manoir, a tower, whose walls go back to the thirteenth century, whose beamed ceilings and furnishings too in part (chests, tables, chairs) date from the seventeenth,— was for sale or for rent. At a very cheap price, but still far beyond the possibilities I could realize in Swiss francs. Then last week one of my friends, who had known this so-called Château de Muzot (pronounced Muzotte) for a long time, one of the Reinharts of Winterthur rented the house in order to place it at my disposal! And now I am moving out there tomorrow and will make a little attempt at dwelling in these rather stern castle circumstances that cleave to one like a suit of armor! I really had to do that, didn't I?, as everything has turned out. The presence of my friend makes possible the running of a little household even before domestic help can be found,—should everything work out, I could then manage for a while with a housekeeper at Muzot. It lies about twenty minutes quite steep above Sierre, in a less arid, happy rusticity with many springs tumbling through it,—with views into the valley, over to the mountain slopes and into most wonderful depths of sky. A little rustic church, situated above somewhat to the left in the vineyards (no longer visible in the picture), belongs to it. The picture does not do Muzot justice, the tree growth in the garden has become much taller in the meantime, also one does not see the magnificent old poplar which should be imagined a few steps farther forward, to the right beyond the edge of the picture, and which is characteristic of the aspect of the little castle from wherever one sees it. I myself say "little castle", for this is the perfect type of the medieval manoir as it still survives everywhere here; these castles consisted only of one strong housebody like this that included everything. The entrance is from the rear where you see the sloping roof jutting out: this floor (that of the long balcony built on in front) includes the dining room, a little boudoir and the guest room; besides the kitchen (in a modern extension); the former kitchen was entirely on the ground floor beneath, a single gigantic room (now abandoned, for the storing of garden tools etc.). On the next story I have established myself. There is my little bedroom which receives its light through the windowpane at the right, but also on the other side sends out a little balcony into the tree. The double window beside it and, around the corner, the next window in the sunlit west front belong to my workroom, which we just about finished fitting out yesterday, all with appurtenances at hand: it has all kinds of promise and attraction for me, with its old chests, its oak table of 1600 and the old dark beam ceiling into which is carved the date MDCXVII; when I say attraction, that is nevertheless not accurate: for actually all of Muzot, while it somehow holds me, yet also drives a kind of worry and oppression into my spirit; as far as possible, I have familiarized myself with its oldest history: the de Blonays probably built it; in the fifteenth century it was in the possession of the de la Tournay-Chastillons; at the beginning of the sixteenth, a year before the battle of Marignan, the wedding of Isabelle de Chevron and Jean de Montheys took place there (all the guests of those three days of continuous festivity are still known and who walked with whom—). Jean de Montheys fell at Marignan and was brought back to the young widow at Muzot. Immediately thereafter the passions of two suitors became kindled for her, who in their fire fell out so violently that they ran each other through in a duel. The unhappy Isabelle, who seemed to have borne the loss of her husband with dignity, did not get over this annihilation of both her wooers, between whom she herself had not yet chosen; she lost her reason and thereafter left Muzot only by night, giving the slip to the solicitude of her old nurse Ursule; almost every night one could see her, "très légèrement habillée", wandering to Miège to the grave of her two hot-blooded suitors, and the legend goes that finally on a winter's night she was discovered stiff and dead in the graveyard at Miège.—So for this Isabelle or for the dead Montheys returning over and over, like a pendulum, from Marignan, one must somehow prepare oneself and may be astonished at nothing. The Château de Muzot, now that we have cleaned it out, has gained everywhere in brightness and homeliness. The rooms, as in all these medieval houses, have about them something honest-farmerish, rude, without arrière-pensées . . . Nevertheless—, and so that I don't forget it, beside my bedroom, in the upper story, the so-called old "chapel" lies out behind, a little white-washed room, accessible from the hallway through a surprisingly low, still quite medieval-gothic doorway, and above it in the wall, as a relief standing sharply out, not, as you might think, the cross, but: a big swastika! So you see me then, Princess, for the immediate future under the spell of this Muzot: I must try it. If you could see it! When one approaches from the valley, it stands there every time like an enchantment above the now already scorched rose paths of its little garden, in its color of ancient hewn stone that has gray and violet tones, but has roasted and browned itself golden in the sun, again like certain walls in Andalusia. . . .

When your first letter reached me in Etoy, I was at the beginning of much that was difficult; it has been, in part, overcome, and perhaps I shall further succeed in not hurting and yet in re-instating what is mine, in a pure equilibrium. My friend will now stay here only so long as her assistance is necessary to me at Muzot. This landscape, which I had first discovered with her last year, says as many notable things to her as it does to me, and I hope her great and charming talent for painting will yet prove itself in many ways on what it offers. . . .

[*162*]

To a Young Girl

. . . You know that I am not one of those who neglect the body in order to make of it a sacrificial offering for the soul, since my soul would thoroughly dislike being served in such a fashion. All the soarings of my mind begin in my blood, for which reason I precede my work, through a pure and simple way of life that is free from irritants and stimulants, as with an introductory prelude, so that I cannot be deceived over the true spiritual joy that consists in a concord, happy and as if transfigured, with the whole of Nature.

. . . A little time yet, and perhaps I shall no longer grasp all the conditions out of which these songs (the Duino Elegies), begun some time ago, arose. If you know some of these works some day you will understand me better; it is so difficult to say what one means.

If I look into my conscience I see but one law, relentlessly commanding: to lock myself into myself and in one stretch to end this task that was dictated to me at the very center of my heart. I am obeying.—For you know that being here I have wanted only that, and I have no right whatever to change the direction of my will before I have ended the act of my sacrifice and my obedience.

I have now done almost all the preparatory work, that is, I have redressed the uncomfortable delays of my correspondence. Think, I have written—I counted them this morning—115 letters, and not one was less than four pages, and many ran to eight, even twelve in close writing. (Naturally I do not count what has gone off to you. That is not writing, that is breathing through the pen.) How many letters! There are so many people who expect of me—I hardly know what: help, advice—from me, who find myself so helpless before the most imperative urgencies of life. And although I know they deceive themselves, are mistaken, still I feel tempted—and I don't believe it is vanity—to tell them something out of my experiences, some of the fruits of my long hours of loneliness. There are young women as well as young girls terribly deserted even in the bosom of their family. Young married women appalled at what has happened to them. And then all these young working people, mostly revolutionaries, who come out of the state prisons without any orientation whatever, take refuge in literature and write drunken, malicious poetry. What shall I say to them? How raise their despairing hearts, how shape their formless will, which under the violence of events has taken on a borrowed, quite provisional character, and which they now carry in themselves like an alien strength, the use of which they scarcely know.

Malte's experiences oblige me from time to time to answer these writings from people I do not know. He, *he* would have done it, if ever a voice had reached him. . . .

Furthermore it is *he* who obliges me to continue this sacrifice, exhorts me to love with all my love's capacities all things to which I want to give form. That is the irresistible force the usufruct of which he left to me. Imagine to yourself a Malte who should have had a lover or even a friend in that Paris that was so terrible for him. Would he then ever have entered so deep into the confidence of things? For these things (he often told me in our few intimate conversations), whose essential life you want to reproduce, first ask you: Are you free? Are you ready to dedicate your whole love to me? To lie with me, as Saint Julian the hospitable lay with the leper, in that ultimate embrace that can never be fulfilled in an ordinary and fleeting love of one's neighbor, but has for its impetus *love*, the whole of *love*, all love to be found on earth? And if a thing like that sees (so Malte told me), if it sees you busy with even a single line of your own interest, it will close itself to you. It will perhaps bestow a rule upon you with a word, make you some slight sign of friendship, but it will forgo giving you its heart, entrusting you with its patient nature and its starlike steadfastness, which makes it so much resemble the constellations of the sky.

You must, in order that it shall speak to you, take a thing

during a certain time as the only one that exists, as the only phenomenon which through your diligent and exclusive love finds itself set down in the center of the universe and which in this incomparable place on that day the angels serve. What you read here, my friend, is a chapter of those lectures I received from Malte, my only friend during so many years full of suffering and temptations, and I see that you mean the same, absolutely, when you speak of your drawings and paintings, which seem to you valid only because of that infatuation with which *brush or pencil carry out the embrace, the tender taking of possession.* Don't be frightened at the expression "fate", which I used in my last letter. I call fate all external events (illnesses, for example, included) which can inevitably step in to interrupt and annihilate a disposition of mind and training that is by nature solitary. Cézanne must have understood this when during the last years of his life he removed himself from everything that, as he expressed it, might "hook him tight", and when, religious and given to traditions as he was, he yet gave up going to his mother's funeral in order not to lose a working day. That went through me like an arrow, when I learned it, but like a flaming arrow that, while it pierced my heart through, left it in a conflagration of clear sight. There are few artists in our day who grasp this stubbornness, this vehement obstinacy. But I believe that without it one remains always at the periphery of art, which is rich enough as it is to allow us pleasant discoveries, but at which, nevertheless, we halt only as a player at the green table who, while he now and again succeeds with a "coup", remains none the less at the mercy of chance, which is nothing but the docile and dexterous ape of the law.

I have often had to take away Malte's writings from young people, forbidding them to read them. For this book, which seems to emerge in the proof that life is impossible, must so to speak be read against its current. If it contains bitter reproaches, these are absolutely not directed against life. On the contrary, they are the evidences that, for lack of strength, through distraction and inherited errors we lose almost completely the countless earthly riches that were intended for us.

Try, my dearest friend, to run through the overabundance of those pages in this spirit. This will not spare you tears, but will contribute to giving all your tears a meaning clearer and, so to speak, more transparent.

[*163*]

To J.H., a worker who had sent
Rilke some poems in manuscript

. . . It would have been hard for me—to put it frankly—to speak up for your poems: they move in the language of a time that is perhaps yours, but into the premises of which I look across only from outside and without finding any abiding contact. A person like myself is not easily to be dissuaded from thinking that the seething mass of productivity that inundates us, as it were, does so not out of abundance—, but from trouble and disorder overflows the banks of everything that has been for us not so much limitation as really limit. I do not want to add to your perplexity and depression in a time when the immediate circumstances of existence are hard and refractory for you; still, we really ought to follow through what you yourself involuntarily call forth. I do not know what métier you have learned—, but as a worker there must in any case be in you the experience of a certain ability to do, and the joy of doing something well cannot have remained so entirely unfamiliar to you. If you will look forth for a moment from this good, reliable ground out onto the rolling sea of your writings, it will not escape you how much chance is playing with you there and how little you have trained yourself to use your pen as *that* which above all it is: an honest, accurately controlled tool for which you are responsible.

You will surely not find it unfriendly if I answer the sincerity with which you were good enough to turn to me, in the same way—that is, sincerely. For the rest, I have the best and most earnest wishes for you; one may always hope that to those moments that seem utterly hopeless and intolerable the change for the better lies closest. May your heart find not only the endurance to wait for the good, but also the disposition to draw it to you.

[*164*]

To Countess Nora
  Purtscher-Wydenbruck   Château de Muzot sur Sierre, Valais
                                  September 25, 1921

. . . Everything turned out worse than I thought. The preparations for my "exact" winter made all sort of journeys necessary (within Switzerland to be sure), and even today I do not know whether Muzot can remain my refuge, or whether I should go to visit friends in Canton Aargau; the chief difficulty now is the lack of a reliable housekeeper: to find such a person seems almost impossible, especially for the somewhat difficult conditions she would have to watch over and manage at Muzot. And the time is passing, and my confidence of being able to realize the seclusion so necessary to me, without compromise, in some remote, wholly congenial place (such as that good Berg was a year ago!), grows less with every day. I say that, not to burden you with even a shadow of my worry, but only because I have no other excuse than this true one for replying so late to what you sent me. And this—let me admit it at once—this really troubles me, that I cannot fulfill your wish that I should provide these poems of yours with a foreword. You would go too far, dear Countess, if you thought to see herein an unfavorable opinion of what you have sincerely done: these verses proceed from the most direct experience, and most of them have a strength of their own to justify them; here and there a most characteristically developed line appears, as though that which had been poured in the mold of good tradition had been allowed to perfect itself under a special handiwork of the heart. All this I have thoroughly felt and understood, and I should be speaking contrary to my most natural conviction did I admit less. And yet: it seems to me one of the fatalities of our time that its penetrating and vehement currents sweep avowals of this sort out of desk-drawers, out of the (oh so pervious!) houses—, and whither, whither? To face a publicity overloaded with a lot of half and false and calculated production, which has no time and no disposition to be more attentive and more receptive to something genuine—where in the crush this is borne toward it—than, say, to something that is conspicuous or by some minor means alluring. Would not interiors (I often ask myself) be again more lived-in, warmer and more intimate, if much that is thus displayed in them were to work back into them again? Consider this: how strong, how full is the potency of your verses inside your own four walls: a power, are they not? a fragrance, an incense—, penetrating everywhere, including and enhancing each thing; and how diluted it would become and lost in the wide windy scattering space of publicity. Whether something brought forth from heart and mind belongs out there seems to me always more and more a question of proportion. Naturally nothing that is sincere and authentic is to be taken lightly; but every such manifestation is served by a particular field of force, and perhaps nothing is so much to blame for the anarchy of the world as just the almost total loss of insight into the measure and fitness of the forces at work. These, which if left in their places would become the center of a circuit controlled by them, see themselves slung out into the open, where all sense of proportion promptly leaves them. Never were squanderings worse or more senseless, and thus too the impoverishments made themselves felt in all the enclosed areas, while space does not gain anything from the tensions pilfered from them only to be lost in it. It is already a hereditary misunderstanding to suppose that, save where just simple communications are concerned, one can "publish" a particular embodiment of the spirit. Each thing of that kind is the center of a smaller or larger sphere, and little as one could keep lastingly private and particular some one thing that by its nature has the characteristics and interrelationships of stars, so little does one increase the force and radiation of some other thing by laying it bare and tearing down all the walls around it. This will be the most essential correction to which a world released into publicity will have to subject itself: that it give back every force to its own scope—, else it must all end in the individual forces being dispossessed, in which case, to be sure, what we now call art and intellect would appear to have been abolished, together with all the inside rooms of the mind and all the heart's equipment.

The friendly service, dear Countess, which at the publisher's suggestion you might have accepted from me, is usually considered so simple and easy to obtain that I am ashamed to set up this enormous apparatus instead of lightly consenting. But you see, I didn't *want* to take it lightly. What sense would a superficial politeness have had between us and in the end what would it have been good for?

Then again I must more and more remind myself that my now nearly ten years' silence lays upon the words with which I want to break it an extraordinary responsibility: those words, indeed all those that I shall ever yet have to form, are made of the stuff of the indescribable hindrances that have been put upon me through the years (and especially since 1914), and they will be heavy and massive by nature. Never was I less in a position to appear with light and pleasant words of an occasional sort. It seems to me as though from now on but one thing, something final and valid, *the one thing that is needful*, would give me the right to speak.

P.S. A private printing of the poems for your friends I would of course fully understand and approve.

[*165*]

To Carl Sieber   Château de Muzot sur Sierre (Valais),
                                          November 10, 1921

. . . if at first it seemed new to you to use toward me the affectionate address that is familiar and natural to Ruth, so to reply in a corresponding sense also causes me, I confess, a certain embarrassment—: only for a moment, however. For already the joy of entering into those relations that Ruth expects of us both outweighs all hesitation and every slowness of the heart; be then, dear boy, through my trust in her, in which you too now belong, heartily and entirely welcome.

When you call me, as Ruth has always called me from childhood up,—Väterchen—it obligates me as it movingly obligated me towards her in a deepest sense: not only as if my child were addressing me, but a human being bound to me in a great and mysterious way, uplifting me by his trust. In such a conception alone could that be compensated which otherwise should be imputed to me as negligence: that I let her forego the really familial, its constant companionship and community. She felt from childhood that this did not happen out of lovelessness, out of arbitrariness, out of thoughtlessness, but because the exclusive call to the *inner* realizations of my life was so great that work on the *external* ones, after a brief attempt, had to be abandoned. I may be reproached that my strength and my concept did not suffice to accomplish *both;* I have nothing to oppose to such censure save the silent indication of those domains into which I have thrown all my abilities, waiting to see whether in the end I am indicted or acquitted.

I write you this in all honesty, my dear future son, in order that, under the name you give me, I may not later seem somehow lukewarm and disappointing: the decisions of my life have long since been cast,—I can belong completely but to *one* thing: to my work, and must for its sake put aside many great and good things that for others, rightly, come before everything.

Now please do not infer from all this that I underestimate the value of what is grounded and established in the family; had I seen coming to me something visible, handed down, I would probably, despite all inner tasks, have recognized the obligation to carry upward and on a worthy growth on the inherited soil. But to our family, which since the thirteenth century has had substantial and at times widely-scattered abodes, it has not been granted to preserve for itself uninterruptedly a fruitful heritage of that sort. Under my great-grandfather, the lord of Kamenitz an der Linde, the last such attempt broke down—, and if to throw a person completely inward a series of heavy deprivations are indispensible, then among the griefs which forced upon me the construction of an inner world one of the greatest was my finding myself no longer established and rooted anywhere in the external.

Ruth's nature (of that I shall sometime be able to tell you privately) was from her earliest days of a strange unifiedness; somehow she was always concentrated in a zest and joy in what is given, tangible, real,—simply and immediately resolved to participate actively in it: how could it not move me deeply, dear Carl, that, in addition to all you are bringing her, you will be able to vouchsafe the dear girl that future as well in which her quiet and strong talents, all of which are those of the fruitful and visible life, may be applied and developed.

Your existence will be a simple, a country one, resting on all those associations which are the really reliable and constant ones of humanity. Even if it should happen that the duties of your profession later kept you temporarily in biggish or big cities, you will have time to create for yourselves a quiet and untorn foundation for your companionship in surroundings most deeply native and familiar to yourself: may Ruth's trusting and happy heart enhance your home to a possession that will now truly be quite immeasurable—, and may the fulfillment with which she is meeting in so manifold a way be rounded out to completeness, since she may now feel beneath her a strong and permanent ground which I was never able to give her and of which she had an anticipation in little Bredenau, receiving this late-acquired sense of home so joyfully and gratefully!

Clara, on her recent card, wrote me greetings from "all the Liebau people". I don't know who all are included in that friendly collective—in any case I beg you: distribute my solicitous and hearty response. Above all I am anxious to present my respectful regards to your mother, to whom you will probably show this letter anyway. What a kind and natural hospitality—I feel from all reports—you must have shown Clara and Ruth at Liebau! I am quite impatient, I can assure you, to have something similar conferred on me.—At present, to be sure, I must first do everything to fortify myself for a solitary (I hope highly industrious) winter here; no small matter to wrest this from the ancient tower of Muzot which for centuries has not been continuously inhabited. This vexation was so time-consuming too that I could not answer you sooner: hastily and briefly I did not want to do it! Goodbye, dear Carl.

Your Väterchen
Rainer Maria

[*166*]

To Frau Gertrud Ouckama Knoop   Château de Muzot sur Sierre
                                         Valais (Switzerland)
                                         November 26, 1921

. . . this Valais (how is it people do not mention it when they enumerate the most famous regions of the earth?) is an incomparable landscape. At first I did not yet truly grasp it because I was *comparing* it—with the most significant of my memories, with Spain, with Provence (to which in fact it bears a blood-relationship, through the Rhone), and only since I have been gazing at it in amazement entirely for its own sake has it revealed to me its great proportions and within these, recognizable little by little, the sweetest charm and the strongest and most ardent tradition. You remember the evenings when one sat as a child before bound periodicals in which travels were described, perhaps not well, but accompanied by alluring pictures, into which one read the whole significance of what it would someday be possible to experience, together with an almost melancholy impatience at being separated from it by so many years of awakening. Indeed, something much deeper may also have been at work in this abandoned gazing, the inexpressible fear that one might die before all this could be grasped and fulfilled. [And now] these very landscapes, with everything that one put into them, as it were, the very landscapes of those Sunday afternoons and winter evenings are being fulfilled here, think of it! Here are their bridges, their gateways, their beautiful, light roads that yet span the hills around which they are swung like silken ribbons, with here and there bits of rustic fencing to right or left, which the draughtsman gave in such interesting foreshortening, and which, just like the fountains, have remained unforgettable. The hills bear castles, and the very towns themselves can, from a certain distance, be gathered into something proud and stately: not just into a romantic concept, but into a reality beyond all dreams. Chapels, mission-crosses at all crossroads, slopes striped with the rows of the grapevines and later all curly with their foliage, fruit-trees, each with its tender shadow, and (right, oh so right!) single tall-grown poplars set out, exclamation marks of space that say: here!—; and not a figure, not a peasant-woman—dressed in local costume, naturally—that does not count as form in it all, as accent or measure; not a cart, not a mule, not a cat, but through its presence everything becomes more distant, open, airy again by far—; and this air in between things, this nowhere-being-empty of the world, how one senses it, even if one could not yet hear the carillon in it, the blessed carillon, which (berry for berry in one's ear!) somehow reminds one anew of the grapes!—Goethe came through the Valais, and I imagine there must be sketches of his, observantly sensitive drawings, in which he would have dedicated his attention to this complete presence of the individual object and how it still leads to the next and the next and on down to the farthest distant.

Perhaps my Muzot occurs—it really ought to—in one of those sketches, not as motif, but as a station on the way to the distance (descending stepwise into the valley), as an interval before the background that is so beautiful, so gentle, so atmospheric, quite without density, almost weightless—although a mountain!—

So much for the Valais. But all the time I have had in mind that what I *really* wanted to talk of was why I should find Munich not so useful. For were there a single person close to me, even a very circumspect and retiring person, I would not have been able to depict all this to you in this way. I would be showing it to him and translating it for him, this close friendly person—, and a little would be left over that I could put into form and communicate, but not much.—This (call it weakness if you must) makes it always more impossible for me to live in any place where I might become so fond of people that I give myself out to them too gladly and variously. The rivalry between intercourse and work became almost relentlessly clear to me during the war years—; before that I lived in Paris, where I saw, spread over the years, some eight people (and people who gave rather than received), the natural isolation (ah, and what provisioning at the same time!) of my inner domain. But now it is really true that I must be strict about my expenditures, for life is passing and some might think that the years which the war and post-war period more or less robbed me of should, according to my age and situation, have been my most responsible working years. (And they are empty! Alas, empty: more than full of horror and distress.) I really don't worry about it in this way. Time and age have grown always less essential to me. Heavens, when I think how the tide comes flowing over the boundaries of my childhood—, and can I say that my youth ever at any time came to an end? And even life and death! How open the roads are to us from one to the other,—how near, how near to the almost-knowing-it,—how nearly expressed in words, this something in which they suddenly become one (in a temporarily nameless unity). So this does not worry me, nor (if one only keeps the grace of giving) the manner of giving, whether to my neighbor, receptive beside me, or in my work—: the difference is perhaps not too distinct in the end. Nevertheless, intercourse with work is still somehow older in me, ineffable memories belong to it in my whole nature,—it stands on its rights and I have indeed to do nothing but yield to it. Now whether the "work" will thereby come to be realized or only the state of mind inwardly corresponding to it in intensity and purity—one would be as much as the other, and the staying alone in my old tower would, in either case, have been to some purpose. For much as the artist in one intends the *work*, its realization, its existence and its continuation on beyond ourselves—, one will not be really just until one understands that even this most urgent realization of a higher range of vision appears, from an at last ultimate view, only as a means of attaining something once more invisible, wholly of the inner world and perhaps not obvious—a more intact state in the center of one's own being. . . .

[*167*]

To Countess M. Château de Muzot sur Sierre, Valais
December 2, 1921

So this time it was *I* who couldn't write! . . .

But: it is the same with all of us: the destructive influences of recent years overtake us now at this place, now at that, just when we might have thought that at last, by a wide lead, we had eluded them: they are still there. And as, toward winter, one may discover in a clothes closet yet another article that the moths have eaten: so one keeps coming upon a new external or internal injury,—upon something or other that is endangered for which the fatalities of yesterday and day before yesterday are to blame. And it requires a very stable confidence indeed to believe in the mending or salvation of so much that is damaged or even to develop in oneself the certainty that most of what has been destroyed and corroded might be replaced by something new and better.— One has only to consider all the conflicts which quite other governing dimensions would have held in check, had not the convulsions of the time intervened with such frightful concurrence in all that bore within it the slightest tendency to decay. Now it would indeed be something wonderful if this opportunity for ruin, so to speak, that shook everything and put it to the test—, were to be followed by a stillness, as of that former famous flood! Un apaisement, un calme nouveau plus grand que jamais l'heureux moment du renouveau, l'aurore d'un commencement pur et universel.—But after so much shaking still to go on being shaken and to see ill-will and bewilderment at work almost everywhere, at a by no means renovated and purged work, but at those very same activities out of which came the boundless doom,—just that is the worst trial after so much evil. Had there been newspapers, that time, long ago, when the flood was ready to subside, as there are today, I am sure the waters would not have fallen, or at best artificially through the invention of an enormous pumping-machine, which, machines being what they are, would have revenged and repaid itself in some other thorough way for the assistance it had rendered human beings.

But all that, dear Countess, means for my special, in general small case only that at the time your letter came, everything had become uncertain for me, Muzot, even the possibility of remaining longer in Switzerland at all and, beyond that, the whither and everything else possible. Really everything. And the remainder of this persevering, equable, generous summer, that would have deserved to be accepted quite unconcernedly out of the fullness it daily offered, consumed itself for me in irksome worry and fore-worry about the months ahead, about the winter for which I thought positively I would have to create circumstances that, similar to those of the last, would be protective and favorable to my work and solitude. Finally, by a favorable providence, all could be saved at the eleventh hour, when a Swiss friend rented Muzot for me and one was able to go about energetically taming and persuading, as it were, the still somewhat unruly house, unaccustomed for centuries to continuous habitation. It isn't even ten days since what was achievable in this connection can be regarded as just about concluded, so that I am no longer exerting and busying myself *with* my house, but (so I hope at least) may begin to be busy *in* it in my—again very interrupted—way.

Over the summer I have seen people now and then; indeed, a close friend of mine even sacrificed herself to facilitate the furnishing and housekeeping of my refuge and as it were to get it going—, she accomplished wonders and worked hard: for on top of everything came the calamity that service was not to be obtained at any price,—and when finally an engagement was concluded and one had with much effort imported from Canton Solothurn what they call in Switzerland a "daughter", this aforesaid daughter turned out to be so inexperienced and unresourceful, that a long schooling and drilling was again necessary in order to acclimatize her to the situation here (which is, to be sure, new and in many ways onerous).

This second person without whom one cannot manage—: what a problem! Last year, in Berg, where simply everything suited me so incomparably, it was solved by a simple natural girl full of tact, decorum and adaptability—, but I knew at once that this was an exception. Had I the strength to isolate myself better, I would of course always prefer the help of an equal, an assistant, to any domestic service (which is really always a dubious business in present-day circumstances and to some extent a subterfuge: since, namely, through social enlightenment, there has been suppressed in people the instinct and the innocence to consider "serving" as blossoming and fecund a form of life as any other employment, if only it proceeds from a lively spirit.) But every equal, human or friendly relation based on help would require of me, being what I am, a degree of association that would promptly betray me again into unpredictable outgivings of the heart and lead almost unavoidably to a rivalry with work. Perhaps it is only in *these* years, where I have so much work and reflection left to catch up, that it is so dangerous for me, but it is becoming ever plainer to me how, truly, I have to decide between human intercourse and work, as if actually I had only just *one* thing to give, which will either communicate itself directly to those nearest me, or else remain preserved more lastingly and in a sense for more general use in the treasury of artistic creation. Other people working at art (so it seems at least) have stores aplenty for close and closest intercourse, yes, far from its consuming them, they increase by its means their assets and their inner span, which then on the other side benefit their artistic achievement. With me that has never been so,—but now there is more and more of a split into a crossroads, as if there were just one *single* thing in me that, in one way or another, after resolute decision, remained to be communicated, but that is not to be passed on in two different ways. And although, from a highest point of view, it might again be indifferent whether a person gave out his ultimate and essential in this way or in that: in the modestly continuing effect of a word to a friend, or, more demonstrable and visible afar, in something that through its transformation is lastingly built into surviving things: nevertheless my entire disposition and the course of my life drive me (certainly not out of vanity!) more toward this last form of expression and transmitting and somehow obligate me to it. But this ever new conflict that arises from such a vocation, and all this talk about the solitude one wants to safeguard and protect for oneself! In Paris it was there automatically and *without emphasis*—, and didn't have to be further justified and defended at all; everyone has it there who needs it, and even a well-known name (which did not indeed threaten one there!) is not necessarily a hindrance to being alone. (Wasn't Baudelaire alone! Wasn't Verlaine . . . ?)—How well moreover one manages for one's entire existence with a few, with five, six, perhaps nine actual experiences which, merely inflected, place themselves again and again in the center of one's heart. Thus I remember, as a young man, having gone through the most amazed embarrassment if I had secured myself an hour of solitude in my room by explaining, in face of the curiosity customary in families, for what *purpose* I needed that hour, what I was planning to do in it: *that* alone sufficed to render useless from the start the limited solitude I had won, to sell it out, so to say, in advance. The tone that had fallen upon this hour nullified its innocence, confiscated it, made it unfruitful, empty, and even before I entered my room my betrayal had anticipated me there and filled it to every corner with bankruptcy, secretlessness and desolation. (And it is something like that even today! Whether because it really *is* so, or because the suggestion of that early experience so strongly influences all that has come later and even today still overwhelms it!) From the standpoint of such experiences must one observe the existence of children, their disappointments and often so incommensurable distresses, of which, while they are happening to them, they still can give no account at all; so that what we now comprehend, retrospectively, could be registered at the time it was suffered only as misliking, misbehavior, as some sort of *mis-*, *mis-*, *mis-* . . .

Well, I still believe we have spared our children many such things or made them easier, quite without credit to ourselves in part, simply because certain facts that have emerged from psychological discoveries have, whether we happen to know it or not, become unconscious reality in us out of which we act far more than out of the principles and moralities that may still cling to us and that as parents, so to say, "for professional reasons" we believed we had to take over. . . .

[*168*]

To Xaver von Moos   Château de Muzot sur Sierre, Valais
                                       December 12, 1921

. . . I am inclined to speak first of your poems: to say so at once, I am surprised and pleased by them. . . . Believe me, it does not often happen that I see myself justified in approving something sent me like this by a younger man: the more pleasing is the exception, when once it may be granted. The happier does it make me, Verhaeren would have written! For happy he was whenever he found something, something that had succeeded; no one who was privileged to experience his grasping of a thing and being moved by it, will have forgotten it; where the mind and vigor of a young artist struck him as convincing he could rejoice over every line standing there clean and firm, and his approval was then unconditional, unshakable, he stood for it bodily, with all his mind, with his whole being. Measure by that *what* his belief, his approval could do for one! I had the good fortune to receive both in the years of our acquaintance; even though my language was a closed book to him and he could not really know any of my works, he *believed* in what I was doing and backed it up in me with his powerful personality. And I don't know but the thing most precious to me was that without any tangible proof, on the basis of what remained inexpressible between us, he had confidence in my work, that it was true, that it was necessary, and treated me accordingly from the first moment. I was indescribably fortified by this great friend and his belief in me bore the more fruit, as it was my lot not to experience masculine friendship until comparatively late. His friendship and Rodin's therefore infinitely touched and stirred me, and I myself would still be far from able to estimate how these two influences affected and stimulated me.

My admiration for Verhaeren was considerably older than our acquaintance,—his earlier books, especially the *Villes tentaculaires*, occupied me constantly in the first years of my (almost twelve-year) stay in Paris. The first of his books, which he came himself to give me, was the volume of *Multiple splendeur*, which I was at heart prepared to accept as out of the common. From then on we saw each other often and yet (since the relentless fact is there, of having to measure it against our loss) not nearly often enough. He lived outside of Paris, in St. Cloud, and only for a few months each winter: sometimes when his way into town had led him into my neighborhood, he unexpectedly (it suited me every time!) dropped in (and his glorious warmth of heart came sweeping over me): sometimes, following a sudden impulse, I (whose life in Paris was of the loneliest) drove out and pulled the old-fashioned bell-rope on the door of his cramped and yet ever friendly apartment. And what a guest one was, the moment one stepped over the threshold; how all traditions of being a guest awoke in one's mind; so large, so open, so complete was his reception that one became a great guest, guest from afar, utterly and entirely guest, guest of all guests, simply in order to keep the balance. . . .

[*169*]

To Robert Heinz Heygrodt
Château de Muzot
December 24, 1921

You have sent me (I received it yesterday) through our mutual friend Dr. Hünich a work that deals most exhaustively and painstakingly with my literary output. You have, so to speak, proved the words written about me in this book by the most thoroughgoing deed: so I will assure you at once that I am wanting neither in belief in your kindly disposition toward me nor in the readiest thanks to you.

Dr. Hünich will have told you that I cannot bring myself to read books and articles that deal with my work; I long held it for a weakness that I could not prevail upon myself to do so, and in part it may actually be nothing else. Meanwhile I have had since about 1907, through an important example (which I shall mention presently), a growing conviction that seems after all singularly to justify this consistent attitude of refusal. For I believe that as soon as an artist has once found the living center of his activity, nothing is so important for him as to remain in it and never to go further away from it (for it is also the center of his personality, his world) than up to the inside wall of what he is quietly and steadily giving forth; his place is *never*, not even for an instant, alongside the observer and judge. (At least not any more in an environment in which the visible everywhere degenerates into the ambiguous and temporary, into a prop, into a scaffolding for anything whatever.) And indeed it requires an almost acrobatic skill to leap from that observation-post back into the inner center again, neatly and unharmed (the distances are too great, the places themselves all to shaky for such an eminently inquisitive feat.) Most artists today use up their strength in this going back and forth, and not only do they expend themselves in it, they get themselves hopelessly entangled and lose a part of their essential innocence in the sin of having surprised their work from outside, tasted of it, shared in the enjoyment of it! The infinitely grand and moving thing about Cézanne (and I have now come to the "example" mentioned above) is that during almost forty years he remained uninterruptedly within his work, in the innermost center of it—, and I hope someday to show how the incredible freshness and purity of his pictures is due to this obstination: their surface is really like the flesh of a fruit just broken open—, while most painters already stand facing their own pictures enjoying and relishing them, violating them in the very process of the work as onlookers and recipients . . . (I hope, as I say, someday convincingly to point out this to me absolutely

definitive attitude of Cézanne's; it might act as advice and warning for anyone seriously determined to be an artist.)

So much for this first point. But there is another thing Dr.
Hünich will not have kept from you: how strongly I resist and
oppose all dragging forth and explaining of my so-called "early
period". In so far as you have started from this point I must dis-
agree with your presentation. Those unfortunately extant experiments cannot really be made use of *for anything*, they are not, in
any, any way the beginning of my work, far rather the most
private end of my childish and youthful helplessness. If I ever
have the pleasure of meeting you some day or of writing you in
more detail, I shall perhaps try to lay before you the reasons for
this situation, which are not only specifically Austrian but also
markedly dated as to time: I have no doubt that you will then be
inclined to agree with me.

Now I did leaf through just these pages about the "young
Rilke" a little bit last evening. Too bad. I remembered the re-
proach that Stefan George (about 1899, the only time we met, in
Florence) thought it well to impress upon me so explicitly: that
I had published too early. How very, very right he was! But even
this publishing . . . well, let us leave that for another time.—
Around page 30 of your book there are a lot of actually untrue
statements. Just as one would be wrong in working *Malte Laurids
Brigge* (as I warned Dr. Hünich) as a mine of biographical material, one should not translate those wretched little stories of
which you occasionally make use into a personal record. *No*, those
intérieurs did not reproduce the milieu of the boy René's surroundings!—Here, as was unavoidable, mistakes and wrong conclusions pile up, the accents are all over the wrong vowels. The
military school: its *enormous* significance, since it became the
early and sole occasion for the "turning around", the way inward even to the inmost center! In short, all the emphasis here
should have been different. But *how*, naturally, and *whence* to
draw the indications for it, since those impotent little products
were only mental pictures, little white lies for the purpose of as-

serting and sustaining oneself against those who were so entirely unable to help one to one's own self-assertion.

You understand, my dear Herr Heygrodt, that with all this *no* reproach is intended. If I were to read the things that deal with me in relation to my life, how many corrections would have to be made! But so far as your book is concerned I am quite sure that, aside from these incidental mistakes, it contains much insight, much understanding and above all much joy in the work as you did it. And that in itself should in any case win out.

Thank you! . . .

[*170*]

To Ilse Blumenthal-Weiss   Château de Muzot sur Sierre
                                             December 28, 1921

. . . So far as the influence of my books is concerned, surely you greatly overestimate its power and effect on you; no book, any more than a helpful word, can do anything decisive if the person concerned is not already prepared through quite invisible influences for a deeper receptivity and absorption, if his hour of self-communion has not come anyway. To move this hour into the center of one's consciousness some one thing suffices: sometimes a book or art-object, sometimes the glancing up of a child, the voice of a person or a bird, even, in certain circumstances, the sound of the wind, a cracking in the floor,—or, when we still used to sit before open fires (which from time to time I have done in my life), a gazing into the changing flames. All this and many slighter things, apparently accidental, can cause and confirm a finding of oneself or a finding-of-oneself-again (such as you are celebrating!). The poets—yes, now and again even they too may be among these good inducements . . . Not out of modesty, not at all, but because his indescribably penetrating art has meant so much to me through the years and has so often led me to collect my own inner faculties, I am inclined to believe that *Jacobsen* deserves much, much more credit for your delightful, happy experiences and progress. Give *him* the honor; and your dear child . . . and, if you absolutely insist, me too, but as one nameless among a hundred unnamable influences. Belief!—there is no such thing, I almost said. There is only—love. The forcing of the heart to hold this and that for true, which we commonly call belief, has no sense. First one has to find God somewhere, experience him as so infinitely, so utterly, so enormously present; then *whatever* one feels toward him—be it fear, be it astonishment, be it breathlessness, be it after all *love*—it hardly matters any more. But for belief, that compulsion to God, there is no room where one has begun with the discovery of God, in which there is then no stopping any more, at whatever point one may have begun.—And you, as a Jewess, with so much most spontaneous experience of God, with such ancient fear of God in your blood, should not have to bother about a "belief". But simply *feel* his presence in yours: and where He, Jehovah, wanted to be *feared*—it was after all only because in many instances there was no other means of contact between man and God except just fear. And fear before God is only, so to speak, the *rind* of a condition, the inside of which does *not* taste of fear, but can ripen to the most ineffable namelessness and sweetness for him who loses himself within it.—You have, do not forget, one of the greatest gods of the universe in your descent, a God to whom one cannot just be converted at any time as to that Christian God, but a God to whom one *belongs*, through one's people, because from time immemorial he made one and formed one in one's forefathers, so that every Jew has been established in Him (and in the one whom none may dare to name), ineradicably planted in Him, with the root of his tongue!

I have an indescribable confidence in those peoples that have *not* come to God through belief but have experienced God through their own race, in their own stock. Like the Jews, the Arabs, to a certain degree the orthodox Russians—and then, in another way, the peoples of the East and of ancient Mexico. To them God is origin, and therefore future as well. To the others he is something deduced, something away from which and toward which they strive as really strangers or as people who have grown estranged—and so they are always needing the intercessor, the mediator, him who translates their blood, the idiom of their blood into the language of the godhead. What *these* people achieve then is indeed "belief"; they must conquer and train themselves to hold for true that which *is* a true thing for the God-descended, and for this reason their religions slip so easily into the ethical,—whereas a God originally experienced does not separate and distinguish good and evil in relation to men but for his own sake, passionately concerned over their being-near-to-him, over their holding- and belonging-to-him and over nothing else! Religion is something infinitely simple, ingenuous. It is not knowledge, not content of feeling (for all content is admitted from the start, where a man comes to terms with life), it is not duty and not renunciation, it is not restriction: but in the infinite extent of the universe it is a direction of the heart. However a man may proceed, wandering to right or to left, and stumble and fall and get up, and do wrong here and suffer wrong there, and here be mistreated and over there himself miswish and mistreat and misunderstand: all this passes into the great religions and upholds and enriches in them the God that is their center. Even the man who lives on the last periphery of such a circle *belongs* to this mighty center, though he may but once, perhaps in dying, have turned his face to it. The Arab's turning to the East at certain hours and casting himself down, that *is* religion. It is hardly "belief". It has no opposite. It is a natural being-set-in-motion inside an existence through which God's wind sweeps three times daily, since this at least we are: pliant.

I think *you* must understand and feel *how* I mean this,—and so may it somehow enter into the calm and open frame of mind you call your convalescence, and there work on to your security and joy!

[171]

To Frau Amann-Volkart   Château de Muzot sur Sierre (Valais)

What a kind idea that was of yours, to present to me so comprehensively and clearly the elements of "catkinology" in your parcel and the supplementary letter; after this there is no need of further or more precise information: I am convinced! So there are no "hanging" pussywillows (strange to say), and even if there were some rare tropical exception, I couldn't use it anyway. The poem passage I wanted to check for factual correctness stands and falls by the reader's grasping and understanding, on his *first* feeling, just this *falling* of the catkin, otherwise the image used there loses all sense. So the absolutely *typical* phenomenon of this inflorescence must be evoked—, and it also became clear to me at once, from the very informative illustrations of your little book, that the bush which, years ago, conveyed to me the impression now used in my work must have been a hazelnut; whose twigs are provided most thickly, *before* the appearance of its leaves, with long, perpendicularly hanging catkins. So I know what I needed to know and have substituted "hazel" for "willow" in the text.

But to you, dear kind lady, I am indebted for this certainty and the helpful surprise whereby it was so unexpectedly brought me. I will fetch various other useful bits of instruction from this little volume, then—in a few days—it will go back to you. . . .

[172]

To Lou Andreas-Salomé   Château de Muzot sur Sierre
                                 Valais, Switzerland
                                 December 29, 1921

. . . Well, it has just been possible to arrange that I am to sit in my strong little tower until further notice; I am really only just beginning to turn its protection, its silence to account, and wish for nothing but a good spell of seclusion and that it may be long and uninterrupted.

Though one cannot escape a certain sense of immobility, still one feels the wholesomeness of neutral territory very much here and added to that this magnificent landscape (reminding me of Spain and Provence). I have done everything to hold myself in it; and in reinforcing this effort the old masonry walls within which I sit have been not unessential. . . .

But above all the quiet winter must first have come and gone. If I am allowed a long and uninterrupted one, I hope to get a little further than last year in Berg,—if not to catch up with myself altogether, still *so* far that I can see myself walking on ahead of myself with space enough between to fetch longer breaths. The interruptions of the war years have left me with an incredible difficulty in concentrating, so that I cannot manage to get through without the support of this most literal being alone. More than ever, every communication becomes for me a rival to my work, which probably comes to be the case with everyone who more and more has in mind only *one thing* and thus in giving, whether to himself or to the world, gives out *this* same one thing. A few days ago I was offered a dog; you can imagine what a temptation that was, especially as the lonely situation of the house makes the presence of a watchdog quite advisable. But I felt at once that even this would result in much too much relationship, through my interest in such a housemate; everything alive, that makes *demands*, hits upon an infinite desire in me to fall in with it, from the consequences of which I must then painfully disengage myself again when I realize that they are using me up completely.

Are you in Vienna, dear Lou? then greetings to Freud—: I see with pleasure how his work is now beginning to have an important effect in France which has so long turned a deaf ear. Not much reaches me thence, save now and then a word from Gide; only the poetry of Paul Valéry really astonishes me, whose "Le Cimetière marin" I managed to translate with an equivalence I scarcely thought could be achieved between the two languages. When I am a little more certain in my own work, I hope to have a try at his prose too; there is a glorious dialogue, "Eupalinos"—, like all Valéry's few works of a serenity, a calm and equanimity of language that you too would entirely appreciate. Paul Valéry stems from Mallarmé; about twenty-five years ago a remarkable article appeared (L'Introduction à la méthode de Léonard de Vinci), which he has now—1919—published with an extraordinarily beautiful introduction; but starting from Mallarmé meant with the next half step landing in silence, dans un silence d'Art très pur, and so it was too: Valéry kept silent and worked at mathematics. Only recently, during the war, 1915 or 1916, did the need for artistic expression arise again, so much the purer, in the man of fifty: and what has since come from him is of the greatest distinction and significance. . . .

I think of you a great deal, it is the time between the two Christmases, the first and the Russian . . . That you *could* get news from there: it almost seems incredible that the one over there is still alive and can still communicate itself to us here. . . .

P.S. A brood of little ladybugs is wintering with me (which might somehow have happened in Schmargendorf too); one, a particularly successful one—they don't all turn out equally well in this parlor-winter—has just wandered across the paper: take it for a good omen!

[*173*]

To Xaver von Moos   Château de Muzot sur Sierre, Valais
December 30, 1921

. . . No, I am not in the least disappointed that you "extremely seldom" write down any poetry and do not give yourself over to hopes of achieving something final and perfect in this field. On the contrary, I am glad to see this restraint in you at a time when the barriers against the realm of artistic achievement have almost all been torn and trodden down by those who want to have everything in common. The taking up of some other definite particular profession (to which will you want to belong?) will surely not prevent you (in whom the tools of constructive language seem already assured and prepared) from confidently producing, when the hour has come, something responsible and necessary. I would like to emphasize that my confidence in you in this respect is extraordinarily sure. And of course you have examples enough, if you needed any, of there being no harm in performing, in a subsidiary office, this, the most glorious high mass of the soul: think of Mallarmé—, or, what lies much closer, of your great Spitteler, whose most enduring poems, if I am not mistaken, were written at a time when he was still far from putting all his energy into this powerful service. And Paul Valéry, who was altogether silent for something like twenty years and, I believe, worked at mathematics, besides carrying on some civil-service job as well,—does he perhaps not owe the repose and finality of his poetic word to this long-suffering abstention?

When my father in his day expected me to carry on as an avocation (alongside the profession of officer or of lawyer) the art to which I felt myself destined, I did indeed rebel most violently and persistently, but that was entirely because of our Austrian conditions and the rather narrow milieu in which I grew up; to put through, with divided energy, anything artistically true and distinctive in such a milieu, with its furthermore so close proximity to the artistic dilutions of the '80s of the last century, would have been entirely unthinkable—, indeed, I had, in order to begin at all, to free myself completely from the conditions of family and home; belonging to those who, only later, in homes of their own choosing, could test the strength and bearing capacity of their blood. Since then so much has changed. Much pioneer work has been done, art has been freed, there was air and room enough (at least before the war) for everyone who inwardly needed them . . . And as I myself have time and again regretted not being in a daily profession which, independent of the currents of grace, can always be carried on, simply, every day, so I would also advise every young person at least to live his way far into tasks of that sort before wholly identifying his existence with the relentless demands of being an artist. . . .

To Ellen Delp   Château de Muzot sur Sierre/Valais
                                            January 4, 1922 (evening)

You will have thought of your letter reaching me on the first
day of the new year (for that matter, along with a mail so big, and
so little superficial, that it was almost too much, all at once: nevertheless it had its place and called forth its special joy here, out of
which I want to thank you at once).

To thank you for complying with, as you write, my "great
desire" . . . yes, but *did* you really?—Into this everyday you
were to describe you continually let in so much space, space and
interspace, sky-space, world-space and all the spaces of the most
open upward glance, that your person contracted in the midst of
them to the tiniest little figure: I was hoping for an interieur, but,
scarcely there, you began mentioning organ. . . and violin, . . .
and again aroused something limitless, merely to vanish quickly in
it. Only in the garden I thought for a moment to catch sight of
you, but you were already surrounded, already covered up from
me by the twenty young creatures and their "distracted" raking.

Well, well. I too, if I could show you how, *how* small I have
been standing here for years, beside what I have in mind or what
has been set for me: I too am immediately covered up by it, the
more so as what wants to be done should have been done back in
1914—, now it has not, to be sure, become bigger, since even then
it was full-grown and really incommensurable—, but the bad
years have rolled me like a pebble into their breakers and have
almost ground away my heart, so that now it stands there, dis-
proportionately diminished, beside its (from eternity) greatest
task.

To translate the magnificent sonnets of Michelangelo, really to
transform them into German, I planned already some years ago,
in protest against the existing translations which are full of inadequacies, a game of childish versifying, with exception of those
few in which Hermann Grimm proved his quiet mastery. No,
naturally, I am *not* expressing anything of my own in them when

I give them to my language to hold; (who am I, that I should be permitted *that*). Also they are not even testimonials of Michelangelo's whole existence; consider what a side occupation they were, and what kind of a work rose beside them into the colossal (now and then they are like a rough sketch of his fatalities,—and perhaps of the fatalities of artistic production itself!) Take them as this, keep them far away from me: it is not with *my* fatalities that they deal. And if I attempted to arrange mine in sonnets, it would be sad: for I would have no other work beside me that would surpass such an undertaking—, even where it justified it.

Yes, things were such that I felt you *very* much in those days: not exactly the most on the tenth, while I was writing: rather a few days previously and soon afterwards—(on the twelfth? I've forgotten now). But in that corner, in which you might have come to me, I intentionally was *not;* I have never heard anyone speak even one verse of mine (with one exception, to be exact: at Hofmannsthal's wish, Lia Rosen, once years ago, recited the poem *The Blind Woman* for me); don't like it: as long as I live I shall know how to do it better and don't want to be disturbed. Indeed, it was wrong of them to place older things (for unity's sake) at the end, especially in my case where almost all that is older, with exception of the Book of Hours, is weak. No, no one can, offhand, mold something whole, round, out of anybody, how then out of me who am just beginning to move, who still have so far to go . . .

And so now you are having winter, you gardener, and are caught. And have, I see, moved into a new prison. Make it wide for yourself in there. Touch something glorious.

[*175*]

To Frau Gertrud Ouckama Knoop   [January ?, 1922]

What shall I say?—Little as you were able recently, after copying those notes, to write me anything besides, so little am I myself now able to communicate myself to you as long as I am still the reader of those pages, bent over them, always, despite all looking up. I had had no idea of all that, I scarcely knew any particulars of the beginnings of that sickness—, and now all at once it was the introduction into something so manifoldly moving, affecting, overwhelming to me. If one were to read this, and it concerned any young girl one hadn't known, it would already be close enough. And now it is Vera, whose dark, strangely concentrated charm is so inexpressibly unforgettable and so fabulously evocable that, at the moment of writing this, I would fear to shut my eyes lest I suddenly feel it quite surpass me, in my hereness and presence.

How much, how much, how much she *was* all that, *that* to which these memories of her suffering bear so deep and irrevocable a witness,—and isn't it true? how wonderful, how unique, how incomparable a human being is! Here there came into being, now that everything was allowed to consume itself, suddenly, which otherwise might have lasted for a long being-here (where?), here there came into being this excess of light in the heart of the girl, and in it became visible, so infinitely illumined, the two extreme limits of her pure intuition: *this*, that suffering is an error, an obscure misunderstanding arising from the physical that drives its wedge, its stony wedge, into the unity between heaven and the earth—, and on the other hand this united oneness of her heart, open to everything, *with* this unity of the existing and enduring world, this assent to life, this—joyous, deeply moved, capable of the ultimate—belonging in the here-and-now—ah, in the here-and-now only? No (which she could not know in these first attacks of break-off and parting!) —into the *whole*, into a much more than here-and-now. Oh how, how she loved, how she reached out with the antennae of her heart beyond all that is graspable and encompassable here—, in those sweet hovering pauses in pain which, full of the dream of recovery, were still vouchsafed her. . .

It seems, dear friend, that fate has set store upon leading you out beyond the common bourn, each time as it were on an overhanging crag of life, to the ravine of death and with heart laid ever barer. Now you are living and looking on and feeling out of infinite experience—.

But for me . . . it has been like an enormous obligation to what in me is innermost and most earnest and (though I attain it only from afar) most blissful, that on the first evening of a new year I was permitted to take these pages into my possession.

[*176*]

To Ilse Blumenthal-Weiss   Château de Muzot sur Sierre
                                              January 25, 1922

There are two of your kind and always beautiful letters to acknowledge; but I am limiting myself from the outset to this page because now a letter-fasting-time, in all strictness, has really begun for me in which, perhaps for several months, I may allow myself only the most urgent exceptions, concentrated into briefest form.

Let the first thing this time be my wish that your indisposition with all its unpleasantnesses may meantime have been overcome; but, with presence of mind, you have won from it something good too in the way of quiet and remaining inwardly occupied, to which *The Notebooks of Malte Laurids Brigge* became an incentive to you: I thank you for the intense sympathy you felt for those pages whose genesis lies far behind me now (as, for that matter, that of all my publications). In so far as what is my own and most my own went into it, it experienced endless transformations and translations; that we should heighten it to the most accessible degree of a certain validity, for that purpose life and destiny are peculiarly entrusted to us artistic workers; if this heightening succeeds, then what actually happened is superseded and no longer worth discussing. And for that matter, even in the experiencing itself, where is the boundary to what is one's own?

He who trains his senses to the purest and most inward participation in the world, *what*, in the end, will he not have been?

Isn't it best and richest to see it thus?

I obey the page which dictates my closing and make use of its little, last space for many good wishes for you.

[177]

To Alwine von Keller   Château de Muzot sur Sierre (Valais),
Suisse
January 26, 1922

Eva Cassirer, our dear mutual friend, admonishes me to send *you* the answer to the letter I just received from her, which I do the more gladly as—since the good lines you wrote me a year ago—your name has been marked on my list; after all, contrary to the prospect and hope of that time, I have never been permitted to thank you personally for so lovely an attention.

Eva Cassirer's letter, you are acquainted with it, engrossed me exceedingly,—I would gladly consider it, but, it can't be helped, I must anticipate in myself the "No" which would have to form the conclusion of all my deliberations.

The experiment she spontaneously proposes is confronted, fairly insurmountably, with practical difficulties—; but it isn't this alone. In this case particularly it would not do to draw close to one the life of a hard-pressed young person, without turning attentiveness and sympathy to his conflicts, indeed, being there outright for them. My nature, even *against* my will, would take *this* attitude; but I may not expose it to the danger of *thus* employing itself at a time when I have set myself inner tasks, for which the least diversion outward would be so hindering that I have had to take upon myself the most rigid solitude; I am living separated from people, whom I neglect with a heavy heart—, that may excuse me if I forbid myself to exercise any influence now of a personal kind, even the most spontaneous—, the bounds of which I would be all too inclined to overstep in the case of a sympathetic young person suffering from himself.

Now that is not to say that this glance into the destiny of young F.H. will not occupy me beyond the moment. Life-weariness, at his age, is indeed only the negative of a great prizing of life which has been so constantly disappointed that his attention has finally remained fastened to the hollow form, because the forces were hemmed in that should have attempted the "cast" of this negative.

Also one is never closer to a "turning" than when existence, even into its smallest and most ordinary aspects, passes for "unbearable"—, just then to wait a while longer should be a task of—curiosity at least.—How much that is beautiful must already have fallen to the lot of this young person for the conviction to become so passionate in him of not having sufficed, that is of having "spoiled" it. Please, help him, dear lady, to see how great is the innocence of the heart and that it is not at all in our power so to disfigure its nature that continually new purity would not spring from it!

Only this today, to be quick; may you find a happy way out—and come to me sometime with report of something confident.

[*178*]

To Lotti von Wedel   Château de Muzot sur Sierre/Valais
                              January 28, 1922

Yes, now, as you say, many a letter will be laid aside that the propitious solitude of Muzot may more and more stand the test even in the sphere of writing—, but yours brings me tidings too friendly, too deeply concerning me, for me to postpone writing you at least a provisional word of thanks.

Chiefly I rejoice in your so strong establishment in a joyous and active situation and promise myself good things from all that will gradually come out of it. Nothing is more gladdening than when one can really put oneself to use again, be it for the benefit of plans or of memories; finest of all, when both work together and joy and freedom arise to carry on the one in the other.—*I* am far from this good turning, still; to "liquidate", so to speak, the obstructions of the war years, to loosen stone by stone from the ring of wall that seemed to separate me as much from what was past as from everything that might yet have come, is still my modest occupation, I don't know for how long; but since after all, for people like us, nothing is really as necessary as patience, even *this* excuse for learning it better cannot but be acceptable to me!

Enough: you tell of the Torre de las Danas—and at once my attention was caught,—and though I have promised myself not even to consider any travel plans before the termination of certain labors,—yet I threw myself with delight over into something beyond what comes next, in the generosity of which a fulfillment of that sort might take place. "Spring 1923" I wrote as the date over my future Granada,—otherwise I could scarcely have endured reading your descriptions. So, I shall then place myself very much in your counsel and under your protection, in order to penetrate there into the "most inaccessible"! *How* you must have lived and taken in all that!

Of the Schack versions I have not the best memory; (in any case I have never opened them again since my student days). If I leave out of consideration the West-East Divan (which absolutely lifted the *happiness* of Oriental discoveries over into the German), my first idea of the Arabian poem is based on those verses which Mardrus copiously inserted into his text of the Arabian Nights. Rodin came over to me sometimes, with the opened book, for the sake of four or six such lines, to let me participate right away in their just having flowered for him; what radiance, blossom or eye or mouth . . . each single poem, no longer than a medical prescription! When later in Tunis and Egypt, I made such rapid progress in the reading of Arabic, alas, *seemed* to make . . . , then there sprang up in me the hope of perhaps one day contributing something of my own to the comprehension and transshaping of such verses . . .

Moreover at that time I had the same experience that you indicate; on the trip back from Egypt, entering my so beloved "Museo" at Naples—: nothing stood up against the pictures by which my memory had been not alone filled, but also broadened in all its dimensions. That magnificent queen. I cannot prevail upon myself to enclose the photographs right off again today; it seems certain to me that I may keep them a few weeks. If not, you will call them back, won't you! What a moment of windlessness was that in the great Egyptian period! What god held his breath, for the people around the fourth Amenophis thus to come to themselves? Whence, suddenly, did they originate? And how, right behind them, did time close again which had granted room for someone "to be",—had "left space for it"?!

Enough! the page dictates it. Warm and grateful remembrances . . .

[*179*]

To Gertrud Ouckama Knoop   Château de Muzot s/Sierre,
                                Valais, Switzerland
                                February 7, 1922

In a few days of spontaneous emotion, when I actually intended to take up some other work, these sonnets were given to me.

You will understand at first glance why it is that you must be the first to possess them. For, undefined as the relation is (only a single sonnet, the next to last, XXIVth, calls Vera's own figure in to this excitation dedicated to her), it dominates and moves the course of the whole and penetrated more and more—although so secretly that I recognized it only gradually—this irresistible creation that so staggered me.

Take them kindly into your hallowed memories.

Were one to let "the Sonnets to Orpheus" reach the public, probably two or three, which, as I now already see, presumably just served the current as conduits (as for example the XXIst) and remained empty after its passage, would be replaced by others. Then we should also discuss in what form you want the name to stand (in the subtitle). In my first draft here too, until your closer agreement, I have just: V.O.K.

[*180*]

To Princess Marie von Thurn
  und Taxis-Hohenlohe

Château de Muzot sur Sierre
(Valais) Switzerland
February 11 [1922], evening

At last,
          Princess,
at last, the blessed, *how* blessed day when—as far as I can see—
I can announce to you

the end
of the Elegies:
Ten!

From the last, the big one (to the opening, begun once upon a
time in Duino: "Someday, emerging at last from this terrifying
vision/may I burst into jubilant praise to assenting angels . . .")
from this last one, which was also meant, even then, to be the
last,—from this—my hand is still trembling! Just now, Saturday,
the eleventh, at six o'clock in the evening, it is finished!—

All in a few days, it was a nameless storm, a hurricane in the
spirit (like that time at Duino), all that was fiber in me and fabric
cracked—eating was not to be thought of, God knows who fed
me.

But now *it is*. Is. Is,
Amen.

So I have survived up to this, right through everything. Through
everything. And just this was what was needed. *Only* this.

One, I have dedicated to Kassner. The whole is yours, Princess,
how could it help being! Will be called:

The Duino Elegies

In the book (for I cannot give you what has belonged to you from
the beginning) there will be no dedication, I think, but rather:

The property of . . .

And now, thanks for your letter and all its communications; I
was anxiously awaiting it.

Of me, only this today, don't you think? . . . It is indeed, at last, "something"!

Farewell, dearest Princess.—

Your

D.S.

Just now, a kind letter from Princess Öttingen. Please, commend me to her. I shall write soon.—All my best to the Prince, Kassner,—etc.

P.S. Please, dear Princess, do not consider it a subterfuge of my laziness when I tell you why I am *not* copying down and sending you the new elegies now: I would be jealous of your reading them. I feel as if it should be *I*, absolutely, who first reads them to you. When? Well, let us hope, soon.—D.S.

[*181*]

To Lou Andreas-Salomé   Château de Muzot sur Sierre
                                 (Valais), Switzerland
                                 February 11 [1922] (evening)

Lou, dear Lou, so now:

at this moment, this, Saturday, the eleventh of February, at 6, I am laying aside my pen after the last completed *Elegy*, the tenth. The one (even then it was destined to become the last) to the beginning already written in Duino: "Someday, emerging at last from this terrifying vision/may I burst into jubilant praise to assenting angels . . ." As much as there was of it I read to you, but only just the first twelve lines have remained, all the rest is new and: yes, very, very, very glorious!—Think! I have been allowed to survive up to this. Through everything. Miracle. Grace.—All in a few days. It was a hurricane, as at Duino that time: all that was fiber, fabric in me, framework, cracked and bent. Eating was not to be thought of.

And imagine, something *more,* in another context, just previously (in the "Sonnets to Orpheus", twenty-five sonnets, written, suddenly, in the fore-storm, as a memorial for Vera Knoop)

I wrote, *made, the horse*, you know, the free happy white horse with the hobble on its foot that once, at the approach of evening, came galloping toward us on a Volga meadow—:

how

I made him as an "ex voto" for Orpheus!—What is time?—*When* is present? Across so many years he sprang, with his utter happiness, into my wide-open feeling.

So it was, one after the other.

Now I *know* myself again. It really had been like a mutilation of my heart that the Elegies were not—here.

They are, they are.

I went out and stroked, as if it were a great old beast, the little Muzot that had sheltered all this for me, that had, at last, *vouchsafed* it to me.

That is why I did not write in answer to your letter, because all the time in these weeks, without knowing toward what, I was keeping silent toward *this*, with heart taken farther and farther inward. And now, today, dear Lou, only this. You had to learn of it at once. And your husband too. And Баба—, and the whole house even down into the good old sandals!

Your old Rainer

P.S. Dear Lou, my little pages, these two, breathlessly written last night couldn't go off, registered, today (Sunday), so I took advantage of the time to copy off for you *three* of the completed Elegies (the sixth, eighth and tenth). The other three I shall then write in the course of days, and send them soon. To me it will be so good when *you* have them. And besides it puts my mind at ease if they exist somewhere else too, outside, in accurate copies, safely preserved.

But now I must for a moment into the air, as long as there is still Sunday sun in it.

Прощай

[*182*]

To Lou Andreas-Salomé   Château de Muzot sur Sierre
                                           (Valais), Switzerland
                                           Sunday [February 20, 1922]

That you are there, dear, dear Lou! to confirm it so joyously into my innermost heart!—In reading your good, knowing letter: how it came over me once again, this certainty from all sides, that now it is *here*, HERE, that which had arisen so long ago, as if it had always been!

I had in mind to copy off the other three elegies for you today since it has already got round to Sunday again! But now, just think, in a radiant after-storm, another elegy has been added, that of the "Saltimbanques". It rounds out the whole most wonderfully, only now does the cycle of Elegies seem to me really closed. It is not added on as the eleventh, but will be inserted (as fifth) before the "Hero-Elegy". Besides, the piece that has hitherto stood there seemed to me, through its different sort of structure, to be unjustified at that place, though as a poem beautiful. This will replace it (and how!), and the supplanted poem will come under the heading of "Fragmentary Pieces" which, as a second part of the book of Elegies, will contain all that is contemporaneous with them, what time, so to speak, demolished before it was brought forth or has so cut off in its development that it displays broken surfaces.—And so now the "Saltimbanques" too are here which actually, even from the very first Paris time, concerned me so absolutely and have ever since been a task to me.

But not enough with that, scarcely was this elegy on paper before the "Sonnets to Orpheus" continued too; today I am arranging this new group (as their second part)—and have also quickly copied off (kept!) for you a few that seem to me the most beautiful. All out of these days and still quite warm. Only our Russian white horse (how he greets you, Lou!) is from the earlier first part, from the beginning of this month.

And with that, finis, for today. I must catch up on letters several of which have accumulated for answering.

I well know that there can be a "reaction"—, after being thrown like this, the falling somewhere; but I am after all falling into the spring which is already nearer here, and then: since I was permitted the patience, the long patience, for what has now been reached—, why shouldn't I be able to manage a little side-patience through baddish days; and finally, gratitude (of which I never had so much) should outweigh in them too everything depressing and confusing!

Thanks for having written me at once in spite of all your work!

Your old Rainer

Elegies 5, 7, 9—: soon!

[183]

To Xaver von Moos   Château de Muzot sur Sierre/Valais
March 2, 1922

. . . As regards the mountains, yes, you are right in being surprised to see me established among them rather than in one of the plains that are inherently more congenial to me; mountains are in fact contrary to my nature, their great conception I formed for myself late, actually only in the presence of the Tel-Atlas at the rim of the desert—: for me the first mountain range that, in its order and sublimity, I "saw into". The Pyrenees also, to be sure, had already been a preliminary step for my insight—, and through them precisely, through Provence and through Spain (countries that have been of great influence on the works just now occupying me) I somehow made the connection again with the wonderful features of the Wallis. It is not its mountains that convince me, but rather the remarkable circumstance that (whether through their configuration or perhaps their special distribution) they are space-creating: as a Rodin sculpture carries within it and sheds about itself a peculiar spaciousness: that is how—to my eye—the mountains and hills in these regions of the Valais comport themselves; space emanates from and between them inexhaustibly, so that this valleyland of the Rhone is anything but confined—, so utterly different from those valleys in

Graubünden (for example, often so picturesque, but so confining to the emotions).—One of my friends with whom, on a particularly broad radiant afternoon in the fall, I strolled toward Loèche-Ville, doubtless meant this, this creativity in space, when looking back he cried out: Ça sort de la création; at all events:— as I experience it, the Wallis seems to me not only one of the most glorious landscapes I have ever seen,—but also capable in grandiose fashion of offering manifold equivalents and correspondences to the expression of our inner world; its never having become the matter for a great painter's unfolding—, actually it has not summoned a poet either—in our sense—to deeper perception: at most one might think of young Louis de Courten, but he is one of those who were interrupted by an early violent death without the presentiment of such a fate having, beyond their years, essentially enhanced and concentrated their achievement. . . .

[184]

To Rudolf Bodländer   Château de Muzot sur Sierre, Valais
                                        (Switzerland),
                                   March 13, 1922

. . . First of all, let me say that I am not to blame for the lateness of this answer. I received your letter yesterday, Sunday, March 12, exactly a month after it was written. The Insel-Verlag, that is, forwards mail arriving for me at its address only in occasional batches and this time had no need to hurry as I was known to be in work and hence averse to all correspondence in general. If, accordingly, I cannot blame them, the most poignant reproach would come up in me against myself were I now to let anything stand in the way of the answer you have been awaiting for weeks—, and to postpone which would also be unnatural to me just because what you write interests me down to the very heart.

Now it is of course another matter whether I might be capable of finding in an after all short letter an answer that will not leave your expectation empty. Also whether such few (and in part counseling) words can really reach you, friend and brother, depends above all upon the passableness and safety of the bridge laid down between us. Now concerning this bridge, I really think I may rely on its full bearing capacity, for the moving words of relation you wrote me are so full of proof and evidence, your familiarity with my works becomes so purely manifest in them, that I think even a letter page, rapid and fragmentary as it is, could not but be received with a certain precision into the contexts you have experienced and prepared. So I will try, with most understanding attention, to speak to you, my friend, concerning the conflict you indicate rather than actually set forth. But I grasp it, I believe, at its center. You call it the discord between "spiritual and worldly duty".

When I now think of myself in my youth, it was for me absolutely a case of *having* to go away at the risk of annoying and hurting. I cannot describe to you our Austrian circumstances of the time which (if one counts in the disastrous falsity and bewilderment of the eighties besides) must have been so hopeless and defunct in themselves that my instinct told me it was utterly impossible, starting from them, for even the most striving strength to grow into, grow out into what life apparently intended for me. Add to this that in the midst of these impossibilities (where almost everything that can be purely experienced seemed barred by subterfuge and prejudice) I was from my tenth year committed to a definite career (that of an Austrian officer);—small as I was, placed on a slippery life track on which every movement caused me to slide ever farther and faster away from that which corresponded to my as yet inarticulate bent and its obscure purposes—, then you will understand that only by the most antagonistic, rebellious deviation was I able to take possession of my blood and spirit.

What I write as an artist will probably to the end exhibit somewhere the traces of the opposition by means of which I set myself upon my own course,—and yet, if you ask me, I would not want it to be *this* which emanated above all from these works: not the challenge to any revolt and liberation, not the deserting of what surrounds and claims them would I wish that young people should deduce from these writings; but rather that they should bear in a new conciliatory spirit with what is given, offered, under certain circumstances necessary, withdrawing from it, not outward, but into greater depth, not so much resisting the pressure of circumstances as exploiting it, in order to become embedded through it in a more compact, deeper, more individual stratum of their own natures.

If today I speak thus and hence advocate rather an acceptance, getting along with, and enduring (which I myself did not achieve)—, this is not (here I am searching myself sternly) the laxity of an older man,—but rather the times have in fact become different; between that most difficult decade of my childhood and the attitude of today (even at its worst) there is a difference scarcely to be evaluated with temporal measures; though the gulf between father and son even now may still be torn open anew every day, certain understandings have become possible across it, indeed so normal that one no longer counts them. And this above all: the young person himself is far from being left alone and forsaken in that sense in which we were in all crucial difficulties: the mere being of the same age has taken on a special meaning and reliability (since 1913 I have held in honor the book of one who died young,—Henry Franck, *La Danse devant l'Arche*—in which for the first time this experience appeared celebrated in the most intense rhythms),—and I believe I do not deceive myself in thinking that, were I young *now*, I would be living upward in richest linkings, swept along by those of my own age, sharing most of their enthusiasms and initiated, from my own mood, into their distresses.

That "taking life heavily" with which my books are filled—, is no heavy-heartedness, dear friend (and this "frightful" and that "consoling" which you, so movingly to me, have acknowledged, will draw ever closer together in these books until finally it will be *one* in them, their sole essential content)—this taking heavily means nothing, does it, but a taking according to true weight, hence according to truth; an attempt to weigh things by the carat of the heart, instead of by suspicion, happiness or chance.

No denial, is it?! no *denial;* oh, on the contrary, how much infinite assent and still more assent to existence!

But now one thing more remains to be considered and said. You do not let me know *what* is demanded of you on the part of your family after final graduation, what profession, what occupation; the, as you say, "only work", the struggle in the direction toward God need not necessarily suffer or wither in the course of an apparently different, more superficial application of one's powers. Do not forget that, for example, in times when manual work was still warm with life, almost all its rhythms and repetitions were able to intensify God in those simple hearts; yes, the one incomparable privilege of man perhaps shows most fundamentally there where he succeeds in introducing into something unassuming, lowly, the hidden grandeur of his inner relations. It has perilously increased the host of perplexities that make difficult for us the reviewing and classifying of the present that the calls of art have so often been understood as calls *to* art. Thus the manifestations of artistic activity—poems, pictures, sculpture and the floating configurations of music—instead of directing their action into life, have called more and more coming young people away from it. This misunderstanding withdraws from life many elements pertaining to it, and the realm of art, in which after all only a few great individuals in the end remain justified, is overfilled with the misled and the fugitive. Nothing does a poem mean less than to arouse in the reader the potential poet . . . , and the completed picture says rather: see, you must not paint; I am already here!

So on *this*, friend and brother, we should, to conclude, come to an exact agreement: that art does not ultimately intend to produce more artists. It does not mean to call anyone over to it, indeed, it has always been my guess that it is not concerned at all with any effect. But while its creations, having issued irrepressibly from an exhaustless source, stand there strangely quiet and surpassable among things, it may be that involuntarily they become somehow exemplary for *every* human activity by reason of their innate disinterestedness, freedom and intensity. . . .

[*185*]

To E. de W.   Château de Muzot sur Sierre (Valais) Switzerland
March 20, 1922

Your letter, so richly communicative, gave me the most sensible joy from its very first lines; I might well fear that the long pause which had grown up over a whole winter might have spoiled the freedom of your tone to me. This—and I thank you for it just as much as I credit it to the nature of our relationship—was not the case: as for me, recently, so for you too, it was natural to interpret the pause as a rhythmic element in our communings through which they were ordered and distributed rather than interrupted. Your reacting this way gives me the cherished guarantee of the lastingness and security of our bond. Let me give myself over to this experience with joy.

The sympathetic understanding of the state which makes its appearance after the termination of a long-sustained artistic tension and purpose (as an at first empty freedom) must indeed have been possible to you by reason of your own work experience; it does not surprise me that you could achieve and share so close a knowledge of it. It is a perilous state (one among the many perilous states of the artistically active person), a becoming light the moment the wings are weary; a becoming *too* light. The upsurge of the spirit toward some surface. In former years that sort of thing could be unspeakably confusing to me, for the vacation quality of this unburdening is only *one* side of it; scarcely felt, it turns into a consciousness of having become superfluous. To protect myself to some extent from such rockings in the too light skiff, I did everything possible to hold in readiness for such released moments a reliable ballast that could always be at hand,— but either because my strength was not great enough to be thus divisible, or because I forced my way too late and against too many difficulties in childhood and youth to the activities most my own, or because the age itself in which I took them up advocated that kind of one-sidedness and limitation to *one thing:* I didn't succeed, despite many studies begun, in developing a really constant counterweight. Later I consoled myself, tant bien que mal, with the fact that art—in any case too long a task for even the longest life—would have suffered from such division, and Rodin's tremendous confirmation in the metier came to me just at the right time for me to implant in my innermost center the will to be *wholly* in *one* thing and there, forever, to justify it. But I did not have Rodin's metier, so helpful in this sense, nor any that would have been capable of standing by me, as something continually at hand, with such daily tangibility and security in the visible,—also I lacked that vitality of the great master which, little by little, had put him in a position to meet his inspiration unceasingly with so many work projects that it could not help acquiescing, almost without a pause coming up, to *one* of those offered. This "accord", brought about with superiority and not without cunning, made the powerful artist so sure of his inspiration that he might simply deny its existence and its intervention: its vibration, always accessible to him, no longer differentiated itself in any way from his own strength, he had it at his disposal as he had himself; only in the last years of his life when the weariness of age finally came upon him, making Rodin inaccurate and exploitingly greedy of what was most his own, did this relationship too avenge itself as every subjection of the *too*-great, of what surpasses us, of the free and unobligated divine must sometime avenge itself: thus he would now and then create with the means of inspiration, but without, indeed against inspiration itself . . . The endangerment of the artist simply is tremendous, and danger grows about him as a manifold of his greatness.

However that may be, dear friend, as things stand today, I am *not* worried about your artistic efforts, on which I place so pure a value, when you inform me that you will for long periods be estranged from this effort so natural to you by a singularly incompatible study. Even though I don't understand what path in the world you propose to open to yourself later through the Doctor of Laws degree, nevertheless it is just this complete contrast in your two activities which seems right to me; for the more differently constituted the intellectual, intentional, deliberate is by its nature and its practice, the more likely is it to protect the inspired, what rises up unpredictably, inspirited from deep within. (Where, on the other hand, two such activities, an artistic one and some other, are somehow neighbored—: as journalism and literature and so many other examples—, there result the most calamitous influencings that bedim and misuse the finer medium.)—For the rest, if I were young today, I would unquestionably have looked about for a daily, very heterogeneous activity and have tried to establish myself in some palpable domain according to my powers. Perhaps one serves art today better and more discreetly if one makes it into an unmentioned affair of certain days or years (which need not mean pursuing it on the side and in dilettante fashion; after all, to mention a highest example, Mallarmé was all his life an English teacher . . .), but the "profession" itself is filled to overflowing with intruders, with those who don't belong, with exploiters of this metier gone hybrid, and its renewal, yes, the giving of new significance, without which this exposure that is hurrying into the sensational will shortly have become absurd, can take place only through those silent *individuals* who do *not* count themselves in and accept none of the practices to which the littérateur has given validity and currency. Now if such an individual be a private person or otherwise keep inconspicuously behind a profession he knows, he will the more readily contribute his part to the correction of circumstances long ago become impossible, since his *silence* as a poet will have a certain significance alongside his profoundest articulation.—It will not, for example, remain unessential for the poet to whom among the Frenchmen of my generation belongs my greatest and most marveling admiration—Paul Valéry—that between his earliest publications and those glorious poems and writings with which he has come forward since 1919, he had the strength to interpose a silence of about twenty-five years. He was, if I am not mistaken, occupied with mathematics, and so widely and clearly oriented in this realm that he was capable of perceiving and expressing the significance of Einstein *before* other French scholars.

What I thought I saw at the time of Malte Laurids Brigge in

relation to the theater—that all its sprouts and shoots would have to be cut back for some years so that it should grow up again bigger and more necessary out of its most fundamental roots—that is now my opinion and warning with regard to all the arts: they have grown rank, and it is not the encouraging gardner they need, nor the fostering, but the one with shears and spade: re-proving— . . .

[186]

To Rudolf Bodländer   Château de Muzot sur Sierre (Valais)
                                              Switzerland
                                          March 23, 1922

How I would like, young friend, to write a good answer to your new little pages too—, but here words have a hard time. On the whole, I think I recognize that you have taken the right stand in wanting to regard that struggle and go through with it as one intimately your own, at pains to learn what physical and spiritual conditions renew the conflict and at which of their in-tersection points it may appear. This is surely the most responsible attitude, only you must absolutely remove from it any incidental accent of reproachful and burdened endeavor. Dear friend, this is important: fight *guilelessly*. No one, nowadays, in our coun-tries "gets through" (as the expression goes) with this struggle—, in each the singular urge gives rise to some group of conflicts,— least of all has the superior bourgeois "overcome" it who admits so many dubious expedients, in contrast to which a deep and si-lent perplexity like this could not but show itself infinitely guilt-less.—We are anyway—do not forget it—entirely in the province of guilt-lessness there.—The terrifying thing is that we possess no religion in which these experiences, being so literal and pal-pable as they are (for: at the same time so inexpressible and so intangible), may be lifted up into the god, into the protection of a phallic deity who will perhaps have to be the *first* with which a troop of gods will again invade humanity, after so long an ab-sence. What then is to support us if religious helps fail—, in that they hush up these experiences instead of clarifying them and would withdraw them from us instead of implanting them in us more gloriously than we dared surmise. Here we are the indescribably forsaken and betrayed: hence our calamity. While religions, going out at their surfaces and depositing more and more burnt-out surface, died away into moralities, they shifted this manifestation too, the innermost of their existence and ours, on to the chilled ground of morality and thereby, necessarily, into the periphery. Little by little people will see that it is *here*, not in the social or economic realm, that our great contemporary calamity lies—, in this expulsion of the act of love into the peripheral; the clear-sighted individual's strength is now exhausting itself in moving it back again at least into his *own* center (if it is not already standing in the common world center, which would have as consequence the immediate flooding of the world's bloodstream with divinities!),—the man who lives blindly somehow delights, on the contrary, in the peripheral, accessible nature of "enjoyment" and takes revenge (clear-sighted in spite of himself) for its being worthless even there, in simultaneously craving and denouncing this enjoyment. Denial in the superficial is *no* advance and there is no sense in straining the "will" (which besides is too young and new a force, measured against the primeval rightness of the instinct) to that end. Denial of love or fulfillment of love, both are wonderful and peerless only where the entire love-experience with *all* its scarcely differentiable ecstasies (so alternating among themselves that just *there* spiritual and physical can no longer be separated) is allowed to occupy a central position: there too then (in the rapture of a few lovers or saints of *all* times and *all* religions) renunciation and fulfillment become identical. Where the infinite enters *wholly* in (whether as minus or plus) the sign, the ah so human sign, as the road that has now been completely traversed, drops away and what remains is the having arrived, *the being!*—It is this, dear friend, more or less, that can (provisionally) be revealed, if one is asked, about our greatest, our innermost secret. I believe it must, if you read it accurately, shift your whole struggle onto a new unravaged plane. (And when sometime you love someone, read this letter *together*, if you do not already know it so well by then that you can invent its contents anew out of yourself!)

If you start thus from the center and from the striving for "being" (that is, for the experience of the fullest possible inner intensity) then your attitude toward any poetic urge that may spring up will also clarify itself. By no means everything must be suppressed there; whatever demonstrates before your gradually strengthening conscience its right to be shaped, to that just give its desired form. The page of a journal may be filled in this way, or a letter come into being (sendable or not, no matter)—or even a creation that has its spontaneous home in the domain of the artistic. Whether a thing belongs *there* is proved not by the wish or urge to make it public or commendable (here too the evil spirit of the peripheral carries on its confusing game—): rather, whether a thing becomes art depends on its *higher* rate of vibration which, by virtue of its nature, surpasses things of custom or expressions of daily intercourse, and as only a secondary consequence of which there appears the intention to provide for such a creation— which exceeds the transitory and, to put it tritely, the private— some situation in which it will endure and survive more lastingly and, as it were, more universally. Of "effect" there is no question anywhere here, not even of the actual becoming public which is only accidental to a phenomenon innately destined for larger circumstances. With such an attitude, whatever you happen to produce, in what profession soever, alongside it or in spite of it, will always have been legitimately written down, and, whether someone now learns or knows of it or not—, every word that has arisen thus will help you and, beyond that, will someday say itself where it belongs.

And this too, in the event that art should be preparing in you, beneath the double floor that your profession will install and fix in your life—remember that it was possible for the most sublime, most "compact" poet of our time, Stéphane Mallarmé, to pass his bourgeois existence as an English teacher. . . .

And so: wishes, dear friend, for confidence and joy.

[187]

To Ilse Blumenthal-Weiss   Château de Muzot sur Sierre
                                    April 25, 1922

. . . The "Fioretti of Saint Francis" are old friendships for my heart, at least in their original text. Years ago, during a whole south Italian winter, I gathered my housemates every morning about my reading aloud of these little and lovely legends; they would always listen to one chapter, that sufficed to set us quite distinctively into the day, which each then utilized or squandered in his own fashion.

And as regards *Beer-Hofmann's* "Lullaby for Miriam", this too, as you mention it now, brings up to me special memories; I have known it practically from its birth. At that time (around 1902) it was the *only* poem Beer-Hofmann had ever written—; later, in the wonderful rarity and discrimination of his work, another, similarly full, second poem was added—, I couldn't say whether the number of these exquisite things has meantime increased. If I admired the "Lullaby" extremely from first acquaintance (when it gloriously appeared in the pages of the "Pan" of that time), I was able (I knew it by heart) to win for it in later years too unqualified admirers. When I lived for six months in Sweden, it went so far that people from other estates would send their carriages for me to our estate, as one sends for a doctor, solely that I might recite the verses to people otherwise strangers who had heard of the extraordinary beauty of this poem—: a request to which I acceded each time deeply moved and with all the joy of my own admiration!

Here I might link up with still another theme touched upon in your letter before last: that of the destiny of the Jew. *Beer-Hofmann* (while so many Jewish people seem to represent this hard destiny only in its splits and evasive twists) was to me always an example of its greatness and dignity, of which even in the long and afflicted exile nothing essential had to be surrendered.—You know from one of my earlier letters (the one about "faith") how very favored the Jew—together with the Arab and the orthodox

Russian, to point no farther into the Orient—seems to me by his innate unity of nationality and religion, which insures him an over and over again manifest head-start. That he had lost the ground beneath him and had to maintain himself on a bit of borrowed earth has its good and its bad aspects; apart from a few great exceptions, he has had to misuse his advantages in order to survive in the contested and foundationless,—he has for the most part misused himself and others. With a cunning to which self-preservation trained him, he transformed his being nowhere attached from a misfortune into a superiority, and where he happens to misuse this dearly bought superiority pettily, greedily and inimically, where—involuntarily—he revenges himself, there he has become noxious, an intruder, a disintegrator. But where the same process, the same survival wrung from destiny has been consummated in a person *grandly* determined, there, out of the same inexorabilities, has arisen that glory of which *Spinoza* would be a famous example.—The mobile and transplantable character of the inner center, its independence (but at the same time rootlessness, unless consciousness leads downward to the root in God)—the truly *transportable* spirit came into the world through the destiny of the Jew: an unheard-of danger and an unheard-of freedom of movement. And according as one stresses one side or the other of this Jewish resource, one will have to fear or extol it; with all of which the fact remains that what has been effected through it is ultimately indispensable to all of us, not to be thought away and not to be wished away. Perhaps this ferment, when it has acted long enough, must be again withdrawn and collected in the vessel most its own. The Zionist consciousness stemming from a purely Jewish impulse would be a beginning for this presumably imperative separating out. This reacquisition of the ancient soil once theirs, this new rootedness, must then be conceived and in-interpreted literally as well as symbolically. If, as is probable, we have known the Jewish people only in its distortions, in its perplexity, in its deflected and sometimes oblique obstinacy, and if we gauge its vigor by its survival, we are at first frightened at imagining the strength it would bring forth were it established, sanctioned, favored!—The growth of these people so fruitful even in their uprootedness would then attain an unrestrainable fruitfulness in God—, the continuation of that history of passionate and weighty harvests which the Old Testament, wherever we open it, makes for us an event, a climate. . . .

[*188*]

To Lotti von Wedel   Château de Muzot sur
                                        Sierre/Valais/Switzerland
                                        May 26, 1922

. . . how should I not be disposed by your letter and its two enclosures to the quickest joyfullest thanks!—

I knew in what good hands I placed my request, and so it doesn't surprise me so very much to see it fulfilled by your father in so favorable a manner; only I am thereby just becoming aware of how presumptuous my demand may have been.

Concerning the magnificent queen, it moves me in a singular way that her picture came back to me and is to belong to me. It belongs in fact—as you rightly say—to those most autonomous things in our daily environment which one may quite disregard, only to be suddenly surprised and overtaken, when unexpectedly sometime the "ignition" comes on, by the undiminished, even renewed intensity of their presence!—So the double portrait again assumes its accustomed place, leaning against the wall on a beautiful old chest . . .

Yes, in view of the late coming of the spring, it wouldn't be so very regrettable that your spring trip to Santa Margherita did not take place, but that now, by the same physical failing, you should be hindered from receiving as it deserved the spring that has come, has caught up with itself with so much strength: to me too that seems altogether unjust. Utterly so, since it is a question of the *Heidelberg* spring.—A Swedish and a Russian friend, both of whom had studied at Heidelberg and then, after about a decade, both married, had met again—years ago at a dinner I heard them exchanging their student memories, rather, one should say, rousing and inciting each other to such memories . . . Time after time I, the listener, who do not know Heidelberg, had to ask myself whether it were really conceivable that a German city was in question, its gardens, its hill-paths, even its skies: what was evoked there had such scenic lavishness, such fullness and southernness, such boundless atmospheric scope, that I might have inferred southern France at least. And now you yourself use outright the word "intoxicating"!

A thinking destiny, one cognizant of us . . . yes, often one has wished to be strengthened and confirmed by such a one; but would it not at once be one that contemplated us from without, observing us, with which we would no longer be alone? That we are set into a "blind destiny", dwell within it, is after all in a way the condition of our own sight, of our gazing innocence.—Only through the "blindness" of our fate are we really deeply related to the wonderful muffledness of the world, that is with what is whole, vast and surpassing us . . .

Yesterday I read a book, the story of a childhood, which seemed extraordinarily beautiful to me. Is there not in its pages the quality that makes Jung-Stilling's childhood so moving, taken up again about a century later, with all the increase in associations possible since then and the inclusion in the "muffled" that has become at once more manifold and everywhere more binding?

When the "Queen" came back, I looked about among my things for a suitable counter-gift; allow me, dear lady, to use as such this timely little book by a person I have long esteemed, and to put it in your hands, particularly for these days of a convalescence that is coming to an understanding with the spring. And may you recover quickly enough still to have some happy share in the blossoming and growing of your tangible surroundings!

[_189_]

To Dory von der Mühll   Château de Muzot
                                          June 23, 1922

. . . It was a deep emotion for me, experiencing the reception
that Princess Taxis gave the Elegies! One day I read her all ten,
next day, the fifty Sonnets to Orpheus, of whose inner unity and
of whose connection with the Elegies, which they gloriously
parallel, I have just become sensible through this listening. Both
works were actually given me as if they were not mine (because
anyhow, by their nature, they are *more* than "*by* me")—, the
Princess was amazed and I, if I may be quite truthful, yes, I was
amazed along with her, tout simplement, with my purest, most
profound astonishment.— . . .

[_190_]

To E.M.   Château de Muzot sur Sierre, Valais (Switzerland)
                                          September 13, 1922

The mere sight, my good and valued friend, of your writing,
before I had even read it, made me fear that some heaviness had
taken possession of you—, and now it proves to be the greatest
heaviness that has come out of the greatest glory: can something
so heavy come from something so purely blissful? For you yourself still know even now *how* this thing, but just now blissful, released you, freed you, gave you wings. Until when? And why
no longer?—

There are two readings of your letter: Yesterday my guess
was that (perhaps reciprocally) you had too long exposed each
other to the strongest radiation of your great emotion, so long
that the same ray that had just called forth growth and fullness
became too much and began to destroy: for which you then involuntarily had to avenge yourself.

Today I understand it differently: As though you, from this
experience in which you still stand and are struggling, should
consider yourself a person who, as a lover (the courting over),

seems to himself sentenced in consequence of inner fatalities to use the means and tools of hatred, just as involuntarily as he would instruments for a deeper, more enigmatical enjoyment . . . This discovery might of course be infinitely painful and confusing to you,—but horrify you it must not: it would merely mean taking up the battle with what is unresolved and erroneous in your innermost nature,—and who knows how far you would be equipped for that very battle by those changes and gains which the affection and devotion of this person opened up and made possible to you at certain periods of your relationship. If you are now afraid of yourself as you grow aware of the way your nature is becoming unbridled and frightening through contact with her, now she is won, and a torment to her—, then to offset that, try to realize that a having-won and possessing of a person, in such a way as to use that person for one's own (often so fatally conditioned) enjoyment, yes: that there is not, may not, can not be such a thing as the using of a person,—and you will see that distance and reverence again establishing itself which will make you measure your excitement anew with those measures that were yours during courtship. It often occurs that a happiness such as that which you, loved and loving, have experienced not only frees new powers in a young man, but also uncovers quite other, deeper layers of his nature, out of which most sinister discoveries break through overwhelmingly: but our disorders have ever been a part of our riches, and where we are horrified at their violence, we are really frightened only at unsuspected possibilities and tensions of our strength—, and the chaos, if we win but a little distance from it, promptly arouses in us the presentiment of new orders and, as soon as our courage willingly participates even to the slightest extent in such presentiments, also the curiosity and the desire to achieve that still unforeseeable future ordering!

I have written the word "distance"; if there is anything like a counsel I find myself qualified to suggest to you, it would be the conjecture that you should endeavor to seek *this*, this distance; both from your present consternation and from those new dispositions and enlargements of your spirit which you indeed enjoyed at the time they took place, but have not as yet taken essentially into your possession at all. A short separation, parting for a few weeks, a beginning of yourself, a new concentrating of your overfilled and unstrung nature would offer the greatest likelihood of salvaging all that seems to be destroying itself in and through itself. Whether now I am right in my first reading or come closer with the second to the reality of your suffering and that which you inflict,—or whether something else entirely should have been understood from your few lines: this single counsel could in no event be wrong. Nothing keeps people so fast in error as the daily repetition of that error—, and how many bound to one another in a destiny finally gone rigid might have been able by short, clean separations to ensure to themselves that rhythm through which the mysterious mobility of their hearts would, in deep proximity to inner world-space, have remained inexhaustible from change to change.

This would be all, this little, with which I may have been able to reciprocate your trust. May you soon feel more confident.—
R.M.R.

P.S. Although your card just this moment arrived recalls and in a sense takes back the letter that preceded it, nevertheless I do not want to retract mine either for that reason. All the better if you have yourself already found and begun what it attempts to say to you: the clear courageous tone of your card permits me to suppose something of the sort.

[*191*]

To Ilse Jahr   Château de Muzot sur Sierre (Valais), Switzerland
December 2, 1922

You dear creature,

A little miracle that your letter finally reached me, for more than twenty years I have not lived at the place to which it was directed. But now, you should know, I delight in its clear voice. How could it be too trivial to me, since every creaking of the floor goes to my heart. You do feel it: My world begins with *things*—, and hence in it even the least human being is already frighteningly big, yes, almost an excess. You are not so small either, you feeling young girl. You should know besides that I never read what "they" write about my works in newspapers or periodicals, or even in books smacking of "science"; I notice nothing of all that, and so every real human voice finds most ample room in my spirit. But now already I direct you further, out beyond me, to the figure I am building for myself, outside, more validly and more lastingly. Hold on to *that*, if it seems big and significant to you. Who knows who I am? I change and change. But *it* is the boundary of my transformation, its pure rim: if it radiates love to you, deeply, *good:* then let us both believe in it.

Rainer Maria Rilke

[*192*]

To Witold von Hulewicz   Château de Muzot sur Sierre (Suisse)
December 14, 1922

. . . For a real and valid estimate of Rodin and his work, what I wrote twenty years ago (the first part of the book does go back that far and the other lies not much nearer) will not be a very essential contribution; apart from my all too youthful attitude, I lacked distance, and the whole nature of my proximity to the master was one-sided, completely determined by whatever it was necessary and helpful for *me* to learn from him. Were I to write today of that great work and its author, admiration—the wish and the compulsion to admire—would certainly still be the measure and means of my conception; but *how* much harder would it not be for this admiration today in view of the calamities by which (seen from a greater remove) Rodin's own existence and his rebellious achievement was besieged and finally overpowered.—But what—in my eyes—assures to those notes of mine even now a kind of justification is, as you correctly recognized—their human devotion to the great example, their conviction that producing art is a most simple and most stern calling, but at the same time a destiny, and, as such, greater than any of us, more powerful and to the very end immeasurable.—And for your wanting to win in your homeland readers and friends for this conviction, for that I thank you most heartily. . . .

[*193*]

To Prince Hohenlohe   Château de Muzot sur Sierre, Valais
                                                December 23, 1922

. . . Proust,—you mention Proust: It pleases me immensely that you have found relish and interest in his work. By a chance, of which I shall tell you sometime, I was one of the first (1913!) to read "Du côté de chez Swann", and hence also one of the first to admire Marcel Proust, which was the natural, immediate consequence of that reading. On the occasion of his death recently, André Gide reminded me of the fact that I have my place among the earliest admirers of this great writer,—and now you can imagine how I had gone along with him in the same state of mind from volume to volume and how strongly the death of this significant man affected me. It is simply not yet possible to foresee *all* that has been opened to us and those to come with these books, they are crammed so full of a wealth of discovery, and the strangest thing is the use, already so natural and in its way quiet, of the boldest and often most unheard-of; anyone else would have been able to risk such lines of connection from event to event only as auxiliary lines,—but in Proust they also at once acquire the beauty of the ornamental, and they retain, even as design, validity and permanence. While by some intuitive stroke he dares the most remarkable connection, it seems again as though he were merely following the existing veins in a polished piece of marble, and then one is surprised all over again at the perfect tact of his interpretation, clinging nowhere, which, playing, lets go again what it just seemed to be holding to and which, with scarcely surpassable nicety, everywhere admits and leaves free that which is sheerly incalculable.—In his cork-slab lined (almost bare) room which he left only now and then at night, this strange soothsayer must have seen life continually open before him like a gigantic hand whose lines he so essentially understood that they could not give him any more surprises—, only, day by day, endless tasks!—How one must love work, once one has got that far! . . .

[*194*]

To Countess Margot Sizzo   Château de Muzot sur Sierre
Epiphany [January 6] 1923

. . . "Woe to them that are consoled", the courageous Marie Lenéru notes something of the sort in her strange "Journal", and here indeed consolation would be one of the many diversions, a distraction, hence at bottom something frivolous and unfruitful. For even time does not "console", as one superficially says, at most it arranges, sets in order—, and only because we later so little heed the order toward which it so quietly collaborates, yes, so little consider it, that what has now become established and assuaged, reconciled in the great whole, we take, instead of marveling at it there, for some forgetfulness of our own and weakness of heart, only because it no longer hurts so much. Ah, how little it *forgets*, the heart,—and how strong it would be if we did not withdraw its tasks from it before they are fully and really accomplished!—Not the wanting to console oneself for such a loss should be our instinct, rather it should become our deep painful curiosity wholly to explore it, the singularity, the uniqueness of this particular loss, to learn its effect within our life, yes, we should cultivate the noble avarice of enriching our inner world by this very loss, its meaning and its weight. . . . Such a loss, the more deeply it touches us and the more violently it affects us, is so much the more a *task* of taking into our possession afresh, differently and finally, what now in the being lost is stressed with hopelessness: *this* then is unending accomplishment that overcomes on the spot everything negative that adheres to pain, all inertia and indulgence that always constitutes a part of pain, this is active, inward-working pain, the only pain that makes sense and is worthy of us. I do not like the Christian conceptions of a Be-

yond, I am getting farther and farther away from them, naturally
without thought of attacking them; they may have their right and
persistence beside so many other hypotheses about the periphery
of the divine,—but to me they contain above all the danger not
only of making those who have vanished more imprecise to us and
above all more inaccessible—; but we too, drawing ourselves yonder in our longing and *away* from here, we ourselves become
thereby less definite, less earthly: which for the present, so long
as we are *here* and akin to tree, flower and soil, we do have, in a
purest sense, to remain, even still to become! As concerns myself,
what has died for me has died, so to speak, into my own heart:
the vanished person, when I have looked for him, has collected
himself singularly and so surprisingly *in* me, and it was moving to
feel that for us he was now *only* there, that my enthusiasm for
serving his existence there, for deepening and glorifying it, took
the upper hand almost at the very moment in which pain would
otherwise have invaded and laid waste the entire landscape of my
spirit. When I remember how—often with extremest difficulty
in understanding and accepting one another—I loved my father!
Often, in childhood, my thoughts would become confused, and
my heart would grow numb at the mere idea that sometime he
might no longer be; my existence seemed to me so wholly conditioned through him (my from the outset so differently oriented
existence!) that to my innermost self his departure was synony-
mous with my own doom . . . , but so *deep* is death implanted in
the nature of love that (if only we are cognizant of it without
allowing ourselves to be misled by the uglinesses and suspicions we
attached to it) it nowhere contradicts love: *whither* after all can
it drive someone we have borne unutterably in our heart save
into this very heart, where would the "idea" of this loved person
be, indeed his ceaseless influence (for *how* could *that* cease which
even while he lived with us was more and more independent of
his tangible presence) . . . where would this always secret influence be held more secure than *in* us? Where can we come
closer to it, where more purely celebrate it, when obey it better,
than when it appears linked with our own voices, as if our heart

had learned a new language, a new song, a new strength.—I reproach all modern religions for having handed to their believers consolations and glossings over of death, instead of administering to them the means of reconciling themselves to it and coming to an understanding with it. With it, with its full, unmasked cruelty: this cruelty is so tremendous that it is just with *it* that the circle closes: it leads right back again into the extreme of a mildness that is great, pure and perfectly clear (all consolation is turbid) as we have never surmised mildness to be, not even on the sweetest spring day. But toward the experiencing of this most profound mildness which, were only a few of us to feel it with conviction, could perhaps little by little penetrate and make *transparent* all the relations of life: toward the experiencing of *this* richest and soundest mildness, mankind has never taken even the first steps,— unless in its oldest, most innocent times, whose secret has been all but lost to us. The content of "initiations" was, I am sure, nothing but the imparting of a "key" that permitted the reading of the word "death" *without* negation; like the moon, life surely has a side permanently turned away from us which is not its counter-part but its complement toward perfection, toward consummation, toward the really sound and full sphere and orb of being.

One should not fear that our strength might not suffice to bear any experience of death, even were it the nearest and the most terrible; death is not beyond our strength; it is the measure mark at the vessel's rim: we are *full* as often as we reach it—, and being full means (for us) being heavy . . . that is all.—I will not say that one should *love* death; but one should love life so magnanimously, so without calculation and selection that spontaneously one constantly includes with it and loves death too (life's averted half),—which is in fact what happens also, irresistibly and illimitably, in all great impulses of love! Only because we exclude death in a sudden moment of reflection, has it turned more and more into something alien, and as we have kept it in the alien, something hostile.

It is conceivable that it stands infinitely closer to us than our effort [would allow] (this has grown ever clearer to me with the years, and my work has perhaps only the *one* meaning and mission to bear witness, more and more impartially and independently . . . more prophetically perhaps, if that does not sound too arrogant . . . to this insight which so often unexpectedly overwhelms me) . . . our effort; I mean, can *only* go toward postulating the unity of life and death, so that it may gradually prove itself to us. Prejudiced as we are *against* death, we do not manage to release it from its misrepresentations . . . only believe, dear, dear Countess, that it is a *friend*, our deepest friend, perhaps the only one who is never, never, to be misled through our behavior and vacillation . . . and *that*, it is understood, *not* in the sentimental-romantic sense of denying life, of life's opposite, but our friend just when we most passionately, most vehemently assent . . . to being-here, to functioning, to Nature, to love. Life always says simultaneously Yes and No. Indeed, death (I adjure you to believe!) is the true yea-sayer. It says only: Yes. Before eternity.

Think of the "Slumbering Tree". Yes, how good that it occurs to me. Think of all the little pictures and inscriptions to it,—how, in youthful innocent trust, you there constantly recognized and affirmed *both* in the world: the sleeping and the waking, the bright and the dark, the voice and the silence . . . , la présence et l'absence. All the apparent opposites which somewhere come together in one point, which at one place sing the hymn of their wedding—and this place is—for the time being—our heart!

[195]

To Lou Andreas-Salomé   Château de Muzot sur Sierre (Valais),
Suisse
January 13, 1923

. . . today must be the Russian New Year! But even the other day, on the western New Year's morning, and between Christmas Eve and it, I was often with you in thought: at that time I still thought, if I put off writing a little, I could lay the Elegies and the Sonnets right in with the next letter: I was far off in my calculations: on the last day of the year there appeared, instead of the first copies, one more Elegy-revision, still fairly faulty, which I could then spread out for myself exactly over the threshold of the year. In the dying note of midnight and in the first stillness of 1923, I was just in the midst of correcting and reading the fifth Elegy! I rejoice that I was allowed to begin thus (if a division is to be granted at all). And you? I am often *greatly concerned*, dear Lou, about *you*, about *all of you*, when I hear and picture how everything in Germany has become more and more absurd and living and living costs practically impossible. It seems—and that was my impression in 1919—, that the only right moment, when everything could have paved the way for understanding, has been missed on all sides, now the divergences are increasing, the sums of the mistakes can no longer be read off, so many-digited have they become; perplexity, despair, insincerity and the opportune wish to draw some profit at any cost out of even these calamities, even yet out of them: these false forces are shoving the world ahead of them . . .

But perhaps the world isn't going along, perhaps *nothing* is going on in politics, scarcely does one get, no matter where, into some layer beneath them, when already everything looks different, and one thinks a most secret growth and its sheer will are using those confusions only in order to keep themselves unharmed beneath and hidden from otherwise occupied curiosity. (In France particularly, among people not politically minded, in those who are inwardly active: *how* many turnings, renewals, wide vistas—, what new orientating of a spirit suddenly, almost against its will, increasingly reflected . . . I don't know whether you have followed Proust, his influence is tremendous—, but not only *his* influence is transforming, but what emanated from him is emanating now from other and younger men . . .) I have the advantage here of being able to follow all this without much difficulty; I translated Paul Valéry and felt my resources so corresponded with his great, glorious poems that I have never translated with such sureness and insight as in this, in itself often very difficult case. (You know that he, P.V., a friend of Gide's, descending from Mallarmé, after a few early publications kept silence through nearly twenty-five years, occupied with mathematics, only since 1919 has he been living into poetry again, and now every line has, added to the pace of it, that deep repose which none of us is able to command. A glory.) And Valéry, although he is completely excluded from Germany by ignorance of the language, wrote me, when he was traveling through Switzerland in the fall on account of lectures: "Vous étiez l'un des objets principaux de mon voyage." How full of premonition and how unrestrainable all real connections are. And for all that, I was unfortunately not able to see him for the silliest of reasons; the impossibility of having Austrian or German money sent out is making me more and more of a prisoner in the old walls of my Muzot, *in* them I have everything for a while yet, but every step outwards, though it be only to Lausanne, is becoming more and more impossible! But how could I help taking this inconvenience comparatively lightly when I think of the distresses that would beset and hem me in at a less out-of-the-way and sheltered spot. One may not now attach much value to freedom of movement; it would only bring one into touch with calamities. In the summer I had all sorts of plans; but so many warnings at once stood at the border of the slightest realization that, quite the reverse, I left no stone unturned in order to be able to go on keeping myself in Muzot. Were the world less awry, a change, at the moment of this for me significant conclusion, would certainly have had sense, and it probably would also have taken place. But as it is, the best thing was to hold fast to the given and tried and to be loyal and grateful to it. Especially as my health is going through singular upheavals: again and again every excitement, even that of work (which often for weeks has not allowed me to eat *quietly*), casts itself upon that center in the pit of my stomach, the sympathetic nerve, the "solar plexus", there I am so truly annihilable, and I am going through remarkable experiences of the rivalries and unisons of the two centers, the cerebral and that more focal one which after all is supposedly our *middle:* as regards the visible as well as the invisible!

Meanwhile: I am not worrying too much about these fluctuations attacking the central organs; at most that I should use my energy to "turn off" for the meal hour the intensive vibrations emanating from mind or mood just as I mostly succeed in doing with regard to sleep. That great god: Sleep; I sacrifice to him without any time-avarice—what does time matter to *him!*—ten hours, eleven, even twelve, if he wants to accept them in his lofty, mildly-silent way! Only unfortunately I seldom manage now to go to bed early; evening is my reading time. The presence of enticing books, the stillness of the old house intensified to the point of improbability, keep me awake for the most part past midnight. The little caring-for-itself of a mouse in the many never-discovered interstices of the deep walls further contributes then to increasing the mystery out of which the tremendous night of the countryside, eternally *without* care, nourishes itself.

Strangely dulled I am, was so, to my astonishment, even in the summer—, toward the countryside itself, the so deeply experienced magnificence of which I must keep before me with an effort and deliberately, in order to participate in it still. Does the leveling of our senses really go *that* far under the continually renewed presence of the surroundings in contact with them? How manifoldly then must habit put us in the wrong toward people and things: one should console oneself with the fact that the curve of delight continues on in one's inner realm: but how follow it there where it will surely be refracted in the density of the medium, perhaps become unrecognizable and display emphasis only *there* where other curves, of just as lost an origin, cross it in the curious vortex of the intersection points. . . .

[*196*]

To "Une Amie" Château de Muzot-sur-Sierre (Valais)
February 3, 1923

So it is to "a friend" that I am permitted to reply this time . . .
She guessed it, in reading her first letter I gave great attention
to her handwriting—not as a graphologist—that I have never
been, for I would consider it indiscreet to force a handwriting
according to a "method" in order in the end to find there the
tenets of ordinary psychology mingled with the actual tools of
this housebreaking. To what purpose? Isn't it preferable to take
what the handwriting *gives* without violence or artifice? Yours,
rapid as it is, finds itself every moment surpassed by you yourself,
by what you call your daily "expectation", you rush out ahead
of each word to see if something is coming . . . That conclusion, isn't it so, I was permitted to draw since you speak of it
yourself. That young, vital impatience, does there anywhere exist
the immense event that could wholly satisfy it? I doubt it. For it
would always want change, what follows, the next surprise. The
adventure? It is on this that I have no valid opinion. I have never
felt myself capable of looking for it, for I lack the principal
quality for coping with it, I mean that dauntless presence of mind
over which they dispose who have the habit of immediate action.
I myself am slow interiorly, I have that intrinsic slowness of the
tree that composes its growth and its flowering, yes, I have a little
of its admirable patience (I have had to educate myself to it
since understanding the secret slowness that prepares, that distills
every work of art), but if I have its venerable measure, I have
nothing of its immobility. Oh, travel! The élan of departing
suddenly, almost without knowing whither, that I know, on that
point we would be admirably in accord. How many times my
life has found itself wholly concentrated in this one feeling of
departure; going far, far away—and that first awakening under
a new sky! And to recognize oneself there, no, to learn more
there. To feel that there too, where one has never been, one is
continuing something, and that a part of your heart, unconsciously

indigenous to this unknown climate, is born and developing from the moment of your arrival and endowing you with a new blood, intelligent and marvelously informed on things it is impossible to know. These experiences have little by little transformed the ardent traveler I was into a colonist who *settles down*. I no longer went into distant countries as a curious visitor, I settled there, I lived in them, and I amply corrected the accident of having been born somewhere by a more vast and more loving birth. (But I see that in speaking to you of these sojourns, I am coming back to the slowness I commend . . .) How delightful it is to awaken in some place where no one, no one in the world, can guess where you are. Sometimes I have stopped unexpectedly in cities that happened to be on my route, just to savor this delight of not being able to be imagined there by any living being, nor reached by any other person's thought. How much that added to the lightness of my soul, I recall certain days in Cordova where I lived as if in a transfigured body, by dint of being completely unknown. Charm of staying in a little Spanish city, simply to enter into relation with a few dogs and a blind beggar (more dangerous, this latter, because he senses you). But after three days, if he hears you coming back at the same hour toward his church, he counts you a someone who from henceforth *exists*, and he repatriates you in his world of sound, and behold you are promoted to a new mystic and nocturnal birth . . .

Knowing these few tastes of my nomad life, do the *New Poems* * still seem so impersonal to you? You see, in order to say what happens to me, I needed not so much an instrument of feeling as I did clay: involuntarily I undertook to make use of so-called lyric poetry to shape, not feelings, but *things I had felt;* the whole event of life had to find place in that shaping, independently of the suffering or pleasure it had at first brought me. That shaping would have been valueless if it had not gone as far as the *trans*-shaping of every passing detail, it was necessary to come through to the essence.

* The *New Poems* and *New Poems—Second Part*, written between 1906 and 1909 approximately, are the last volumes of verse I have published.

"Form-Dichter", I do not know what that is . . . Also, happily, for more than twenty years I have never read a single line of what might be said about my works. Not out of contempt, certainly not. Only this critical profession is so removed from mine, it nowhere touches on anything I do. Also I have no need of being enlightened on my writings; all my interior action, since I have been in possession of my resources, *holds*, and no voice, be it the strongest and most authoritative, could influence the precision and the error of my intimate balance. And as regards the efforts of others, I do as my great friend Verhaeren did: I have my admiration with which to measure their élan and to consent, infinitely, to their victories!

And this too brings us closer together, that you did not want to judge a work of art save by its intensity. One can be mistaken, of course; but how much more touching and more vivifying an error of that sort remains than an error of criticism! . . .

[*197*]

To Ilse Jahr Château de Muzot sur Sierre (Valais) Switzerland
February 22, 1923

Dear girl, many a sun and many a candle's light has shone since Christmas through your luminous silhouette and has made it gay and warm to me, the figure in it, yours and your tall grasses and your moon and your stars . . . ; often, when I looked through, it was like your growth's green blood, you young flower, that was stirring inside there, your trust even into sorrow and your joy in everything that is life's. At last I must tell you all that was not lost on me, though I was silent: all along this winter I have been a bad letter writer despite my great solitude and my long evenings. That comes from the fact that my pen—(it is unfortunately the same that has to manage the work and also the paths of communication by letter!)—exhausted itself last winter in endless labor and now, this year, suffices only for the translations I have set myself, and for the most necessary in the epistolary line, which, with my enormously expanded correspondence, is still considerable.

But I am sure you understand me, you dear girl stirred to your innermost heart, when I beg you to keep your speaking-to-me (though it be only something you feel or now and then write) independent of my visible response; with your attitude, you cannot fail to feel me responding and answering, even if at first, even if for a long time I am silent.

Perhaps too you are turning not so much to the person that I *am;* perhaps you are addressing and rejoicing with the man I was twenty years ago when I wrote those books that became closest to you, immediately yours, so that through them you first became open and flowing toward human beings, toward the fraternally human. This, this linking with human neighborhood and nearness did not happen to me either until very late, and without certain periods in my youth passed in Russia, probably would scarcely ever have been vouchsafed me as purely and as completely as one really must be allowed to experience it in order to be set in without false rivets into the whole, into the glory of life. I began with *things,* which were the true confidants of my lonely childhood, and it was already a great deal that I managed, without outside help, to get as far as animals . . . But then Russia opened itself up to me and bestowed on me the brotherliness and the darkness of God, in whom alone there is community. So I *named* him at that time too, the God who had broken in upon me, and lived a long time in the anteroom of his name, on my knees . . . Now you would scarcely ever hear me name him, there is an indescribable discretion between us, and where once nearness was and penetration, there stretch new distances, as in the atom, which the new science also conceives as a universe in the small. The comprehensible escapes us, is transformed, instead of possession one learns relation, and there arises a namelessness that must begin again with God in order to be complete and without evasion. The experience of feeling recedes behind an endless longing for all that can be felt . . . attributes are taken away from God, the no longer expressible, fall back to creation, to love and death . . . ; it is perhaps only that again and again which took place in certain passages in the Book of Hours, this ascent of God out of the breathing heart, with which the sky is covered, and his falling down as rain. But every confessing to it would already be too much. The Christian experience enters less and less into consideration; the ancient God outweighs it infinitely. The view that one is sinful and needs ransom as premise for God is more and more repugnant to a heart that has comprehended the earth. Not sinfulness and error in the earthly, on the contrary, its pure nature becomes essential consciousness, sin is surely the most wonderfully roundabout way to God,—but why should *they* go on pilgrimage who have never left him? The strong, inwardly quivering bridge of the Mediator has sense only where the abyss is granted between God and us—, but this very abyss is full of the darkness of God, and where one experiences it, let him climb down and howl in it (that is more necessary than to cross over it). Only to him for whom the abyss too has been a dwelling place do the heavens before him turn about and everything deeply and profoundly of this world that the Church embezzled for the Beyond, comes back; all the angels decide, singing praises, in favor of earth!

You are too young, dear girl, to understand now, on the spot, what I mean; but, do you see, one thing is more important to me now than all the rest, to be *precise*. I did not want your dear heart to seek me where I no longer am; you are not for that reason to lose me, on the contrary, your affection, even for my onetime heart, can clarify itself only if you know in what spirit it has been unfolding—. The mysteries are greater than you can yet surmise, but you already know much about them since you could write that on your "beloved God's earth", all was beautiful, only all was just "differently beautiful". Take that conception very broadly and don't let yourself be frightened or confused.

[*198*]

To Leopold von Schlözer   Château de Muzot sur Sierre (Valais)
Switzerland
March 30, 1923

. . . To preserve tradition—I mean not the superficially-conventional but what is of real descent (even if not around us, where circumstances tie it off more and more, then *in* us)—and to continue it cleverly or blindly, according to one's disposition, may for us (who will now once and for all remain those sacrificed to transitions) be the most crucial task. The impulse to contribute to its fulfillment something of my own, something comparatively precise, urged forth last year, in a few days, a number of sonnets which today I am sending to you (and your good wife) as a little reply to the great friendliness of your gift. Much in these poems might, without the cognizance of certain premises and some incidental information concerning my attitude toward love and death, be difficult to grasp, but much that is quite fully matured will open itself completely to you (who are not indeed without some closer dispositions toward and associations with me and for years have accompanied my changes in kind sympathy). My inclination to establish this very link with the greatest and most powerful part of tradition, yes, obedience to the inner indication to set *this* attempt within my work above every other, will serve moreover to elucidate for you many passages that deny themselves on first or second glance; regarded from such an angle then, the structure of the whole (unpremeditated, based entirely on inner dictation) as well as the parallelism of the first and second parts might become more intelligible. But enough, it would seem presumptuous of me to plague you with further "introductions"! I only wanted to be allowed, in this giving, to be genuinely giving and communicative.

[*199*]

To Xaver von Moos   Château de Muzot sur Sierre/Valais
April 20, 1923

. . . You mention the Sonnets to Orpheus: these may confront the reader, now and then, rather ruthlessly. They are perhaps the most mysterious, even to me, in their way of arising and imposing themselves on me, the most enigmatical dictation I have ever sustained and achieved; the whole first part was written down in a single breathless act of obedience between the second and fifth of February 1922, without one word being in doubt or having to be changed. And that at a time when I had braced myself for another great work and was also already occupied with it. How could one help growing in reverence and infinite gratitude, through such experiences in one's own existence. Even I myself am penetrating only gradually into the spirit of this mission, as which the Sonnets appear. As for their comprehensibility, I am now—at Easter time when I enjoyed the visit of friends here, I was able to make the test—fully capable, reading aloud, of conveying these poems accurately, there isn't one that then eludes the understanding of the whole context. To test that out, recently, filled and satisfied me extraordinarily. . . .

[*200*]

To Clara Rilke   Château de Muzot sur Sierre, Valais
April 23, 1923

I learned of Schuler's death by chance, from a little letter from Lilinka Knoop-Claus where it was just casually mentioned; wrote the very same day to her mother with a request for fuller particulars; meanwhile, before the answer could get here, I received them, as detailed as could be desired, through Hedwig Jaenchen-Woermann (with whom Schuler enjoyed staying during the last two summers).—But now you, with your intense and genuine experience, have implanted in me his reconciled and accepted going, as it will remain in me, a completion and confirmation of his personality, in which mystery was *there*, the way I always divine it, *as existence*. I thank you for these good tidings, which in so large a sense informed me about you too,—it was like an offering placed before Schuler's memory, everything you have there assembled together under his name,—and that you did not forget the smile he would allow at thought of me or speaking of me, the as you say (so wonderfully clearly to me) "lighted-up smile", makes me especially grateful to you. To know *this* more than anything else about him, was after all what I needed.—In memory of him I have just got a few newly opened narcissus and placed them on the altar of the abandoned rustic chapel (beside Muzot) which I take care of;—on account of its decrepitude no mass is read in it any more, and so it is now given back to all the gods and is always full of open simple homage.

In the Sonnets to Orpheus there is a lot that Schuler too would have granted; yes, who knows whether my expressing much in them at once so openly and so cryptically does not come across to me from my contact with him; I myself have only now, in reading aloud, gradually grasped these poems (which, when they un-expectedly came—the whole "First Part" came into being be-tween the 2nd and 5th of February 1922—, burst over me so that I had only just time to obey) and learned to convey them pre-cisely;—with little helps that I am able to interpolate in com-municating them, I now know very well how to serve the in-telligibility of the whole, the continuity everywhere establishes itself and where a darkness remains, it is of such a kind as to de-mand not illumination but submission. If you ever have questions about any of the poems, I will do my utmost to answer them. Isn't it lovely that the white horse (The "Ex-Voto", first Part, 20th sonnet, p. 26), which I "experienced" with Lou on a meadow in Russia, in 1899 or 1900, leapt through my heart again?! How nothing is ever lost! . . .

Spring, the Wallis is not a country where it can really draw breath, or reach its own peculiar depths, for which its being able to hesitate is the premise. The sun, already too powerful in March, draws all vegetation, as if with corkscrews, out of the hard gray earth. And then this climate has the frightful superstition of admitting no rain; it is rain-shy to a degree I would not have held thinkable; any means of thwarting and dissipating rain is agreeable to it,—in the summer that sometimes has its pleasant side, in that one almost always manages not to get wet—, but *now,* when it longs to rain silently and fruitfully, long letters that the sky would like to write to the earth, one almost despairs over the daily angers of the storm that with indescribable virtuosity hurls the good clouds over the mountains. That often tugs at one's nerves and, even more, at the poor flowers in the beds which, senselessly whipped and flogged, lose their heads.

And I, personally, have all sorts of physical indispositions that occasionally spoil a day or a night for me—, but none that I have not known long enough to get along with, as best I can. My pen has been thoroughly harnessed, these weeks, copying down the rather numerous translations this winter has brought in,—glorious poems of Paul Valéry—, and never, it seems to me, have I been more accurate and happy in translation. . . .

[*201*]

To Clara Rilke   Château de Muzot sur Sierre (Valais), Switzerland
December 21, 1923

. . . You could scarcely guess to what reading I have belonged with quite zealous absorption these last evenings. My housekeeper was presented with the letters and diaries of Paula Becker which I did think I knew; but this edition, which seems to have been little by little considerably enlarged (it is the fifth edition I have before me) gives so much more rounded and more deeply coherent a picture of her mature personality that to me the reading was like new and infinitely moving. Only now can that fabulously pure linking of destiny and task be perceived; only now does one understand the measure of quiet exclusion and equally quiet assent vested in her, and admire, once again, the way she used it, almost undoubting, reverently and joyfully.

I had the feeling in reading that I should lay my two books

somewhere in a niche to her memory, so that she may now pardon me my "unjoyousness" and so much else. And with you too, dear Clara, she would be pleased and in accord and would remind you that, nearly twenty-five years ago, she noted down that whatever might befall you, it would always be for your best good! . . .

[202]

To Nanny von Escher   Château de Muzot s/Sierre/Valais
December 22, 1923

. . . In you, Nanny von Escher, are combined such ancient and pure qualities of this manifold land that I feel a sort of satisfaction in showing by these books what I have achieved upon its righteous ground and under its protection. Much in the course and continuity of these verses—about this I have no illusions—you will find difficult of approach. Not as if I thought I was representing another time, for you are of those who have not grown away from younger people (and, incidentally, I may count myself among the generation of grandfathers, hence in common parlance among the "old") . . .

But it lies in the nature of these poems, in their condensation and abbreviation (in the way they frequently state lyric totals instead of listing the figures that were necessary for the result) that they seem more designed to be grasped in general by means of the inspiration of those of like direction than by what one calls "understanding". Two inmost experiences were decisive for their production: The resolve that grew up more and more in my spirit to hold life open toward death, and, on the other side, the spiritual need to situate the transformations of love in this wider whole differently than was possible in the narrower orbit of life (which simply shut out death as the Other). Here, so to speak, would be the place to look for the "plot" of these poems, and now and then it stands, I believe, simply and strongly in the foreground. . . .

[203]

To Gertrud Oukama Knoop   Château de Muzot s/Sierre (Valais)
Switzerland
February 13, 1924

I thank you from my heart for not wanting to wait until this late Easter to bestow upon me a few tidings which I received with attentiveness and real need; to me too, my silence toward you had long been too great—, but although the exchange here provides no diversions (at most when the dismal necessity occurs of pouring a flood of Czech or Austrian kronen or even marks! into the franc mold . . .), still there were other things preventing, dismal for me and on the whole unaccustomed; physical indispositions, of distant origin, with which however I have always been able to deal myself, have since summer become so importunate that twice (shortly after Christmas again) I had to seek out sanitariums; in this getting involved with doctors there is something indescribably confusing to me, just as though I were to find myself in the situation of dealing with my soul by the roundabout way of a priest: for the communication with my body, for twenty-five years, has been so direct and of such strict understanding, that I feel as if this medical interpreter were driving his way like a wedge into our neat adjustment. On the other hand it would be a new and somehow painful thing for me were I required with hitherto unused mental superiority to disregard in some measure a flagging body. In this I have never developed an antithesis, on the contrary, I was convinced that all the elements of my nature acted together toward a pure harmony, at the high points of which achievement then resulted from this surplus of common (physical and spiritual) gladness. My body, as an initiate into everything, has always had power of attorney too, it was permitted, like its partners in responsibility, to sign for the whole "firm". An upset in this business order would be a désastre for me; for however many great, indeed powerful counter-examples one could hold up to me, pointing to infinite results that could issue from the overcoming of the physical, from ignoring it, even from exploiting its indispositions, it would not be *my* way of arriving at such things, and I do not know what solution I would have to work up to for myself, being as I am, in a situation of that sort. Well, perhaps it hasn't permanently got that far, and I may, if enough has been imposed on me, continue in the old frame of mind and by means of it achieve a few more results! . . .

Russia: that "face of the mother of God", yes, there too: may those who are aware of its ascent not retreat too soon, but be sparing, sparing of it, hide it and cover it until its radiance has become ripe and time void! I don't doubt for a moment that the division as which we must see the war, facilitates new beginnings, but one trembles for them lest they show themselves too early and fall into the hands of the exploiters. The days of the profiteers would first have to be over.

If only I could be at your home for some tea hour, of a Sunday, in my habitual deep armchair, and tell you of all the wonderful things that are coming out of France; I am surrounded by them here. All I can lay by I use for the purchase of books now appearing; for many of them are of the kind one should not only read but open again and again. There the frontiers have now really fallen; having found itself again in a new vital way, the French spirit no longer fears to assimilate what is foreign and remote: suddenly, as never happened from that quarter, the Italian or Spanish, Russian or Scandinavian genus, but also the English and even the German—, is being recognized and characteristically evaluated; and the influences they thought before the war they could dispense with (or, being themselves intellectually localized, would have misunderstood) . . . , these influences now appear already quite taken up into the works of the youngest generation, those for whom the war has been something like a heroic puberty. There would be no sense in my citing names now: but there are ten or more books that give reality to inner events and hence (one may believe) are preparing from a distance, from the farthest distance perhaps, the corresponding external events . . . My confidence is great in this direction. . . .

[204]

To Alfred Schaer   Château de Muzot s/Sierre/Valais
                                       February 26, 1924

. . . In my *earliest* period, twenty-five or thirty years ago, one might indeed speak of "influences" that can be easily and specifically cited. The name of Jacobsen alone signifies here a quite definite epoch in my life: he was really the "year's regent" of my planetary-terrestrial year. And when I think of Bang (of the *Gray* and the *White House*), a star of the first magnitude might be indicated there, by whose appearance and position I found my way for a long while in the darkness of my youth (which was differently dark and differently twilit from periods of youth today). Liliencron's name was very wonderful to me in those years, Dehmel's hard and significant; Hofmannsthal's existence somehow proved to one that the most absolute poet was possible as a contemporary—, and in Stefan George's relentless creating one sensed the rediscovered law which henceforth no one, if he is concerned with the magic of the word, would be able to ignore. Into these experienced relationships worked the Russians, Turgeniev first, and the man who had directed me to this master, Jacob Wassermann, through his personality as well as through his first, already singularly controlled works. To recognize the Michael Kramer of Gerhart Hauptmann, with whom I also had personal relations, was a pride of those years. With my first trip to Russia (1899) and my learning of the Russian language in which I then experienced quickly and almost without hindrance any more, the spell of Pushkin and Lermontov, Nekrassov and Fet and the influence of so many others . . . , with these decisive inclusions the situation then changes so basically that a tracking down of influences seems absurd and impossible: they are countless! How many things had effect! One by its perfection, another because one at once understood that it should be better or differently done. This, because one immediately recognized it as akin and exemplary, that, because it obtruded itself antagonistically without being comprehensible, indeed, almost without being bearable.

And life! The presence of the suddenly exhaustlessly disclosed life which in Russia opened up to me still like a picture book, but in which, since my moving to Paris (1902), I knew myself included, everywhere com-municating, co-imperiled, co-endowed! And art . . . the arts! That I was Rodin's secretary is not much more than an obstinate legend that grew up out of the circumstance of my once, temporarily, for five months (!), assisting him in his correspondence. . . . But his *disciple* I was in a much better and much longer sense: for at the bottom of all the arts there operated the one, same challenge which I have never received so purely as through conversations with the powerful master who at that time, although of a great age, was still full of living experience; in my own metier I possessed a very great and praiseworthy friend, Emile Verhaeren, the poet so human in his hard glory,—and as the most forceful model, from 1906 on, there stood before me the work of a painter, Paul Cézanne, every trace of which I pursued after the death of the master.

But I often ask myself whether that which was in itself unaccented did not exercise the most essential influence on my development and production: the companionship with a dog; the hours I could pass in Rome watching a ropemaker who in his craft repeated one of the oldest gestures in the world, . . . exactly like that potter in a little Nile village, to stand beside whose wheel was, in a most mysterious sense, indescribably fruitful for me. Or my being granted to walk with a shepherd through the countryside of "Les Baux", or in Toledo, with a few Spanish friends and their women companions, to hear sung in an impoverished little parish church an ancient novena that once, in the 17th century, when the carrying on of this custom had been suppressed, was sung in the same church by angels . . . Or that so incommensurable an entity as Venice is familiar to me, in such degree that strangers could ask me successfully among the manifold turnings of the "calli" about any destination they sought . . . , all this was "influence", wasn't it?—, and the greatest perhaps still remains to be mentioned: my being permitted to be *alone* in so many lands, cities and landscapes, undisturbed, exposed, with all the diversity, with all the hearkening and heeding of my nature, to something new, willing to belong to it and yet again compelled to detach myself from it.

No, into these simple transactions that life performs with us, books, at least later, cannot extend entirely decisive influence; much from them that lays itself in us with its weight may simply be outweighed by meeting with a woman, by a shift in the season, yes by a mere change of atmospheric pressure . . . , through, for example, a "different" afternoon unexpectedly following upon such and such a morning—, or something else of the sort that is continually happening to us.

The question about "influences" is naturally possible and admissible, and there may be cases where the answer carries with it the most surprising disclosures; however, no matter how that answer reads, it must promptly be rendered again to the life from which it stems and in a sense be newly dissolved in it. Pursuant to this feeling, I have tried here, in order to answer at all, to prepare something like a "solution". May it appear not too diluted in your test-tube, my dear Doctor, and may it manifest a few more properties which will repay the investigation and observation you wish to expend upon it.

[205]

To Lou Andreas-Salomé   Château de Muzot sur Sierre (Valais)
Switzerland
Thursday after Easter, 1924 [April 22]

My dear, dear Lou, I cannot tell you what a great, a grand Easter you provided for me with your letter to which I joyfully looked forward, the longer it was delayed, as to something only the more sure and rich! Now it has been added to these days of celebration and was ripe with good tidings and affection as nothing that has befallen me for a long time. Only presently, when I have recounted to you the history of my past (third) Muzot-winter, will you see how wonderful it is that you can just now report *this* to me about your patients: I keep reading it over and over and draw from it an indescribable security. That I needed to confirm this will of itself tell you that my winter has been not a good one, indeed almost a hard one. What you had foreseen after that enormous capability of the first winter at Muzot, the reaction, has set in, and for a moment it was so violent and confusing that, shortly after Christmas, I left Muzot and went into the Val-Mont Sanitarium (above Montreux), unable (for the first time in many years) to deal with myself. They were curious weeks. Physically, the transverse colon had become the affected spot, more and more, but from there everything had gone awry. I was in Val-Mont three weeks. Unfortunately only on the next-to-last day, just before my departure, the attentive and well-intentioned doctor discovered on top of all this a goitre on the left side, which he indeed assured me was ten years "old" and had been compensated, but which, once discovered, nevertheless worked into my consciousness, all the more as there also emanated from the transverse colon, through upward pressure of air, swallowing and breathing difficulties of which I then, with the additional cause, became even more aware and suspicious. But that is already "case history" which I will sketch out for you better another time, dear Lou; for just now the house is full of guests, and visitors upon visitors are coming in relays in the next few days (an after all not unwelcome change after the loneliness of the long winter) . . . But also I have not recanted what I wrote you that time two years ago: that after the magnificence of this achievement I will gladly bear what may be imposed upon me in the way of reaction. I am holding out. And in so doing have also not been altogether inactive: a whole volume of French poems (to me remarkable; a few times I even set myself the same theme in French and in German, which then, to my surprise, developed differently from each language: which would speak very strongly against the naturalness of translation) came (somehow irresistibly) into existence, several things besides, and my reading all winter long was lively and of most rewarding intake. The location of my old tower is such that French books above all came to me; there is no end to my amazement at all that is now coming from there. Proust in first rank, who must certainly be wonderful to you too. You know how I was translating Paul Valéry all winter before last: this year he was one of my first visitors at Muzot, two weeks before Easter Sunday!

Since your letter came, Lou, do you know what I think? That *you* will sometime be here with me, this year! Why shouldn't that be possible? (except in the hottest time, when it would not be good for you and when I too shall probably go away). You know I have a guest room, a dear mansard, though with very small windows. Let us keep that in prospect when occasion arises? Yes?

Perhaps too, I must soon exchange the present rather special and exposed solitude for that in Paris which is nourished and permeated differently; perhaps everything here is beginning to be no longer necessary to me in the same measure, and as regards climate too is making itself oppressive. The local sun works only on the wine, that is its metier: everything else, plants and people, it forces too much, burdening them with the weight of its brooding which is perfectly adapted to wine country. And so, in time, a change, at least temporarily, will be necessary.

Since November second I have a granddaughter, a strong and sturdy little Christine. Ruth asked me particularly to tell you too. From her therefore, many good things; from Clara wonderfully good things even (from within) and such fine mitigations and illuminations . . .

[206]

To Anton Kippenberg   Muzot
                                            before May 22, 1924

. . . how happy I am that I hardly need increase at all the count or countlessness of the letters that crowd upon you on this (as custom has it) more stressed day of celebration; that rather I may, to say most of it, allude to a very recent reunion and all its dependabilities.

What I have wished for you in so many years, in the moments of greatest mutual trust and joyfullest understanding, and that wordlessly: today, as you read this, may it all, from me to you, wordlessly, be in effect.

Which might perhaps be expressed:

May everything lovingly achieved in home and profession and in the clear circle of your affection and duty make itself felt for an instant in your consciousness, so that you instinctively come to rest in it, repose upon it; and if then in a so festively appointed today the desire stirs to continue tomorrow something so manifoldly begun, may you, friend of ever more and more developed measure, at the same time discern in the force of this wish both the impatience of youth and the generously serene reflection of riper years.

So much for the sayable; the other may remain between us in use and suspension. In use and suspension let that too be kept which binds me to you indescribably, my gratitude.

It would be to interrupt a feeling like that in its course, my good friend, were I to try suddenly to designate it with words. But allow, dear, loyal friend, allow its current to carry to you a simple notebook—no dedication, nothing called forth or determined by the "occasion"; nevertheless something written down in this year, that of your fiftieth birthday.

You have long been acquainted with that peculiarity of my nature of falling back now and then upon an earlier tone; such relapses hardly advance what between us we may in confidence call the work, and they cause him to whom they happen a certain surprise and embarrassment. When I was looking through these sketches from two winter evenings again recently, I came near destroying them; but then it seemed to me that they might prove to be directed—if to anyone—to my friend. For him who has so often, on some urgent human or civic occasion, been called upon to exert himself in quick participation, may there perhaps be here provided a playground, an hour of relaxation for his sympathy.

And to close, this besides: my dear Kippenberg, you who are so practiced in supporting me, apply *this* too now for my support, that you are a year ahead of me, and give me an example of how one makes one's own, in a comprehensive and progressive sense, this turn beyond one's fiftieth year. Before I try it myself, let me in the conception of this be your pupil.

[207]

To Anton Kippenberg   Muzot sur Sierre (Valais) Switzerland
May 28, 1924

. . . Clara Rilke told me a great deal about her work, showed me pictures too (especially significant to me was the Schuler bust fashioned with such strange validity from memory and out of comprehensive inner experience); but most of all I let her report to me about Ruth and about little Christine and we mutually supported and furthered each other as best we could in the simplest and most elementary exercises of grandparenthood.

Not to forget this either, dear friend: on the twenty-second we thought again and again of you; in the afternoon Clara Rilke wanted to send you another telegram, and then in the evening, in the Bellevue, I drew you completely into our little circle. Since, for the guest period, the old ice of my going without alcohol is of course broken, I took advantage of it at once and had a half bottle of Pommery brought in which we drank up very gaily to your honor and happiness.

Clara Rilke, I must further add, was very moved that, despite hindrances, you had made it possible to see her in Leipzig; she still always does do things rather on the spur of the moment, but behind the disconnected decisions there really is developing in her, more and more, a reliable constant in which gradually the separated and interrupted elements of her nature might—one hopes—come together in such a way as to be at her disposal at any given moment. . . .

[*208*]

To Countess M.   Château de Muzot sur Sierre/Valais
                                    August 9, 1924

I have just come from Ragaz and although, after largely ne-
glecting my correspondence for six weeks, a mountainous letter
landscape awaited me on my table, I am allowing precedence over
all the rest to writing you my convalescence wishes. . . .

You were able in so lively and direct a way to comprehend
my difficult books, despite the endless inevitable difficulties these
verses entail (not so much on account of their obscurity, but because their points of departure are often concealed, like a tangle
of roots)—since quite without help you were so able to comprehend, something really almost like a reunion, it seems to me,
has taken place between us, at which however you made a severe
effort and I (as far as I am personally concerned) was severely
eliminated! But it can scarcely be said to what degree one is
able to carry oneself over into an artistic condensation as intense
as that of those Elegies and certain individual Sonnets; often, on
the thinner days of life (the many!), it is a strange situation for the
person who brings them forth to feel beside him *such* essence of
his own existence in its indescribable outweighing. The actuality
of such poems stands out singularly above the flatness and in-
cidentalness of daily life out of which nevertheless this greater,
more valid thing was wrested and derived, how one scarcely
knows oneself; for hardly is it done before one belongs again in
the general blinder destiny, among those who forget, or know as
if they didn't know, and who through a facile vagueness or being-
imprecise contribute to increasing the sum of life's mistakes. Thus
every big artistic achievement, into its last possible success, is both
distinction and humiliation for him who was capable of it. The
poetic word of course has about it an atmosphere of freedom that
is wanting to us; it has no neighbors, save in turn other equivalent
formations, and between it and them a spaciousness may evolve
similar to that of the starry sky: enormous distances and the un-

predictable movements of a higher order for which we lack any comprehensive view. . . .

[209]

To Nora Purtscher-Wydenbruck   Château de Muzot sur Sierre,
Valais
August 11, 1924

. . . If your whole letter, my dear Countess, was a subject of interest to the Princess, her quite special attention went to those strange lines in which you allude to your experiences with mediumistic writing. You remember that at the Taxis', whenever a reliable medium was there, they held very serious and often continuous séances—, in Ragaz we were just in the process of reviewing former and more recent results of these sessions, a part of which was still unknown to me, and so what you kindly wished to tell me landed in an atmosphere that allowed each of your words to work and to take effect with all its surmise, in all its seriousness. Only we would have liked to know so much more!

The Princess bade me tell you to go ahead quietly and carefully; perhaps those communicating powers may finally permit us to write down and preserve their manifestations (whereas it is certainly important to enter into *no* relations with metaphysical societies!) if one undertakes to keep these confidential and not use them in a way displeasing to them. It is indeed of the greatest value to be able to reread those communications the sense or validity of which comes out only gradually.—As for myself, my own impressions in this mysterious domain stem, with very few exceptions, from those experiments in the Taxis circle at which I was often present as an observer until about ten years ago. Later it was unfortunately never possible for me to connect with a reliable medium, otherwise I would certainly have been eager to increase on suitable occasions the very singular experiences that had fallen to my lot. I am convinced that these phenomena, if one accepts them, *without taking refuge in them*, and remains willing again and again to fit them into the *whole* of our existence, which is indeed full of no less wonderful mysteries in all its happenings—, I am, I say, convinced that these manifestations do not correspond to a false curiosity in us, but in fact *indescribably concern* us and (if one were to exclude them) would still be capable of making themselves repeatedly felt at some place. Why shouldn't they, like everything not yet recognized or indeed recognizable, be an object of our effort, our amazement, our perturbation and reverence?

I was for a while inclined, as you now seem to be, to assume "external" influences at these experiments; I am no longer so to the same degree. Extensive as the "external" is, it scarcely bears comparison, for all its sidereal distances, with the dimensions, *with the depth dimensions of our inner being*, which does not even need the spaciousness of the universe to be in itself almost immeasurable. If then the dead, if then those to come are in need of an abode, what refuge should be more pleasant and more proffered to them than this imaginary space? It appears to me more and more as if our customary consciousness inhabited the apex of a pyramid whose base in us (and in a sense beneath us) spreads to such breadth that, the farther we find ourselves capable of letting ourselves down in it, the more generally do we appear to be included in the given facts, not dependent on time and space, of terrestrial, of, in the broadest sense, *worldly* existence. Since my earliest youth I have entertained the conjecture (and have also, as far as I sufficed, lived by it) that at some deeper cross-section of this pyramid of consciousness mere *being* could become an event for us, that inviolable presentness and simultaneity of all that which, at the upper "normal" apex of self-consciousness, it is granted us to experience as mere "sequence". To suggest a personality that would be capable of perceiving what is past and what has not yet come into being simply as presentness to the last degree was, even then, in the time of the "Malte", a necessity to me, and I am persuaded that this conception corresponds to a state which is real though it may be retracted by all the terms of life as we practice it.

Now those séances, with all their disturbing or confusing attendant manifestations, with their fatal clumsinesses, halfnesses and (there can be no doubt about it) their countless misunderstandings . . . , lie on the road to such insights,—and could not pass me by as, intuitively, these insights were already prefigured in me; they have not, since I always inclined to assume a totality of the possible, in any way altered my conception of the world: it is just that I would simply have missed things of that sort *not* occurring. But just because, in a sense, the naturalness of this tremendous thing was already included in my inner assents and concessions, I also declined to side with such disclosures *more* than with any other mysteries of existence; they are to me *one* mystery among countless mysteries, all of which have more share in us than we in them. Whoever, within poetic creation, is initiated into the fabulous wonders of our depths, or at least is, like a blind and pure tool, somehow used by them, must arrive at developing for himself in marveling one of the most essential applications of his spirit. And there I must confess my greatest, my most passionate marveling goes to my own achievement, to certain activities in Nature, *even more* than to any mediumistic happenings, deeply as they have now and again stirred me. But regarding precisely these, while accepting them obediently, seriously and reverently, it is my strange instinct, when they pass over and into me, at once to waken counterweights to them in my consciousness: nothing would be more foreign to me than a world in which such powers and interferences had the upper hand. And strangely: the more I act thus (at pains after every nocturnal session, for example, immediately to hold the sight of the starry, still night just as grandiose and valid . . .), the more I believe myself in agreement with what is essential in those happenings. They want, it seems to me, rather to be tolerated than recognized; rather not rejected than summoned; rather admitted and loved than questioned and exploited. I am, luckily, quite unusable as a medium, but I do not doubt for a moment that in my own way I keep myself opened to the influences of those often homeless forces and that I never cease enjoying or enduring their association. How many words, how many decisions or hesitations may be laid to the score of their influence! Moreover, it is one of the original inclinations of my disposition to accept the mysterious *as such*, not as something to be unmasked, but rather as the mystery that, to its innermost being, and everywhere, is *thus* mysterious, as a lump of sugar is sugar throughout. Possibly, thus conceived, the mysterious on occasion dissolves in our existence or in our love, while otherwise we achieve only a mechanical breaking up of the most mysterious, without its actually passing over into us. I am (that would perhaps be the only spot in me where a slow wisdom could begin) completely without curiosity toward life, my own future, the gods . . . *What* do we know of the seasons of eternity and whether it just happens to be harvest time! How many fruits that were meant for us or whose weight would simply have entailed their falling to our share,—how many such fruits have inquisitive spirits interrupted in their ripening, bearing off a premature, untimely knowledge, often a misunderstanding, at the price of a (later) edification, or nourishment destroyed.

But I must close, dear and valued friends, after attempting to describe so wide an orbit. Take from it something that is yours and, if circumstances allow, always communicate with me about the particular jolts and movements that translate themselves to you from the unknown. You too will not manage without the awakening of counterweights: which luckily you do not lack, since artistic work, house, family, Nature—and, not least, the animals fervently occupy your heart and your interest. These indeed, who are privy to the whole, animals, which have their self-evidentness in a broader cross-section of consciousness, are again the most apt to lead—yonder and are close to the medial state . . .

To Professor Hermann Pongs   Château de Muzot sur Sierre, Valais
August 17, 1924

. . . When I recognized your letter in last evening's mail, I
was prepared for a (how well justified) reproof; now you have
made this so exceedingly charming in the form of the most understanding resignation that I would in any case have gone back
to your earlier letter. But how distances always refute themselves
in matters of the mind: perhaps at the very time you were writing
me just now, I had been occupied with that letter, and since then
it has lain on top of one of my piles of arrears (for here is also
my excuse: I was absent from home for more than seven weeks
and forced myself, during this vacation, to leave my letter pen
switched off. Which now is naturally having its reaction).

But to that letter before last and its questions. Whenever I took
it up, even three days ago, I was filled with the same distinct
regret: that this, for us both, toilsome expression by letter could
not be replaced by a few hours of living conversation. Not that I
shunned any toil in face of your detailed interest,—but the information you seek would yield itself fully only under the stimulus of
counter-questions interrupting and luring it on. Especially taking
into consideration my poor memory, which would perhaps not be
so poor if it were not a question of—in a sense—repressed years
on which, in view of my disinclination to have to do with their
recollections, no real opinion could take shape in me.

I am certainly grateful to you for not expecting of me any
biographical paraphernalia, and must now nevertheless bring up
a few matters of this sort myself, to make my aversion to my
earliest productions intelligible to you. The years you are now
thinking of followed immediately upon some of which I never
understood how they could have been survived. Around my
seventeenth year I was so unprepared for life and the work I was
to realize for myself as can possibly be imagined. A five-year training in a military school had finally, on account of the state of my
health and my spirit, become so flagrantly absurd that it had to

end with a break. A further year passed in sickliness and perplexity. The lower military academy and later the upper academy at Mährisch-Weisskirchen—however good a reputation the two institutions may have had in professional circles—had brought me nothing of what could have served my inclinations and talents; moreover the conditions there had become so damaging to my health that in the last year and a half I had not been able to follow even the very one-sided and flimsy instruction customary there. Besides this, the segregation of the boys in those strict educational institutions was so complete that I knew neither the books that would have been nourishing and suitable to my age nor any bit of simple reality working into life. The return home—to Prague—seemed at first like a liberation full of infinite possibilities; actually there resulted from it nothing but embarrassments and confusions. These kept increasing the more manifest it became to what inclinations I wanted to give myself over. My father needed the support of all of his great love for me in order to concede that the officer's profession might not be the most fitting for me. How might one ask him to consent to a vocation that stood in contradiction to everything he called profession. Yet, after long hesitation, it was arrived at that I should make up grammar school; they could not possibly put me among the ten-year-olds at its beginning where I had to start. Advantageous private instruction was granted me which, as I was now setting about things with a certain determination, took me so far that I got through the first six classes of the Latin School in one year; a slower pace then made easier the remaining two classes (which, as a reward, I was allowed to complete under the same private arrangement) and I at last matriculated at a public grammar school not much later than I would have come to the final examination in a normal school course.

These years, beset by efforts of every sort, were at the same time those of my earliest, often, despite all duties and tasks, quite lively productivity; my first publications date from it—, all those experiments and improvisations which, a little later, I could only wish I had had the discretion to retain in my school desk drawer.

That they nevertheless got out, indeed that I forced them out by every means, was due to the same cause that today makes them seem to me so inappropriate to denote the beginnings of what I was little by little to achieve. If I was foolish enough to want to play out those nullities, I was driven to it by the impatient wish to prove to my antagonistic environment my right to such activity—, a right for which, these attempts once displayed, others also might show a notable inclination to intercede. Indeed more than anything I was probably hoping for this: to find among the public such people as could help me achieve the connection with those intellectual movements from which in Prague, even under better circumstances than mine, I believe myself fairly shut off. It is the only time in my life when I did not struggle within my work, but with its miserable scrapings went out after recognition: this above all was probably what brought it about that, shortly thereafter, when (about a year before the first Russian journey) for the first time I found myself implanted in a provisional center of my real nature, I disowned that early period with a certain shame, though its dust still lay upon my books. In so doing I condemned to be sure my own attitude only and did not forget the helps that had fallen to my share. Among the Prague people, Alfred Klaar, Friedrich Adler, of the younger men Hugo Salus and the painter Orlik, had noticed my efforts, and August Sauer had turned to even my earliest attempts an attention they could not have deserved. But the strongest hand I was permitted to cling to had been extended to me from the north, and as long as I did not let it go, I may sincerely have boasted about it. I shall never forget that it was Detlev von Liliencron who was one of the first to encourage me to the most unforeseeable projects—, and if occasionally, he furnished his cordial letters with the generous salutation which, read aloud, spelled: "My splendid René Maria", it seemed to me (and I was at pains to present this conviction to my family) that in these lines I possessed the most reliable indication of the boldest future!

Moreover the poetic influence of Liliencron's work must have taken very penetrating effect in me; he on the one hand, on the other Jacobsen, had first confided to me in my immaturity and isolation how it is possible from what is closest, from things that are at hand under all circumstances, to take the leap into the most spacious; and how through it one could brace oneself for the experience of that wonderful feeling of self in which one's own highly insecure ego acquired a relative value that seemed more decisive than any possible recognition.

But as to J. P. Jacobsen, even later, during many years, I still experienced through him something so indescribable that I find myself in no position to determine without delusion and invention what he may have meant to me in those earliest years. Even far into the Paris period, he was a companion in my mind and a presence in my heart—; that he was no longer living seemed to me at times an unbearable deprivation, but just this strange compulsion still to have known him, early bred in me freedom and openness toward the dead writer, an attitude which particularly in his, Jacobsen's, homeland and in Sweden was to experience the most singular corroboration.

Here, for example, are places, dear Dr. Pongs, where I miss your counter-questions for tracing further with you narrower, almost overgrown paths. So to remain at what can be simply grasped: I first made Jacobsen's acquaintance (*Niels Lyhne* and the *Six Short Stories*) in the sympathetic oldest translation of Maria von Borch—(Reclam)—, which still remained the most pleasing to me when I had fitted myself to some extent for mastering the Danish texts.

For the rest, it was Jacob Wassermann to whom I ascribe the first, almost severe pointing-out of these books (as well as of Turgeniev); the lyric vagueness in which I was moving made him, who had already learned to value and to practice working and reworking in art, impatient—, and so one day in Munich, as a kind of task, he put into my hands these works which he himself had just previously set us as criteria. That I, on my own, was incapable of finding such accessible books reminds me of my dreadful helplessness in reading; without the famous book-stands along the Seine, which lay the books of all periods at the very border of one's life—, what would I ever have found!

Even those early days in Munich were of no special service to me so far as reading goes; the *Pages for Art* for example even then remained unobtainable or unknown to me, so that I cannot have read much of Hofmannsthal. The enchantment that emanated from the little I could make my own had of course no equal. Of Stefan George the *Year of the Soul* was significant to me from the beginning; but it revealed itself as overwhelming only from the time I had heard the poet reciting his imperious verses in the Lepsius circle.

When I think of other "influences" it would be difficult to call them all to mind; you mention Jacobowski; a Baltic writer, Reinhold Maurice von Stern, and a number of others who appeared in the little periodicals read and besieged by all, could be mentioned with just as much justification. The, for a while, parallel efforts of Wilhelm von Scholz and E. von Bodmann had intermittent exemplary or comradely significance—, but then Russia came into it, two years before I traveled there, through a person close to me who embraced it all in her nature, and with that, as you rightly recognize, was prepared the turning into what was really my own.

The "Cornet" was the unforeseen gift of a single night, an autumn night, written down in one impulse by the light of two candles flickering in the night wind; the drifting of clouds over the moon provoked it, after the subject had been inspired in me some weeks before by first acquaintance with certain family papers I had inherited.

The "Angel Songs", the "Maidens' Songs" were conceived in Tuscany, in Florence and by the Ligurian Sea; a few individual ones were probably even written down right there, in Viareggio, where years later a part of the *Book of Hours* came to precipitation. To speak of the religious terms out of which those songs unfolded would require going too far back; for the high point of my Catholic-accented emotion is located in the upheavals of that hard military-school period which had imposed upon me, among five hundred boys, a (for my age) more than life-sized experience of loneliness. Immediately after it, or already during it, began a ruthless putting-to-use of that relation to God which is not to be characterized as denominational.

Enough: I herewith enclose your letter, the earlier one, so that, beside my attempts to reply, you can recall your own questions. In this I am not concealing from myself the inadequacy of my information. Do not let it discourage you nevertheless from coming to me again; perhaps I shall succeed another time in being more instructive. I would then suggest simply getting up a kind of questionnaire on which you would leave me room to enter the answer right beside your inquiry; this practice recently, in corresponding with my Polish translator, proved sufficiently convenient and fruitful to be recommended in similar cases. In closing let me further assure you that I could follow your concept or occasional surmise very well. I never read what is published on my books, but if in some essay insights are expressed as strong and reliable as those you show me, I must almost regret having imposed absolutely on myself this (for the rest necessary) restriction.

I feel in duty bound to be grateful, to remain grateful to you for bestowing such deep attention.

Yours sincerely,

R. M. Rilke

P.S. I have just noticed a further unanswered postscript on the margin of one of your letter-pages. Unfortunately I have no remembrance of the creation of the poem: "I would not like to die in spring" (do not, please, draw any conclusions from this rather vague assertion *).

* that of the poem!

[*211*]

To Captain Otto Braun   Château de Muzot sur Sierre (Valais),
Switzerland
September 3, 1924

. . . If my wish to make the acquaintance of Niederlangenau had not been already lively enough, your kindness, in writing me as you did, would have found the happiest means of intensifying and arousing it. The history of our family has interested me since my childhood, indeed, there was a time then, in my eighth or ninth year, when this interest had grown to a kind of passion that was unequaled. The head of our family, my father's eldest brother (Dr. Jaroslav von Rilke-Rüliken) had in those years, for the benefit of his son especially, renewed with extraordinary vigor the investigations that had always been going on. It is probably thanks to this circumstance that the reports you most kindly handed on were all known to me already, though naturally I no longer remembered specific dates. Shortly thereafter, through the early death of his son, my uncle lost all interest in such discoveries—, but the result of those archival labors which had been pursued by several commissioned specialists, a big bundle, came to me from his estate, unfortunately to the most uncertain destiny: it is to be assumed that these papers, with all the rest of my property that had remained there, were auctioned off and sold for a song in Paris . . . For the rest, my great-grandfather, who at the beginning of the last century had again come into landed property (he possessed the extensive estate of Kamenitz an der Linde in Bohemia), had undertaken zealous researches into his family's past: to him is probably attributable the handing on of that tradition which would trace our family back to the family of the ancient Carinthian nobility called Rilke, Rilcke) in the various spelling cited in Weiss, *Old Carinthian Nobility*). The State Assembly House in Klagenfurt does, in fact, show above this name, anciently established there, a coat of arms akin or fashioned similarly to ours. From thence (the Carinthian Rilkes, if I am not mistaken, appear from 1276 on as liegemen of the

Carinthian dukes) branches are said to have emigrated even at an early period to Saxony and Bohemia, always into mining districts, as indeed the possessions in Carinthia too were located in regions in which mining had been indigenous from earliest times. All that is of course to be taken more or less as legend, for the establishment of an unbroken genealogy has not been possible to any of the investigators.

Furthermore, a Rilke branch must have existed for some time on one of the Saxon estates . . . ; I remember finding mention in those archival transcripts of a Magdalena Rilke, born von Hartitzsch, who appeared there as late as 1718, which date indeed also seems to have been that of the final collapse of the onetime prosperity of the family in Saxony.—Mention was made also, as I recall, of the Griebes: at all events I knew that this family had succeeded to a part of the former Rilke estates; nevertheless you mention to me in this connection a whole series of remarkable details that were certainly not recorded there. And you point out to me too, also concerning the past of the Rilkes, something further in the way of tradition; what joy it will mean to me to look over things like that with you sometime; there may indeed be much that is altogether new to me among them. However, it will be almost more important to me to see the countryside itself: I think it should bring to awakening something in me that has never yet been called upon; after all I have never had a chance to visit any of the places (I do not know Carinthia either) which we assume belong to our family's past, and hence too have contributed, with the countless influences of soil and surroundings, to its making. . . .

[212]

To Professor Hermann Pongs   Château de Muzot s/Sierre
(Valais), Switzerland
October 21, 1924

An imminent journey, matters to be wound up and preparations in connection with it, compel me to be briefer and to use more trite phrases than I otherwise would in dealing with the ideas suggested to me by your letter and the "questionnaire".

I must restrict myself to the most factual and then, after filling out the answer-side, will start tying in some supplementary material with the answers that refer to individual passages in your letter or its enclosures.

First the questionnaire:

Prague period. Final school examination 1894	(or 1895)
As student in Prague until middle of 1896?	Yes
Memories of professors? Painting? (Klimt?)	—: none at all. Painting played no role, except that (very incompetently) I myself tried my hand at it. Klimt? thinnest gilt paper, even at that time.
Perhaps Ernst Mach's Philosophy?	Have never read philosophers except perhaps in those years a few pages of Schopenhauer (aversion to that sort of systematization).
What impressions were behind the strong social inclinations that came to expression in *Wild Chicory?*	The inclination to give away "Wild Chicory" may have been not so much "social", as rather brotherly and human; arising from my having myself been cut off from books and intellectual connections.

Wouldn't it be worth while to collect and re-publish the prose pieces of the whole early period?
    "Hoar Frost" 1897
    Without Present
    (Drama) '98
	For reasons I have already indicated recently, this early production is without lasting value; besides which I, like most of those who were first carried away by the poem, was incapable of writing even a tolerable prose. The proof, that I could let

Along Life's Way
(Short Stories) '98
Two Prague Tales '99
Everyday Life 1902
The Last 1902
About God 1900
or any others?

Munich Period.
How long? Memories of
modern painting?

Stay in Italy 1897

When is the Worpswede
period?
When the first Russian
journey? 1899?
When the second? When
with Tolstoy?

When and through what
did the "White Princess"
come into being?

myself go in the "Cornet" to inter-
mingle these two widely separated
forms, a tastelessness which for
years made that little improvisation
of a single autumn night unendurable
to me, until finally I again gave it
credit for the naïveté of its youthful
manner.

Munich 1896 till Fall 1897 with interruptions.
Painting, yes, but wrongly seen,
from the point of view of subject.
Uhde, with whom I had the opportunity of becoming personally acquainted.

First stay in Italy 1897 (after having
already at the age of eight visited our
Italian Littoral [Görz and surround-
ings]. Since then have spoken and
occasionally read the language).

First Russian journey 1899; longer
stay in Russia the following year.
Called on Tolstoy both times. (1899
in Moscow, 1900 at Yasnaia Poliana.)
Learning of Russian between the two
journeys, without a teacher; reading
Tolstoy (the great novels).
Westerwede near Worpswede: residence from 1901 to 1902 (from my
marriage, which provided the reason
for settling there.)

Removal to Paris: fall 1902; residence there until 1914; with many
journeys, for example, winter 1904

When for the first time Paris?

How long with Rodin?

What French painters preferred?

(Van Gogh?) (Cézanne?)

When in Sweden?

to 1905 (almost a year) Rome. Appended to that the months in Copenhagen and Sweden (Skåne).

What came between parts I and II of the *Book of Hours?* (1899 and 1901?) What between parts II and III? (1902 to 1903) (in the way of works and travels) (study of mysticism?)

Is the dense rhymeless style of the Requiem determined by a particular model?

Between Book of Hours I and II therefore came Russia; the 2nd part came into being in Westerwede, the 3rd (coming from Paris) at Viareggio in Italy, where, in the glorious pinete I did a great deal of work. Mysticism I read as little as philosophy.

What gave the first incentive to translations? Even before 1908? (E. Browning?)

The Sonnets of Elizabeth Browning were translated in honor of a friend who was of English descent on her mother's side and loved these poems above everything. Sole attempt in English, the most remote and alien language to me.

When first acquainted or acquainted at all with Simmel's works? And with which?

With Georg Simmel I came in contact only socially (1908–1900) [1899–1900]; at that time I was living in Schmargendorf near Berlin.

How (after a four-year interval) did the "Life of Mary" come about?

The Life of Mary (see letter)

(1913?) through what impressions? Perhaps through plastic art?

What impressions produced the occult incidents in Malte?

The "occult occurrences" in Malte: in part accurately recounted experiences of childhood in Prague, in part things experienced and heard in Sweden. Here moreover one of the reasons why the fictitious figure of M. L. Brigge was made a Dane: because only in the atmosphere of the Scandinavian countries does the ghost appear ranged among the possible experiences and admitted (which conforms with my own attitude).

Besides Jacobsen is another prose now also contributive? (Maeterlinck?)

From the time I read Danish, besides Jacobsen, Bang; Maeterlinck probably too for a time, but not as an element contributing to the development of my prose.

What personal impression of the late pictures of Paula Modersohn?

Paula Modersohn I last saw in Paris in 1906 and knew little of her works of that time or her latest, with which even now I am not yet acquainted.

Your inner relation to things? Relation to Van Gogh?

Only in passing, the great event to me in painting was Cézanne, whom however I began to study only after his death. Previously the great French impressionists had had an effect, and, in passing, Cottet, Lucien Simon, Zuloaga.

Tolstoy: it would be wrong to attribute to those visits to him an influence on my works of that time; ultimately he confirmed for me only the discovery of Russia, which was decisive for me. His figure was to me the embodiment of a fatality, a misunderstanding, and it struck me so by reason of the fact that, for all the obstinate injustice this tremendously restless man inflicted upon himself and was constantly ready to inflict upon others, that (I say) it still affected one as so touchingly protected and valid in his desertion of the tasks that were his greatest and at which he was most skilled. Only thus could a young person, who had already resolved to pursue art all his life long, comprehend that contradictory old man, who in himself was working at the constant repression of what had in the most divine sense been imposed upon him; who disavowed himself with infinite effort right into his own blood and never mastered the tremendous forces that were inexhaustibly renewing themselves in his repressed and denied artistic genius. How high (and pure!) he stood above those, the majority in Europe, who, on the contrary, worried all their lives about these forces and were determined, by practice and falsification (by "literature"), to conceal the occasional slackening or defection of their fruitfulness. The meeting with Tolstoy (whose moral and religious naïvetés exercised no attraction whatsoever upon me,—shortly before my second trip the disgraceful and silly pamphlet *What Is Art* had in all superfluity come into my hands—) so thus strengthened in me precisely the opposite of the impression he may have wanted to leave with his visitors; infinitely far from bearing out his conscious renunciation, I had seen, even into his most unconscious behavior, the artist secretly retaining the upper hand, and particularly in view of his life filled with refusals, the conception grew within me of the positiveness of artistic inspiration and achievement; of its power and legitimacy; of the hard glory of being called to something like that.

Only the meeting with Rodin, vouchsafed me two years later, and the years of close association with him, could still further strengthen this so grandly conceived idea, could bear it out more thoroughly. Here an error that has become more and more ingrained might incidentally be corrected. I was, strictly speaking, *never* (as your question sheet expresses it) "with Rodin", if by that a kind of position is meant. When I moved to Paris in 1902, Richard Muther had suggested that I write about Rodin; for his work (though even then of plastic art little, according to its true value, had as yet become significant to me), I seemed prepared, inasmuch as my wife has the right to consider herself a pupil of Rodin's; through her, who as a young girl had been allowed to bring him her weekly work for many months (and later again and again), a turning had been prepared in me: I had become more capable of comprehending works of art from the standpoint of *form* and seemed a trace more safeguarded against chance over-powerings by mere relations of content, which act upon the un-prepared person, even through the most inadequate handling of form, if they in any way touch him.—At the time I came to Paris, one could get to know Rodin's work, with exception of the few pieces that even then belonged to the Luxembourg Museum, almost only at his own place; so it was natural for me to go out often that fall, finally every day to Meudon. Out of our from the very beginning quite lively conversations, a real relation-ship rapidly developed, the funds for which on the one side my gradually increasing admiration sufficiently provided, while to meet this self-probing feeling a response grew up on the Master's side which, without presumption, even at the end of the first year, I might call one of friendship. If journeys kept me away then, how often it was an unexpected, sympathetic word from Rodin that came to strengthen me in my own work. In 1905 [1904], during my stay at a little Swedish castle in the neighborhood of Lund, there reached me from several German and Austrian cities invitations to lecture on Rodin; I did not see myself capable of completely satisfying these demands without previously coming into new contact with his continually growing work, and de-cided, in agreement with Rodin, to return to Paris earlier than had actually been my intention. To my inquiry whether I should find him in Meudon, Rodin had replied in the affirmative, more-over with the invitation to lodge this time with him. Scarcely had I declined this, when, I remember, a telegram arrived from Rodin's secretary which repeated the invitation so pressingly that I had no further scruples about accepting. This telegram read: Monsieur Rodin y tient, pour pouvoir causer. And so with that began those five months when I really was "with Rodin"; first as a guest in his house, later, as I did not want to stretch this hospitality further without also (my own work, part two of the Rodin book, had meanwhile been concluded) being somehow useful to him, when I devoted my free time to assisting him with his extensive correspondence, which was continually far in arrears, I cannot boast of the letters I wrote for him at that time. This occupation for which my pen, which knows no haste, was not the most apt, soon grew up over my head and—what was worse—it threatened to force our association out of its natural course in that it compelled me often to substitute for our otherwise fluent discussions the most irksome reminders of letter-debts and other obligations of correspondence, leading of necessity to a distortion of our relationship, which it was infinitely crucial for me to keep sound and fruitful. So by May of the following year I moved back to Paris, completely my own master, and my relations with Rodin, which had passed into a curious region, fell back into their earlier channel which they were then, through the years, to fill in a stronger or weaker stream. Here once again(gathering from your questionnaire how much you are further looking about for "influences") I will linger and emphasize how far this direct and manifold influence of the great sculptor outweighed anything that stemmed from literature and in a sense made it superfluous. I had the good fortune to meet Rodin in those years when I was ripe for my inner decision and when on the other hand the time had arrived for him to apply with singular freedom the experiences of his art upon everything that can be lived. The opposite of what I had observed in Tolstoy took place here: A man who had assented fully and actively to the inner mission of his creative genius, the infinite divine play, was taking possession, by means of the insight there acquired, of more than just his art; it looked for a while as if everything for which, his hands bound in the work, he had been unable to reach, were of its own volition giving itself to him as well . . . And so it may be too, not only for the artist of highest intent, but for the simple craftsman, if only he has once bitten open the kernel of his métier: the intensity arrived at within his characteristic achievement appropriates to him (automatically, one might say) everything that is and has been which corresponds to the same degree of intensity. From thence stems the wonderful wisdom of craftsmen (which is being lost), thence the spiritual spaciousness in shepherds' souls . . .

And now (we are not so far from it) the difficult attempt to do justice to your striking reflections on "rich" and "poor". The turns your letter takes are not entirely intelligible to me, which may well be due to my not finding your point of departure, and so having to join your thought along the way, without knowing from whence it may have started. If it comes from the conception of the "social"—as it appears to—then I must at once assert that one would be wrong in classifying any one of my efforts under this rubric. Something of a human likemindedness, something brotherly is indeed spontaneous in me and must have been laid down in my nature, otherwise the liberating of this characteristic under the influence of the Russian example would not have moved me so deeply and familiarly. But what absolutely differentiates so joyous and natural a tendency from the social, as we understand it today, is the utter disinclination, even aversion, to changing anyone's situation or, as they say, to bettering it. The situation of no one in the world is such that it could not be of peculiar use to his soul . . . And I must confess that, where I have been required to participate in the destiny of others, this above all has always been important and urgent to me: to help the person oppressed to recognize the peculiar and special conditions of his plight, which each time is not so much a consolation as an (at first unapparent) enrichment. It seems to me to create nothing but disorder if the general effort (for that matter an illusion!) should presume schematically to alleviate or remove oppressions, a thing which injures the freedom of the other person much more drastically than does the plight itself, which with indescribable adaptations and almost tenderly confers upon him who entrusts himself to it, indications of how—if not outwardly, then inwardly—it could be escaped—. To want to better the situation of a human being presupposes an insight into his circumstances such as not even the poet possesses concerning a figure of his own invention. How much less still the so infinitely excluded helper, whose scatteredness becomes complete with his gift. Wanting to change, to improve, a person's situation means offering him, for difficulties in which he is practiced and experienced, other difficulties that will find him perhaps even more bewildered. If at any time I was able to pour out into the mold of my heart the imaginary voice of the dwarf or the beggar, the metal of this cast was not won from the wish that the dwarf or the beggar might have a less difficult time; on the contrary, only through an extoling of their incomparable destiny could the poet, suddenly bent upon them, be true and fundamental, and he would have to fear and avoid nothing so much as a corrected world in which the dwarfs are stretched and the beggars enriched. The God of completeness sees to it that these varieties do not cease, and it would be most superficial to regard the joy of the poet in this suffering multiplicity as an esthetic pretext. So I too have a conscience clear of any reproach of having prevaricated if, faced with the concepts "rich" and "poor", I unquestioningly claim for my poem the justified impartiality of artistic expression. It can never have been my intention to play off the poor against the rich or to espouse the one with more conviction than the other. But the task may well have been set me of measuring poverty and wealth for a while with their purest measures,—for, even here again, how should one not come to praise both when one discerns them rightly.

In a world which tries to resolve the divine into a kind of anonymity, that humanitarian over-estimation must come into effect which expects of human aid what it cannot give. And divine goodness is so indescribably linked with divine hardness that a time which undertakes, in advance of Providence, to dole out the former, at the same time also drags forth the oldest stores of cruelty among men. (We have experienced it.)

I have finished; or rather I must decide to do so. Glancing over your pages once more, I notice I have still left two points unconsidered, or three, or more . . .

Quickly still to these. (Concerning the letter:) No, it would have little sense for you to lay a *Book of Pictures* before me for the dating of the individual poems and poem-groups; my own memory is too unreliable and inadequate here. Most to be recommended would be a comparison of the first edition with the later ones, which would show you what works of later origin were little by little taken into the whole. (I am never provided with my own books and possess none of these editions to assist you in this survey.)

The origin of the *Life of Mary*, with which (in the winter of 1912) I resumed an older tone I had long since got beyond, was quite externally conditioned: I learned at that time that Heinrich Vogeler, in whose guest-book I had occasionally written Mary poems in those Westerwede years, was intending to publish those (early) verses with his drawings. To prevent this and at least to furnish him, in case he were to stick to his intention (which did not happen), with better and more connected texts, I wrote in a few days, consciously feeling back, these (except for one or two) unimportant poems, for which the painters' book of Mount Athos with its picture-legends served as objective support.

How difficult it often is to make credible the causes out of which a poem arises! You ask about the "White Princess". At Viareggio, I lived in a big villa facing the sea with a stately garden. In this there appeared, while I was standing at the window one afternoon, a friar collecting for his brotherhood, the white hood drawn before his face; he evidently did not dare enter the house but, in expectation of making his presence felt, kept at some distance on the garden path. Now whether he noticed me at one of the tall windows or not, the fear seized me that the uncanny stranger with the veiled face might take my slightest movement for a sign and enter. And from this fear I fell into a strange, paralyzing numbness. Moreover on the same evening (something which makes the day unforgettable to me) a dachshund belonging to the house died; that morning I had been surprised to find the animal, which was friendly with me and otherwise disposed to be playful and interested, sitting close up to the house, motionless, his long face turned as if in boundless meditation to the wall . . .

Mustn't we be (you say it yourself) strangely constituted if from these two occasions, lifting itself up by them as it were, a year later, the poem could come into being that is called "The White Princess"?

And now, as a real close, a greeting to your little four-year-old son who has accorded my name the most beautiful and most direct recognition. This "poem" has the virtue of being short; should he ever want to memorize it, I would prefer for this effort the expression they have for it in French: qu'il le saurait "par coeur"!

See whether his spontaneous "conjuration" has brought you in something serviceable and elucidating, and continue to regard me as

Yours sincerely,

R. M. Rilke

Postscript, the following day:

I am making use, dear Dr. Pongs, of this remaining fourteenth page to append one more contribution to the theme of "rich and poor". The little incident here reported (the greatness of which for the rest one may judge for oneself) expresses what my personal attitude would be, if I were to give thought to it, so completely and so validly that I should have nothing to add to it.

Does the name *Jammersminde* (Danish, translated by the expression "memory of suffering") remind you of anything? These are the journals, very widely circulated in Denmark, even taken up in schools, of Countess Leonora Christina Ulfeldt, a daughter of King Christian IV, drawn up for her children and grandchildren during her twenty-six-year imprisonment in the blue tower of Copenhagen. Her husband, Imperial Steward Korfitz Ulfeldt, charged with high treason, had managed to save himself in time by his flight to the Tirol; the Danish government deemed it in order to assure itself at least of the Countess, who remained loyal to Ulfeldt. She was at the English court seeking help for her husband. There they knew how to reach her and on some pretext or other to invite her onto a Danish ship where she believed herself to be a guest while in reality she was already the prisoner of her custodian. Into this moment is to be set the little scene which is reported in the introduction to *Jammersminde* (in the Danish edition at least). One of the younger officers of the ship, in his youthful zeal, thought he would advance himself when he prematurely approached the still unsuspecting Countess and respectfullly but definitely demanded the jewelry she was wearing on her person. One can imagine the astonishment of the person thus addressed. It cannot have been quite easy for the young lieutenant to sustain with grace the look his covetousness brought him. But then the beautiful and stately lady who, in accordance with the mode of the time, was richly adorned with jewels and chains, stepped up to the mirror of her cabin and slowly, without haste, one after the other, removed the rings, the pendants, the brooches, the bracelets and earrings that piled up, warm and heavy, in the frightenedly outspread hands of the officer. When, already quite uncertain, he went with this royal booty before his commandant, the latter's surprise and finally his rage knew no bounds. He did not doubt that his secret intentions were now discovered and the whole bold undertaking had miscarried. Flaring up at his lieutenant with the hardest words, he refused all responsibility and left it to the unfortunate man to make good his arbitrary and disastrous rashness—, he could find out for himself how! Pale, trembling, the fabulous abundance even yet on his overladen hands, the annihilated officer again appeared before the tall lady. Stood, stammering . . . She left him, regally, for a suitable moment in his state of despair, but only (though she must really have understood all that would follow) to step again to her mirror and, slowly, as if from the hands of a servant, to take and put on the manifold trinkets with precisely the same serenity she had previously shown in giving them away, and already absorbed in her reflection as it festively completed itself again in the glass.

P.S. Reading over my pages, though it is superfluous (for you already, I think, understand me correctly) I would nevertheless like to have noted down one thing more: I am never giving *judgments* here of the manifestations and things you questioned me about, but am showing them, most one-sidedly in the perspective of the digressions from them that I may at times have made. As "judgment" most of it (for instance the Tolstoy item) would be awry and laughable. But it was a question here of the explanation of a specific situation interesting you at the moment (which for that matter makes me ashamed of taking it so seriously). I have tried my utmost to satisfy your wishes and am once more, as already yesterday, your:

R.M.R.

[213]

To Clara Rilke
Bellevue Palace & Bernerhof, Bern
November 17, 1924

Your last letter reached me here on September 21st—, and now I am writing you for the 21st of November: two months! I don't quite know how it could get to be so long, or I know only in part: somehow it paralyzed me that I should be unable to fulfill your financial wish this time, and from that there arose a first little silence that further circumstances came to extend. Once again I was on bad terms with my letter pen and had not a good period in other ways either, indeed as far as I can recall, the remainder of this summer and the fall has been one of my worst and inwardly most difficult times. This at first from the physical . . . ; but somehow it then becomes scarcely possible to distinguish whether a physical indisposition is disturbing the free movements of the soul, or whether these, in their standstill, are holding the indisposition fast. In short, there were not-good weeks, one after the other. My second Ragaz visit I had given up, partly because too much miscellaneous writing had awaited me at Muzot—, also it bothered me to leave house and roses so soon again; from Ragaz came word that it was overrun with visitors, and, in contrast to the beginning of the season, full of unpleasant people. And finally, I hoped by this renunciation to lay by something for a that much greater mobility later on, secretly counting on starting for Paris around October 15. Of that, as you see, nothing came either. I did not feel well and active enough, sat the time away in Muzot where, by way of compensation for the scarcely favorable summer, there were three truly radiant weeks in which the Wallis was itself again. Work too progressed in many directions: I wrote down for my own pleasure a little volume of Wallis verses, "Quatrains Valaisans", in which one or another experience of this landscape lightly took shape, and in addition a whole little cycle, "Les Roses", likewise French. All that only like cakebaking; but then quickly (while for ten days and really for quite other writing purposes I had a secretary) there came into being the first provisional version of a translation of Valéry's magnificent *Eupalinos* dialogue, from which you will get much that is close and significant to you, when sometime you can read it in my version. So, for all the despondency, the time has not been badly handled, but I miss Paris extraordinarily, I am just noticing now how firmly I had counted on getting there—, and I still have left a little hope of going thither, regardless of the now already rather late season. I discovered in myself a lively need of meeting quite new people and of coming into contact with new circles—, a result probably of the long-observed, complete solitude. From Paris I would certainly bring with me a hundred reasons for wanting this state again which has indeed nothing forced about it for me, and new means of making use of it. Two weeks ago I saw my doctor in Val-Mont who even recommended the trip—, but then there was again a series of bad days, and finally a whole complication of dental disorders on which account I went Tuesday to Bern, and with the overcoming of which I am just now absorbed, for two days what is more with a swollen cheek, which spares me from explaining to Bern acquaintances what has brought me here.

There, dear Clara, you have a brief summary of my recent history; it is just about complete if I record one more ruthless encroachment that has grieved and upset me. Farmers, to whom it belonged, quite unexpectedly, on the morning of October 15, felled the beautiful old poplar at the crossroads in front of Muzot, simply because they found that the roots of the tree were impoverishing their meadows at the borders of which it stood. I got up late that day and came too late to save the beautiful tree: I would have been able to, I learned later—, and that now makes the destruction all the more painful to me. The landscape, you can imagine, has been much changed thereby—, that strong vertical drew it upward and gave it lift and lineage. Even here I am haunted now and then by the sadness that such an alteration creates in one.—But now it is difficult to make a birthday letter out of all this. Well, you see and feel that I remember the date, and our meeting is added to that to assure you that on the 21st I shall get up with heartfelt and strong wishes for you . . .

[214]

Dory von der Mühll   Hôtel Foyot, Paris
                                        January 17, 1925

To you, above all, I must announce that now (at last!) I am here. In Paris: whither I believed myself to be on the way since the middle of October, detained by one annoyance after another. I came directly from Val-Mont and on a sudden decision to convert the attention which there—without much success—I had to direct upon my condition, into a brusque opposite: namely to ignore it, to disregard it entirely. Perhaps that will be of more help, since the other method has failed. Wavering and unsure from the long indecision, the much lying down, the baths—, I made my first outings here, in the vehemence of the streets and the turmoil of the street crossings feeling like the wretched campagnard I have become—it seems—from my long Muzot. And my first encounter, at a coiffeur's by the Madeleine, was with your brother who, from his seat, could recognize me in three mirrors. That gave me, at my début, a feeling of security, to know he is here; now indeed he has moved over to the rive droite, but I feel him present and accessible, that does me good. . . .

Which was your room in the Foyot? The rooms have already been quite worn with use and occupancy since 1920, when I found them immediately after restoration; mine leaves much to be desired in the way of propreté, but nevertheless I cannot make up my mind to go elsewhere. I hope to be here at least through January. . . .

Valéry is full of friendship for me. Have you read the October number of *Wissen und Leben* which was the first to publish a few of my translations with the text of the original facing them? . . .

[*215*]

To Anton Kippenberg   Hôtel Foyot, 33 rue de Tournon,
                                     Paris VI
                                     February 12, 1925

It was a real blessing for me that my letter found you still in the midst of the "Insel", and I thank you for all the active looking into my affairs that you promptly did out of the fullness of your friendly readiness. The *Kreditanstalt* has already notified me of the extraordinary increase in my account, and I am happy to have at my disposal for the immediate future some resources which allow me to make things here more comfortably mine. For the rest (I must rectify) it is not so, Paris could not have altered essentially. The conditions of its greatness seem to be so basic and constant that again and again something extreme and unsurpassable seems to emerge from them as from the root, and I recognize continually what caused me bliss and dismay years ago, and in the face of it am experiencing the being no less overpowered. At most the current that flows over these essentials has become thicker, more ruthless, more hurried (but beneath it the outlasting nature of this incomparable city is conserving itself all the more secretly). If, for hours now and then, I have to grant the change, it is because this time I myself occasionally drift along in this superficial current—, but how gladly I sever myself from it, to belong to the other Paris that is still the Paris of Villon or Charles-Louis Philippe, the Paris of Gérard de Nerval and Baudelaire, that complete Paris which, in the infinite spirituality of its space, comes into all its heritage and includes in itself all vibrations: the only city that could become a landscape of life and death beneath the exhaustless affirmation of its magnanimous and weightless skies . . .

˙[216]

To Lou Andreas-Salomé   (transcript from the Notebook)

"Later he thought he remembered certain moments in which the strength of this one was already contained, as in the seed. He thought of the hour in that other southern garden (Capri), when a bird-call was there, both in the outside and in his inner being, concordantly, so to say, since it did not break at the boundary of his body, but formed of the two together an uninterrupted space in which, mysteriously protected, only one single spot of purest, deepest consciousness remained. At that time he had closed his eyes in order not to be confused in so magnanimous an experience by the contour of his body, and the infinite passed over into him from all sides so trustfully that he might believe he felt in his breast the light reposing of the stars that had meantime entered there.

"It came to him again too how much it meant to him, leaning in a similar posture against a fence, to become aware of the starry sky through the mild branchings of an olive tree, how facelike in this mask the universe confronted him, or how, when he bore such awareness long enough, everything passed so completely into the clear solution of his heart that the savor of creation was in his being. He thought it possible that such abandonments might be recalled as far back as his opaque childhood: he had only to be reminded of the passion that had always seized him when it came to exposing himself to the storm, how, striding over great plains, excited in his innermost soul, he broke through the wind-wall continually renewed by himself, or standing forward on a ship, blindly let himself be carried on through dense distances that closed more tightly behind him. But if, from the beginning, the elemental rushing of the air, the water's pure and manifold behavior, and whatever was heroic in the procedure of the clouds, moved him beyond measure—indeed, quite like fate took possession of his soul who had never been able to grasp such things in the human—he could not fail to see that now, since the most recent influences, he was as though conclusively committed to such relationships. Something gently dividing maintained between him and other people a pure, almost shining interspace, through which indeed single things could be handed over, but which sucked up every relationship into itself and, overfilled with it, like murky smoke deceived one figure with another. He did not yet know how far this isolation impressed itself on others. As concerned himself, it alone granted him a certain freedom toward people,—the little beginning of poverty, by which he was the lighter, gave him among those whose hopes and cares lay in each other, who were bound in life and death, a peculiar flexibility of his own. The temptation was still in him to hold out his lightness to their weightedness, though he already perceived how he deluded them in this, since they could not know that he had arrived at his kind of self-conquest, not (like the hero) in all their ties, not in the heavy air of their hearts, but outside, in a spaciousness so little adapted to humanity that they would not call it anything but "empty". The only thing with which he might turn to them was perhaps his simplicity; it was reserved for him to speak to them of joy, where he found them too much caught up in the opposites of happiness, also to impart to them perhaps single things out of his intercourse with Nature, things they missed or took only incidentally into consideration."

[217]

To Witold von Hulewicz   Muzot sur Sierre (Valais)
                                  November 10, 1925

I do not like doing anything, whatever it may be, in a hurry, but this time I *ran* through your questionnaire, pressed by the enormous lateness and all the other equally enormous arrears by which I have been besieged since my return . . . In the *Malte* there can be no question of specifying and detaching the manifold evocations. The reader should not be in communication with their historical or imaginary reality, but through them with Malte's experience: who is himself involved with them only as, on the street, one might let a passer-by, might let a neighbor, say, impress one. The connection lies in the circumstance that the particular characters conjured up register the same vibration-rate of vital intensity that vibrates in Malte's own nature; as for instance Ibsen (let us say Ibsen, for who knows whether he really felt that way . . . ?) or a playwright of yesterday seeks out visible evidences of the happening that has become invisible to us, so young M. L. Brigge too longs to make life, which is continually withdrawing into the invisible, intelligible to himself through evocations and images; these he finds now in his own childhood memories, now in his Paris surroundings, now in the reminiscences of his wide reading. And all that, *wherever* it may be experienced, has the same valency for him, the same duration and presentness. Malte is not in vain the grandson of old Count Brahe who regarded everything, past as well as to come, simply as "present"; thus Malte too regards as present those stores of his spirit derived from three ways of receiving: his period of distress and the great period of distress of the Avignon popes, where everything broke out externally that now turns fatally inward, are equated: it is of no consequence to know more of what is evoked than just what the searchlight of his heart lets one recognize. They are historical figures or characters of his own past, but *vocabula* of *his* distress: that too is why one should now and then let pass a name that is not further elucidated, like a bird voice in this nature of his in which the inner wind-stillnesses are more perilous than the storms.

That is why it could only become confusing to set forth more specifically the merely indicated figures; let each find references for them in his own way, and whoever is unable to do so will still be sufficiently informed by the tension of these anonymities. . . .

This book is to be accepted, not taken-in in detail. Only *so* will everything come to its right emphasis and overlapping. I wish you could await the French translation before you impart your final "Imprimatur" to the Polish text. It will be thoroughly responsible, and would, with the unambiguousness and logic of that language, perhaps serve you in helping to make clear the meaning of single places that are still further questionable and especially the word-relationships. *There*, I believe, it will not be possible to misunderstand a number of things that were dark to you in the German. I have great confidence in this French version, which was to be out *before* Christmas. (You will get the volume anyway, as soon as it appears.)

I must now quickly to other things!

In closing, take the hand offered you in spirit with all friendship and always the best thanks for your loyalty and effort.

[*218*]

To Witold von Hulewicz   [postmarked Sierre,
                                            November 13, 1925]

. . . And am *I* the one to give the Elegies their proper explanation? They reach out infinitely beyond me. I regard them as a further elaboration of those essential premises that were already given in the *Book of Hours*, that in the two parts of the *New Poems* tentatively played with the image of the world and that then in the *Malte*, contracted in conflict, strike back into life and there almost lead to the proof that this life so suspended in the bottomless is impossible. In the *Elegies*, starting from the same postulates, life becomes possible again, indeed, it experiences here that ultimate *affirmation* to which young Malte, though on the difficult right path "des longues études", was as yet unable to conduct it. *Affirmation of life-AND-death appears as one in the "Elegies"*. To grant one without the other is, so it is here learned and celebrated, a limitation which in the end shuts out all that is infinite. *Death* is the *side of life* averted from us, unshone upon by us: we must try to achieve the greatest consciousness of our existence which is at home in *both unbounded realms, inexhaustibly nourished from both* . . . The true figure of life extends through *both* spheres, the blood of the mightiest circulation flows through *both: there is neither a here nor a beyond, but the great unity* in which the beings that surpass us, the "angels", are at home. And now the place of the love problem, in this world extended by its greater half, in this world only now *whole*, only now *sound*. I am amazed that the *Sonnets to Orpheus*, which are at least as "*difficult*", filled with the same essence, are not more helpful to you in the understanding of the *Elegies*. These latter were begun in 1912 (at Duino), continued in Spain and Paris— fragmentarily—until 1914; the War interrupted this my greatest work altogether; when in 1922 I ventured to take them up again (here), the new elegies and their conclusion were preceded, in a few days, by the *Sonnets to Orpheus*, which imposed themselves tempestuously (and which had *not* been in my plan). They are, as could not have been otherwise, of the same "birth" as the *Elegies*, and their springing up, without my willing it, in connection with a girl who had died young, moves them even closer to the source of their origin: this connection being one more relation toward the center of *that* realm whose depth and influence we share, everywhere unboundaried, with the dead and those to come. We of the here and now are not for a moment hedged in the time-world, nor confined within it; we are incessantly flowing over and over to those who preceded us, to our origins and to those who seemingly come after us. In that greatest "*open*" world all *are*, one cannot say "simultaneous", for the very falling away of time determines that they all *are*. Transiency everywhere plunges into a deep being. And so all the configurations of the here and now are to be used not in a time-bound way only, but, as far as we are able, to be placed in those superior significances in which we have a share. But *not in the Christian sense* (from which I am more and more passionately moving away), but, in a purely earthly, deeply earthly, blissfully earthly consciousness, we must introduce what is *here* seen and touched into the wider, into the widest orbit. Not into a beyond whose shadow darkens the earth, but into a whole, into *the whole*. Nature, the things of our intercourse and use, are provisional and perishable; but they are, as long as we are here, *our* property and our friendship, co-knowers of our distress and gladness, as they have already been the familiars of our forbears. So it is important not only not to run down and degrade all that is here, but just because of its provisionalness, which it shares with us, these phenomena and things should be understood and transformed by us in a most fervent sense. Transformed? Yes, for it is our task to imprint this provisional, perishable earth so deeply, so patiently and passionately in ourselves that its reality shall arise in us again "invisibly". *We are the bees of the invisible. Nous butinons éperdument le miel du visible, pour l'accumuler dans la grande ruche d'or de l'Invisible.* The *Elegies* show us at this work, at the work of these continual conversions of the beloved visible and tangible into the invisible vibrations and excitation of our own nature, which introduces new vibration-frequencies into the vibration-spheres of the universe. (Since different elements in the cosmos are only different vibration-exponents, we prepare for ourselves in this way not only intensities of a spiritual nature but also, who knows, new bodies, metals, nebulae and constellations.) And this activity is curiously supported and urged on by the ever more rapid fading away of so much of the visible that will no longer be replaced. Even for our grandparents a "house", a "well", a familiar tower, their very clothes, their coat: were infinitely more, infinitely more intimate; almost everything a vessel in which they found the human and added to the store of the human. Now, from America, empty indifferent things are pouring across, sham things, *dummy life* . . . A house, in the American sense, an American apple or a grapevine over there, has *nothing* in common with the house, the fruit, the grape into which went the hopes and reflections of our forefathers . . . Live things, things lived and conscient of us, are running out and can no longer be replaced. *We are perhaps the last still to have known such things.* On us rests the responsibility not alone of preserving *their* memory (that would be little and unreliable), but their human and laral value. ("Laral" in the sense of the household gods.) The earth has no way out other than to become invisible: *in* us who with a part of our natures partake of the invisible, have (at least) stock in it, and can increase our holdings in the invisible during our sojourn here,—*in* us alone can be consummated this intimate and lasting conversion of the visible into an invisible no longer dependent upon being visible and tangible, as our own destiny continually *grows at the same time* MORE PRESENT AND INVISIBLE in us. The elegies set up this norm of existence: they assure, they celebrate this consciousness. They cautiously fit it into its traditions, in that they claim for this supposition ancient traditions and rumors of traditions and even in the Egyptian cult of the dead evoke a foreknowledge of such relationships. (Although the "Land of Lamentation" through which the older "lamentation" leads the young dead is *not to be identified with* Egypt, but is only, in a sense, a mirroring of the Nile country in the desert clarity of the consciousness of the dead.) When one makes the mistake of holding up to the Elegies or Sonnets *Catholic* conceptions of death, of the beyond and of eternity, one is getting entirely away from their point of departure and preparing for oneself a more and more basic misunderstanding. The "angel" of the elegies has nothing to do with the angel of the Christian heaven (rather with the angel figures of Islam) . . . The angel of the *Elegies* is that creature in whom the transformation of the visible into the invisible, which we are accomplishing, appears already consummated. For the angel of the Elegies all past towers and palaces are existent, *because* long invisible, and the still standing towers and bridges of our existence *already* invisible, although (for us) still persisting physically. The angel of the Elegies is that being who vouches for the recognition in the invisible of a higher order of reality.—Hence "terrible" to us, because we, its lovers and transformers, do still cling to the visible.—All the worlds of the universe are plunging into the invisible as into their next deepest reality; *a few stars immediately intensify and pass away in the infinite consciousness of the angels—, others are dependent upon beings who slowly and laboriously transform them, in whose terrors and ecstasies they attain their next invisible realization. We are,* let it be emphasized once more, *in the sense of the Elegies, we are these transformers of the earth; our entire existence, the flights and plunges of our love, everything qualifies us for this task* (beside which there exists, essentially, no other). (The Sonnets show details from this activity which here appears placed under the name and protection of a dead girl whose incompletion and innocence holds open the gate of the grave so that, gone from us, she belongs to those powers that keep the one half of life fresh and open toward the other wound-open half.) Elegies and Sonnets support each other constantly—, and I see an infinite grace in the fact that, with the same breath, I was permitted to fill both these sails: the little rust-colored sail of the Sonnets and the Elegies' gigantic white canvas.

May you, dear friend, perceive here some advice and elucidation and, for the rest, help yourself along. For: I do not know whether I ever could say more . . .

[219]

To Clara Rilke   Château de Muzot sur Sierre (Valais)
November 17, 1925

. . . *where* will your birthday be celebrated? I had better send off these lines somewhat ahead of time in case they should have to follow you somewhere; and I almost wish they *would* have to do that, preferably to Ruth and Christine, where everyone would make you feel your birthday most naturally and warmly.

From me, dear Clara, come all good wishes: the beautiful and good thing with you is that one feels how you will interpret and use them in a right sense: determined as you are to see and affirm the *good* in everything, you cannot help regarding good wishes as something very good. Please, do so with reference to this impulse of mine which I hope, despite my persistent silence, you may feel and love.

Yes, I have been silent, silent for a long time, in all directions, Ruth indeed was made to feel this behavior amply too. It seems as though one's fiftieth year did signify a kind of crisis; for me in any case it will have been one, the most fundamental of my life; I do not yet see how and where I shall get out beyond it. But since nothing stands still and remains as it is, that cannot but be found. I can in no way express myself about what is insurmountably difficult for me, it comes from the side of my health which seems more centrally affected than the doctors have hitherto been willing to recognize. But probably I am also meeting this increasing fact with the falsest attitude: instead of seeing bright, as you have learned to do, I see black, and that throws confusion and gloom over everything. But enough, enough of this outpouring, so thoroughly inappropriate in a birthday letter and, besides, after so long a silence on my part, not exactly comprehensible.

Ruth had for a moment the sweet thought of paying me a quick visit while I was in Ragaz; it was, you can imagine, not easy for me to say no: but finally I had to: in Ragaz they were already closing, staying in the completely empty hotel was not comfortable, besides which for Ruth I would after all like to be really gay and quite *myself:* toward that I am working and so it will come to pass, I hope in the not too distant future, that I can sometime call the children here. I read with great regret that their move to Liebau is possibly impending, what a pity, what a pity about the good old house at Alt-Jocketa behind its magnificent chestnut trees!

So read here above all my good thoughts and wishes and take them, aside from the state of mind out of which they rather murkily proceed, purely from heart to heart!

[*220*]

To Anton Kippenberg Château de Muzot sur Sierre (Valais)
December 7, 1925

My dear, good friend Kippenberg,

My telegram has told you how much both of you were included, from its first hour on, in the day people wanted to celebrate for me. You actually opened it for me when, coming down into the dining room for breakfast, I was really overwhelmed by a big basket of most beautiful cyclamens standing on the deep window seat in the pure winter sun, a rose-colored island of joy! It came, in a way at first incomprehensible to me, from you: discovering with it your joint card and at the same time learning that the Bellevue had just sent it up, I fell upon my coffee: for I thought, for the beginning of a moment, that, hurrying down, I could in a half hour embrace you there, in Sierre. But there beside my cup lay piles of letters and among the first your handwriting, which then, alas, restored distance by assuring me in another way of your loyal presence.

It is, my dear friend, the value of a day like this that one may receive a few wishes that accord, in impulse and direction, with one's own inner wishings. How much your wishes and those of the Mistress belong to this rare group, I do not have to prove to you. Without this validity of understanding would we have come to such retrospects as these into which you let me gaze (as through the certain little hole of a birthday penholder): 25 years of Insel-association and 20 years of mutual personal trust—: I lingered gratefully and attentively before these perspectives, and the deep vistas in the imaginary penholder, held against the light, were not lacking in clear and endearing details, to which something best and most enduring was inviolably attached.

On the same fourth I received also the rest of what you sent: the *Inselschiff* above all, which, so richly pennanted and laden, sails this time under my flag—, the requested Valéry volumes (together with Bertram) and the little word that came so quickly to consider and fulfill my business queries. Effectively and vitally as you always reply to it, my trust can never turn into mere habit: it is always a new act, the most recent gesture of a feeling that as a whole has become great. A basic feeling, dear friend, dear friends, and heavy or light, as life may bring it, I give myself over to the durability of your friendship.

Your

Rilke

P.S. I still haven't by a long shot looked through all that has arrived; quite a large basket, once procured for one of our apple harvests, goes on filling up with correspondence and telegrams; I shall be able to answer only the smallest part. There caught my eye, decked out with numerous signatures, a big communication from the "German Department" of the University of Edinburgh.

[221]

To Berta Flamm   Muzot sur Sierre (Valais), Switzerland
December 9, 1925

Your letter has just reached me, I thank you for having written it. The privilege of giving joy is conferred more rarely than one thinks, partly in consequence of our so rigid inability to receive, partly because the imprecision and vagueness between people, that may always have been a hindrance, has in perplexing times still further increased. Finally even the most appropriate gift still requires an extreme adaptation on the part of the recipient, but where the giving is "in keeping" this achievement belongs right in with the natural gesture of those on whom gifts are bestowed.

That some things from my books have been able to benefit one so sorely afflicted speaks much more for him, for your son, than for the books: how easily he could have denied and closed himself to them. But (as you let me see) he has consolidated the victory in himself, the most difficult and secret victory, which consists in little by little, from a place in life most painfully contested and circumscribed, nevertheless reaffirming all of that

somehow innocent life! This indescribably secure achievement
will have its reward in him and in you, his mother and his
brother, who were both there to back up his fight. Since the
great pure linking of his heart and his spirit seems to have been
rescued, the measure of all his relationships will now be so special
and personal a one that, in certain moments of indescribable
being-included, he will almost have something of an advantage
over those who achieve their participation out of more ordinary
and easier conditions. These few lines, intended for all of you
together, but especially for your patient, merely repeat, con-
jecturally, what he already knows and lives!

And so I send him and you my greetings. One or two books I
hope to send along shortly; very busy, I cannot at the moment
tell what things of mine are here. These lines, at least, should be
with you quickly.

[222]

To Arthur Fischer-Colbrie   Château de Muzot sur Sierre
(Valais) Switzerland
December 18, 1925

So I thank you for a sympathy that, straight and strong as it is,
is the outcome of such long experience with my books: Your letter was full of evidences of true interest, how should I not want
to answer it with equally true thanks.

I never read what my works call forth among the critics in the
way of opinions, either in newspapers or periodicals: these voices
do not seem to me to belong among those reactions that I would
have to take into consideration again: also they are indeed
destined altogether for the reader and must, as you yourself mention, reckon with *his* resources. However (as I was laying it with
the rest of its kind) my glance fell on the first lines of your article.
Let me, in confidence, clear up what you were impelled to point
out there.

To President Masaryk I offered my respects, not this time indeed, but on an earlier occasion, through his Bern representative

of that time: this feeling existed long before the revolutions of 1918 raised him to that more conspicuous position; how could I help feeling called upon to give approval when a man of universal intellectual significance assumed the topmost place in my native country, from which I am sufficiently detached to be loyal, independently, to its particular destinies.

As to the other point: I have lived since 1921 in an old tower of this French canton; Switzerland in general, its soil, the relationships that have supported me here, and not least the event of the grandiose landscape of the Wallis to which I have become more deeply attached with every year: all these facts together constitute that which, after the evil interruptedness and all the confusion of the war years, has become a salvation of my life and of my work. I cannot enumerate the individual circumstances that make my being taken in here seem the most marvelous dispensation, but it is easier to prove that it has been the most productive. One has only to consider that the *Elegies* (begun at the war-destroyed Castle of Duino in 1912, continued fragmentarily until August 1914 in Spain and in Paris . . .) had been left interrupted by the external circumstances into which the fortunes of wartime had plunged me and even more through my inner torpor; nowhere but here, in the Wallis, a country then completely unknown to me, could such a store of unforseeable supports have been assembled: for here took place, and everything was conducive to it, in the rigorous solitude of the winter of 1921–22, the reuniting I scarcely hoped for any more with the breaks in my work of 1914, and it was so clean and so passionate, and at the same time of such mildness in the healing together, that out of a few weeks of indescribable devotion the whole of the Elegies arose as if it had never been broken off, even gone rigid in its separate pieces. That a person who through the wretched harassings of those years had felt himself split to the roots, into an Aforetime and a dying Now not to be united with it: that such a person should experience the grace of perceiving how in yet more mysterious depths, *beneath* this gaping rift, the continuity of his work and his soul re-established itself . . . , seems to me more than just a private event; for with it a gauge is given of the inexhaustible stratification of our nature, and how many, who for one reason or another believe themselves cleft apart, might draw from this example of possible continuation a singular comfort.

(The thought readily suggests itself that this comfort too may somehow have entered into the achievement of the great Elegies, so that they express themselves more completely than they could have done without endangerment and rescue.)

Enough: out of all this should be understood merely that I have remained bound in a special way to this landscape in which I have met with the fullness of grace. Although I had seldom before become resonant through incentives of environment—, but here my glad and lively joining, together with the complete seclusion of my life, brought with it my setting down verses in the language which surrounds me and which is not accidentally that of these hill vineyards, the series of those "Quatrains Valaisans" around which other French poems, in most irrefusable dictation, have gradually arranged themselves. I saw no reason to ward off this spontaneous resonance that imposed itself on me in all purity, nor yet to resist when later, in Paris, it was proposed that I fill a little book with these examples of a happy inspiration. I was glad to give back to the country this most native gift in return for its eager and rescuing hospitality: with this is told the story of that "writing in French" which, as I learned little by little from various rumors, had occasioned such curious interpretations on the part of the public. It is enacted, this most incidental story, on quite different stages of the spirit from those they wanted to assign to it.

I know (to come back to your article) that you took up that version of the "discord" only for the sake of "accord", because this was after all the easiest insight that could perhaps be made attainable to the reader. Yet at this price particularly, I would least like to be more considerately handled. I know nothing of any discord, any more than I have ever known of any disapproval, any "disapproving attitude of German literary circles". My work was dependent upon such reactions to a certain unavoidable degree only when I first published. Even at twenty-three, at the time of the *Book of Hours,* I ceased bothering about applause or disapproval, and since then individual voices at most have reached me which, whether they applauded or rejected or were undecided, work back into life and (unlike mere criticism) are resolved in it. I would be in a sad way if in my fiftieth year, in the domain of my art, I permitted anything to appear out of disillusionment or "rancune", and it is the strangest misunderstanding that this suspicion so foreign to my nature should happen to throw its sullen shadow on the producing of those French poems, which for me signifies the brightest happiest having-been-given!

Do you think that by such "helps" the reader will become more capable of dealing with my books? But that is not meant as a reproach to you. Only you yourself, in view of your relationship to me, you yourself, that is what matters to me, should be among those who know better, those who truly know *with* me. The suspicion has crossed my mind that you too believed a bit in the possibility of a (how shall I say) revenge: well, that would be taking this innocent and spontaneous product, which I have with astonishment and delight seen appear out of my being's mystery, far too seriously and besides (how much!) misjudging it and me in it!

Straighten this out (with yourself)
and my grateful greetings:
Rainer Maria Rilke

P.S.: In Linz of course no one could give "information" about me; the unhappy months spent there comprise a time when I was quite unrecognizable to myself: how very much then I must have been so to others!

[*223*]

To Georg Reinhart   Château de Muzot sur Sierre (Valais)
December 19, 1925

The "real" simply has a quite indescribable advantage over all that is invented and inventable: where the latter projects possibilities into imaginary space and so furthers and in a sense trains

and exercises our imagination—, this otherwise so stimulating ability yields, relaxes before the evidences with which the consummated overtakes it, and yet feels no offense: for how much it
participated in the living achievement in which it now seems to
be surpassed, surpassed by life itself, bearing, affirming life that
passes on and ramifies the impulses. I could, last evening, think of
no story that would have touched me more closely and carried
me along more briskly than this history of the House of "Volkart", which really, factually as you have handled it, contains
only dates, simple statements of what has been achieved, all along
from its origin to its expansion.

What a document is given one in this book; what an example
of harmonious common effort, what an ideal association of com-
bining forces! And how reality has from the beginning and again
and again kept saying "yes" to this genuine venture that did not
take place for the sake of profit but proceeded from the grandly
recognized need of being united, of barter, the weighing of
foreign against familiar things. And when profit *did come* and
reward the precise and timely cleverness of those enterprises and
measures, with what self-command the leaders of such expanded
undertakings knew how to convert it into energy again, so that
it could not for a moment "grow rank" but continually served
the healthiest and happiest growth.

When I entered your Winterthur offices for the first time, I
felt plainly enough, but less expressibly, what now strikes me anew
from this book: the idea of commerce in its human directness and
purity. This language the continents of the world speak among
themselves, whose vehicles are things used and evaluated; materials, and that which may in painstaking ways be gained and derived
from them. And how this idea, with all its infinite realizations and
unavoidable complications through the centuries, has forfeited
nothing of its spontaneity and youthfulness: how the charm of
the foreign and remote is still active in it, the hearty curiosity of
joy in barter and the inexhaustible amazement at—finding a product brought from afar so different, so essentially precious, so pure
in its structure, so one with its own fragrance. And *this* joy too,

of giving some native thing for it, something plainer and less conspicuous in accord with the climate, but besides that too all the clever and subtle inventions and constructions of the European mind, which in turn may excite amazement and satisfy or surpass naïve curiosity among people of different birth . . . All this appreciated and striven for according to its real usefulnesses, and everywhere attended by all that which, here and yonder, over and above the merely useful, fills and alters whatever pertains to the human sphere; and only at the end: profit, and this never bursting forth in arrogance, but again and again turned inward and led back into the ramifications of the work: creating wealth in the work itself—, and ultimately in its final effects, irrepressible, admitted by the managers of so many objects and destinies linked with the common effort as something personal and to be owned . . . And here, in the realm of the most personal, once again held a responsibility, placed at the service of recognized great values and used as only those can use it who in their profession have trained themselves to that which is genuine and true, that which is lasting.

You see, my dear Herr Georg Reinhart, the little factual book invites to excursions and interpretations; I could fill up more than these two pages with them. But may I in closing voice a request? I am probably right in assuming that your publication is reserved for friends and is not to be purchased in bookstores. Now I would so like to have presented a copy of this commemorative book to my publisher and friend, Professor Kippenberg. This able and active owner and director of the Insel-Verlag, renowned besides (as you know) for his important Goethe collection—the biggest private collection of manuscripts and pictures belonging to Goethe and those around him—, would (I am sure), as the great and fortunate merchant of spiritual values that he is, take the liveliest pleasure in possessing your publication; he, in his way, would have the finest instinct for admiring the history of this traditionary rise, and to him (as to me) a document of that kind would be nothing short of consoling in an age that overestimates its "being-new" as against the continuable. How the old Goethe,

who also through conversance with the structural elements of the
world and out of the need for universal relations developed his
own great conception of the genuine and his reverence for the
traditional . . . , how the old Goethe would have held your
memorial in honor—one hears him commenting on it to Eckermann! . . .

[*224*]

To Leonid Pasternak   Val-Mont par Glion sur Territet
                                         (Vaud) Switzerland
                                         March 14, 1926

No, I cannot write you in Russian, but I did read your letter
. . . and even if I could no longer read Russian (I still can quite
well, but unfortunately seldom get to it . . .) but, even if I no
longer could, the joy and the great surprise of reading you, dear
valued friend, would, for a moment, have given me back all my
knowledge: *this* good letter I would have understood in all circumstances and in all languages. And now I want to assure you at
once how *your language* and all that concerns the old Russia (the
unforgettable secret Skaska), and how everything of which you
remind me in your note has remained close, dear and sacred to me,
forever embedded in the substructure of my life! Yes, we have
had to let much change pass over us, your country above all: but,
even if *we* are no more to experience it in its resurrection, the deep,
the real, the ever surviving Russia has only fallen back into its
secret root-layer, as once formerly under the Tartarshchina; who
may doubt that it is *there* and, in its darkness, invisible to its own
children, slowly, with its sacred slowness, is gathering itself together for a perhaps still distant future? Your own exile, the
exile of so many most loyal to it, is nourishing this in a sense subterranean preparation: for as the real Russia has hidden itself
away under the earth, in the earth, so all of you have only gone
away in order to remain true to its momentary hiddenness; how
strongly, with how much emotion, dear Leonid Ossipovitch Pasternak, I felt that last year in Paris: there I saw again old Russian

friends and found new ones, and the young fame of your son Boris touched me from more than one side. Also, chronologically, the last thing I tried to read there were poems of his, very *beautiful* ones (in a little anthology of Ilya Ehrenburg's, which I then unfortunately gave to the Russian dancer Mila Sirul; unfortunately: because at times since I would have liked to reread them). Now it moves me to know that not only *he*, Boris, the already recognized poet of a new generation, has not ceased to know about me and to be familiar with my work, but that with you and yours too my existence has remained in your hearts and sympathies, that you, dear friend, have let your memory and affection for me prosper and grow in your family, infinitely increasing in this way something good that has remained dear to me.'

To know you living and working in comparatively normal circumstances, surrounded by a part of your family, is a good happy knowledge to me! And prejudiced though I am against having my portrait made, if proximity in space permits and we see each other again, I shall be proud to occupy a modest place in the ranks of your models. But it is much more likely that you will see Clara Rilke, who still lives in Germany, near Bremen, or with our daughter, who is married and living on an estate in Saxony and already something over two years ago made me a grandfather by the arrival of a granddaughter! . . .

[225]

To Georg Reinhart Still Val-Mont par Glion sur Territet (Vaud)
March 19, 1926

You gave me great pleasure in sending me back the address that so clearly resumes the spirit of your anniversary volume and that of your life work as well: in your words (not one is superfluous) there comes most vividly and directly to life what was set forth, in such a lucid accounting, in that historical survey; there, the past appeared, preserved and temporarily outlined by the boundaries of the present: these, these boundaries, your animated words everywhere set vibrating. Yes, with your happily im-

provised space-curve you did something further; you bent into
a globe the planisphere of the Volkart Brothers' world-map and
so brought the stereometric problem of the firm's activity within
the grasp of all your co-workers present at the celebration, that
none could become aware of the manifold task uniting you and
themselves without an enrichment of his own inner sense of space:
that is, without a spontaneous increase of freedom and felicity. I
who have always stood in the midst of my work, as a single and
solely responsible individual entrusted with both plan and execu-
tion, nevertheless possess intuition enough to be able to imagine
what it may mean to each one, from the humblest to the most
indispensable, working into the whole, to belong to such an immense like-minded association; but I feel it a special privilege too
that I was permitted to gain this convincing experience through
such a great and happy example.

Even here Switzerland, as through so much, has become in a
peculiar way communicating to me and well suited to introduce
me, not only to new people whom I have quickly learned to value
and love, but to conditions also which, in their significance and
universality, work together on my view of the world, its measure
and its expanse. And I am proud, I may say, not only to be personally connected in warmth and gratitude with you and your
brother Werner, but also to reach—learning, marveling and admiring—to the wide domain of your work.

Surely to you too, who are accustomed to take the attentive
interest of an all-round adept in the chemistry of any given life-
moment, in its composition, the contrasts crowding in it, . . .
surely it has at times occurred to you too of what curiously com-
pounded, conflicting or mutually complementary constituents the
incoming mail of a single day is made up. It would perhaps turn
out a not so confused book, if one decided to treat as a unit such
a complex of letters, driven together from the most varied origins:
The recipient alone, his occupations and interests, should suffice
to embrace under a single relation the most heterogeneous elements consorting on his table, and many a question would find

itself solved or further developed in an entirely unsuspecting neighbor-letter concerned with something else.

[226]

To Hans Ulbricht   temporarily: Val-Mont par Glion sur Territet
(Vaud) Switzerland
March 24, 1926

Since your letter came I have often pondered what that would be friendly I could give you to take along on your new way: what, above all, that would be useful? Your letter, as well as one and another (particularly the last) of your lyric attempts, does contain passages of personal and individual expression that make you come through more recognizably; but there exists between the two utterances (the one of artistic and the one aiming at communication) too great a similarity.

So it only (once again) became clear to me how depressing and hopeless an occupation the lyric poem represents at a certain age, just because it works with the medium of language and does not offer sufficient craftsmanship to develop in it something independent (I mean this not in the artistic sense but in the purely vital). What life exhales continually reacts upon life again—, an existence that by this means tries to unburden, burdens itself rather with the intensified expression of all that is unbearable to it, remains crowded about by its own distresses that have passed through an apparent removal and release, is more at their mercy than if it had never been caught up and condensed in a lyric consciousness. Even where an early talent comes to the assistance of this effort or in a sense anticipates it (Heym or Trakl), the result has had too little substance to overcome to delight by transubstantiation; a Trakl (one should consider) who could have exercised his genius in painting or in music instead of in poetry would not have perished under the excessive weight of his work, under the darkening with which it overhung him.

Since life, as you tell me, will shortly require of you changes of all kinds: may they be—it remains for me to wish—*such* as will thrust into your hands something immediately tangible, an occupation in the most concrete sense. At the risk of your being for a while not able to try yourself out in poems. But should you find a pen in your hand nevertheless, forbid it to write down "emotionalisms", oblige it to note facts of your own and preferably of more remote life, and, in any case, provide for yourself, besides the pen that is destined to convey to friends a sign of your welfare and activity, a second pen that you handle like a tool: and do not let your self be moved by what proceeds from this second pen, be hard toward the least of your productions. What you have put out as a craftsman, to which this other pen gives contour, should react no further on your own life, should be a shaping, a transposition, a transformation, to which your "ego" was only the first and last impetus, but which from there on remains standing across from you, originating from your impulse but at once removed so far from you to the level of artistic estrangement, of thinglike solitude, that you feel your part in the completion of this mysteriously objective thing to be but that of a person calmly carrying out some order.

In any case this is important for you: that you get away beyond this neighborhood of your lyric poems, that you do not go about letters as you would poems and do not merely take life as an occasion for moods and unreliabilities of feeling. It is so much more. And it would be too bad if, overtaken by words, you would in the end have to have borne only the perplexities of youth without knowing what it was to be overwhelmed by the being-young, which is sheer existence.

[227]

To Dieter Bassermann   for the present, Val-Mont par Glion,
                              Territet (Vaud) Switzerland
                              Easter Monday [April 5] 1926

The announced numbers of your professional journal have unfortunately not arrived, only (by the same roundabout way they must have taken) your letter: it interested me exceedingly, and I am glad of the assurance you expressed in it. I have always thought that some poem, by the very extremeness of its nature, could suddenly extend quite directly to the domain of the precision instrument, settling out of its world space, as it were, like pure dew, on the surface of a problem.

I cannot say whether, outside the kind of framework within which the various categories of the exact come to an understanding among themselves, I would be capable of intentionally expressing myself on the theme you propose. Perhaps after all I lack conversance with the mechanical achievements up to now; for only on a certain familiarity with the accomplishments of the talking-machine might conjectures about its task and its future be set up. Younger people may be better fitted for this purpose. Nevertheless I do not yet want to say no. If you wish to send me once more (to the address given above) the copies that didn't arrive, it is not impossible that I might be able to form an impression.

My yes, on the other hand, applies even today to your courteous intentions of occupying the readers of your periodical when occasion offers with my "Primal Sound" essay (the title is not mine). Why should I not confess my weakness for those notes in which, after years, I had laid down what in a certain unforgettable intuition had appeared to me as not even "so fantastic". Since the nature of the phonograph derives from the graphic projection of tones, why should it not be feasible to transform into sound manifestations lines and drawings of elemental origin that occur in Nature?

The so special course of the coronal suture, for example, transposed into the depth dimension, should it not really emit a kind of "music"? And would it not be something unheard-of (and immediately thereafter accepted) to set to sound the countless signatures of Creation which in the skeleton, in minerals . . . at a thousand places persist in their remarkable versions and variations? The grain in wood, the gait of an insect: our eye is practiced in following and ascertaining them. What a gift to our hearing were we to succeed in transmuting this zigzag (in which chance after

all represents merely a stock company founded by laws) into
auditory events!

Already once, years ago, I learned that someone thought of
making the suggestions I had provisionally set down in the "Primal
Sound" essay the point of departure for technical experiments;
whether this took place, and with what result, I have never
learned. The idea however still seems to me so remarkable that I
am grateful to anyone who may linger over it a while: even error
turns out so often to be the step of a little platform on which a
footing can then be found. . . .

[228]

To Dieter Bassermann Val-Mont par Glion, Territet (Vaud)
Switzerland
April 19, 1926

Unfortunately I was able after many hindrances only yesterday,
Sunday, to look through the proposed texts: I would have no
objection to their being printed in this form. At most this: it dis-
turbs my ear for language a little to feel a letter passage, which is
by nature of a different density, joined as a direct supplement to
the older essay. I should prefer to have you indicate by a few dots
the not quite definitive character of the prose pages taken from
the *Inselschiff*, in order to append the passage from my letter to
you with more visible differentiation, after a more emphatic break,
to the preceding text. In this typographical setting it would round
out the former even better, in that the interval would become apparent which separates a note going back years ago now from my
attitude of this very day, which is still similarly oriented; thus the
curious persistence with which this idea, in a sense, keeps overtaking me, becomes more striking.

Meanwhile not only have the numbers of your periodical I
asked to have sent again reached me, but, via my permanent address, the copies previously sent have also found their way to me.
I have looked through them attentively. What surprises me is to
find the talking-machine praised almost exclusively as a repro-

ducer of musical material, as if it had so far concerned itself little
with the spoken *word*. And yet, through its exact repetition, it
could render strict control services to those whose business it is
to give a speech or recite a poem, just as it does, in his sphere, to
the practical musician. The talking-machine could further contribute, in the service of the poetic word, to a new orderly sense
of responsibility toward the *reading aloud* of a poem (by which
alone its whole existence appears). How many readers still miss
the real relationship to the poem because in running over it silently
they only graze its individual qualities, instead of bringing them
awake. I picture to myself (after some resistance) a reader who,
reading along with a poetry book in his hand, listens to a talking-
machine in order to be better informed of the existence of the
poem in question; that would surely be no mere "artistic pleasure",
but very penetrating instruction, somewhat as certain tabulations
in the school-room present and charge the eye with something
in its relative proportions that is otherwise invisible. The prerequi-
site for such an exercise would in any case be that the talking-
machine had received the sound picture of the verse sequence
from the poet's own lips and not indirectly by way, say, of the
actor. On the contrary, this means of education would not be
unsuited to making the actor innocuous as an interpreter of poems
(he almost always errs and goes astray). Preserved in the disks, the
poem would then persist, to be called up at any time in the form
intended by the poet: an almost inconceivable advantage! But
of course for *us* to whom certain revelations seem to get their
most indescribable quality of greatness, melancholy and humanity
from their fabulous uniqueness, such a mechanical survival of the
most mysterious and rich form of expression would be almost unbearable. It is still (besides being a need) also a strength and a
pride of our soul to consort with the unique and irretrievably
transitory.

[229]

To Beppy Veder   Hôtel Hof-Ragaz, August 9, 1926

Not our hours alone . . . , their further bringing me this postscript in the evening has been in a special way good and comforting to me. And as for the joy, nothing could easily happen that
might diminish it. Even if my entire occupation, if all my pref-
erences, if every object of my inner zeal turned out to be foreign
to you, there would still remain what, *before* any words, with the
first handclasp you laid in my hand: an infinitely joyous trust in
your very life itself, this applying of yourself, spending out of
the stores of a spirit which even through distress, pain and disappointment will never be impoverished, because deep, happy
springs feed it and keep it in freshness and fullness, whatever may
happen to you. But now may favorable things befall, so that the
art to which you now want to belong may take from within you
that rise for which space and sky about you are prepared.—R.M.R.

P.S. Today Herr Wunderly-Volkart arrives, then tomorrow
my friends leave . . . , and then I hope to see you not "once",
but, up to that too-near Thursday, just as much as you ever will
allow me.

[230]

To Beppy Veder   Ragaz, August 23, 1926

Now each of the so different people to whom you have been
an ever-sure joy here has had had time to practice his deprivation:
mine is of so special a kind that I have as yet been unable to write
you. Perhaps because I was so adjusted to your being-here that it
confuses me to learn another way of association, a less direct
one, that accommodates itself to the measure of distance. Perhaps,
too, because I still somehow remain caught in our farewell. Can
you understand that?

I think this letter has confirmed something in advance, for only
after this summer have the great blows of fate come upon our

sunny family and into my existence. *Nevertheless* I am convinced that they have made us richer, if one has the strength to take them.—R.M.R.

[231]

To Rudolf Kassner   Wednesday, December 15, 1926

My dear Kassner, so this it was of which my nature has been urgently forewarning me for three years: I am ill in a miserable and infinitely painful way, a little-known cell alteration in the blood is becoming the point of departure for the most horrible occurrences scattered through my entire body. And I, who never wanted to look it squarely in the face, am learning to adjust myself to the incommensurable anonymous pain. Am learning it with difficulty, amid a hundred resistances, and so sadly amazed. I wanted you to know of this condition of mine which will not be of the most passing. Inform the dear Princess of it, as much as you consider well. I learn through Princess Gargarine that Princess Taxis will settle down in her beautiful apartment in the Palazzo Borghese for the winter. And you, dear Kassner? How was Paris for you? I was happy to find the Eléments de la grandeur humaine in the issue of *Commerce!*

All love, Kassner!

I think much, much of you.

Your

Rilke

[232]

To Jules Supervielle
(in French)   Clinique de Val-Mont sur Territet
                               par Glion (Vaud)
                               December 21, 1926

My dear, dear Supervielle,

Gravely ill, painfully, miserably, humbly ill, I recover myself for an instant in the sweet consciousness of having been able to be reached, even here, on this indeterminable and so little human plane, by your message and by all the influences it brings me.

I think of you, poet, friend, and in so doing I think still of the world, poor broken fragments of a vase that remembers being of the earth. (But this abuse of our senses and of their "dictionary" by the pain that goes leafing through it!)—R.

Notes and
List of Correspondents

NOTES

Rilke was born in Prague, December 4, 1875, and died at Valmont, near Glion, Switzerland, December 29, 1926.

———

ABBREVIATIONS USED IN THE NOTES

A.W.   *Ausgewählte Werke* (1938), the two-volume edition of selected works.

D.E.   *Duino Elegies,* translated by J. B. Leishman and Stephen Spender (W. W. Norton & Company, Inc., New York, 1939).

Cornet   *The Tale of the Love and Death of Cornet Christopher Rilke,* translated by M. D. Herter Norton (W. W. Norton & Company, Inc., New York, 1932).

G.W.   *Gesammelte Werke* (1927), the six-volume standard edition of collected works.

J.O.S.   *The Journal of My Other Self (Die Aufzeichnungen des Malte Laurids Brigge),* translation by John Linton (W. W. Norton & Company, Inc., New York, 1930).

Letters: *Letters of Rainer Maria Rilke, 1892–1910,* translated by Jane
1892–1910   Bannard Greene and M. D. Herter Norton (W. W. Norton & Company, Inc., New York, 1945).

M.L.B.   *Die Aufzeichnungen des Malte Laurids Brigge,* known in English as *The Journal of My Other Self* (see J.O.S. above).

Salis   J. R. von Salis, *Rainer Maria Rilke's Schweitzer Jahre* (Huber & Co., Frauenfeld und Leipzig, 1936).

S.G.   *Späte Gedichte.*

S.O.   *Sonnets to Orpheus,* translated by M. D. Herter Norton (W. W. Norton & Company, Inc., New York, 1942).

S.O.G.   *Stories of God (Geschichten vom lieben Gott),* translated by M. D. Herter Norton and Nora Purtscher-Wydenbruck (W. W. Norton & Company, Inc., New York, 1932).

T.P.   M. D. Herter Norton, *Translations from the Poetry of Rainer Maria Rilke* (W. W. Norton & Company, ınc., New York, 1938).

Y.P.   *Letters to a Young Poet,* translated by M. D. Herter Norton (W. W. Norton & Company, Inc., New York, 1934).

[The number in brackets is that of the letter, the page number that of the page on which the reference occurs.]

[1]   p. 15   Venice: Rilke was staying at the Hotel Regina.

à mon insu: unconsciously.

Carlo Zeno: (1334–1418), a great figure in the history of the Venetian state, commander of both land and sea forces, diplomat, orator, devotee of the sciences and music. (See the article on him by Bettina Seipp in *Inselschiff*, Christmas 1935, 17 Jahrgang.) Rilke's project of making his life the subject of a book was never carried out. (See also [26].)

Duino: Rilke had just been visiting at the old family castle of Princess Marie von Thurn und Taxis-Hohenlohe (see next letter and note), situated near Nabresina on the Austrian Littoral, above Trieste and below Monfalcone and Sagrado.

Kassner: Rudolph Kassner (1873–   ), critic, essayist, philosopher, physiognomist, author of many books. Rilke was both attracted and alarmed by his severe and penetrating mind, but his dedication to him of the Eighth Duino Elegy testifies both to deep affection for the man and to respect for his thought. Kassner's own observations on Rilke in his *Buch der Erinnerung* (Insel, 1934) are friendly but far from uncritical.

[2]   p. 16   Princess Marie von Thurn und Taxis-Hohenlohe: A truly cultured grande dame, and from now on one of Rilke's greatest and most generous friends, whose circle included some of the ablest and most gifted personalities of the time. Rilke had met her the previous December in Paris, and a warm sympathy had sprung up between them which lasted to the end of his life. Her *Erinnerungen an Rainer Maria Rilke* (Corona, 1933) is an invaluable account of their friendship.

His restlessness on the increase, Rilke had gone from Venice to Paris resolved to bury himself in work again. But in July he set out once more, first for Oberneuland to visit Clara and Ruth, thence to the Princess' Bohemian home, Lautschin, and finally, via Prague, to this near-by castle of Janowič. Rilke's first visit here to the Nadhernys is described in [187] of *Letters: 1892–1910*.

Prince Pasha: son of the Princess.

p. 17   Malte Laurids: *The Notebooks of Malte Laurids Brigge*, *G.W.* V; *A.W.* II; *J.O.S.*

p. 17   Kierkegaard: Sören Kierkegaard (1813–1855), the Danish religious thinker and philosopher.

the three children: Baroness Sidie Nadherny and her two young brothers.

[3]   p. 18   Countess Lili Kanitz-Menar: a member of the von Schwerin circle which had played so prominent a part in Rilke's earlier life (see *Letters: 1892–1910*).

Raskolnikov: the protagonist of Dostoievsky's *Crime and Punishment*.

[4]   p. 18   rue de Varenne: see note to [193] in *Letters: 1892–1910*.

Algiers: A group of friends, among them a huntswoman, Frau Oltersdorf, were to be Rilke's traveling companions.

p. 19   the death of Tolstoy: Tolstoy had died on November 7 at the railway station of Astapovo.

[6]   p. 20   you two: Clara and Ruth.

souk: Arab word meaning market.

gebba: a flowing outer garment.

gandourah: a kind of sleeveless shirt worn in the Near East.

[7]   p. 21   Kairuan: was founded sometime before 670 A.D. by Sidi Okba ibn Kafi as a rallying place for Mohammedans in Africa.

the mosque: Called after its founder, the Mosque of Sidi Okba has special significance to the Mohammedan world in that, according to tradition, it was set by divine inspiration absolutely true to Mecca.

[8]   p. 22   temple world of Karnak: cf. *Sonnets to Orpheus* II, 22 (*G.W.* III, 367; *A.W.* I, 300); S.O., 112–113.

O die eherne Glocke, die ihre Keule	O the brazen bell that daily
täglich wider den stumpfen Alltag hebt.	lifts its bludgeon against the dull quotidian.
Oder die *eine*, in Karnak, die Säule, die Säule,	Or the *one*, in Karnak, the column, the column
die fast ewige Tempel überlebt.	that outlives almost eternal temples.

Also the poem "In Karnak Wars" published in the Insel-Almanach for 1923 as "from the poems of Count C.W."

[9]   p. 23   Prince Alexander von Thurn und Taxis: the husband of Princess Marie.

p. 23   Heluan: Rilke was now with Baron Jacob and Baroness May Knoop.

[10]   p. 24   Rilke left Africa in March and returned to Paris after a week in Venice with the Princess.

[11]   p. 24   Frau Lili Schalk: The brilliant wife of the Viennese conductor Franz Schalk and daughter of the Bavarian poet Hopfen.

p. 25   Petrarch on Mont Ventoux: In a letter of April 26, 1335, Petrarch wrote:

> "I opened the compact little volume [St. Augustine's *Confessions*], small indeed in size, but of infinite charm, with the intention of reading whatever came to hand, for I could happen upon nothing that would be otherwise than edifying and devout. Now it chanced that the tenth book presented itself. My brother, waiting to hear something of St. Augustine's from my lips, stood attentively by. I call him, and God too, to witness that where I first fixed my eyes it was written: 'And men go about to wonder at the heights of the mountains, and the mighty waves of the sea, and the wide sweep of rivers, and the circuit of the ocean, and the revolution of the stars, but themselves they consider not.' "

(Cf. *Petrarch, The First Modern Man of Letters: A Selection from His Correspondence*, J. H. Robinson and H. W. Rolfe, G. P. Putnam's Sons, 1909, p. 317.)

[12]   p. 26   Sermon on Mary Magdalene: "L'Amour de Madeleine," a 17th-century French sermon, "Drawn by the Abbé Joseph Bossuet from MS QI 14 in the Royal Library at St. Petersburg," which Rilke had just translated (*G.W.* VI, 71–102).

Guérin Centaur: "Le Centaur," the fragmentary prose poem of Maurice de Guérin (1810–1839). For Rilke's translation see *G.W.* VI, 51–69; *A.W.* II, 323–336.

p. 27   Eugénie de Guérin: (1805–1848), sister of Maurice. The *Lettres d'Eugénie de Guérin*, edited by G. S. Trébutien, were published in Paris in 1863. Rilke's library includes only her *Journal et Fragments*, 25ième ed., Paris, 1869, published by the same editor.

[13]   p. 28   Helene von Nostitz: Frau von Nostitz-Wallwitz (born von Hindenburg), an author, wife of the chief magistrate of Auerbach in the Saxonian Vogtland, mentions Rilke (pp. 150–151) in her *Aus dem alten Europa* (1925).

Lautschin: See [2] and notes.
We then drove: The Princess enthusiastically describes this

trip with Rilke in her car on August 20th (*Erinnerungen*, p. 23).

p. 28 Bettina: Bettina (Brentano) von Arnim (1785–1859). See *Letters: 1892–1910*, [194] and note.

Duchess Anna Amalia: mother of Goethe's friend and patron, Duke Karl August of Sachse-Weimar and regent during his minority, resided at the old ducal Wittumspalais, 1774–1807. Outstanding at the time in her respect for the German language, she engaged Christoph Martin Wieland as tutor for her two sons.

[14] p. 29 Frau Elsa Bruckmann: born Princess Cantacuzène, wife of Hugo Bruckmann, the Munich art and book publisher.

Duino: It was during Rilke's stay here from October 1911 to May 1912, with exception of two brief excursions to Venice, that the first two Duino Elegies and fragments of others were written. The complete series (*G.W.* III, 259–308; *A.W.* I, 227–260; *D.E.*) was not finished until 1922.

remis à neuf: freshened up.

Karst: (Carso) the terrain forming the hinterland of Trieste, which, with its predominance of limestone, is characterized by subterranean channels and caves.

[15] p. 30 your friend: Artur Hospelt.

[16] p. 32 Lou Andreas-Salomé: Rilke's oldest close friend. See numerous letters to her and note to [8] in *Letters: 1892–1910*.

two Christmases: the Western and the Russian Christmas did not fall on the same day owing to differences in the calendars.

Gebsattel: Rilke was considering the possibility of undergoing an analysis with Emil Baron von Gebsattel, a psychiatrist.

Ellen Key: Swedish reformer, feminist and writer (1849–1926); see note to [44] in *Letters: 1892–1910*. She and Rilke had formerly been warm friends.

p. 33 Rodin: reference to Rodin's affair with the Duchesse de Choiseul (see *Letters: 1892–1910*, [206] and note).

p. 34 My best Paris time: the period between May 1908 and January 1910, when *New Poems* II, the *Requiems* and the *Notebooks* were being written.

p. 34 Ilya of Murom: chief hero of the Russian Bylinie or Hero Songs. Cf. the poem cycle "The Czars" in Book of Pictures II, *G.W.* II, 97–106, *A.W.* I, 121–129.

Zwei fremde Pilger riefen einen Namen,	Two stranger pilgrims called a name,
und aufgewacht aus seinem langen Lahmen	and wakened out of his long laming
war Ilija, der Riese von Murom.	was Ilya, the Giant of Murom.

p. 35 Baudelaire poem: "Confession" from *Les Fleurs du Mal.*

que c'est un dur métier etc.: what a hard calling it is to be a beautiful woman.

[17] p. 36 elder Prince Taxis: the father-in-law of Princess Marie.

p. 37 evenings on Capri: Rilke had twice visited Capri, in the winter of 1906–07 and in the spring of 1908.

two elderly women and a young girl: his Capri hostess, Frau Alice Faehndrich, Julie, Baroness von Nordeck zur Rabenau and the former's niece, Countess Solms-Laubach.

p. 38 *New Poems:* Part I was written and published in 1907, Part II in 1908.

rue Cassette: After his break with Rodin in May 1906 Rilke had taken a room in a little hotel at number 29.

p. 39 ancient tombstone: Cf. passage from the Second Elegy (*G.W.* III, 267–268; *A.W.* I, 237; *D.E.,* 33):

Erstaunte euch nicht auf attischen Stelen die Vorsicht menschlicher Geste? war nicht Liebe und Abschied so leicht auf die Schultern gelegt, als wär es aus anderm Stoffe gemacht als bei uns?

On Attic stelês, did not the circumspection of human gesture amaze you? Were not love and farewell so lightly laid upon shoulders, they seemed to be made of other stuff than with us?

and the lines from the poem in *The Life of Mary* (*G.W.* II, 314; *A.W.* I, 223; *T.P.,* 222–223.

| Sie hatten nicht nötig, sich stark zu berühren. Er legte ihr eine Sekunde kaum seine nächstens ewige Hand an die frauliche Schulter. | They had no need firmly to touch each other. He laid for a second scarcely his soon to be eternal hand to her womanly shoulder. |

[18] p. 40 Countess Manon zu Solms-Laubach: see note to [17].

p. 41 a woman being able to pursue art: see [202] in *Letters: 1892–1910*.

[19] p. 41 Emil Baron von Gebsattel: see note to [16].

p. 42 Marthe: a young factory girl, a kind of protégée of his, who remains a mysterious figure in Rilke's life. In her *Erinnerungen* (p. 27), Princess Thurn und Taxis-Hohenlohe says she was closer to him than any other woman and that all his letters about her have a tone she finds nowhere else. Cf. [43].

Madame W.: Frau Wenderl, the woman under whose care Rilke had placed Marthe.

p. 43 through the hardest stone: cf. *Book of Hours, G.W.* II, 269, *A.W.* I, 85.

> Vielleicht, dass ich durch schwere Berge gehe
> in harten Adern, wie ein Erz allein;
> und bin so tief, dass ich kein Ende sehe
> und keine Ferne: alles wurde Nähe
> und alle Nähe wurde Stein.

> Perhaps I am going through heavy mountains
> in hard veins, like an ore alone;
> and am so deep I see no ending
> and no distance: all has become nearness
> and all nearness, stone.

[21] p. 46 Annette Kolb: (1875–   ), a writer, interested chiefly in Catholicism and the broadening of cultural relations between European countries.

mais moi . . . : but I, in reality I hardly think at all, I swallow my thoughts whole without noting the taste in detail, I have them in my blood before drawing from them the immediate profit that imposes itself.

those who have died young: Cf. 1st Elegy (*G.W.* III, 262, ll. 4–6, and 263, ll. 7–9; *A.W.* I, 233, ll. 4–6 and 29–30; *D.E.*, 24–27).

p. 46 the woman who loves: this theme recurs again and again in Rilke's poetry. Cf. 1st Elegy (*G.W.* III, 261, ll. 8–18; *A.W.* I, 232, ll. 18–28; *D.E.*, 22–23.)

p. 47 Gaspara Stampa: (1523–1554), a Milanese lady, whose unhappy love for Collatino, Count of Collalto, she made the subject of some two hundred sonnets. See preceding note.

p. 47 Lyonnaise Labé: Louise Labé (1526–1566), a lady of Lyons, famous for her poetry, her beauty and her eccentric behavior (at sixteen, disguised as a captain, she for a time followed the troops of Francis I). Rilke's translations of her poetry are to be found in *G.W.* VI, 187–210 (*A.W.* II, 348–350, includes but four).

Marianna Alcoforado: the Portuguese nun whose letters to her unfaithful lover Rilke had translated (*G.W.* VI, 103–148). See [117] and note in *Letters: 1892–1910*.

Chamilly: the Marquis de Chamilly, Marianna's lover.

[22] p. 49 To her cousin, Franz Schoenberner, Lou describes her attempt very cautiously to analyze Rilke while they were traveling in Russia, and her sudden awareness that since his genius was rooted in what she recognized as a neurotic complex, the effort to cure his neurosis might mean destroying the poet in him (*Confessions of a European Intellectual*, Macmillan, 1946, p. 268).

p. 50 You know analysis so intimately: Lou was a close friend of Sigmund Freud, and, with his permission, actually practiced analysis herself.

new little "Life of Mary": *G.W.* II, 295–318; *A.W.* I, 211–223; *S.P.*, 194–231.

[23] p. 51 M.L.B.: Malte Laurids Brigge.

[24] p. 52 Dai Bog Zhizn!: God give life!

Angela da Foligno: (1248–1309), foundress of the Third Order of St. Francis and beatified by the Catholic Church, a mystic whose *Instructions* Rilke had been reading.

telyega: Russian peasant cart.

p. 53 Kassner's infirmity: Kassner was a hunchback.

Indian Idealism: Der indische Idealismus (Bruckmann, Munich, 1903), not to be confused with *Der indische Gedanke* (Leipzig, 1913), the book of essays published by Insel-Verlag.

Bruckmann: Hugo Bruckmann. See note to [14].

p. 54 fi de la vie . . . : to the devil with life,—don't speak to me of it any more.

proshchai: Russian for "good-by."

[25] p. 54 difficult for me where dogs are concerned: Cf. *Sonnets to Orpheus* I, 16 (*G.W.* III, 328, *A.W.* I, 278) and Rilke's note, also *S.O.*, 46–47 and translator's note on Rilke's attitude toward dogs.

p. 55 Brahms version: a portion of the *Harz Journey* is used as text for the *Alto Rhapsody*, Op. 53.

acquiring admiration for Goethe: for an earlier stage of Rilke's feeling for Goethe, see [70] in *Letters: 1892–1910*.

returns the compliment of Herr Dr. Kannegiesser: the latter had sent Goethe his commentary on the *Harz Journey*. By way of acknowledgement, Goethe not only complimented Kannegiesser on the accuracy of his interpretation, but himself wrote a four- or five-page analysis of the poem, a document which is included in the notes to most editions of Goethe's poems.

[26] p. 57 grandmother: Frau Caroline Enz (born Kinzelberger). In *René Rilke* (Leipzig, 1932) Carl Sieber states that until her death in 1927 at the age of ninety-eight, this robust old lady continued to celebrate Christmas "with punch and sweet-meats."

p. 58 letters to "Gustgen" Stolberg: Of Goethe's very intimate letters to Countess Auguste Stolberg, whom he had never met, Rilke wrote (August 3, 1912) to the Princess: ". . . what magnificence! How born into the earthly this man really was, how he understood, with what spiritual ingenuity, what can be made of it. And then one was young and took it amiss, dear heaven, yes, and time didn't wait to be told twice and went—"

Venetian history: see [1] and note.

sandals: always kept for Rilke at Lou's house.

[28] p. 60 Alfred Walter von Heymel: (1878–1914), poet (*Gesammelte Gedichte*, Leipzig, 1914), founder of the Insel-Verlag and onetime editor of the *Insel Almanac*, known for a remarkably accurate and able translation of Marlowe's *Edward II*.

p. 61 Schlegel's translation: the Shakespeare translation by August Wilhelm von Schlegel (1767–1845), famous for its extraordinary excellence.

Froissart: A copy of *Les Chroniques de Sire Jean Froissart* (Buchon, 1842, Paris, 3 vols.) was found in Rilke's library.

[29] p. 61 Tasso: Goethe's play on the life of Torquato Tasso (1544–1595), author of *Gerusalemme Liberata*.

p. 61   Marianna: Marianna Alcoforado. See note to [21].

p. 62   Raskolnikov: See note to [3].

        Lepanto: the great naval battle (1571) in which Spain and Italy destroyed the Turkish sea power.

[30] p. 62 From May to September Rilke was in Venice, living for the greater part of the time in the Princess' palace.

p. 63   Casino dei Spiriti: presumably the Casa degli Spiriti. Horatio Brown, a friend of Princess Marie, whom Rilke had met at Duino, suggests, in his *Life on the Lagoons* (London, 1900), that its name and its reputation for being haunted sprang from the fact that bodies bound for burial on the island of San Michele were deposited there at night for purposes of autopsy by medical students.

        Duse: Eleonora Duse, the actress. Rilke had wanted for years to meet her.

p. 64   experience with Rodin: see [16] and note.

        Moissi: Alexander Moissi, the actor, Italian by birth, who made his reputation in the German theater under Reinhardt.

        Reinhardt: Max Reinhardt, the theatrical producer.

p. 65   Placci: Carlo Placci, the actor, whom Rilke had met at Lautschin the previous summer.

        D.S.: Princess Marie had begun, in the summer of 1911, calling Rilke Doctor Seraphicus or Dottor Serafico because she found "Rainer Maria Rilke" too long, "Rilke" too short, and "Rainer Maria" not respectful enough (*Erinnerungen,* pp. 19–20).

[31] p. 66 Voilà où nous sommes: that is where we are.

        The White Princess: G.W. I, pp. 365–401. A dramatic sketch, written with Duse in mind, which in its final form dates from 1904. See [212], also Letters: 1892–1910, [60].

[34] p. 69 Anton Kippenberg: director of the Insel-Verlag and Rilke's publisher from 1906 until the poet's death. He was not only a warm personal friend but was also most generous with financial support over these years.

        Rilke's interest in Spain, which he himself dates from "those Roman days" (winter and spring 1903–04), but which the published letters suggest as having begun somewhat earlier (see [45] in *Letters: 1892–1910*), stems almost certainly from his meeting with Ignacio Zuloaga in Paris and his enthusiasm for the painter's work. Later the impact of Greco's paintings had come to reinforce this feeling for Spain and to lend greater urgency to his desire to go there. At a spiritualistic séance (described by the Princess in her *Erinnerungen*, pp. 60–63; see also note to [35]) held during his visit to Duino, probably just about the time this letter was written, Rilke received a message apparently forecasting a trip to Spain. For a full discussion of the subject see Hans Gebser, *Rilke und Spanien* (Zürich, 1940).

[35] p. 70   The bridges and the walls with chains: At the above-mentioned [34] séance in Duino (see also note to [36]), the planchette had communicated the following messages, to Rilke: "the bridges, the bridges with towers at beginning and end", also, "red earth—glow—steel—chains—churches—bloody chains—".

[36] p. 72   Jesuit Ribadaneira: Pedro A. Ribadeneira (1527–1611), a hagiologist, an early follower of Ignatius Loyola. His most important work was his *Life of Loyola*, 1572.

Dr. R.: Dr. Rziha, librarian at Duino.

p. 73   Salone della Ragione: the great hall of the Palazzo della Ragione in Padua (because of it the palace itself is often called the "Salone"), the walls of which are covered with fifteenth-century frescoes representing the influence of the seasons and the constellations on human life.

Cividale as a promise of the Tajo: Rilke felt the picturesque ravine of Cividale del Friuli, a town of Venetia in the province of Udine, to be a preparation for the great gorge of the Tagus (Tajo) river in Toledo.

gigantic Cristóbal: the so-called Cristobalón, a figure 46 feet high painted on one of the walls of the Toledo Cathedral. Probably the inspiration for Rilke's poem "St. Christopher" (*S.G.*, 9–10).

p. 74   un cabochon énorme . . . : an enormous cabochon set in this terrible and sublime reliquary.

the way you translate: the Princess had been making Italian translations of the Elegies.

our Unknown: the spirit supposed to have sent the message described in the note to [35]. She was purported to have been a woman named Rosemonde Trarieu from Bayonne. Rilke even stopped off at Bayonne en route to Spain in a vain search for vestiges of the mysterious figure.

p. 74 the Bulgarian . . . master in Constantinople: on November 10, 1912, Bulgarian troops had entered Constantinople.

[38] p. 77 his dream picture: Pasha had had a dream in which Rilke had said he would not remain in Toledo but would go farther south to a walled city (*Erinnerungen*, p. 63).

p. 78 Blessed Angela: Angela da Foligno. See note to [24].

quand tous les sages . . . : though all the sages of the world and all the saints of paradise were to heap upon me their consolations and their promises, and God himself his gifts, if he did not change me myself, if he did not begin at the bottom of me a new operation, instead of doing me good, the sages, the saints, and God would exasperate beyond all expression my despair, my fury, my sorrow, my pain, and my blindness.

p. 79 "Elective Affinities": Goethe's novel, *Die Wahlverwandtschaften*.

Old Men's Home: cf. "The Spanish Trilogy", *G.W.* III, 446–448.

[39] p. 81 Moses when he came from the mountain with horns of light: In many early paintings as well as in such works as Michelangelo's statue, Moses is portrayed with horns, a curious tradition deriving from a mistranslation in the Vulgate of the Hebrew word meaning both "horn" and "irradiation". The Latin Bible gives "quod cornuta esset facies sua" where the King James version reads, "he wist not that the skin of his face shone."

p. 82 au lieu de me pénétrer . . . : instead of penetrating me, impressions pierce me.

p. 83 Ellen Key: See note to [16]. Rilke had visited her in 1904.

Fabre d'Olivet: Antoine Fabre D'Olivet (1768–1825), an eccentric literary figure, whose books Rilke had first met with in Toledo. Among other treatises he published *La Langue hébraïque restituée et le véritable sens des mots hébreux rétabli et prouvé par leur analyse radicale*, 1816.

Your husband: Professor Andreas was professor of Oriental languages at the University of Göttingen.

To this letter Rilke appended copies of "To the Angel" (*G.W.* III, 449) and "The Assumption of the Virgin" (unpublished), noting that they had been "written down in the meadowland, walking, this afternoon: and felt at once that you should have them."

[40]   p. 84   Cf. [120], [216] and notes.

Two Elegies: the first two of the Duino Elegies. While in Spain Rilke also wrote the greater portion of the sixth Elegy and some of the ninth.

Book of Hours: *G.W.* II, 175–293; *A.W.* I, 5–83.

[42]   p. 86   Annette Kolb: see note to [21].

Rundschau: Die Neue Rundschau, published by S. Fischer.

Exemplar: Annette Kolb's novel, *Das Exemplar* (1913), which first appeared serially in the *Rundschau.*

Tycho Brahe: (1546–1601), Danish astronomer, who on the night of November 11, 1572, first observed the celebrated "new star" in Cassiopeia.

Mariclée: heroine of *Das Exemplar.*

p. 87   Portuguese Nun and Angela da Foligno: see notes to [21] and [24].

car ce beau livre, etc.: for this beautiful book isn't literature, it is quite simply a state of grace—isn't that enough for you?

[43]   p. 87   Paris: Rilke had returned to Paris at the end of February.

à quelques exceptions près: with a few exceptions.

p. 88   la mort du pauvre . . . : the death of the poor man who dies, his head on one of these stones, is perhaps sweet after all.

Marthe: see note to [19].

Bullier: the bal Bullier, dance hall in the Latin Quarter.

* . . . *. The passage between asterisks, pp. 88–90, was written in French.

p. 90   the little heron of Egypt: probably the cattle-egret or buff-backed heron that picks ticks off the backs of cattle.

prétend que . . . : claims that blood came up in her throat.

Verhaeren: Emile Verhaeren (1855–1916), the Belgian poet.

p. 91   Mme. de C.: The Duchesse of Choiseul, an American by birth. See note to [16].

[44]   p. 92   Jean-Christophe: Romain Rolland's long novel.

p. 92   ce n'est pas de l'essence de rose . . . : It isn't essence of roses, certainly, but it is a tisane which has had time to be infused and which, if one lets it drip [sips it] slowly and with abandon, sometimes comes to remind you of the sweet intimacy of the blissful little flower.

Ancient music, an epitaph: The grave-inscription of Seikilos, near Pralles in Asia Minor, discovered in 1883, is one of the few complete examples extant of Greek music. Presumably the "spring melody taken from a Gregorian mass" would be the very similar melody of a Gregorian antiphon for Palm Sunday, *Hosanna filio David*, which has been assumed to be not so much a reproduction of this ancient piece as an adaptation to their own uses, such as would have been entirely natural to later composers, of a melody-type current in antiquity. (Cf. [120]).

[45]   p. 93   Leipzig: Rilke was staying with his publisher, Anton Kippenberg. He had left Paris in June to spend a month at Bad Rippoldsau in the Black Forest for his health, thereafter visiting Lou in Göttingen.

[46]   p. 93   Ellen Delp: a young friend (not actually Lou's daughter!). The issue of *Philobiblon* (Vol. 8, No. 10, 1935) commemorating Rilke's sixtieth birthday contains her "Erinnerung", a brief reminiscence of Rilke.

p. 94   Heiligendamm: an old watering place near Mecklenburg. Rilke was there in the company of Herr and Frau von Nostitz.

[47]   p. 94   Eva Cassirer: author of a comparative study of some of Rilke's early poems ("Mir zur Feier—die Frühen gedichte: ein Vergleich", *Die Frau*, 1911/12, pp. 612–624).

Munich: Rilke was in Munich from early September until the beginning of October.

Tolstoy letters: Correspondence with Countess Alexandrine Tolstaia.

p. 95   personal contact: Rilke had met Tolstoy in Russia in 1899 and 1900. See [15] in *Letters: 1892–1910*.

Werfel: Franz Werfel (1890–1945), poet, dramatist, perhaps most widely known in this country as the author of *The Forty Days of Musa Dagh*, *The Song of Bernadette*, etc.

The Carrion Way: "Jesus and the Carrion Path". See *Gesänge aus drei Reichen* (Leipzig, 1917) and *Franz Werfel: Poems*, translated by Edith Abercrombie Snow, Princeton University Press, 1945.

[48] p. 95 Rilke had just returned to Paris.

p. 96 Hellerau métier: Rilke had recently seen Claudel's "L'An-nonce faite à Marie" performed at an experimental theater in Hellerau (Leipzig), "a kind of laboratory disturbing only because it is not fitting to assemble in a laboratory with such solemnity and emphasis and from afar; one should carry on in there, each with apron and protective glasses, as inconspicuously as possible and watch the investigations unfolding in this light-retort under blue-green radiation." (November 4, 1913, to Helene von Nostitz.)

p. 97 "The Stranger": G.W. III, 231; A.W. I, 180.

Und dies alles immer unbegeh-	And to let all this go
rend	ever undesiring, seemed to him
hinzulassen, schien ihm mehr	more than his
als seines	life's delight, possession, fame.
Lebens Lust, Besitz und Ruhm.	

[49] p. 98 Geheimrat Martersteig: then superintendent of the City Theaters in Leipzig.

"tranquille, mais bien armée": "calm, but well armed".

[50] p. 98 Reinhard Johannes Sorge: (1892–1916), a young writer of half-mystical dramas, a Catholic convert, especially drawn to Franciscan ideals, killed in the first World War before he had reached full development.

"Emmaus": G.W. III, 386; "Journey to Hell": G.W. III, 384; A.W. I, 330.

Jacopone da Todi: (1230–1306), Franciscan mystical poet. These lines (p. 99) are from Lauda LXXXX:

> Love, Love that has so wounded me
> Nothing can I do but cry Love;
> Love, Love, with thee I am united,
> Nothing can I do but embrace thee.

[51] p. 101 Schrenck-Notzing: Albert, Baron von Schrenck-Notzing, (1862–1929), the spiritualist, who had been investigating a number of well-known mediums who were using methods he himself had devised.

you *know* something of these things; the Princess had for years been a member of the Society for Psychical Research.

[52] p. 102 Thankmar, Baron von Münchhausen: son of the poet Bör-ries von Münchhausen.

p. 103   Deubel: Léon Deubel (1879–1921), French symbolist poet.

poètes maudits: The subjects of a series of critical essays by Paul Verlaine, later revised and published under this title in 1884, include: Tristan Corbière, Arthur Rimbaud, Stéphane Mallarmé, Marceline Desbordes-Valmore, Villiers de l'Isle-Adam, and Pauvre Lélian who was Verlaine himself.

cette misère revêche qui s'entête: that harsh misery that obstinately persists.

heur and malheur: good fortune and bad.

[53]   p. 104   Tolstoy's correspondence: see [47] and note.

aunt of Tolstoy's: probably the wife of Nikolai Tolstoy, a distant relative of Leo Tolstoy, with whom Rilke and Lou Andreas-Salomé stayed in July 1900, on their second trip to Russia.

p. 105   Prince Myshkin: hero of Dostoievsky's novel *The Idiot*.

[54]   p. 107   passages concerning Charles the Bold: *G.W.* V, 224–232; *J.O.S.*, 180–186.

[55]   p. 108   comme tout change . . . : how everything changes, and one doesn't know when one diminishes . . . It is always that that frightens me most.

"malade un peu": slightly ill.

Meudon: where Rodin had his studio and where Rilke had lived during the brief period of his so-called secretaryship.

incident of last spring: Rodin, for political reasons, had broken his agreement to let Clara Rilke do a bust of him.

p. 109   "Retour de l'enfant prodigue": Gide's story, "The Return of the Prodigal Son", which Rilke translated (*G.W.* VI, 151–184).

Insel-Bücherei: The Insel-Verlag's popular series of little, figured-paper–bound books.

[56]   p. 109   "Swann": *Du côté de chez Swann*, published in November 1913 by Bernard Grasset at Proust's own expense, had received little notice and was accounted a failure. Rilke was one of the few immediately to recognize its significance.

[57]   p. 110   Rilke had left Paris in April and had just been to Duino.

the Mezzanino: The Princess's apartment in Venice, in the palace of her friends the Valmaranas.

p. 110 Il faut que . . . : I must recover, find myself again, that will take a long time and I do not think it will happen here.

p. 111 how far I am from the "poverello": for Rilke's earlier attitude toward St. Francis, see closing verses of the *Book of Hours, G.W.* II, 291 ff.; *A.W.* I, 103–104.

que nous importe . . . : which is what the good heart of that little market town of Umbria means to us.

"lovely", "charming": Rilke uses the English words.

[59] p. 111 Paris: Rilke returned at the end of May for what proved to be his last visit to Paris before the first World War.

p. 112 A kind of future is past: Rilke had just passed through the intense experience of his relationship with Magda von Hattingberg. Many of his letters to and conversations with her have been included in *Rilke und Benvenuta, ein Buch des Dankes* (Wilhelm Andermann Verlag, Vienna, 1946). The letters are beautiful, but seemed not suitable for inclusion in this book, out of their proper context. For similar reasons we have not included the letters to Elya Maria Neva (*Freundschaft mit Rainer Maria Rilke* [1918–1923], Albert Zust Verlag, Bern, 1946) and Claire Goll—"Liliane" —(*Briefe an eine Freundin, 1918–1925*, published in a limited edition in *Aurora VI*, Herbert Steiner, editor, 1944).

p. 113 exuberant "S": Rilke refers to his writing of the letters in German script, which at that time was exaggeratedly long, expressing his gay mood.

p. 115 Stefan George: (1868–1933), the German poet.

The Star of the Covenant: published in 1914.

Elberfeld horses: Maeterlinck's essay was also published in a volume entitled *The Unknown Guest*, New York, 1914. These highly trained animals, said to be capable of such feats as counting, had excited considerable interest at this time.

[60] p. 116 "Turning": *G.W.* III, 460–462; *A.W.* I, 309–310.

p. 115 dolls: Rilke's essay, "Dolls", inspired by the wax dolls of Lotte Pritzel, *G.W.* IV, 265–277; *A.W.* II, 265–273. Illustrations of eleven of these dolls or puppets appear in *Das Puppenbuch* (E. Reiss, Berlin, 1921) in connection with Theodor Däubler's article on "Die Puppen der Lotte Pritzel".

[61] p. 117 The outbreak of the first World War found Rilke staying with the Kippenbergs in Leipzig. On July 9 he had written Herr Kippenberg from Paris that he was working regularly, scarcely leaving his room "except for a little exercise under the depressing trees of the Luxembourg which since the last hot-spell stand there quite parboiled and almost leafless", and Frau Kippenberg reports that when he arrived in Leipzig he did not look well. One evening he read the parts of the Duino Elegies that had already been written. Then came the news of Russia's mobilization, of which Rilke, "like the political child he was", remarked that it was "surely just a gesture". Next day Germany was under arms. While they waited for Herr Kippenberg to bring further news from the city that night, Rilke fetched his Bible and read aloud "about Elijah, from the Book of Kings, hesitatingly, softly and with long pauses."

As an Austrian, Rilke risked internment if he returned to Paris. On August 1, accordingly, he left instead for Munich.

p. 117 verses: two of the "Five Songs, August 1914", which first appeared in the Insel Almanac for 1915 (*G.W.* III, 389; *A.W.* I, 322). Rilke wrote down these five songs in the volume of Hölderlin (see [63] and note) which he carried about with him at Irschenhausen (together with a sixth, "Thee will I praise, flag", not included in the first published edition nor in *G.W.*, but now *S.G.*, 36, and *A.W.* I, 328). As Frau Kippenberg suggests, the excitement of his departure from Leipzig—the crowds, the bulletins and rumors, the first sight of soldiers on the move—and what he saw in that day's journey across southern Germany—the armed men, the singing, the farewells of women, old farmers hastening near to wave their caps to the soldiers in the passing train—these must have swept Rilke into the current of exalted excitement and caused him to give vent to these only—and quickly deprecated—war poems.

p. 118 an officer: young von Münchhausen was serving as a lieutenant of Hussars.

[62] p. 118 Anna, Baroness von Münchhausen: Thankmar's mother.

[63] p. 119 my doctor: Dr. Emil von Stauffenberg, on whose advice Rilke was spending three weeks in Munich.

friends in Bohemia: the Prince and Princess von Thurn und Taxis.

p. 119   the Hölderlin volume: a privately circulated selection from Vol. IV of Norbert von Hellingrath's edition of Hölderlin. In it Rilke also wrote down the lines "To Hölderlin" (now *S.G.*, 37; *A.W.* I, 328). He had written von Hellingrath (July 24) that Hölderlin's "influence on me is large and generous as only that of the richest and inwardly most powerful can be."

Hyperion: Hölderlin's novel.

[64]   p. 120   Freiburg: Rilke had again been playing with the idea of studying at a small university, this time at Freiburg.

p. 121   pages written in August: again the five war-poems.

[66]   p. 122   mournful news: the death of Prince Taxis' mother.

[67]   p. 123   From Berlin, whither he had hastened at the news that Heymel (see [28] and note) was dying, Rilke wrote his friend Hans Carossa, the doctor-writer, on the evening of November 24, describing in some detail the sick man's condition and treatment (he died on November 26). At the beginning of the war, Heymel had temporarily triumphed over a spreading tubercular infection, served for five weeks, on horseback—"and there the end eluded him, only to eat him away so horribly here . . . Dear Carossa, do you sit at *such* bedsides!?"

[68]   p. 124   Johannes Kalckreuth: son of the painter Leopold Kalckreuth.

[69]   p. 124   Karl and Elisabeth von der Heydt: a banker and poet, and his wife, whom Rilke had met through Countess Schwerin and who had been very generous to him in earlier days (see *Letters: 1892–1910*). Part I of the *New Poems*, published late in 1907, was dedicated to them.

p. 125   leaving all my possessions: in April 1915, at the instigation of his Paris landlord, all Rilke's belongings were auctioned off and scattered (see [84])—"not maliciously,—he simply wanted to get his rent, for no one could assure him that I still existed and would pay." Friends managed to reassemble a few boxes. The daguerreotype of his father, subject of the poem "Portrait of My Father as a Young Man" (*G.W.* III, 69) was restored to him after the war and is now in the Rilke Archive at Weimar.

[70]   p. 126   Written as postscript to a letter of the preceding day. Rilke was on his way to Würzburg with the thought of studying there.

p. 126　The *Cornet:* The narrative prose-poem, *The Tale of the Love and Death of Cornet Christopher Rilke* (*G.W.* IV, 5–34; *A.W.* II, 309–322), though written in 1899, was not published until 1906.

[71]　p. 126　"I, who for years have not harbored one, have a large Christmas tree, as though a child were invisibly here or I should rejoice like a child—; dear friends did this for me, and I took possession of it, was aware of it in my heart's purview, into which nothing enters very easily these days." (To Anton Kippenberg, December 28.)

[73]　p. 127　the music to the Cornet: This setting by Kasimir von Pászthory (Kistner und Siegel, Leipzig) was performed at Leipzig, "once before a large number of people, the other time at a little Schlösschen near L.", and again in Vienna, in the palace of Prince Franz Auersperg.

Frau von Hattingberg: see note to [59].

[74]　p. 128　Ludwig von Ficker: editor of the Brenner Verlag's fortnightly publication. A week later, as nothing fresh had come to his mind, Rilke sent von Ficker the lines from his notebook beginning "Straining so against the strong night" ("So angestrengt wider die starke Nacht", *G.W.* III, 398), saying he had hesitated over a title and finally let it go, but asking that particular attention be paid to his punctuation marks and to the lower-case letters at the beginning of lines.

[75]　p. 128　The Cornet: as many comments throughout his correspondence reveal, Rilke did not entertain a very high opinion of this youthful work. Learning that a first edition of the *New Poems*, not yet out of print, had brought 370 marks at the Heymel auction and the "old Cornet" three times that amount, he remarked that "people are simply crazy in this respect too" (to Clara Rilke, November 4, 1917).

[76]　p. 130　A man otherwise quite a recluse: Alfred Schuler (d. 1923), whose only published writings are contained in the privately printed "Alfred Schuler, Dichtungen. Aus dem Nachlass." Schuler's ideas must have impressed Rilke more than superficially, since their influence, as Rilke himself was aware (see [200]), may be traced in the *Duino Elegies* and *Sonnets to Orpheus.*

[78]　p. 132.　The finest Picasso: Rilke had asked Frau Hertha Koenig, owner of the "Saltimbanques", whether he might stay at

her apartment while looking for the right little house in the country: "I would beg for a bed in the guestroom for myself, a bed for my housekeeper, the kitchen, and permission to work at your magnificent desk—; everything else would remain locked up; at most I would on some afternoon sit for a long time before the Picasso, which gives me courage for this beginning, just as the certainty does that in your good rooms perhaps in a hand's turn I would fall into that disposition to work which I have not known for months." He remained here until after October 10. The picture (Paris, 1905) is now at the Art Institute in Chicago on extended loan from the Chester Dale Collection. It is reproduced in Werner Wolff's *Rainer Maria Rilkes Duineser Elegien* (Heidelberg, 1937), and in *D.E.* It was the chief inspiration for the Fifth Elegy, which is dedicated to Frau Koenig.

[79] p. 132 News about Duino: Later the castle was badly damaged. The Princess, returning in 1918, found it "but a phantom."

Wozzek: The play by Georg Büchner (1813–1851), one of the creators of German expressionist drama, provided the text for Alban Berg's opera of that name, performed in Philadelphia and New York in 1930 under the direction of Leopold Stokowski.

[80] p. 134 Le monde . . . : "the world is terrible . . ."

[81] p. 135 the reading: Rilke had written Frau Bruckmann (July 13) that rereading the *Book of Hours* (written 1899–1903, now *G.W.* II; *A.W.* I) had so "lifted and built him up" that he thought it might, if he could read it "resolutely and convincingly", be of similar influence on others now.

[82] p. 136 Regina Ullmann: A Swiss writer. According to her *Erinnerungen an Rilke* (St. Gallen, 1946), their friendship began in 1908 when she asked Rilke for his opinion of her "Field Sermon". His enthusiastic response gave her confidence to pursue her career. He also was largely responsible for the inclusion of the work in the Insel-Bücherei.

[83] p. 138 Marthe: See note to [19].

Il n'y aura . . . : there will be before me only disasters, terrors, indescribable anguish; it is with you that the good things of my life finish—

[84] p. 140 the "*Unknown*": see note to [36].

p. 140　qui n'est pas une auberge . . . : which is not an inn but a fine crossroads just the same.

p. 141　restons dehors: let us stay outside.

et moi, si j'ai . . . : and for myself, if I still have any future, it will be by starting again humbly that I shall arrive at it.

Paris belongings: see note to [69].

p. 142　voyez quel débris: you see what rubbish.

Je suis un enfant . . . : I am a child who would like about him only more and more adult childhoods.

[85]　p. 143　irritating press: it may be well to remind ourselves of what went on in these times by reading an account of the press reports manufactured by *all the warring nations,* like that in Joseph Ward Swain's *Beginning the Twentieth Century* (pp. 454–456).

[87]　p. 145　On leaving Widenmayerstrasse, Rilke lived at the villa of Frau Renée Alberti, in Schwabing, near the Englischer Garten. He had been obliged to remain in Munich waiting for his class to be called up: "Nothing is more torturesome to me."

[88]　p. 146　This letter was first published, together with one to an imaginary worker of the postwar period, in the little volume *Über Gott* (Insel-Verlag, Leipzig, 1933).

p. 150　Wilhelm Fliess: The book referred to is probably *Vom Leben und Tod,* Lectures in Biology (2nd ed., 1914), by William Fliess. Fliess evolved a theory about the numerically determinable periodicity of certain dates important to the course of people's lives. His principal work was *Ablauf des Lebens* (1906).

The "hideous cup": see the poem "Death" (*G.W.* III, 413; *A.W.* I, 339), written at this time (November, 1915).

[89]　p. 151　Saonara: the villa of Countess V., near Padua, whither the Princess had driven Rilke on one of their numerous expeditions from Duino, in September 1912.

[90]　p. 152　Turnau: in German Bohemia, where, as Rilke was born in Prague, he might presumably have been sent for his military training.

p. 152   Rilke was now on four days' leave from Vienna (where he had stayed until the middle of January with his "extremely kind and helpful friends the Taxis'" in the Victorgasse), to find some seventy letters piled up on his desk in Munich, the accumulation of two months' correspondence. According to his military pass, the examination in Munich on November 24 had shown him, contrary to all expectation and much to the concern of his friends, fit for armed service in the reserve. At the subsequent examination in Vienna (February 15) his physical unfitness was acknowledged, but only after the barracks experience. Finally, at the instigation of Frau Kippenberg, who, in the name of the Insel-Verlag, sent to the Austrian ministries of war and defense a petition signed by many well-known intellectuals, he was granted indefinite leave of absence from service (June 9, 1916). Frau Kippenberg reports that during this period he struck perhaps the lowest point of his life's curve: in his discouragement he wanted to give up writing and again seriously considered becoming a doctor.

p. 153   Michelangelo: Rilke's translations of the Sonnets of Michelangelo (*G.W.* VI, 213–271; *A.W.* II contains only two; also separately published in No. 496 of the Insel-Bücherei). See [174].

[91]   p. 154   Hugo von Hofmannsthal: (1874–1929), the Austrian poet. Frau Kippenberg writes that "when Hofmannsthal heard of Rilke's plight . . . he exclaimed with wonderful sympathy, 'the poor child!', striking to the black depths of the situation as only poets can."

p. 155   Your Picasso: the picture—an early self-portrait, high in color, on a blue background—still belongs to von Hofmannsthal's daughter, Frau Christiane Zimmer.

Rilke returned to Munich in July, but on September 18 wrote Kippenberg that the "seven months of disconnection" had so fundamentally unsettled him that he might, somewhat reluctantly, have to seek a change of place, perhaps offer his services to the Insel-Verlag in Leipzig, though his hopes still clung to "this desk and the three folders of MS in a certain drawer".

[92]   p. 155   Jacobsen: Jens Peter Jacobsen (1847–1885), the Danish poet. See [204], [210].

[93]   p. 156   Imma von Ehrenfels: the fiancée of Norbert von Hellingrath (see note to [63]), who had fallen before Verdun, December 14, 1916.

[94] p. 157 the military school: Rilke refers again and again throughout his correspondence to the five years of his life spent at military schools: September 1886 to September 1890 at St. Pölten, September 1890 to April 1891 at Mährisch-Weisskirchen. See [150] and the introduction to *Y.P.*

translations: presumably of the Michelangelo Sonnets (see [90]).

[95] p. 158 Franz Marc: the German painter, born in 1880, is perhaps best known in this country for his Red Horses (about 1909) shown with other of his works at the Museum of Modern Art in New York in 1931.

[96] p. 159 Chiemsee: Rilke had spent the last two weeks of June at this Bavarian lake, and had made up his mind to give up his Munich apartment and go for the rest of the summer to Gut Böckel bei Bieren, Westphalia, the estate of Frau Koenig.

these poems: over a year later (September, 1918) Rilke gave the manuscript of what there was of the Elegies to Herr Kippenberg for safekeeping, remarking that he would probably never finish them. The Princess Thurn und Taxis-Hohenlohe reports that when she saw him in June, 1921, at Rolle, in Switzerland, he read her some further fragments, new to her though written some time earlier, and that in his profound discouragement he had almost decided to let the Insel-Verlag publish the material as it was.

[97] p. 160 Stifter: Adalbert Stifter (1805–1868). *Indian Summer,* his most celebrated novel, was a favorite with Nietzsche, who kept it at his bedside.

Herr von Kühlmann: Richard von Kühlmann had also been councilor of the German Embassy in London for the six years preceding the war (see note to [102]).

[99] p. 162 Countess Mary Gneisenau: A writer (*Aus dem Tale der Sehnsucht, Der Tod Adrian Guldenkrons,* etc.) and an old friend of Rilke's (see [117], [120], [127] in *Letters: 1892–1910*).

Gut Böckel: The house at Böckel was an old moated Westphalian manor behind a high screen of lindens; the landscape was strange, the weather wet, but Rilke enjoyed his tower-room and its two roomy alcoves with old windows deeply recessed in the masonry walls.

p. 163   correspondence with a child: the correspondence of Bettina (Brentano) von Arnim and Goethe. See [13] and *Letters: 1892–1910*, [194] and note.

Gustave Sack: born 1885, fell in Rumania in 1916.

[100]   p. 163   Dr. Wolf Przygode: editor of *Die Dichtung*, in the first number of which (Roland-Verlag, Munich, 1918) appear the five poems in question: "From a Spring" ("Aus einem Frühling [Paris]"), "The Doves", ("Die Tauben"), "One must die because one knows them . . . [old Egyptian papyrus]", ("Man muss sterben, weil man sie kennt . . . [altägyptischer Papyros]"), "Lament" ("Klage" [*G.W.* III, 409–412; only the last in *A.W.* I, 321]), and "Christ's Journey to Hell" ("Christi Höllenfahrt", [*G.W.* III, 384–385; *A.W.* I, 330]).

[102]   p. 165   Rilke was "half against his will" spending some nine weeks in Berlin, "seeing over and over again people of all sorts, in order to take instruction from them in current events and changes which, even if I have to breathe among them, remain for me a theme indescribably inflected."

Since the Russian Revolution, unrest had been increasing in Central Europe. Germany's political system had for some months been giving way under the strain of war. Bethmann-Hollweg had fallen in July. The Center and Majority Socialists had passed a peace resolution in the Reichstag and Kühlmann (see note to [97]), who was to fall in June 1918, over the question of a negotiated peace, had been made foreign minister.

p. 166   Keyserlingk: Rilke's correspondence with young Count Keyserlingk has unfortunately been lost.

Uexküll: Baron Jacob J. von Uexküll, the naturalist. He mentions Rilke in his *Niegeschaute Welten* (Berlin, 1936).

[103]   p. 167   Rodin's death: at Meudon on November 17, 1917.

Grandmother: Clara's mother, Frau Westhoff.

[104]   p. 168   Bernhard von der Marwitz of Friedersdorf: (1890–1918), a young poet whose journal was published in 1924, and a volume of his letters and war-diaries (edited by Harald von Königswald under the title *Stirb und Werde*, W. G. Korn, Breslau) in 1931. He greatly admired Hölderlin, Rodin, Rilke and Paul Claudel, and was translating some of Claudel's poems into German when he was called to the colors.

p. 168   the poems: probably the translations of the Michelangelo Sonnets (see [90] and note and [174]), on which Rilke had been working at intervals for some time. "I won't be hurting anybody by it, for since the few masterly translations of Hermann Grimm no attempt of any value has come to anything" (September 12, 1916). Grimm's translations are scattered through his *Leben Michelangelos* (1860–1863).

    Claudel: Paul Claudel, the French poet and dramatist, later ambassador to the United States.

[105]   p. 169   your little book: *Drei Briefe an einen Knaben* (1918) written for her son. Rilke had read it in 1914 and had written Lou his impressions of it (February 20, 1914).

    the maternal body: see Eighth Elegy, lines 43–65 (*G.W.* III; *A.W.* I; *D.E.*).

[107]   p. 171   household of my own: Rilke had left the Hotel Continental for his new apartment at Ainmillerstrasse 34 IV, out in Schwabing and next door to Paul Klee, the painter.

    The rising cost of living and the exceptional demands of getting settled made very welcome a large money order from the Insel-Verlag, besides which Frau Kippenberg had sent a hamper of linen and bedding which delighted the soul of Rosa, the housekeeper.

[109]   p. 174   Bernhard von der Marwitz had died of wounds in a field hospital near Valenciennes on September 8. See note to [104].

[110]   p. 176   Marie von Bunsen: author of books of travel in the Far East and in Germany, *The Lost Courts of Europe*, and *The World I Used to Know—1860–1912* (in which Rilke is twice mentioned in passing).

    Ansbach: Rilke had been to the beautiful little medieval town in his search for a "protected and lasting refuge", had even expressly advertised for "a quiet garden apartment or garden pavilion". But, feeling that such a place is better happened upon than sought after, and that the moment had perhaps not come, he was now considering a journey to Switzerland as a way of stirring himself out of his creative immobility.

p. 177   people through whom the past remains connected with us: elsewhere in this letter, Rilke speaks of his regret at having missed some hours with Richard Voss, the dramatist and novelist (1851–1918), and more particularly, the chance of meeting Lady Blennerhasset (Charlotte Julia von Leyden, 1843–1917), whose essays in the history of literature he was just reading and whose steadiness through the difficult years could have helped him, he was sure, if he could only have listened to her occasionally for half an hour.

[112] p. 179 Unrest had been fast increasing in Germany and the request for an armistice led to further chaos, political and mental. Just before the fall of the Imperial Government at Berlin, revolution broke out in Munich. Kurt Eisner, Independent Socialist, was released from prison in time to organize his forces; on November 5 he demanded a republic; on the 6th, while the soldiers' and workers' council was being set up, the King of Bavaria fled; on the 7th Eisner formally proclaimed the Bavarian Republic with himself as president.

p. 181 Grandmama Phia: Rilke's mother was still living in Prague, where the Czech national council was setting up the new republic of Czechoslovakia.

[114] p. 182 Herr von Kaufmann's proposals: concerned the resumption of personal relations between individuals of the various countries that had been at war.

[115] p. 182 Concerning Rilke's military service, see [90] and note.

[116] p. 183 the revolution: See note to [112].

[117] p. 184 First published in the *Berliner Tageblatt*, December 29, 1936. "We have known each other for *two* years, Anni Mewes. Only acquaintance with me has become a sad business, not easily put into effect. My, how I enjoyed you in those days in Vienna, and here too in your rooms in the Pension Romana, where you kept me so protectingly warm!" (Good Friday, 1918).

[118] p. 185 *Baroness Schenk: A niece of Frau Alice Faehndrich at whose Capri villa Rilke had been a fellow guest in 1907. See *Letters: 1892–1910*, [196] and note, and [207].

p. 186 Caroline Schlegel-Schelling: (1763–1809), daughter of Professor Michaelis, oriental scholar at Göttingen, was closely linked with the leaders of the German Romantic school. She married Wilhelm Schlegel, older brother of Friedrich, in 1796, and F. W. J. Schelling in 1803. The reference is to *Caroline, Briefe aus der Frühromantik*, enlarged edition, after Georg Waitz, by Erich Schmidt (Leipzig, 1913).

[119] p. 186 your cuff links: This reference suggests that the addressee is Emil Lettré, the artist-goldsmith (1876–) author of *Kleinodien* (1923).

four of my contributions: See [120] and note.

[120] p. 187 *The Insel Almanac:* for 1919.

sad event: the death of the Countess' husband, Dr. von Stauffenberg (see note to [63]).

p. 188 the Comtesse de Noailles's lovely poem: *Les vivants et les morts:* "Tu vis, je bois l'azur", which Rilke had translated (*G.W.* VI, 340; *A.W.* II, 355).

two little experiments: "Death" (see [88] and note) and "Narcissus" (*G.W.* III, 416).

"An Experience": (*G.W.* IV, 280; *A.W.* III, 256) describes a state of mind Rilke experienced—while leaning against a tree in the garden of Duino where, according to his habit, he had been walking up and down with a book—in which he seemed to have "come out on the other side of Nature", more keenly understanding objects because remote from them, as though in his present embodiment experiencing a kind of return, a looking out over things from the recess of a deserted window (Cf. [40], [216] and notes). Carossa recalls that when Rilke was reading this piece aloud to him, in the studio in Munich, the maid coming in with tea slipped and the tray crashed; she picked up herself and the pieces, disappeared, and presently returned with fresh tea things—the quiet reading never ceased, Rilke seemed never even to have noticed the disturbance.

a fragment of ancient music: See [44] and note.

[121] p. 189 Verhaeren: See note to [43]. The poet met his death in a railway accident in the station at Rouen, November 27, 1916.

"Flammes hautes": (in *Choix de poèmes*, 1916, Mercure de France) opens:

> Dites, quel est le pas
> Des mille pas qui vont et passent
> Sur les grand'routes de l'espace,
> Dites, quel est le pas
> Qui doucement, un soir, devant ma porte basse
> S'arrêtera?

p. 189　A single translation (1919) from Verhaeren, "The Dead", appears in *A.W.* II, 365.

[123]　p. 190　the malicious agitation about Rodin: the acquisition of some bronzes, by a well-known amateur and an *artiste parisienne*, from Rodin's usual caster, had given rise to the question of the authenticity of the pieces and hence to the "affaire des faux Rodins" (see "A propos des faux Rodins", by "un sculpteur", *Revue de Paris*, xxvi, no. 6, March 15, 1919).

[124]　p. 192　The socialist republican government of Bavaria had set up a provisional constitution; but on February 21, the day the Diet was to meet, Eisner was shot dead in the street by a reactionary Nationalist officer.

[126]　p. 193　infringements and interferences: from February to April, Germany was torn by civil war, great strikes taking place in the Ruhr, in Berlin, in Württemberg. In Munich, the murder of Eisner had led to communist uprisings and the establishment on April 6 of a soviet or councils republic (Räte-Republik). This rule lasted until about May 1, when it was overthrown after fierce fighting, and the former socialist republican government, with Hoffmann as minister-president, again took charge, a new constitution being laid before the Diet on May 5 and put into effect August 14. During May a sort of White Terror reigned. (Wilhelm Hausenstein, the art-historian, says, in *Stimmen der Freunde*, ed. by Gert Buchheit, 1931, that Rilke was aroused at five o'clock one morning by the tread of army-boots and the knock of a rifle butt, and accused of being a "bolshevik", and that it was this experience that drove him from Munich and from Germany. He was also said to have been labeled "a Czech perverting the German language.")

p. 194　not gained much in health: before Rilke left for Switzerland early in June he happened on Carossa, returning slightly wounded from the front. Knowing Rilke's custom of fasting when he did not feel well, the doctor suspected from his appearance that he had had an involuntary overdose of this treatment, and before even examining him as Rilke asked him to do, filled out the formulas necessary for getting seriously sick patients extra allowances of the milk, butter, eggs and flour which Rilke's "vegetarian" diet made necessary.

[127]　p. 194　Rilke left Munich about June 11, and the cities he "had to do with" were Geneva, Bern and Zurich. On July 24 he

went to visit the painter R. R. Junghanns and his wife
Inga, Danish translator of *M.L.B.*, in Sils Baselgia in the
Upper Engadine. Frau Junghanns tells how her husband
wondered whether Rilke would still be able to laugh, and
how, as the first evening wore on in the long and intimate
talk of friends reunited, the two men began capping each
other's funny stories about the North German fisherfolk,
until they were all laughing "as they had not laughed for
three years." He left here after four days by the mail coach,
to drive over the Maloja Pass to Soglio in the Bergell, in a
southern valley of Graubünden. Here he lived at the Pension Willy, the former Palazzo Salis.

[128] p. 199 quand-même, la vie . . . : even so, life, destitute as it
seems, has astonishing generosities.

p. 200 an old room full of books: the library was opened to him
as a refuge, the quietest part of the *Gasthaus*, where the
noise of playing children could not reach him.

the poets: Albrecht von Haller (1708–1777) and the lyri-
cist, Johann Gaudenz, Baron von Salis-Seewis (1762–1834).

[129] p. 201 Elisabeth von Schmidt-Pauli: author of *Rainer Maria
Rilke, ein Gedenkbuch* (Basel, Benno Schwabe & Co.,
1940).

p. 202 (travail repoussé): repoussé work, relief designs hammered
on metal from the reverse side.

[130] p. 203 Vogeler: Heinrich Vogeler, painter and illustrator, to
whom he dedicated the *Life of Mary* (see note to [22]),
was an old friend of Rilke and his wife from the early days
among the Worpswede artists who form the subject of
the profusely illustrated monograph *Worpswede* (1910).
Rilke's letters to Vogeler are unfortunately lost.

[131] p. 204 Gertrud Ouckama Knoop: wife of the novelist, Gerhard
Julius Ouckama Knoop (1861–1913), and mother of the
young Vera to whose memory the *Sonnets to Orpheus* are
dedicated (see [175] and note).

[132] p. 207 Rilke left Soglio toward the end of September, and after
meeting Marthe at Begnins, went to visit friends in Nyon.
But here there were too many people for his taste, and he
resumed his wanderings, to Zurich, then Locarno.

[133] p. 208 (. . . my first Zurich reading): Rilke had "just put an end
to my curious public behavior on Friday in Winterthur,
reading in a little old theater, before a green curtain, by the

light of two candles, within the frame of an old-fashioned stage-set, flanked right and left by a Biedermeier muse. I broke through this milieu to some extent . . . In Bern I read in the great Council Hall from the president's desk . . . had the people in my palm like a four-in-hand" (to Countess M., December 1, 1919). Various plans had fallen through, but he reports to Anton Kippenberg that his "evenings" have made him some good Swiss friends who are also thinking about his living problem.

p. 208   The patrician Burckhardts: See [152] and note.

p. 209   *Inselschiff:* the quarterly publication of the Insel-Verlag.

[134] p. 209   Dr. Hünich: Fritz Adolf Hünich, author of the Rilke Bibliography (Insel-Verlag, 1935).

that general introduction: the introductory talk to Rilke's reading of his poems before the Hottingen Reading Circle in Zurich (in October) is preserved as MSS 293/4 in the Rilke Archive.

p. 210   Aksakov Chronicle: Sergiei Timofeivitch Aksakov's *Family Chronicle,* the Russian classic (German translation, Insel-Verlag, 1919).

the "Bibliotheca Mundi": a new undertaking of the Insel-Verlag to put out books in their original languages.

tower room: the room Rilke always occupied when visiting the Kippenbergs at Leipzig.

[135] p. 211   very important book: *Die Elemente der menschlichen Grösse* (1921).

[136] p. 212   so large a "W": the play on the German letter and word "W" (*Weh*), pain or suffering (or woe), is lost in translation.

[137] p. 213   Leopold von Schlözer: author, editor of the little *Rainer Maria Rilke auf Capri: Gespräche* (Dresden, Wolfgang Jess, 1931).

p. 214   par hasard plutôt: rather by chance.

p. 215   C'est le monde etc.: It is the world that is sick, and the rest is a matter of suffering.

[138] p. 215   Dory von der Mühll: sister of Carl Burckhardt (see [152] and note). Rilke was now staying at the old family residence of the Burckhardts.

[139] p. 216 Rilke had gone to stay with the Princess Thurn und Taxis-Hohenlohe at her apartment in Venice, in the palazzo of the Countess Valmarana.

        p. 217 Giudecca: one of the islands of Venice.

[140] p. 219 energetic influence of a friend: Count Zech, the Austrian Ambassador, without whose intervention Rilke would have been unable to return to Munich, since through the partition of Austria he had become a citizen of Czechoslovakia.

              Fürstenbergs': Prince Egon Fürstenberg had, at Frau Kippenberg's instigation, offered Rilke a little house in a park in the Euganean hills, near Padua.

[141] p. 220 my own life there: Rilke stayed on in Venice after his hostess had left.

        p. 221 the biography of Dostoievsky: *Dostojewski geschildert von seiner Tochter* (Erlenbach-Zürich, 1920).

[142] p. 221 Oswald von Kutschera: Rilke's nephew.

              Paris: it is not clear whether Rilke had any concrete plans to go there; in fact, as late as August 21, he speaks of his expected return to Munich early in September, begging Herr Kippenberg's support of this move, as it will in many ways be so difficult for him.

[143] p. 222 Helene Burckhardt-Schatzman: sister-in-law of Carl Burckhardt (See [152] and note).

              "Peintres Genevois": The Genoese painters, title of a book by Band-Bovy (Geneva, 1903–04).

        p. 223 Liotard: Jean Etienne Liotard (1702–89), a portrait painter born in Geneva, who spent five years in Constantinople, assuming the clothes and customs of the Turks. On returning to Europe he continued to wear the exotic dress; a self-portrait shows him with turban and flowing beard, but in time he married and thereafter the portraits are beardless.

              lace: see "Lace" ("Die Spitze"), *G.W.* III, 54; *A.W.* I, 163; also *M.L.B.*, *G.W.* V, 162–165; *A.W.* II, 116–117; *J.O.S.*, 129–131.

              Agasse: Jacques Laurent Agasse (1767–1849), the animal painter, likewise a native of Geneva.

              Saint-Ours: Jean Pierre Saint-Ours (1752–1809), another Genevan and a painter of genre, historical scenes and portraits.

[144] p. 224   my little house: on the Princess' estate in Bohemia, which seemed too far out of his present way to be practicable.

        j'en conviens: I agree.

        Pitoeff: George Pitoeff, (d. 1939), the Russian director, then working in Geneva. Elsewhere Rilke wrote of him, "How I love him, how I admire him," and expressed the desire to work with him "as secretary or somehow."

[146] p. 226   la même plénitude . . . : the same fullness of life, the same intensity, the same justice even in the wrong.

     p. 227   ma vie . . . : my life, from eternity my own.

[147] p. 227   "My departure from Geneva had been set for the 11th even before they had told me that all rooms were taken next day for the League of Nations delegations . . . Promptly on the 12th I moved into my new life." (To Anton Kippenberg, November 17, 1920.)

        Schloss Berg: on the Irchel, an old, vine-covered house in a rather neglected-looking park, "for centuries the country seat of the Eschers vom Luchs, whose coat-of-arms still occurs all over." Rilke lived here as the guest of Colonel Ziegler and his wife, of Thun.

     p. 228   donc, retraite absolue: so, utter seclusion.

[149] p. 230   pièce d'eau: pool or pond.

     p. 232   original home of the family: see [211] and note.

[150] p. 233   your letter: In his letter (of October 5, 1920), Major-General Sedlakowitz recalls himself to Rilke's memory as the German-language teacher in the military school at St. Pölten (which Rilke entered at the age of ten; see [94]); admits to too much red ink and irony in the marking of Rilke's compositions, but declares that he had sympathy for the bookworm as well as for the bad gymnast; says that he became aware through a lecture of Ellen Key's of the rising lyric poet Rilke, that he has enjoyed many of his poems and wishes in spirit to offer his hand and to express his gratitude at having been privileged to encounter the "noble poet" in his "golden youth".

     p. 236   letter of 1892: (December 30), a good example of what Rilke had to outgrow: "By the way, Friend Poetry is not altogether idle—the strings of my lyre are not rusting, my busy hand awakes in them the reconciling harmony of beautiful sound and it rings purer than ever. (Nebstbei ruht Freundin Poesie nicht ganz aus, die Saiten meiner Leier rosten nicht, die tätige Hand erweckt in ihnen des Wohllautes versöhnende Harmonie, und sie erklingt geläuterte als je.)"

[151] p. 237 This letter, first published in the "Inselschiff" (12 Jg., H. i, Christmas 1930, 1–2) is the only letter to his mother, who survived him, in the collected *Briefe*. From Rilke's own descriptions of her nature, in which the unreal and the superficial were strangely combined with fanatical religious piety, the possibility of any genuine filial feeling on his part seems to have been precluded. (See *Letters: 1892–1910*, [2] and the striking passage in [61].)

Rilke's last Christmas letter to his mother (1925, published in the *Inselschiff*, Christmas 1936) again recalls "our six-o'clock hour", when he always thinks "the bells must still be audible that Papa knew how to ring at the most exciting moment in so festively heralding a manner. I believe that all the joys of my life have had *this* voice, just as all of them, at whatever time of year they may have come to me, reminded me of Christmas: so much has that fulfillment, that series of fulfillments, which once upon a time, breathless, my heart pounding up into my throat, I found there under the radiant Christmas tree remained a criterion for all the bestowals, later, of life! . . . If later on my existence, under the dreadful pressure of the Military School, in a sense overflowed into my own, often so weak and bewildered hands—at that time, at the time of those Christmases, I did not yet hold it, but gave it to you to hold sometimes, to you and Papa, and it certainly became decisive for me that you were able and determined to lift it up then under the protection and the splendor of this festival as high as possible into the jubilance, into that jubilance which has given me the angels, the consciousness of whom, far indeed from having been lost to me, has grown with me at every stage of my life. . . ."

[152] p. 239 Professor Carl Burckhardt: Rilke's good friend, who was later to become League of Nations Commissioner for the Free City of Danzig and universally respected for his efforts to preserve the peace during the fateful events of the late summer of 1939.

p. 240 the forty drawings: done in secret by the little son of Madame Baladine-Klossowska (see [161] and note)—as a sort of diary, a year after his first great sorrow, the loss of his cat—were published in *Mitsou: Quarante images par Baltusz* (Préface de Rainer Maria Rilke, Rotapfel-Verlag, Erlenbach-Zurich, 1921).

p. 241 "Prince": the Burckhardts' shepherd dog at Schönenberg.

Hofmannsthal's Beethoven lecture: given on the occasion of Beethoven's 150th anniversary, before the Hottingen Reading Circle in Zurich, December 10, 1920 (published only in the *Neue Züricher Zeitung*, December 19, 1920, No. 2099, p. 5), was based on the *Rede auf Beethoven* in Vol. III, Pt. 3, of his *Reden und Aufsätze*.

[153] p. 241 Inga Junghanns: see note to [127]. Rilke's *Briefe an R. R. Junghanns und Rudolf Zimmerman* have recently been published in a limited edition by the *Vereinigung Oltner Bücherfreunde* (1945, 61 pp.).

[154] p. 242 Seckendorff: Götz von Seckendorff, the young painter, was killed in the war in August 1914. In Berlin, in October 1917, Rilke had attended a "Herrenabend" at the official residence of Herr von Winterfeldt, *Landesdirektor* of the Province of Brandenburg, and had seen a lithograph by Seckendorff, an Awakening of Lazarus which seemed to him very close in feeling to his own "Christi Höllenfahrt" ("Christ's Journey to Hell") of 1913 (see [100] and note). Von der Marwitz notes in his war diary that he is concerned at not hearing anything from Seckendorff: "Were he not to come back, our whole hope would be destroyed."

[155] p. 243 Flaach: Salis notes that, some weeks later, in one of his journal-letters from Etoy to Frau Nanny Wunderly-Volkart, Rilke amused himself with the idea—perhaps inspired by the opening of a correspondence on religious questions by the vicar of Berg—of what it would be like if he, Rilke, were to become "the vicar of Flaach"!

[157] p. 246 strong leaning toward expression in painting: A number of drawings by the very youthful René have been preserved in the Rilke Archive. Their subjects recall the passage in the *Notebooks* just before the child's discovery of the mysterious hand under the table, for they are of knights and steeds—preferably in the midst of battle "because then one only had to make the smoke enveloping everything." He seems also to have had a knack for caricature. See also [212].

[158] p. 249 Neuburg: the monastery of Neuburg on the Kammel.

[160] p. 250 Baron von Ungern-Sternberg: German translator of the *Stances* of Jean Moréas (1856–1910), the French symbolist

poet, leader of the école romane. In this letter Rilke goes on to discuss some of the verses Ungern had sent him and encloses his own translation (*G.W.* VI, 351) of No. VI from Book III, which Ungern included in his publication (Wir-Verlag, Berlin, 1922, 300 copies), dedicated to Rilke.

About the middle of May Rilke was obliged to leave, in part, apparently, because of some personal crisis. Zurich friends drove him to Etoy near Morges on the Lake of Geneva, and here he spent a sort of holiday of several quite happy weeks, in the old house—part of a thirteenth-century Augustinian priory—of a Mademoiselle du Mont, who lived there "alone with a friend, looks after pigeons and bees and discreetly takes in a few pensionnaires". He read many modern French works at this time, among them *A la recherche du temps perdu* (see [56] and note, and [193]), and from now on, in French Switzerland, the language of his diary notes becomes a mixture of French and German.

[161] p. 252 This old manoir: In the window of a coiffeur near the hotel, Rilke had happened on a photograph of the little castle of Muzot, beneath which stood the words "à vendre ou à louer" (for sale or rent).

presence of my friend: Mme. Klossowska. While in Geneva (see [144]) she and Rilke had hit upon the plan of doing a group of "window"-poems for which she was to provide the illustrations. Rilke had conceived the idea of the window as a symbol, thinking of its forms, its significance, characteristically developing it as he had the fountain, the rose, the mirror. The book appeared some years later as *Les Fenêtres* (Librairie de France, Paris, 1927, since included in *Poèmes français* and *Gesammelte Gedichte*, but in neither *G.W.* nor *A.W.*).

little rustic church: the white chapel of Saint Anne, situated a little above Muzot.

magnificent old poplar: In a letter to Frau Nanny Wunderly-Volkart (quoted in *Salis*, p. 77) Rilke described this poplar as standing at the edge of the road in front of Muzot "like a landmark again and an exclamation mark, as if it said, confirmed: see, this is it!" (Cf. [213]).

p. 253 Battle of Marignan: in which Francis I (1515) defeated an army of Swiss mercenaries in the pay of Duke Maximilian Sforza of Milan, thereby conquering that city.

p. 254 très légèrement habillée: very lightly clad.

a big swastika: it must be remembered that since prehistoric times the swastika has been used by mankind in many parts of the world as a religious symbol and a token of good luck and benediction.

[162] p. 255 This letter (included in the *Briefe aus Muzot* in the German translation of Kilian Kerst) was first published in the *Nouvelle revue française* (Vol. 14, no. 161, Feb. 1, 1927), where it is followed by two verses composed for the recipient, "Saturday, while I was walking in the admirable allée of the Château of Hollingen".

[164] p. 259 Countess Nora Purtscher-Wydenbruck: niece of Princess Marie, wife of the Austrian painter Aloys Purtscher, an author in her own right, co-translator of *S.O.G.*

[165] p. 261 Carl Sieber: Rilke's future son-in-law, co-editor with his wife Ruth (and later Ernst Zinn) of the letters, custodian, until his recent death, of the Rilke Archive in Weimar, author of *René Rilke* (Leipzig, 1932).

p. 262 Väterchen: diminutive for "father".

p. 263 Bredenau: Clara Rilke's house in Fischerhude.

On November 25, Rilke wrote his publisher asking him to send Ruth in his name whatever sum could be spared to meet the demands of her approaching marriage.

[167] p. 267 Un apaisement, etc.: a lull, a new calm greater than ever the happy moment of renewal, the dawn of a pure and universal beginning.

[169] p. 272 The book in question is Heygrodt's *Die Lyrik Rainer Maria Rilkes: Versuch einer Entwicklungsgeschichte* (J. Bielefelds Verlag, Freiburg, 1921).

Dr. Hünich: see note to [134].

p. 273 Cézanne: Rilke never did write the proposed study which was so much in his mind. See *Letters: 1892–1910*, [179] through [187].

p. 274 my so-called "early period": again and again Rilke discouraged attempts to drag forth his youthful writings (Cf. [210] and [212]). Included in *G.W.*, however, are both *First* and *Early* poems, which he himself planned with Anton Kippenberg "even to details of content and typography", and which in his mind were the only poems of his youth worthy of survival. See [9] and note in *Letters: 1892–1910.*

[170] p. 276 the *rind* of a condition: Rilke's use here of the simile of the fruit recalls Sonnets XIII–XV in Part I of the *Sonnets to Orpheus*, as that in [169] recalls *"Death of the Poet"* ("Der Tod des Dichters", *Neue Gedichte*, I), while the "berry for berry" of the carillon in [166] brings to mind the last verse of "Quai du Rosaire—Bruges" (*Neue Gedichte*, I).

[171] p. 278 This letter, undated, is placed by the German editors in December 1921. Since it concerns a detail of the Tenth Elegy, which, from Rilke's own evidence, was set down in a burst of inspiration in February 1922 (see [181]), either the editors have been in error or—which is perhaps more likely!—the letter casts an illuminating sidelight on the creative processes that preceded the actual writing down of the elegy. The point of the letter, furthermore, is indicative of the accuracy of Rilke's descriptions of natural phenomena.

the poem passage: This passage (*G.W.* III, 308; *A.W.* I, 264) is most significant for the close of the *Elegies:*

Aber erweckten sie uns, die unendlich Toten, ein Gleichnis,
siehe, sie zeigten vielleicht auf die Kätzchen der leeren
Hasel, die hängenden, oder
meinten den Regen, der fällt auf dunkles Erdreich im Früh-
    jahr.—

Yet more they, the endlessly dead, to waken for us a likeness,
see, they would point perhaps to the catkins of empty
hazels, hanging, or else
think of the rain that falls on dark earth in the early spring.—

[172] p. 279 I was offered a dog: See [25] and note, [152] and especially *Eine Begegnung* (*G.W.* IV, 233; *A.W.* II, 251).

the poetry of Paul Valéry: Rilke had made the acquaintance of the French poet's work only in the spring of 1921, but it had an important and lasting effect upon him. "I was alone," he said later, "I was waiting, my whole work was waiting. One day I read Valéry; I knew that my waiting was at an end." (Quoted in *Salis*, 93, from Monique Saint-Hélier, *A Rilke pour Noël*, Bern, 1927.)

"Le Cimetière marin": appears as "Der Friedhof am Meer" in Rilke's translations of poems by Valéry (dedicated to Herr Werner Reinhart "by a grateful guest") in *G.W.* VI, 288. Rilke also translated (Insel-Verlag, 1927) Valéry's

Socratic dialogue, *Eupalinos, ou l'architecte. Précédé de l'Ame et la danse.*

p. 280 Schmargendorf: Rilke had lived at Schmargendorf, near Berlin, from 1892 to 1900, and he comments at the opening of this letter that his present study and small bedroom somehow "in their layout, in their proportions, in something I can't quite describe, especially toward evening" remind him of his rooms of those days in the Villa Waldfrieden.

Mallarmé: Stéphane Mallarmé (1842–1898) earned a small income as professor of English in a French college.

[173] p. 281 Spitteler: Carl Spitteler (1845–1924), the Swiss poet-philosopher, worked as schoolteacher and editor until he settled down as an independent writer in 1892.

[174] p. 282 sonnets of Michelangelo: see [90] and note.

p. 283 Die Blinde: a poem in dramatic dialogue, written in Schmargendorf, November 25, 1900 (*Book of Pictures* II, *G.W.* II, 153–158; *A.W.* I, 134–138).

[175] p. 283 those notes: Frau Knoop's account of the last illness of her daughter Vera, to whose memory *Sonnets to Orpheus* are dedicated. Though he had scarcely known the girl, her death two years before had made a profound impression on Rilke, and he had asked Frau Knoop to send him some little object she had cherished. Writing to Frau Wunderly-Volkart early in January 1922, Rilke said that this document had been as moving to him as "Montaigne's impressions at the bedside of his grievously and distortedly dying friend" (quoted in *Salis*, p. 94).

[178] p. 287 Lotti von Wedel: Frau von Wedel (born von Gwinner) gives an account of her meeting with Rilke at the Karl von der Heydts' in Berlin in 1917 and her recommendation to him of Soglio and the Pension Willy (*Neue Schweizer Rundschau*, Zurich, 1938, N.F., Jg. VI, 495–499).

p. 288 Torre de las Danas: probably Torre de las Damas, one of the fortified towers around the Alhambra in Granada.

Schack versions: a German translation of Omar Khayyam, *Strophen des Omar Chijam* (1878) translated by Adolf Friedrich Count von Schack (1815–1894).

that magnificent queen: the bust of Nefertiti in the Berlin museum, of which Frau von Wedel had sent photographs.

[179] p. 289 a few days of spontaneous emotion: the first series of *Sonnets to Orpheus* was written between the second and fifth of February.

the XXIVth sonnet: XXV of Part I in the final version, "But you now, you whom I knew," is still the next-to-last, a further sonnet having been inserted as XXIII. In the second series, which came later, the next-to-last sonnet also specifically evokes Vera.

the XXIst: "O the new, Friends, is not this" was later included in *S.G.*, 97. On February 9, Rilke wrote Frau Knoop asking her to paste over this one a new sonnet, the "Child's Spring-Song", XXI in the completed cycle, as the original poem stood "like a blemish on his conscience".

(the subtitle): in the published *Sonnets*, the subtitle reads, "Written as a memorial for Vera Ouckama Knoop".

[180] p. 290 On the afternoon of February 9, Rilke telegraphed Frau Wunderly-Volkart: "Seven Elegies completely finished—the most important at any rate—joy and miracle." The eighth and ninth took shape in his mind on the way back from the telegraph office. Late that same night he wrote Anton Kippenberg a letter quite similar to this one, but expressing his overwhelming gratitude to his publisher for having waited so patiently for ten long years.

one . . . dedicated to Kassner: the eighth.

[181] p. 291 *the horse:* in Sonnet XX of the first series.

p. 292 баба: grandmother

Прощай: (proshchai) goodby.

[182] p. 293 the "Saltimbanques": the elegy inspired by Picasso's painting, the "Acrobats" (see [78] and note).

the piece that has hitherto stood there: presumably the poem on pp. 68–70 of *S.G.*

"Fragmentary Pieces": this plan was not to be realized. After Rilke's death, the material intended for this volume was included in *S.G.*, and in part in *G.W.* III ("Letzte Gedichte und Fragmentarisches") and *A.W.* I (poems of 1913–1926).

[183] p. 295 Ça sort de la création: that comes out of creation.

p. 295 Louis de Courten: the de Courtens had been a prominent family in the region. The Hotel Bellevue in Sierre was originally a palace built by Count Jean François de Courten.

[185] p. 300 tant bien que mal: as best I could.

[187] p. 305 Beer-Hofmann: Richard Beer-Hofmann (1866–1945), author of the uncompleted dramatic trilogy, "Jaákobs Traum".

"Lullaby for Miriam": "Schlaflied für Mirjam", *Pan* IV, p. 88. This beautiful poem is included in the small volume, *Verse,* published in New York in 1941 (Bermann-Fischer Verlag).

six months in Sweden: from June to December 1904.

[188] p. 307 The magnificent queen: see [178] and note.

p. 308 Jung-Stilling: (d. 1817), a friend of Goethe's youth, first a doctor, later a political economist, part of whose autobiography, *Heinrich Stillings Jugend,* was published in 1777.

[189] p. 309 Dory von der Mühll: sister of Carl Burckhardt; see note to [152].

the reception that Princess Taxis gave the Elegies: According to the Princess (*Erinnerungen,* 93–95), Rilke, at his "Stehpult" (standing desk) in Muzot, read the Elegies aloud, the first seven in the morning, the last three in the afternoon; next day, in her room at the hotel in Sierre, he read her "the twenty-seven [sic!] sonnets",—after which Rilke bent down to kiss her hand, and she kissed him on the forehead, "as a mother her son, a wonderful son".

In July the Kippenbergs, and later Frau Baladine-Klossowska, were visitors at Muzot. Frau Kippenberg vividly describes Rilke's reading of the Elegies (*Rainer Maria Rilke, Ein Beitrag,* Insel-Verlag, 1935, pp. 186–187).

[190] p. 309 The latter part of August and early September, Rilke spent with Madame Klossowska and her family at Beatenberg above the Thurnersee.

[192] p. 312 Witold von Hulewicz: Von Hulewicz, Rilke's Polish translator, was preparing an edition of the *Rodin* (*G.W.* IV, 299–421) to be published in 1923, and had sent the manuscript to Rilke.

[193] p. 313 Prince Hohenlohe: brother of Princess Marie.

Proust: see [56] and note.

[194] p. 314 Countess Margot Sizzo: This letter is not included in the *Briefe* and has presumably not been hitherto published.

Marie Lenéru: (1875–1918), a French writer of psychological dramas. At the age of 11 she began to keep a diary, published in 1922 as *Journal de Marie L.*

[195] p. 318 Paul Valéry: Rilke was at the time translating Valéry's volume of poems, *Charmes*.

p. 319 "Vous étiez l'un des objets etc.": "You were one of the principal objects of my trip."

[196] p. 321 This letter, written in French, and not included in the *Briefe*, was published in an Alsatian periodical, *Le Point*, XVI, Sept. 1938, 3e année, 6 rue Rapp, Colmar.

"Form-Dichter": literally, "Form-Poet".

[198] p. 326 your gift: von Schlözer had sent Rilke a copy of his book, *Dorothea von Schlözer (Dorothea von Rodde), der Philosophie Doktor, ein Deutsches Frauenleben um die Jahrhundertwende 1770 bis 1825*, 1923.

[200] p. 327 Schuler: see [76] and note.

p. 329 physical indispositions: After the spring and early summer, with frequent visitors at Muzot and several trips to various parts of Switzerland, Rilke's physical condition, growing progressively worse, forced him reluctantly to seek medical help, and he spent a few weeks of the late summer in a sanitarium on the Vierwaldstättersee. There he had to submit to massage treatment, "and thus occurs the grotesque case of an old man meditatively promenading over my body on his hands every morning. A circus number." (to Frau Wunderly-Volkart, August 23, 1923, quoted in *Salis*, 126–127). He returned to Muzot in November.

[201] p. 329 Paula Becker: Paula Modersohn-Becker (1876–1907), the painter. See *Letters: 1892–1910*, particularly [17] and note and [202]. After reading an earlier edition of her journals, Rilke wrote that though her death had for years made him feel that death outweighed life, they had been to him a proof that "she, since she was so vibrantly devoted to the future, foresaw more than earthly joy in her open heart." (To Dr. Kurt Becker, Easter Monday, 1913.)

[203] p. 331 shortly after Christmas again: Rilke went this time to the sanitarium in Valmont, near Montreux, three hours from Muzot, where he remained for three weeks under the care of Dr. Haemmerli, who was to look after him until his death. On January 21, he wrote Frau Wunderly-Volkart what he called a "confession sans retenue" showing a full awareness of the gravity of his condition: "I was as if raised up to another plane of life, perhaps on that where the incurables are".

p. 332 habitual deep armchair: Rilke had been a frequent guest at the Knoop house in Munich during the war years.

[204] p. 333 Alfred Schaer: Privatdozent (unsalaried lecturer) at the University of Zurich.

Bang: Hermann Joachim Bang (1858–1912), the Danish impressionist writer, author of *The White House* (1898), *The Gray House* (1901).

Liliencron: Detlev von Liliencron (1844–1909), the poet.

Jacob Wassermann: (1873–1934) author of *The World's Illusion* (*Christian Wahnschaffe*) and *The Maurizius Case* (*Der Fall Maurizius*), novels which have had some circulation in this country. He is taken to be the prototype for Thalmann in *Ewald Tragy*, a "novelle" dating from around 1899 but not published in Rilke's lifetime, recently brought out (Johannespresse, New York, 1944) as the first in a series of three volumes (*Rainer Maria Rilke im Jahre 1896*) edited by Dr. Richard von Mises.

Lermontov: Mikhail Yurevich Lermontov (1814–1841), Russian poet and novelist.

Nekrassov: Nikolai Alexeievich Nekrassov (1821–1877), Russian poet.

Fet: Afanasi Afanasievich Fet (1820–1892), Russian poet.

p. 334 ropemaker in Rome, potter in the Nile village: Cf. Ninth Elegy, ll. 57–58 (*G.W.* III, 300; *A.W.* I, 259; *D.E.*, 77):

> Er wird staunender stehn; wie du standest
> bei dem Seiler in Rom, oder beim Töpfer am Nil.

> He'll stand more astonished; as you did
> beside the roper in Rome or the potter in Egypt.

"Les Baux": see [205] in *Letters: 1892–1910*.

[205] p. 336 volume of French poems: presumably *Vergers*, written in February.

p. 336 Valéry's visit: Valéry writes of this visit: "My imagination could not help but hear inside you the endless monologue of a quite isolated consciousness that nothing distracts from itself and from the feeling of being unique. I could not conceive of so separate an existence, of eternal winters in such an abuse of intimacy with silence, so much freedom offered to your dreams, to the essential and too-concentrated spirits that are in books, to the inconstant genii of writing, to the powers of memory. Dear Rilke, you seemed to me enclosed in pure time and I feared for you the transparency of an all too uniform life that through the round of ever-like days allowed one clearly to see death." (in *Reconnaissance à Rilke*, Cahiers du Mois 23/24, Paris, 1926.)

[206] p. 337 The Kippenbergs had again been Rilke's guests at Muzot a month before. He greatly needed people now and had a steady stream of visitors. "No spring at Muzot", he wrote to Dory von der Mühll, "was ever so blessed with them as this late, hesitant one . . ."

p. 338 a simple notebook: "Three Poems", included in *Briefe VI* (*an seinen Verleger*).

[207] p. 339 Clara Rilke had, with her brother, made a visit to Rilke. They had not seen each other for years, and this was to be their last meeting.

[208] p. 340 Ragaz: the health resort, where Rilke had spent several weeks.

[209] p. 341 Again the first part of the summer had been spent in visits and outings with friends in various parts of Switzerland.

experiments in the Taxis circle: see note to [34].

p. 344 who are privy to the whole: cf. 8th Elegy, (*G.W.* III, 293; *A.W.* I, 254; *Duino Elegies*, p. 67):

> das freie Tier
> hat seinen Untergang stets hinter sich
> und vor sich Gott, und wenn es geht, so gehts
> in Ewigkeit, so wie die Brunnen gehen.

> the free animal
> has its decease perpetually behind it
> and God in front, and when it moves, it moves
> in eternity, like running springs.

[210] p. 345 Professor Pongs has made several important contributions to the field of Rilke criticism, among them "Rainer Maria

Rilkes Umschlag und das Erlebnis der Frontgeneration,"
Dichtung und Volkstum, 1936; "Rainer Maria Rilke, ein
Vortrag", *Euphorion*, 1931.

In his foreword to the three letters from which this
letter and [212] are taken (first published in "Drei un-
veröffentlichte Briefe Rilkes," *Dichtung und Volkstum*,
Stuttgart, 1936, no. 1, Sonderheft, 37) Dr. Pongs says the
correspondence had opened with his request that Rilke
read to his students, adding that he was young and shy at
the time and did not ask such probing questions as he
might have.

p. 346 a further year: at Linz; see note to [222].

private instruction: financed by Rilke's uncle, Jaroslav
Rilke.

my earliest productivity: see [9] and note in *Letters: 1892–
1910*.

p. 347 Alfred Klaar: (1848–1927), writer and teacher.

Friedrich Adler: (1857–   ), poet.

Hugo Salus: (1866–1929), doctor and poet.

Orlik: Emil Orlik (1870–   ), to whom Rilke dedicated the
poem "Peacockfeather" (*G.W.* I, 172. See [25] in *Letters:
1892–1910*).

August Sauer: (1855–1926), professor of literature at the
University of Prague.

Detlev von Liliencron: see [204] and note.

René Maria: Rilke had not yet changed his name to Rainer
Maria.

p. 348 Jacobsen: see [92] and note.

Jacob Wassermann: see [204] and note.

Munich: Rilke went there to study in 1896.

p. 349 *Pages for Art: Blätter für die Kunst*, a periodical founded
by George and published from 1892 to 1919, one of the
most significant literary organs of the time.

Year of the Soul: a volume of poems published in 1897.

Lepsius Circle: Reinhold Lepsius (1857–1922) and his
wife, Sabine (1864–   ), both portrait painters, had evenings in their Berlin home at which their friend George
read his poems. In her book, *Stefan George, Geschichte*

einer Freundschaft (Berlin, 1935), Frau Lepsius mentions Rilke's presence at one of these (in November 1897) with Lou Andreas-Salomé.

p. 349   Jacobowski: Ludwig Jacobowski (1868–1900), poet, novelist, dramatist and editor of several literary periodicals.

Reinhold Maurice von Stern: listed elsewhere as Maurice Reinhold von Stern (1860–), a poet with a social and political slant.

Wilhelm von Scholz: (1874–), dramatist. Almost certainly he was the prototype of Wilhelm von Kranz in *Ewald Tragy* (see note to [204]).

E. von Bodmann: or Bodman (1874–), a poet and a Munich friend. See [24] in *Letters: 1892–1910*.

a person close to me: Lou Andreas-Salomé, who was Russian by birth.

the "Cornet": see [70], [73] and notes; also [212].

"Angel Songs": *G.W.* I, pp. 273–281; "Maidens' Songs": *G.W.* I, pp. 305–323.

Tuscany, etc.: Rilke was there in 1898.

p. 350   "I would not like to die in spring": "Ich möchte nicht im Frühling sterben", from *Life and Songs*, 1894, 67. Not in *G.W.*

[211] p. 351   the history of our family: see Carl Sieber's *René Rilke* (Insel-Verlag, Leipzig, 1932) which is the chief source of information; also [44] and note in *Letters: 1892–1910*.

[212] p. 353   Klimt: presumably Gustav Klimt (1862–1918), a prominent Austrian commercial artist.

Ernst Mach: (1838–1916), physicist and philosopher, professor of physics at Prague in Rilke's day.

Wild Chicory: a literary pamphlet (3 numbers were printed) containing pieces by Rilke and other young artists which was not sold but distributed among the poor. See [4] and note in *Letters: 1892–1910*.

Hoar Frost, Without Present: published in *Aus der Frühzeit Rainer Maria Rilkes. Verse. Prosa. Drama* (1894–1899), Leipzig, 1921.

p. 354   *Along Life's Way, Two Tales of Prague, The Last:* stories published in *Erzählungen und Skizzen aus der Frühzeit*, Leipzig, 1928.

p. 354   *Everyday Life:* a drama in two acts, Munich 1902.

       About God (Stories of God): *G.W.* IV, pp. 39–178.

       Uhde: Fritz von Uhde (1848–1911), painted scenes from the life of Christ.

       "White Princess": see note to [31].

p. 355   Requiem: *G.W.* II, 321–345.

       Elizabeth Browning translations: *G.W.* VI, 5–50; *A.W.* II, 352–354 (contains only Nos. 6, 35, 39, 22).

       Simmel: Georg Simmel (1858–1918), philosopher and sociologist.

       Paula Modersohn: see [201] and note.

       Van Gogh: see *Letters: 1892–1910,* especially [172] and [173].

p. 356   Cottet: Charles Cottet (1863–1925), landscape painter, pupil of Puvis de Chavannes.

       Lucien Simon: (1854–), painter of Breton scenes.

       Zuloaga: see note to [34].

p. 357   "What is Art?": published in 1896.

p. 359   This telegram: Monsieur Rodin insists, so that you can talk. (Cf. [86] in *Letters: 1892–1910.*)

p. 361   imaginary voices of the dwarf or the beggar: *Book of Pictures* II, "The Song of the Beggar", "The Song of the Dwarf", *G.W.* II, 122, 130; *T.P.,* 112, 126.

p. 362   Mt. Athos: The mountain on the Macedonian peninsula of that name is largely populated by monastic communities noted for their valuable collections of documents and their treasures of Byzantine art.

p. 363   the most beautiful and direct recognition: Pongs's little son had said on hearing the name, "Rainer Maria Rilke, that sounds like a poem."

       Qu'il le saurait "par coeur": that he should know it "by heart".

[213] p. 365 my second Ragaz visit: Rilke had hoped to return there in the fall.

p. 366   "Quatrains Valaisans": *Vergers suivis des Quatrains Valaisans*, 1926.

I had a secretary: Marga Wertheimer, who later wrote *Arbeitsstunden mit Rainer Maria Rilke* (Zurich, 1940).

"Eupalinos": see [172] and note.

p. 367   beautiful old poplar: cf. [161] and note.

[214] p. 367   Val-Mont (Valmont): Rilke had been at the sanitarium again from the end of November into early January.

your brother: Carl Burckhardt.

The last paragraph of this letter was written in French.

Rilke was to remain in Paris for eight months. At intervals the thought of Muzot tempted him to return, but, in addition to his old affection for Paris, he now, being no longer an unknown author in France, allowed the claim of many social engagements, perhaps in large part because of his deep awareness that the disease from which he was suffering had incapacitated him for the rigors of solitude and creative work. When he finally left Paris in September, medical care had become imperative. After spending some time in Ragaz and consulting doctors in Meilen and Zurich, he returned to Muzot in October, where he immediately wrote out the will (see p. 449) which he sent to Nanny Wunderly-Volkart. He had meanwhile engaged a new housekeeper, the faithful Frieda Baumgartner having been obliged to leave. A selection from his letters to Mademoiselle Ida Walthert (published in the Swiss magazine *Annabelle*, Jg. 8, No. 94, Zurich, Christmas 1945) shows his meticulous thoughtfulness for the care of the little house and of visitors, as well as his dependence on and consideration for the person charged with looking after his needs.

[216] p. 369   The accompanying letter has been lost. This quotation, evidently related to the fragment "An Experience" ("Erlebnis": see [120] and note, also [40]) written in Spain in 1913, presumably also belongs to that earlier period, though Rilke appears to have sent it to Lou only in 1925.

a bird call was there . . . concordantly: Cf. *S.O.* II, 26, and "Die Spanische Trilogie" (*S.G.* 153; *G.W.* III, 446):

> Da steht er nächstens auf und hat den Ruf
> des Vogels draussen schon in seinem Dasein
> und fühlt sich kühn, weil er die ganzen Sterne
> in sein Gesicht nimmt, schwer— . . .

> Then he stands up and already has the call
> of the bird outside in his being
> and feels bold because he takes
> all the stars into his vision, heavy— . . .

leaning in a similar posture: Cf. the same poem:

> Warum muss einer dastehn wie ein Hirt,
> so ausgesetzt dem Übermass von Einfluss,
> beteiligt so an diesem Raum voll Vorgang,
> dass er gelehnt an einen Baum der Landschaft
> sein Schicksal hätte, ohne mehr zu handeln.

> Why must one stand there like a shepherd,
> so exposed to the excess of influence,
> so taking part in this space full of happening,
> that, leaning against a tree in the landscape,
> he had his destiny, without more doing . . .

[217] p. 372   the French translation: *Les Cahiers de Malte Laurids Brigge*, (Emile-Paul, Paris, 1926), one of the many Rilke translations by Maurice Betz.

confidence in this French version: In *Rilke Vivant* (Paris, 1937) Betz speaks of having worked with Rilke on this translation.

[218] p. 372   This much-quoted letter has formed the basis of most recent Rilke criticism. It begins with Rilke's answers to a questionnaire from von Hulewicz and concludes with the pages here translated.

p. 373   des longues études: of long study.

The War interrupted this my greatest work altogether: The Fourth Elegy, however, had been written in Munich in November 1915.

p. 374   Nous butinons éperdument . . . : We pilfer distractedly the honey of the visible to collect it in the big golden hive of the invisible.

p. 375   "Land of Lamentation": see Tenth Elegy.

[219] p. 376   Christine: Rilke's granddaughter.

[220] p. 378   Rilke had turned fifty on December 4. Despite the tone of cordial appreciation in this letter, he was harassed rather

than pleased by all the greetings and remembrances that poured in. He had asked Frau Wunderly-Volkart beforehand to discourage such things, and when letters and telegrams had piled up notwithstanding, he wearily wrote, "Quelle corvée, quelle inutilité! (What a bore, what futility!) . . . Naturally, if one looks at it justly, there was something dear in it, but where is the love that does not make more trouble?" (Quoted in Salis, p. 179). For his own part, Rilke had commemorated his birthday by giving a thousand francs toward the restoration of the nearby Chapel of St. Anne.

Bellevue: the hotel in Sierre; see note to [183].

rose-colored island: a play on the name of the publishing house, Insel (Island).

[221] p. 379 Frau Berta Flamm had asked Rilke to send words of encouragement to her son, wounded in the war. The son recovered and later became a doctor.

[222] p. 380 Following the publication of the first of Rilke's French poems in *Commerce* in 1924, German journalists launched a series of attacks charging him with betrayal of his native language and country.

p. 382 "disapproving attitude of German literary circles": The influential George circle had never recognized Rilke and had refused to publish his poems in the famous *Blätter für die Kunst*. (See [210] and note).

p. 383 Linz: After the fiasco of the military school, Rilke had spent a no less disastrous winter (1891–1892) at the Linz Commercial School.

[223] p. 383 Georg Reinhart: elder brother of Werner Reinhart, the owner of Muzot, and a member of the well-known importing house of Volkart Brothers in Winterthur.

[224] p. 386 Toward the end of December, Rilke was forced to return to Valmont, remaining for five months.

Leonid Pasternak: (1862–1945), painter and professor at the Moscow Art School, through whom Rilke had met Tolstoy on his first visit to Russia.

Tartarshchina: the Tartar rule.

p. 387 your son Boris: Boris Pasternak (1890–). His autobiographical sketch, "Safe Conduct" (*Boris Pasternak: The Collected Prose Works*, London, 1945), is inscribed, "To the Memory of Rainer Maria Rilke". *Accent* published his short story "The Death of Mayakovsky" in autumn 1946, and translations of two poems in spring 1947.

[226] p. 389 This letter was first published in *Die Literarische Welt*, Berlin, Jg. 3, Nr. 22, June 3, 1927, p. 5.

Heym: Georg Heym (1887–1912) was drowned skating.

Trakl: Georg Trakl (1887–1914) committed suicide.

[227] p. 390 Dieter Bassermann: author of the essay on Rilke's letters which introduces the new edition of the *Briefe*, also of an excellent study, "Engel und Orpheus", in *Die Neue Rundschau*, April 1939.

professional journal: the *Schallkiste*.

p. 391 "Primal Sound": ("Urgeräusch", *G.W.* IV, 285 ff.; *A.W.* II, 274 ff.) In this essay, written at Soglio in 1919, Rilke speculates upon what sort of music might be produced if the coronal suture of the human skull could be treated like the sound-track of a phonograph record.

[228] p. 392 proposed texts: passages from these letters of Rilke's were printed in the June 1926 number of the *Schallkiste*, p. 9, under the title "Eine Anregung".

[229] p. 394 Rilke left Valmont the end of May, but was unable to live continuously at Muzot and at intervals stayed at the hotel in Sierre. The middle of July he went to Ragaz, bearing with him the final Valéry translations, the "Fragments du Narcisse", which he was to read there to the Princess.

[231] p. 395 His health was sufficiently good to enable him to make various visits in September to friends at Ouchy on Lake Geneva, where he saw Valéry once more, and to Lausanne. But after his return to Muzot in October, his condition became so poor that when he scratched his finger cutting his favorite roses, the slight wound not only did not heal but became seriously infected and was exceedingly painful. This was the first symptom of the disease which was soon to be diagnosed as acute leukemia. Early in December, he went once more to Valmont. On the eighth, in a laborious and uneven hand, he penciled to Frau Wunderly-Volkart (in French):

". . . day and night, day and night: . . . Hell! one will have known it! . . .
"Thank you, that with all your being (I sense it) you are

accompanying me into these anonymous regions. . . . "The most serious, the longest way: is to abdicate: to become 'the sick person'. The sick dog is still dog, always. We, after a certain degree of insensate suffering, are we still ourselves? One must become the sick person, learn this absurd métier under the eye of the doctors. It is long! And I shall never be clever enough to 'turn it to account'; in this affair I am losing." (*Salis*, p. 201.)

[232] p. 395 Supervielle: Jules Supervielle, the French poet (born at Montevideo, Uruguay, in 1884), whose acquaintance Rilke had made during his last stay in Paris.

In the days that still remained Rilke was closely attended by the doctors (particularly Dr. Haemmerli), his nurse and (until the final stages) by Frau Wunderly. Dr. Haemmerli has testified to the intense agony he underwent and to the fact that he refused any drugs that might deaden his awareness. The medical interpretations of his illness he did not want to hear, but the problem of dealing with a suffering body and of the interrelationship of the physical and spiritual were constantly in his thoughts. "We were such wonderfully good friends, my body and I, I don't know at all how it happened that we separated and became foreign to each other" (Salis, p. 204). He wrote letters to Lou, always hoping that she might give him the answer to the riddle. But of the firm courage he maintained to the end, the most moving testimony is in his words to Frau Wunderly, "Never forget, dear friend, life is a glory".

Early in the morning of December 29 he died, and on January 2, 1927, in the presence of a handful of friends, he was buried, as he had wished, in the little graveyard by the old church at Rarogne (Raron).

RILKE'S TESTAMENT

[Quoted in full from Salis, who gives it (pp. 174–175) with the permission of Frau Wunderly-Volkart and Dr. Werner Reinhart]

A few personal instructions in the event of an illness that more or less deprives me of my reason.

(Muzot, October 1925)

1. Should I fall into a serious illness that in the end also destroys my mind, I beg, even *implore* my friends to keep from me any priestly as-

sistance that might be pressed upon me. Bad enough that in the physical afflictions of my nature I have had to accede to the mediator and negotiator in the doctor; to the movement of my soul, toward the open, any spiritual intermediary would be offensive and repugnant.

2. Should I happen to die at Muzot or anywhere in Switzerland, I wish to be interred neither in Sierre nor yet in Miège. (It is this last perhaps that, after the unintelligible pronouncement of the unknown old lady, we might *not* do, in order not to arouse anew the restless night wandering of poor Isabelle de Chevron.)

3. Rather I should prefer to be buried in the graveyard situated high up beside the old church at Rarogne. Its enclosure is one of the first places from which I received the wind and light of this countryside, together with all the promises it was later to help me, with and in Muzot, to realize.

4. Now I abhor the geometrical arts of the present-day stonemasons; it will perhaps be possible to acquire an old stone (of the Empire for instance) (as happened in the case of my father's grave in Vienna). When the earlier inscriptions are planed off, let it bear:

the coat of arms
> (in the older form used by my great-grandfather that is repeated in the silver seal recently brought with me from Paris)

the name
and, at a little distance, the verse lines:
> Rose, oh pure contradiction, desire
> to be nobody's sleep beneath so many
> lids.

5. Of the furniture and objects at Muzot, I regard *nothing* as my actual personal possession; except for what is there in the way of family pictures: which as such go to my daughter Frau Ruth Sieber, Alt-Jocketa Farm near Jocketa (in Saxony). Of all the rest, in so far as it does not belong as a matter of course to the house, Frau Nanny Wunderly-Volkart in the Unteren Mühle at Meilen, in agreement with her cousin, Herr Werner Reinhart, Rychenberg-Winterthur, my generous friend and the owner of Muzot, would have the disposal.

6. Since, from certain years on, I was accustomed occasionally to direct a part of the creativity of my nature into letters, nothing stands in the way of the publication of my correspondence that may have been preserved in the hands of the addressees (should the Insel-Verlag propose something of the sort).

7. Of my pictures I regard none as essentially valid save those evanescent ones still surviving, in feeling and memory, with a few friends.

Château de Muzot   RAINER MARIA RILKE
    on the evening of October 27, 1925.

LIST OF CORRESPONDENTS

(The numbers refer to the Letters)

Amann-Volkart, Frau, 171
Amie, Une, 196
Andreas-Salomé, Lou, 16, 17, 20, 22, 24, 26, 39, 40, 45, 48, 59, 60, 64, 105, 172, 181, 182, 195, 205, 216
Aretin, Erwein Baron von, 158, 159
Attems, Countess Viktoria, 157

Bassermann, Dieter, 227, 228
Baumgarten, Fräulein A., 85
Blumenthal-Weiss, Ilse, 170, 176, 187
Boddien, Hedwig von, 56
Bodländer, Rudolf, 184, 186
Braun, Captain Otto, 211
Bunsen, Marie von, 110
Burckhardt, Carl, 152
Burckhardt-Schatzmann, Helene, 143
Burschell, Dr., 113
Bruckmann, Elsa, 14, 81

Cassirer, Eva, 47, 53

Delp, Ellen, 46, 86, 87, 174
Dietrichstein, Countess Aline, 92, 97, 111, 127

E. de W., 185
E. M., 190
Ehrenfels, Imma Baroness von, 93
Escher, Nanny von, 202

Ficker, Ludwig von, 74
Fischer-Colbrie, Arthur, 222
Flamm, Berta, 221

Gebsattel, Emil Baron von, 19, 23
Gneisenau, Countess Mary, 99

Hethey, Margarete, 114
Heydt, Karl von der, 69
Heydt, Elisabeth von der, 69, 125

Heygrodt, Robert Heinz, 169
Heyl zu Herrnsheim, Baroness, 124
Heymel, Alfred Walter von, 28, 67
Hofmannsthal, Hugo von, 91
Hohenlohe, Prince, 193
Hulewicz, Witold von, 192, 217, 218

J. H., a Worker, 163
Jahr, Ilse, 191, 197
Junghanns, Inga, 153

Kanitz-Menar, Countess Lili, 3
Kassner, Rudolf, 231
Keller, Alwine von, 177
Kippenberg, Anton, 34, 41, 71, 90, 94, 96, 107, 126, 133, 134, 140, 206, 207, 215, 220
Knoop, Gertrud Ouckama, 131, 166, 175, 179, 203
Koenig, Hertha, 108
Kolb, Annette, 21, 42
Kutschera, Oswald von, 142

L. H., 88
Ledebur, Dorothea Baroness von, 116, 136
Lettré, Emil, 119

M., Countess, 123, 128, 132, 139, 146, 149, 156, 167, 208
Mewes, Anni, 117, 130
Münchhausen, Anna Baroness von, 62, 63, 73
Münchhausen, Thankmar Baron von, 52, 61, 65, 75, 78
Marwitz, Bernhard von der, 104, 106
Moos, Xaver von, 168, 173, 183, 199
Mühll, Dory von der, 138, 189, 214
Mühll, Hans von der, 145

N. N., 15, 25, 27, 29, 32, 37

451

Nordeck zur Rabenau, Marietta Baroness von, 101
North Austrian Government, Presidency of, 115
Nostitz, Helene von, 13, 49, 54, 55, 68, 80

Pasternak, Leonid, 224
Pongs, Professor Hermann, 210, 212
Purtscher-Wydenbruck, Countess Nora, 164, 209
Przygode, Dr. Wolf, 100

R. S., 148
Reinhart, Georg, 223, 225
Rilke, Clara, 1, 4, 5, 6, 7, 8, 70, 102, 103, 112, 200, 201, 213, 219
Rilke, Phia, 151

Schaer, Alfred, 204
Schalk, Lili, 11
Schenck zu Schweinsberg, Elisabeth Baroness, 118
Schlözer, Leopold von, 137, 198
Schmidt-Pauli, Elisabeth von, 129
Schönburg, Prince, 135
Sedlakowitz, Major General von, 150
Sieber, Carl, 165

Sizzo, Countess Margo, 194
Solms-Laubach, Countess Manon zu, 18
Sorge, Reinhard Johannes, 50, 58
Stauffenberg, Countess, 120, 121, 122
Stoecklin, Francisca, 155
Supervielle, Jules, 232

Taubmann, Elisabeth, 95, 98
Thurn und Taxis, Prince Alexander von, 9, 66
Thurn und Taxis-Hohenlohe, Princess Marie, 2, 10, 12, 30, 31, 33, 35, 36, 38, 43, 44, 51, 57, 76, 77, 79, 83, 84, 89, 141, 144, 147, 161, 180

Ulbricht, Hans, 226
Ullmann, Regina, 82
Ungern-Sternberg, Baron von, 160

Veder, Beppy, 229, 230

Wedel, Lotti von, 178, 188
Winterfeldt-Menkin, Joachim von, 109, 154
Wolff, Hanna, 72

Young Girl, a, 162

INDEX

To Volume I, 1892–1910, and Volume II, 1910–1926

acceptance, II 297
actor, II 224, 393
admiration, I 240, 279—II 229, 312, 323
Adler, Friedrich, I 347
affirmation, II 317, 372, 378-89
affliction, II 103
Africa, II 101
Aksakov Chronicle, II 210
Alcoforado, Marianna, I 227, 228, 273, 332—II 47-49, 87; *see also* Portuguese Nun
Algiers, II 18, 20, 25, 35
Al Hayat, I 282
Allah, II 20
almond tree, II 84
alone, I 103, 149, 171, 202, 203, 239, 267, 336—II 211, 335
Amalfi, I 117
Amenophis IV, II 288
America, II 374
Americans, I 351—II 218, 374
Amsterdam, I 67
Anacapri, I 258, 260, 262, 265
Andalusia, II 254
Andreas, Prof., II 83, 292
Andreas-Salomé, Lou, I 34, 40, 186, 187, 243-46—II 36, 122
Andrée (atlas), I 254
angels, I 85, 107, 137, 347, 245—II 48, 72, 97, 102, 136, 146, 257, 325, 373 ff.; and devils, II 49, 51; Chartres, I 198; singing, I 208—II 334; three last, I 349
Angela of Foligno, II 52, 78, 87
animals, I 103, 118, 122, 161, 166, 178, 287—II 16, 121, 161, 344
Anna Amalia, Duchess, II 28
Ansbach, II 176
antique moderation, II 55
antiquity, I 90, 91, 122, 128
Aphrodite, throne of, I 133, 135, 186
Arab, II 277, 305
Arabian Nights, I 270—II 18, 20, 288
Arabic, II 22, 35, 83, 288
Arco, I 159

Arnim, Bettina von, I 331, 335—II 28, 163
art, I 24, 27, 28, 126, 261, 347—II 31, 41, 45, 159, 161, 229-30, 298; and the church, II 112; and conscience, I 318; evaluation of, II 247; as forgetting or insight, II 155-56; Gorky on, I 278; and intellect, II 261; and life, I 84, 126, 159—II 244-45, 255-58, 259-61, 269-70, 285, 295-98, 299-302, 302-304, 357 ff., 360, 394; and Nature, II 17, 41, 159, 391; Rodin on, I 82; poetic, I 63; plastic, I 270—II 242; Tolstoy on, II 357; transformation, not selection, I 347
art, Italian Renaissance, I 28
art, works of, I 95, 276, 279, 285, 340, 355—II 156, 223, 241, 275, 358
art-craft, I 63—II 360
art critics, I 299
art dealers, I 83, 299, 312, 314
artist, I 28, 36, 261, 278, 285, 286, 316, 339—II 31, 36, 95, 158, 281, 285, 295-98; Chekhov, I 35; myself an, I 28; not insurrectionist, I 278; insights, I 289, 316; situation of, I 339; suffering, I 76
artistic achievement, activity, etc., I 123, 269, 274, 318, 347—II 168, 280, 283, 340; appraised, II 229, 241, 247
artistic point of view, II 111
artistic observation, I 314
arts, the, II 132, 246, 334
Assisi, I 117
Atlas Mountains, II 20, 198, 294
Auerbach, II 28
Austria, II 130
Austrian subject, being an, II 212, 215
autumn, I 171, 176, 183, 229, 230, 310—II 140
Avignon, I 348—II 348, 371

Bach, I 171
Baedeker, II 70
Balkan disorder, II 74

Balzac, I 306, 307—II 138
Bang, Hermann, I 177—II 336, 356
Basel, II 208, 239
Bashkirtseff, Maria, I 54, 281
Bastien-Lepage, I 281
Baudelaire, I 108, 314, 315—II 35, 270, 369
Bavarian republic, II 181
Bavarian temperaments, II 180
beauty, I 82, 118, 193, 240—II 197, 202, 205
Becker, Paula (Modersohn), I 210, 267, 280, 334—II 329, 356
Beer-Hofmann, II 84, 305
Beethoven, I 171, 331, 352—II 134, 241
being, II 144, 304, 353, 374
Belgian coast, I 227
Belgium, I 271
belief, II 276-77
Belvedere, II 28
Bergson, II 115
Berlin, I 77, 185, 225, 228, 361, 364—II 28, 126, 142
Bern, II 198, 202, 206, 208, 366, 367
Bernheim jeune, I 281
Bertram, II 378
Bibersberg, I 32, 33
Bible, The, I 29, 93, 107, 134, 201—II 129; Genesis, II 71, 72; Gospels, II 105; Job, Book of, I 108; Moses, Books of, II 83; Old Testament, I 149—II 39, 139, 307; Psalms, II 126
Bibliothèque Nationale, I 89, 91, 92, 112, 124, 292
Bie, I 272
biographical paraphernalia, II 233-37, 266, 345-50, 353-56, 362, 383
birds, I 23, 49, 128, 157, 173, 179, 201, 231—II 88, 100
bird call, II 369
bird voices, I 67—II 79, 82, 275, 371
birth, I 345—II 322
Biskra, II 20
Bjerred, I 169
Black Forest, II 83
blindness, II 229-30
bliss, I 241, 332, 334—II 59, 96, 103, 107, 147, 309
Bodmann, von, II 349
Bohemia, I 98, 145, 146, 324—II 28, 119, 145, 146, 352
Bohemians, I 306

Bojers, I 97
Bolshevism, II 221
Bonnier, I 276
books, I 134, 162, 275, 356—II 15, 83, 126, 156, 274, 332, 335, 348
booksellers, secondhand, I 300, 301
Borch, Maria von, II 348
Borghese, I 134, 135
Boscoreale murals, I 138
Bossuet, II 99
Botticelli, I 29, 90, 219
bouquinistes, I 308—II 348
Brahe, Count (Chamberlain), I 315, 327, 337—II 371
Brahe, Tycho, II 86
Brahms, II 55, 56-57
Brandenburg, I 98
Brandes, Georg, I 104
Bremen, I 63, 64, 70
Brémond, Madame, I 305, 306, 307
"Brenner," the, II 127
Brescia gallery, II 92
Breslau, I 325
brotherhood, II 203, 360
Browning, E. B., I 277—II 355
Bruckmann, II 53
Brussels, I 192
Büchner, Georg, II 133
Buddha, I 194, 208, 335, 336
Bulgarian, the, II 74
Bullier, the, II 88
Burckhardts, II 208
butterfly, II 28-29, 100

Cairo, II 22, 35
Calé, Walter, I 260 ff.
Capri, I 231-37, 240, 241, 272, 284—II 37, 39, 83, 186, 214, 369
Capri priest, I 356
Caraccis, I 29
Carinthia, II 232, 250, 351-52
Carossa, Hans, II 158
Carpaccio, I 163
Carrara, I 96
Carriera, Rosalba, I 303, 340
Carrière, I 103, 193, 194, 200, 280
Carthage, II 21
Casino dei Spiriti, II 63
Cassiopeia, II 86
Cassirer, Eva, II 286
cathedrals, I 89, 198—II 80, 96

Catholic, I 51, 102, 146—II 99, 100, 349, 375
catkins, I 137—II 277
Cellini, Benvenuto, I 219
censorship, II 135-36
Cézanne, I 302-21, 323, 324, 337—II 158, 208, 257; attitude, II 273-74; color, I 309, 311, 314, 315, 316, 319; death, I 317; influence, II 242, 334, 356; objectivity, I 314, 323; and Rodin, I 307; paintings, I 312, 313, 314, 320, 323; a prophet, II 134, 138; turning point, I 313
Chaika, I 33, 35
Chamilly, Count de, I 332—II 47-48
change, I 310, 353, 358—II 64, 85, 107, 114, 132, 152, 165, 311, 312
Chantilly, I 182
Chardin, I 304
Charles the Bold, I 315, 360—II 107
Charlottenlund, I 182
Chartres, I 91, 198
Chekhov, I 34-36
Cherny, I 323
cherry-blossom flower, II 94
Chevalier, Etienne, I 219
Chiemsee, II 159
child, I 48, 70, 322; as a, I 38, 62, 71, 102, 340
childhood, I 26, 98, 102, 111, 173, 181 —II 120, 134, 143, 152, 308, 370
children, II 270, 275
Chinese pheasants, I 200
Choiseul, Madame de (Marquise), I 351, 352—II 91
Christ, I 19, 332—II 52, 77, 89, 125, 237
Christianity, II 76, 77, 99
Christian Beyond, II 314, 325
Christian church, II 112
Christian country, II 76
Christian experience, II 324
Christian faith, II 112
Christian God, II 275
Christian heaven, II 375
Christian sense, II 374
Christians, American, II 76
Christmas, I 54, 93, 137, 247 ff., 248 ff. —II 20, 21, 32, 80, 105, 126, 127, 212, 237-39, 280, 317
Church, the, II 325; today, II 99; Christian, II 112

churches, II 213, 334; with chains, II 70, 71; in Russia, II 45
Cividale, II 73
Claudel, II 90, 168
Clouets, I 219
Cluny, I 210
Colarossi, I 280
Colmar, II 120
colors, I 29, 50, 218, 236, 303, 310, 311, 322, 353—II 20, 137, 254
columns, II 21, 22, 80
Communion, II 38
companionship, I 330
Condés, I 218, 219
conscience, I 318, 319, 347—II 63, 229, 361
consolation, II 139, 314, 316
constellations, I 245, 336, 355—II 74
Constantinople, II 74
continuities, II 133, 170
convalescence, I 346—II 35, 119
conversation, I 172, 175, 327, 332
Copenhagen, I 153, 160, 164-65, 171, 182—II 355
Cordova, II 75, 76, 78, 81, 152, 323
Cottet, II 356
Courten, Louis de, II 295
cows, II 136
craftsman, I 287—II 360, 390
creation, II 72, 391
critic, I 95
criticism, I 293, 294, 318—II 323, 383; never reads, I 291—II 273, 312, 323, 350, 380; examples of Rilke's, II 258, 259-61, 271-72, 389-90
cruelty, II 361
Czechs, I 146—II 181, 381

Dahlem, I 135
Daniel in the lion's den, II 73
Danish language, I 161, 164, 170, 177, 276—II 348, 356
D'Annunzio, I 159
Dante, I 241—II 48
dauphine, II 54
dead, the, II 21, 45, 72, 130, 174, 342, 375
death, I 49, 51, 52, 63, 74, 151, 353—II 17, 123, 124, 146-51, 197, 316, 317; Cézanne's, I 317; Chamberlain Brahe's, I 315, 327, 337; changes, I 353; influence of, I 338; life and, *see*

456

death (*Continued*)
  life; and love, II 169, 314-17; Malte's, I 337; Schuler's, II 327-28; Rilke's attitude toward, I 329-30—II 373 ff.
Dehmel, II 333
desert, I 255, 259—II 22
destiny, I 110, 126, 223, 244, 345—II 20, 31, 38, 43, 138, 308, 329
Deubel, II 103
devotion, I 228, 246, 261, 315—II 60, 129, 132
diary, quoted, II 83-84, 369-70
Diefenbach, I 124
difficult, the, I 153, 181, 197, 245, 246, 340—II 19, 59, 75
Diriks, I 288
distance, I 44, 57, 58, 86, 263, 309—II 310, 311
distress, I 346—II 45, 51, 73, 131, 237, 371
divine, the, I 281, 336—II 47, 78, 105, 201, 300, 361
divine face, II 147
doctors, II 34, 50, 76, 331, 366, 377
dogs, I 208, 216, 299, 301, 304, 308, 309 —II 54-55, 60, 78, 179, 241, 322, 334, 362-63
dolls, II 54, 115
Don Quixote, II 80
Dostoievsky, II 105, 221, 235
Dostoievskaia, Liubov, II 221
Drechsel, Countess Sophie, II 68
Dresden, I 64
Duino, II 15, 16, 73, 81, 87, 115, 130, 131, 132, 139, 140, 188, 210, 214, 227, 291, 381
Duncan, Isadora, II 107
Durand-Ruel, I 138
duration, II 232, 233
Dürer, I 226
Duse, I 234—II 49-50, 63-66, 68-69, 107, 218
duty, I 244, 246
Duval, I 215

Eaden, Mrs., II 217
earthly and heavenly, the, II 67
Easter, I 141, 146, 248
easy, the, I 197
Ebenhausen, II 120
Eckehart, Meister, I 184
Eckermann, II 386

economy, I 284
education, I 70
Egypt, I 265, 268, 287—II 18, 25, 35, 90, 186, 288, 375
Egyptian journey, I 265
Ehrenburg, Ilya, II 387
Einstein, II 301
Eisner, II 181
Ekdal, Hjalmar, I 217
Elective Affinities, II 79
endurance, I 315, 346—II 133
English descent, II 355
English genus, II 332
English language, I 177—II 60
English love poems, I 277
English people, II 77
error, II 311
Erzia (Marthe's Russian), II 88-90
eternity, I 291, 295—II 67, 112, 218
Etoy, II 252, 254
Europe, II 91, 357
everyday, the, II 114
Exemplar, II 86
existence, I 315-16, 355—II 29, 43, 81, 85, 95, 179, 188, 328, 390
experience, II 22, 41, 62, 142, 146-51; of things, I 295; and religion, II 302
expressionist, the, II 204
externality, II 62, 108, 146, 342

Fabre d'Olivet, II 83
Faehndrich, Frau Alice, I 232
failure, I 343—II 64
faith, I 66, 103—II 189
family, I 145-46—II 250, 262, 281, 395
fate, I 74, 97, 228—II 394
father, II 249, 297
feminine heart, II 47
Fet, II 333
"Field Sermon," II 136
Fischer, I 233
Flaack, II 243
flamingos, I 200
Flaubert, I 315—II 129, 138
Fliess, Wilhelm, II 150
Florence, I 31, 117, 127, 159—II 349
Fontainebleau, I 222
Fouquet, I 219
Fra Angelico, I 31
France, II 96, 279, 307, 318, 332
Franck, Henry, II 297
Frankfurt, I 225

457

Freiburg, II 120
French language, I 87, 131, 164, 172, 275
French books, II 332, 336
French impressionists, II 356
French people, I 217, 292—II 215, 248, 301
Frenhofer, I 306
Freud, II 44, 279
Freyhold, II 190
friar, II 362
Fribourg, II 211
Friedelhausen, I 190, 203, 231, 265
Frisell, Stina, I 220
Froissart, II 61
Fujiyama, I 106, 236
Furnes, I 226
Fürstenberg's, II 219
future, II 112, 119, 123, 125, 138, 140, 156, 178, 179, 186, 190, 192, 204; open, II 163, 171; past and, II 125, 132, 177, 183
Furuborg, I 180, 182, 183, 348

Gargarine, Princess, II 395
Garschin, I 141
Gauguin, I 217, 286
gazelles, I 282
gazing, I 118, 216—II 82, 86, 116, 178
Gebsattel, II 32, 44, 45, 49, 50, 80
genealogy, I 168-69—II 351-52
Geneva, II 198, 223-34, 228
Genoa, I 96
George, Stephan, I 175, 278, 279—II 115, 333, 349
German dictionary, see Grimm's Dictionary
German language, I 276, 278—II 26, 61
German literary circles, II 382
German scholars, I 292
German youth, II 174-75
Germans, I 129, 158—II 158, 248, 332
Germany, I 362, 363, 364—II 83, 180, 207, 211, 219, 318
Gibraltar, II 77
Gibson, Frau Lizzie, I 348
Gide, I 358; II 108, 109, 279, 319
Giotto, II 111
giving, I 27, 340—II 209, 266, 279
Giudecca Gardens, II 217 ff.
Gleichen-Russwurm, Baron von, I 291
God, I 55, 73, 185, 240, 247, 315, 332,

334, 348—II 79, 86, 87, 102, 107, 136, 171, 224; Beethoven and, I 331; beggars and, I 32; Botticelli and, I 29; Cézanne and, I 308; in Christianity, II 112, 276-77, 306-307; creating, II 27; condition made by, I 224; everywhere, I 55; for, I 281; in human history, II 146 ff.; lover of, I 354—II 90; measure, II 85, 105-106; Mohammed and, II 77; no opposite, I 268; owe, I 291; Portuguese Nun and, II 48; relation to, II 324-25, 350; R. Rolland and, II 91; Russian, I 255 —II 324; St. Angela, II 78; service to, I 214; take potion to, I 336; Toledo, II 70; Verhaeren, II 189
gods, I 254, 270, 333, 355—II 24, 106, 125, 134, 139, 147, 203, 230, 288, 302
Goethe, I 175, 216, 335—II 55, 58, 265, 385, 386; and Bettina, I 335—II 28
Gogh, van, I 238, 281, 286, 300, 307, 310; Letters, I 238, 317; paintings, I 217, 281, 299; portfolio, I 208
Gogol, I 141
Goncourts, the, I 165
Gonzales, Eva, I 302
Gorky, I 241, 277
Göteborg, I 153
Gothic, I 117, 122, 161, 187, 198
Göttingen, I 185—II 83, 93
Gourvitch, Mlle., I 333
Goya, I 238
Granada, II 288
granddaughter, II 337, 387
grandmother (Westhoff), II 167
grandmother, maternal (my), II 57
grandparents, I 269—II 205, 375
Graubünden, II 295
gray, I 319-20
great-grandfather, II 263
greatest, the, I 339—II 139
greatness, I 270, 339—II 131, 138
Gréban brothers, II 98
Grecian sea, I 258, 262
Greco, II 69, 70, 74; paintings, I 341—II 29, 69, 73
Greece, II 229, 231, 265; horror and beauty of, I 265
Greeks, I 18, 135
Greek sculptors, I 135
Greek works of art I 265; tradition (music), II 93

green, I 218, 296
Green Vault, the, I 340
Gregorian chants, I 351, 352
Gregorian mass, II 92, 188
grief, II 249
grilles, II 74
Grimm, Hermann, II 282
Grimm's Dictionary, I 125, 161, 164
growth, I 289
Guardi, I 303
Guercino, I 135
Guérin, Maurice de, II 26, 27
Guérin, Eugénie de, II 27, 67, 68
guest, II 272
Guibert, Count de, I 284

habit, II 320
Hainbund poets, I 187
von Haller, II 280
Hamburg, I 67, 127
handwork, I 82, 120, 121, 124, 125
handworker, I 118
happiness, I 241—II 131, 178, 288, 310, 370
Harz, the, I 187
Haseldorf, I 67, 69, 76
hatred, II 62, 310
von Hattingberg, II 127
Hauptmann, Gerhart, I 131—II 333
heart, human, II 106
heather, I 295-96
Heidelberg, II 307, 308
Heiligendamm, II 94, 134
Heller, I 323, 328
Hellerau, II 96
Hellingrath, Frau von, II 146
Hellingrath, Norbert von, II 156, 157
helplessness, II 67, 141, 144, 222, 232
Heluan, I 268, 275
here-and-now, the, II 87, 149, 284, 373 ff.
Herxheimer, I 221, 280
Heydt, Karl and Elisabeth von der, I 190, 220—II 166
Heym, II 389
hideous cup, II 150
history, II 133, 140, 146, 176
Hofmannsthal, I 125, 175, 273, 327, 328 —II 29, 158, 226, 241, 283, 333, 348
Hokusai, I 106, 126, 174, 315
Hölderlin, II 119, 129
holiness, I 315

Holmström, I 178
home, I 43, 46, 94—II 76, 232, 250, 281
honey, I 152
horror, II 88, 147
horses, I 168, 170, 178, 282—II 161, 291-93, 328
Hôtel Dieu, I 109
Hottingen (Reading Circle), II 194
Hugo, I 89
Hulewicz, II 350
human, the, I 336—II 65, 78, 84, 133, 176, 336; and divine, I 281
human, becoming, II 17
human affairs, II 137, 188
human approaches, II 108
human beings, I 174, 312—II 38, 39, 112, 145, 174, 312, 360
human heart, II 106
human history, II 146
human kindness, II 129
human life, II 105
human matters, II 86, 139
human mind, II 148
human models, I 287
human relations, II 112, 149, 188
human spheres, II 37
human things, II 46, 65
human world, II 163
humanity, II 138, 139, 164, 171, 189, 192, 203
Hünich, II 209, 272, 273, 274
hypnotism, I 25

Iberian Madonna, I 32
Ibsen, I 217—II 19, 371
ideals, II 192
idleness, I 179
illustration, II 246-47
Ilya of Murom, II 34
immortality, I 145
indisposition, II 85, 215, 329, 331-32, 365
individual, the, II 125, 134, 148, 183-85, 204, 214, 222, 301
infinite, the, II 16, 17, 47, 112, 133, 157, 303, 369
influence, I 46, 264, 279, 316—II 37, 333-35, 345-50
Ingegneri, II 91
Ingres, II 24
inner alterations, II 162
inner being, II 144, 159, 342, 369

inner center, etc., II 126, 142, 306
inner conditions, II 85
inner equivalents, II 145
inner events, II 332
inner experience, II 62
inner existence, II 105
inner intercourse, II 95
inner ownership, II 109
inner tensions, II 41
inner world, II 179; of crystals, II 93
inner world-space, II 311
innocence, II 67, 138
Insel Almanac, I 273—II 125, 159, 164,
    187
Insel-Bücherei, II 109
Inselschiff, II 209, 378, 392
Insel-Verlag, I 256, 271, 288, 311—II
    120, 232, 295, 368, 378, 385
insight, I 263, 316, 353—II 41, 64, 144,
    147, 155; increases of, II 125; Lou's,
    II 122; into the saint, II 106; spirit-
    ualistic, II 343
intellectual, the, II 195-96, 222, 300
intermediary, without an, I 214
internality, II 62
invisible, the, I 330—II 102, 111, 125,
    159, 267
Isar (river), II 140
Isenheim, II 191
Islam, II 21
Italy, I 98, 132, 158, 284; first in, II 354
Italian life, I 132
Italian sojourn, etc., I 117—II 305
Italian influence, I 157
Italian genus, II 332
Italian things, I 157, 237
Ivanov, I 141

Jacob, II 88
Jacobowski, II 34-39
Jacobsen, I 144, 160, 177, 240—II 155,
    274, 336, 348, 356
Jacopone da Todi, II 98-99
Jaenecke, Anna, I 336, 338
Jaffé, Professor, II 180
Jammersminde, II 363-64
Jammes, Francis, I 164, 201
Janovič, I 324—II 142
Japanese, the, I 303
Japanese collection, I 281
Japanese color, I 317
Japanese prints, I 179, 322

Jean-Christophe, II 92
Jehova, II 276
Jew, II 53, 276-77, 305-307
jewelry, II 223
John (the Baptist), II 169
journalism, I 101—II 301
Jouven, I 216, 280, 298
judging, judgment, I 311—II 67, 229,
    365
Juncker, I 104
Jung-Stilling, II 308
justice, I 212—II 104-105, 266

Kairuan, II 21
Kalkreuth, II 124
Kamenitz an der Linde, I 98, 325—II
    263, 351
Kannegiesser, Dr., II 55
Kant, I 189
Kappus, I 173
Karst, the, II 30, 36, 42
Kassel, I 225
Kassner, II 15-16, 17, 52, 53, 102, 105-
    106, 157, 173, 224, 290; Elements of
    Human Greatness, II 211, 395; In-
    dian Idealism, II 53; and Kierke-
    gaard, II 53; quotation from, II 115
Kaufmann, von, II 182
Key, Ellen, I 130, 165, 166, 180, 183,
    194, 220-23, 276—II 35, 83; corre-
    spondence with, I 130; letters, I 177;
    Lifslinjer, I 184; in Capri, I 271; in
    Paris, I 215, 220-23
Keyserling, Hermann, II 133
Keyserlingk, Count Paul, II 166, 177
Kierkegaard, I 161, 359—II 17, 53
kindness, II 129
Kippenberg, II 120, 385
Kleist, I 51
Klimt, II 353
Klossowska, Madame Baladine-, II
    252, 254
Klossowski, Balthasar, II 240
kneeling, I 32—II 170, 238
Knoop, Vera Ouckama, II 284, 289,
    291
Koran, II 76, 83
Kuropatkin, I 141

lace, I 67, 167, 209, 326—II 223
lament, II 67, 75, 129
lamentation, I 228, 375

language: great cultural, I 276; one's own, I 275-76; plastic, I 161; development, II 31; tools of, II 280; *see also* specific languages
Larsson, Frl. Hanna, I 168, 169
Last Supper, I 301
Latour, I 304
Lausanne, II 319
Lautschin, II 16, 17, 27, 28, 123, 224, 228
Lebossé, II 191
Leipzig, I 117, 363, 364—II 28, 120, 127, 128, 194
Pauvre Lélian, II 103
Lenbach, I 81
Lenéru, Marie, II 314
Leonardo, I 90, 126, 219, 315
Lepanto, I 62
leper, I 315—II 256
Lermontov, II 333
Les Baux, I 349-51—II 334
Lespinasse, Mlle. de, I 285
Libyan Mountains, II 22
lies, II 143, 144
Liebermann, I 81
life, I 161, 222, 245, 246—II 105, 146 ff., 161, 334; affirmation, etc., II 41, 284, 298, 373 ff.; breadth, I 318; creative, I 77; and death, II 121, 130, 146-51, 188, 266, 284, 330, 370, 373 ff.; and poetry, II 389; provisions, etc., of, II 159, 178, 179, 195; real, I 174; renewal, I 173; rhythm, I 343; self-transformation, I 151; simplicity, I 288; taking heavily, II 297-98; whole, I 152, 260
life task, I 343
Liliencron, II 333, 347
lineage, II 250, 367
Linz, I 21, 26—II 383
Li Tai Po, I 292, 315
literary, the, II 87, 242
literature, I 101, 287—II 143, 301, 357
littérateurs, I 287, 325—II 301
living, I 159, 291, 296; art and, II 269-70; earning, I 66, 159; inner tensions of, II 41; in oneself, I 152
living, the, II 72
Ljungren, Ellen, I 103
Loèche-Ville, II 295
London, I 177
Longwy, II 126

Lord, our, II 30, 100
loss, II 314
Louvre, I 89, 128, 135, 210, 225, 280, 302, 305
love, I 20, 21, 22, 103, 150 ff., 240, 261 —II 59, 119, 129, 146-51, 242, 309-11; beyond, I 311; conventions of, I 335; and death, II 149, 169, 314-17, 324; without deceit, I 332; denial, II 303; disdained, I 228; God, the Jew, II 276-77; must *learn*, I 152; life, art, II 255-58; man's inadequacy, II 47-48; and marriage, II 309-11; miracle, I 297; and parting, I 353-54; perfect, II 157; place of, I 152; Portuguese nun, I 273—II 46-49; extreme possibility of, I 315; Strindberg, II 138; great task, I 358; Tasso, II 61-62; Tolstoy, II 95; transformations of, II 330; in work, painting, I 311
lovers, I 354—II 46-49, 149, 303, 309-11
Lucerne, II 208
Ludovisi Museum, I 133, 186
Lund, I 170, 175—II 358
Luxembourg Museum, I 91—II 358
Luxembourg Gardens, I 86, 87, 92, 196, 210—II 27, 227
Luxor, II 22

Madrid, II 71, 74
Maeterlinck, II 115, 356
Mallarmé, II 280-81, 301, 304, 319
Maillol, I 287—II 24; works of, I 281
Malte Laurids Brigge, I 337, 343, 360-62, 364—II 17, 32-34, 37, 62, 141, 147, 225, 255 ff., 356
man, II 46-49, 140, 144, 170, 197, 201
Manet, I 281, 303, 308, 320
Manets, II 238, 280
Mangwa, the, I 174
mankind, II 46, 189, 316
Marburg, I 187, 189
Marc, Franz, II 158
Marcus Aurelius, statue of, I 133, 136
Mardrus, II 288
Maria Grubbe, I 144, 164
Mariclée, II 86, 87
Marienbad, I 127
Marlowe, II 60-61
Marly, II 24
marriage, I 57, 61, 74
Martersteig, Geheimrat, II 98

Marthe, II 42, 88-90, 138, 152, 207
Mary Magdalene, II 26
Masaryk, President, II 380
maternal body, the, II 169
Mecca, II 21
Mediator, the, II 325
mediums, II 341-44
Meier-Graefe, I 217
Meiningen, I 31, 33
metamorphoses, I 336
metaphysical, the, II 147
metaphysical societies, II 343
Meudon, I 78, 80, 86, 118, 188, 190, 203, 236—II 108
Michel, Wilhelm, I 97
Michelangelo, II 54, 283
Michelet, I 61, 164
military school, II 157, 345-46, 349
mind, human, II 148
Minne, I 200
miracle, I 250, 261, 297—II 52, 77
misery, II 61, 76, 88, 103, 113, 125, 131, 134, 165, 215
modelé, I 83, 84, 264, 270, 287
models, human, I 287
Modersohn, Otto, I 194
Modersohn, Paula, see Becker, Paula
Mohammed, II 21, 76
Moissi, II 64, 65
von Moltke, II 167
Mona Lisa, I 216, 219, 226—II 100
money, I 103, 280, 285—II 111, 120
Monfalcone, II 130
monkeys, I 199, 303
Montaigne, II 129
Monte Solaro, I 258
Mont Valérien, I 236
Moors, the, II 77
morality, II 303
Mordvin (language), II 89
Moreau, Gustav, I 217
Moreau-Nélaton, I 280
Morice, Charles, I 193
Morisot, Berthe, I 281, 302
Moscow, I 31, 39, 141, 146—II 105
Moses, I 24—II 81
mother, I 46, 48, 283—II 170, 249
mountains, I 294—II 22, 61, 72, 77, 78, 82, 119
Mühsam, II 180
Münchhausen, Thankmar von, II 166
Munich, I 58, 64, 76, 117, 127, 238—II

41, 43, 45, 119, 120, 137, 141, 171, 180, 201, 205-207, 219, 228, 348, 349, 354; apartment, II 182, 194; not congenial, II 211, 213, 214, 265
music, I 119, 172, 296, 324, 352—II 91, 92, 152-53; and word, II 127, 128, 246, 391
musicians, I 171
Muther, Richard, I 75—II 358
Muzot, II 252-54, 264-65, 268, 292, 319, 328, 335-37, 366-68
mysteries, II 325
mysticism, II 355

Nadherny, I 324, 325, 327
Naples, I 232, 235, 237, 239, 284—II 39, 40; museum, I 238, 284—II 288; National Gallery, I 238
Nature, I 200, 279, 309, 310, 311, 355—II 23, 67, 68, 112, 149, 157, 195, 235, 238, 374; and art (see art); Cézanne and, I 311; cruelty in, II 197; descriptions, II 72, 77-78, 205-206; influence of, II 120, 145; Rilke's relation to, II 40, 119, 145, 161, 178, 196, 213, 214, 235, 240, 370; Tolstoy's experience of, II 150
nature, our, I 263—II 382
near and far, I 263—II 16, 149
Nefertete (magnificent queen), II 288, 308
Nekrassov, II 333
Nerval, Gérard de, II 369
Neuburg, II 249
Neva, the, I 38
newspapers, I 291—II 74, 100, 130, 144, 170, 171, 179, 194, 208
Niederlangenau, II 351
Niels Lyhne, I 76, 107—II 34
nightingales, I 67, 148, 158, 208-209, 263
Nike of Samothrace, I 89, 90, 128
Nile, the, I 254—II 22, 35, 375
Noailles, Countess de, II 188
Nonna, Frau, I 275
Norlind, I 172, 178
nothing that is real, I 145
Notre Dame de Paris, I 89, 198, 280—II 53

Oberneuland, I 53, 116, 221
observation, aesthetic, II 220

Obstfelder, I 181
Oby, I 183
"occult occurrences," II 356
Odenhausen, I 189
Odysseus, I 258
old lady, I 301-302
old maids, I 97
old men, II 79
open, the, II 35, 56, 219
open, to be, II 24
open future, II 163, 171
open world, II 166, 174, 178, 214, 250, 373 ff.
opération, la nouvelle, II 78, 81
organs, II 74, 80
Orient, II 35, 306
Orientals, II 23
Orlik, Emil, I 58—II 347
Öttingen, Princess, II 291

Padua, II 73
pains, II 88, 102, 113, 395, 396
painters, I 76, 77, 314, 316, 353—II 273
painting, II 159, 162, 242, 353, 354
Palestrina, I 141—II 91
Paris, I 54, 82, 88 ff., 92, 108 ff., 132, 160, 161, 213, 226, 232, 281, 285, 326, 356-58 —II 46, 91, 132, 166-69, 212, 214, 266, 348, 381, 382; admiration for, I 269, 284; belongings auctioned, II 141, 351; difficult, I 93, 140, 281—II 19, 96, 102, 107; favorable, I 232—II 24, 26, 34, 186, 224; great, II 368-69; Malte Laurids Brigge and, I 217, 282, 362 —II 371; my, II 247-48; reading in, I 124, 163; solitude in, I 257—II 337; task, I 274; visit, 1902, I 70, 75, 76, 77 ff., 117, 292—II 334, 354; visit, 1903, I 105; visit, 1905, I 188, 191; visit, 1910, II 15; visit, 1911, II 29; visit, 1914, II 120, 232; visit, 1920, II 182, 221, 225, 226, 228, 230-32, 240; visit, 1924, II 366-69
past, the, II 125, 200
Pasternak, Boris, II 387
Pasternak, Leonid, I 39—II 386
Paszthory, Herr von, II 127
patience, I 19, 107, 159, 261, 264, 268, 313, 316, 332, 346—II 51, 67, 85, 153, 204, 215, 287, 294; always good, I 204; long, I 144, 341, 342, 343—II 33, 233

peace, II 166, 184
Peintres Genevois, II 223-24
people, I 22, 50, 92; Paris, I 109-115, 118, 122, 129-30, 145, 147, 268, 313, 332— II 111, 112, 142, 164-65, 176, 320; at Capri, I 240; "in hell," I 352; other, II 100, 202, 370; rejected, II 37, 39, 46, 141, 184, 213; in Vienna, I 326, 327; wanted, II 34, 37-39, 107, 185, 266; who love, I 353-54—II 23; young, II 257, 286, 296-98
Peronnet, I 304
perseverance, II 67
persons, II 24, 43, 49, 83, 102
Peter Michel (Huch), I 95
Petersburg, I 38, 80
Petrarch, II 25, 62
Petri, I 171
philosophy, I 23, 261—II 355
Picasso, II 132, 144, 155, 158, 293
pictures, II 156, 224, 298
Pierrot, II 54-55, 60
Philippe, Charles-Louis, II 369
Pinakothek, the, II 29
Pisa, I 96
Pissaro, I 305, 316
Pitoeff, II 224, 225
Placci, II 65, 91
Plato, I 300
Poe, Edgar Allan, I 171
poems, I 29, 30—II 298, 353
poet, I 76, 77—II 103, 104, 168, 200, 275, 298, 301, 361
poeta ignoto, II 151
poètes maudits, II 103
poetry, II 343; criticism, II 258, 259-61, 271, 389-90; lyric, II 323, 389-90
Poles, I 146
Poletti, Mme., II 64, 66, 68, 98
politics, II 79, 248, 318
Pollaiuolo, I 219
Pompeian, I 237, 238, 304
poplar, II 265, 367
Portuguese Nun, see Alcoforado, Marianna
possession, I 263, 330—II 111, 114, 173, 257, 310, 324
possessions, II 33, 141, 142, 232, 351
potion, prepare the, I 336
poverty, II 33, 84, 111, 360-61, 363-64, 370

Prague, I 73, 98, 103, 322-26—II 16, 57, 346, 347, 356
prayer, I 50, 173, 224, 285
pre-Greeks, I 128
press, the, II 143, 192
prisoners, II 143
prophets, I 315—II 72, 134, 138
Prophet, the (Mohammed), II 21, 76
prose, I 342, 344—II 353-54, 356
Protestants, II 76
Proust, II 109, 110, 313, 318, 336
Provence, I 91, 348-49; and Spain, II 251, 264, 279, 294
psychoanalysis, II 42-45; arguments against, II 34, 42, 51; devils and angels, II 49, 50, 51; in Switzerland, II 206
psychology, I 23—II 271, 321
publishing, I 278—II 303, 304
Pushkin, II 333
Pyrenees, II 294

Quidde, Ludwig, II 180

R., Dr., II 72
Rabenau family, I 188
Ragaz, II 340, 341, 365, 366, 377
rain, I 138, 289, 301, 310—II 73, 83, 105, 140, 325, 329
Rameses, II 22
Raphael, I 219
Raskolnikov, I 315—II 18, 62
Ratibor, Prince, II 74
Ravello, I 117
ravens, I 169
readers, I 347—II 246, 383, 392
reading, II 129, 215, 305, 320, 336, 393
real, the, I 145, 246, 295, 330—II 56, 111, 383
reality, I 46, 144, 241, 244, 247, 263, 295, 296, 297, 323, 339—II 62, 114, 151, 375 ff.
recognition, mistrust of, I 312
Redeemer, I 29
Reinhardt, II 64, 107
Reinhart, Werner, II 252, 268, 388
relationships, I 151, 316, 330—II 39, 112, 149, 168, 186, 188, 324
religion, II 277, 302-303, 316
Rembrandt, I 219, 225, 235—II 24
Renaissance, I 28, 91—II 246

Renan, I 268
Reni, I 135
renunciation, II 303
responsibility, I 245
Resurrection, I 36
Reventlow, I 326
revolution, II 183, 184, 187, 195, 381
revolutionary, the, I 278—II 196, 204, 256
Rhone, I 349—II 225, 251, 264, 294
Ribadaneira, II 72
rich and poor, II 360-61, 363-64
riding, II 162
Rilke, Christine Sieber, II 337, 339, 376
Rilke, Christopher, II 129
Rilke, Clara, I 69, 88, 132, 143, 147, 153, 185, 229, 231, 232, 241, 243, 269—II 42, 45, 120, 263, 337, 339, 358, 387; see also Westhoff, Clara; Rilke, Rainer Maria—wife
Rilke, Ruth, I 66, 69, 74, 82, 84, 97, 116, 137, 143, 144, 165, 216, 220, 221, 231, 247-49, 275, 285, 296, 325, 356—II 21, 120, 261-63, 337, 339, 376-77, 387
Rilke family, history of, I 145—II 351-52
Rilke, Grandmama Phia, II 181
Rilke, Jaroslav von Rilke-Rüliken, II 351
Rilke, Rainer Maria: art, I 32, 61, 88, 100, 121, 124, 283—II 16; books, I 30, 107, 165, 204, 233—II 32, 120, 141, 274, 297, 324, 340, 379, 380, 383; childhood, I 18, 32, 96, 150, 244, 322, 340—II 107, 266, 297, 299, 315, 356; development, I 72, 233, 347; education, I 70, 72, 100, 163; expression, I 145; family, I 98, 145, 146, 180; father, I 28, 98, 99, 103, 117, 127, 180, 203, 329—II 125, 281, 315; grandfather, I 98; great-grandfather, I 98; health, I 96, 184, 232, 338—II 319, 377; home, I 43, 138 (see also Russia); homelessness, I 244; house (women of), I 145; insights, I 337—II 85, 96; inner world, II 141, 152; landscape, I 46; life, I 77, 126, 140, 190, 239, 240, 360—II 25, 33, 39, 43, 81, 93, 113, 114, 217, 234-37, 272-75, 296; loneliness, I 19, 106, 175—II 350; love, I 129—II 90; marriage, I 70, 74, 100; melancholy, I 238; mother, I

Rilke, Rainer Maria (*Cont.*)
19, 46, 98, 99, 104, 147, 325—II 57, 90;
mother-in-law, I 143, 149; nature,
I 32, 340, 346—II 36, 42, 85, 139, 266,
286, 395; observation, I 157, 325, 327;
parents, I 98, 99; poems, I 121, 311,
347; powers, I 94; relation to Nature,
II 40, 119, 145, 161, 178, 196, 213, 214,
235, 240, 370; reverence, I 107,
124; secret mind, II 48; solitude, I
239, 257—II 106-107; surroundings,
I 45; what is mine, I 99, 104, 124—II
158, 213; wife, I 63, 64, 69, 102, 117,
155, 203, 212, 360; work, I 71, 75, 76,
88, 121, 124, 146, 155, 159, 175, 179,
224, 341, 344—II 26, 152, 153, 245-46,
338, alone with, I 203, 220, 293,
anonymous, I 311, in, I 241, 361,
laborious, I 290, neglected, I 211,
never read about, I 293 (*see also*
criticism), own, I 202, 204, 213,
turning point, I 313; youth, I 150—II
296, 324
Rilke's works: "Alkestis," I 272; "Angel Songs," II 349; "Assumption of
the Virgin (unpubl.), I 409; "Blind
Woman, The," II 283; *Book of
Hours,* I 202, 256, 270, 310, 348, 357—
II 84, 135, 139, 283, 325, 349, 355,
372 ff., 383; *Book of Pictures,* I 80,
165, 199, 210, 214, 219, 295—II 362;
"Carrousel, The," I 326; "Christ's
Journey to Hell," II 98, 164; *Cornet,*
I 210, 214—II 126, 127-29, 359, 354;
"Corrida," I 298; *Daily Life,* I 291;
Days of Celebration (unpubl.), I 31;
"Death," II 88; "Doves, The," II 164;
Dreamcrowned, I 30; *Duino Elegies,*
II 74, 102, 131, 153, 159, 255, 290-93,
309, 317, 318, 340, 372 ff., 381, 382;
"Emmaus," II 98; essay on letters of
Marianna Alcoforado, I 273; "Ex-
perience, An," II 188, 369-70; "Fenê-
tres, les," II 433; "Five Songs, Au-
gust 1914," II 117, 121, 125, 168; frag-
ment on the Lonely (unpubl.), I
311; *Fragmentary Pieces,* II 293;
French Poems (*Vergers*), II 336, 382,
383, 440; "From a Spring," II 164;
"Gazelle," I 290; *In My Honor,* I
165; "I Would Not Like to Die in
Spring," II 350; "Ivan the Terrible,"

I 326; "Lament," II 164; "Last Judgment," I 80; *Life and Songs,* I 30;
Life of the Virgin Mary, II 50, 98,
355, 362; "Maidens' Songs," II 349;
"Marionette Theater," I 290; "Mari-
tana" (unpubl.), I 20; military novel
(unpubl.), I 160; "Narcissus," II 419;
New Poems, Part I, I 271, 273, 288—
II 34, 38, 97, 323, 372 ff.; *Notebooks
of Malte Laurids Brigge,* II 18, 25,
32-34, 37, 38, 51, 69, 107, 146-47, 285,
301, 343, 356, 371, 372 ff.; *Offerings
to the Lares,* I 30; "One Must
Die . . .", II 64; "Orpheus, Eury-
dike, Hermes," I 257; "Panther,
The," I 186; Preface to Mitsou, II
240; "Primal Sound," II 391-92;
"Prayers," the (unpubl.—*see also
Book of Hours*), I 160, 165; Quatrains Valaisans, II 366, 381; *Rodin,* I
75, 93, 97, 102, 104, 117, 122, 186, 191,
221, 229, 231, 268, 288, 324—II 312;
"Rosebowl, The," I 272; *Roses, Les,*
II 366; single poems, II 153; *Son-
nets to Orpheus,* II 289, 309, 318, 325,
326, 330, 340, 372 ff.; *Stories of God,*
I 55, 73, 107, 153 ff., 165; "Straining
So against the Strong Night," II 417;
"Stranger, The," II 97; three poems,
II 338; "To the Angel," II 409;
Translation of Chekhov, I 33; Trans-
lation of Gide, II 109; Translation of
Michelangelo, II 153, 157, 168, 192,
282; Translation of Valéry, II 279,
366, 368; Translation of Verhaeren,
II 426; "Visions of Christ" (unpubl.),
I 20; "White Princess, The," I 145—
II 362, 363; *Wild Chicory,* I 30—II
353; *Worpswede,* I 102
Rippoldsau, I 348
rivers, I 140, 190, 245—II 251
Riviera di Levante, I 96
Robbias, the, I 155
Rodaun, I 328
Rode, Helge, I 276
Rodenbach, I 358
Rodenbach, Madame G., I 217
Rodin, I 69, 76-86, 90, 91, 94, 118-24,
126, 128, 131, 132, 190-207, 209, 212,
260, 315, 331-34, 336, 352, 355—II 19,
91, 108, 109, 134, 248, 288, 312, 358-
59; Americans, I 351; art, I 119, 198;

and Cézanne, I 307; communication resumed, I 323, 328; conversation, I 287; daughter, I 82; death of, II 167; exhibitions, I 323; figures, etc., I 145, 179, 254—II 294; first came to, I 77, 118; forgeries, II 190-91; a friend, I 194—II 272; going wrong, II 33, 64; at the home of, I 82, 188; insight, I 193; Jacobsen and, I 144; learned from, I 123, 135, 229—II 242, 334; leaving, I 204, 213, 215; on love, I 332; marveling, II 245; not meeting, I 288; metier, II 300; and Pitoeff, II 224; reality, I 289, 333; and St. Christopher, I 333; solitude, I 118; things, I 122; words, I 160, 307; work, I 88, 93, 79, 117, 288, 300
Rodin's works, I 238; Age d'airain, I 192—II 191; Balzac, I 332; Bust of a Woman, I 91; the Hand, I 78; Morning Star, I 78; Porte de l'Enfer, I 79; la Prière, I 79
Rodin, Madame, I 80, 81, 189, 192, 193, 195, 196
Rolland, Romain, II 90, 91, 92, 188
Rome, I 117, 127, 132-35, 147, 148, 155-58, 177, 201, 203, 206, 248, 258, 263-64, 267, 359, 364—II 62, 69, 130, 186, 214, 334, 355
Ronda, II 77, 79, 81, 93
Rongac, I 38
Rosa, II 193
roses, I 86, 158, 167, 289, 357, 364—II 151; equilibrium, I 227; make words of, I 290; yellow, I 242
Rosen, Lia, II 283
Rothenstein, I 210
Rouen, I 91—II 96
Rousseau, Henri, II 158
Russia, I 31, 44, 45, 70, 101, 132, 146, 182, 224, 278—II 69, 186, 203, 324, 329, 332, 357, 386-87; artists, I 278; Bolshevism, II 221; as home, I 45, 131, 178—II 214; journey in, II 69, 354-55; music, I 352; pictures, I 34; war, I 141
Russian genus, 332
Russian influence, II 235-36, 334, 349, 360
Russian language, I 41, 75, 164—II 333, 354, 386; poems in, I 275
Russian officer, I 142

Russians, I 128, 129, 246, 247, 277, 278—II 307, 333
Russian studies, I 50, 75
Russian things, I 32, 50, 70, 132, 164

Sack, Gustav, II 163
Sagrado, II 130
saints, I 239, 315, 364—II 48, 76, 84, 86, 87, 89, 104-106, 303
St. Angela, II 52, 78, 87
St. Anne (Leonardo), I 216
St. Augustine, II 25
St. Christopher, Cristóbal, I 333—II 73
St. Francis, I 117, 292, 299—II 84, 98-99, 111, 305
St. Gall, II 208
St. Julien-l'hospitalier, I 315—II 256
St. Margarita of Cortona, II 93
St. Theresa, I 341—II 46
Sakkhara, II 22
Salis-Seewis, II 198
Salomé, I 350
Salon, I 302, 303, 309, 321, 341
Salus, Hugo, II 347
Salvatierra, Marquis de, II 79
Salzböden, I 189
Salzburg, I 26
Saonara, II 151, 152
Sappho, I 335
Saul, I 310, 315
Savior, the, II 237
Saxony, I 98—II 352
saying, I 311
Scandinavian, II 332, 356
Sceaux, II 88
Schloss Berg, II 227, 228, 230, 231, 239, 240, 250, 259, 269, 279
science, I 161, 162—II 310
sculptors, sculpture, I 76, 77—II 156
Schack (versions), II 288
Schlegel, II 61
Schlegel-Schelling, Caroline, II 186
Schmargendorf, I 134, 300—II 83, 280, 355
Scholz, Wilhelm von, II 349
Schönaich, I 163
schools: commercial, I 21, 26, 99; Latin, II 346; military, I 20, 27, 102, 103, 153; Primary, I 18, 19
Schopenhauer, II 353
Schrenck-Notzing, II 101-102

Schuler, II 130, 327, 328
Schwarzwald, I 348—II 120
Schwerin, Countess, I 232, 329
seagull wings, I 178
séances, II 341-44
Seckendorff, II 242
Seine (river), I 77, 89, 91, 92—II 19
self-abasing entreaty, I 228
self-surrender, I 228, 283
self-transformation, I 151
sermons, I 185—II 26
service, I 43, 214, 250—II 136, 247, 269, 301
Seville, II 76, 79, 80, 81
sex, I 332—II 303-304
Shakespeare, II 60-61
sharings, the true, I 66
Shaw, George Bernard, I 205-208
Shaw, Madame, I 205, 206
short stories, I 29, 30
sickness, II 35, 71, 114, 140
Sierre, II 225, 251, 378
silence, II 136, 213
Simmel, Georg, II 355
Simon, Lucien, II 356
singing, I 280, 289
Sion, II 225, 226, 251
Sirul, Mila, II 387
Slavdom, I 146
Slavic blood, I 145
Slavs, the, II 89, 235
Småland, I 183
smile, II 63-64, 87, 88, 107, 198
socialism, II 184, 360
society, I 268
Soglio, II 207, 209, 210, 212, 213
solitude, I 56, 117, 129, 203—II 37, 38, 39, 270, 286, 390; go into, I 172; guard, I 57, 58, 65; an inner affair, I 269; neighboring, I 150
Sorrento, I 234-36
sorrow, II 67, 134, 156, 249
Spain, I 160—II 69, 76, 77, 89, 99, 145, 188, 212, 322, 381; and Provence, II 251, 252, 264, 279, 294
Spanish genus, II 332
Spanish influence, II 200, 202, 334
Spanish journey, II 69, 81, 82, 85
Spanish language, II 74
spheres, human, II 37
Sphinx, I 255, 270
Spinoza, II 306

spiritualism, I 25—II 101-102, 115, 341-44
Spitteler, II 281
Stampa, Gaspara, II 47
Stauffenberg, Dr., II 120, 121, 140, 173
Stern, Rheinhold Maurice von, II 349
Stieler, Kurt, II 127
Stifler, Adalbert, II 160
Stockholm, I 165
Stolberg, "Gustgen," II 58
Strassburg cathedral, II 55
Strindberg, II 54, 129, 133, 138
student, the, I 282
Subiaco, I 117
suffering, I 56, 76, 241—II 67, 76, 107, 113, 146 ff., 163, 165, 215; an error, II 284; *Jammersminde*, II 363-64; war, II 124, 132, 133, 139, 140
Sund, the, I 167, 171
Sweden, I 165, 166, 203—II 83, 305, 348, 355, 356
Swedish cities, I 165
Swedish language, I 153, 168, 276
Swiss sojourn, II 219
Swiss people, II 202, 206, 208
Switzerland, II 187, 190-92, 197-99, 202, 204-206, 212, 213, 217, 225-28, 232, 251 ff., 268, 330, 381, 382, 388; history, II 202, 206; mountains, II 198, 205

Tajo, the, II 73
talent, II 31
talking-machine, II 392-93
Tangiers, II 77
Tante Alla, I 284
Tante Gabriele, I 18, 268
tasks, I 315—II 113, 146, 170, 282, 329
Tasso, II 61-62
Taubmann, Elisabeth, II 158, 161
Taxis, *see* Thurn und Taxis
Taxis circle, II 341
technique, II 162
Teniers, I 226
terrible, the, I 347—II 139, 197, 376 ff.
theater, II 98, 132, 133, 143, 224-25, 302
Thiel, I 23, 24
thing, the *one*, I 131—II 261, 262, 269, 279, 299, 317
things, I 122, 127, 128, 347—II 16, 46, 67, 320, 323, 374; enduring of, I 103; experiencing, I 294-95; foreign, I

263-64, 269; great, I 253, 276; human, II 46, 65; important, I 260; made by Jacobsen and Rodin, I 144; make out of fears, I 115; old, II 176, 200, 211, 213, 231; Rilke's relation to, II 121, 228, 312, 324; Rodin and, I 82, 118-22; small, I 336; transcend the sexual, I 332

Thisted, I 160
Thurn und Taxis-Hohenlohe, Princess Marie, II 15, 122, 123, 216, 309, 341, 395
Thurn und Taxis, Prince, II 93, 101, 102
Thurn und Taxis, Prince, the elder, II 36
Thurn und Taxis, Prince Pasha, II 70, 72, 77
Thyssen, I 210
Tiefurt, II 28
Tiepolo, I 303
tiger (antique), I 90, 91, 128
time, I 94, 330—II 94, 266, 373 ff.
time, the, II 93, 163, 164, 177, 181, 184, 191
Tintoretto, I 303
Titian, I 303
Toledo, II 69, 70-74, 81, 87, 145, 334
Tolstoy, Count, I 36, 39 ff., 133—II 138, 168, 173, 354, 356-57, 359 ff., 365; and death, II 150; and Ibsen, II 19; letters, II 94, 95, 104-105
Tolstoy, Countess, I 39 ff.—II 104
tradition, II 325
Trakl, II 389
transformation, I 151, 291, 310, 335, 347, 348—II 162, 330, 374 ff., 390
transiency, II 373 ff., 393
translating, I 177—II 329, 336; Chekhov, I 33; Michelangelo, II 153, 157, 168, 192, 282; Valéry, II 279, 318, 329, 337, 366
toujours travailler, I 124
travel, II 23, 51, 100, 220, 288, 323-24
Tre Fontane, I 135
Tretiakov Gallery, I 34
Trieste, II 71
Trinity, the, I 185
Trocadero, I 91
troubadours, II 48
Troubetzkoi, I 199
Tula, I 42

Tunis, II 18, 25, 35, 186, 212, 288
Turgeniev, I 238—II 333, 348
Turin, I 96
Turnau, II 151, 152
turnings, II 115, 179, 274, 287, 318, 349
"Turning," II 116
Tuscany, I 117, 156—II 349

Uexküll, I 259—II 166
Uhde, II 354
Uhlfeldt, Countess Leonora Christina, II 363-64
ultimate, the, I 276, 343, 345—II 78, 95, 284
Uncle Vanya, I 34
understanding, not, II 214
Unknown, the, II 74, 101, 130, 140
universities, I 162—II 35, 45, 83, 142, 378

Valais (Wallis), the, II 225-26, 251-54, 264-65, 294-95, 328, 366, 381
Valéry, Paul, II 279 (see also translating), 280, 281, 302, 378
Val Fleury, I 78, 86, 134
Valmarana, Countess, II 216
Valmaranas, II 110, 217
Val-Mont, II 336, 366-67
vegetarian, I 225, 338, 357
Velhagen, I 93
Venetians, I 303, 305
Venice, I 117, 127, 329—II 24, 47, 58, 81, 87, 98, 216-18, 220, 221, 335
Venus (throne of), I 186
Venus de Milo, I 89, 216
Venus (Petersburg), I 80
Verhaeren, Emil, I 194, 213, 216, 315—II 90, 91, 167, 189, 271-72, 323, 334
Verlaine, I 313, 322—II 103, 270
Versailles, I 192 ff.
Vesuvius, I 236, 262
Viareggio, I 116, 145, 157, 206—II 349, 362
victory, II 165, 323
Vienna, I 323, 326-27—II 152, 157, 211
Villa des Brillants, I 189
Villon, I 315—II 369
Virgin Mary, I 315—II 72, 80, 98
visible, the, II 112, 125, 170, 250, 320
visible-invisible, II 320, 371, 373 ff.
visible world, II 62, 106
visibility, II 114

visions, II 72, 139, 145, 267
Vittoria, II 91
Vogeler, I 70, 74—II 203
Vogüé, I 70
Volga (river), I 45, 255
Volkart Brothers, II 384, 388
Vollmoeller, I 235
Vollmoeller, Mathilde, I 280, 309, 320, 321, 334

Wachholderhöhe, I 321
walks, I 308—II 72, 79, 82, 120; barefoot, I 103, 261—II 52, 83, 87, 102; in avenues, I 210, 211
Wallis, see Valais
war, II 79, 92, 119, 123, 124, 125, 126, 131, 132, 133, 134, 137, 143, 158, 164, 167, 170, 184, 189, 190, 195-96, 214, 249, 332; archives, II 153, 154, 155; Russian, I 141, 142
war god, II 125, 134
war years, II 266, 287, 373
Wassermann, II 333, 348
Watteau, I 219, 303
Weber, II 180
Weimar, II 28, 29
W(enderl), Madame, II 42, 88
Werfel, II 95, 129
West-East Divan, II 288
Westerwede, I 63, 74—II 354, 355, 362
Westhoff, Clara, I 51, 64, 70, 74; see also Rilke, Clara
Whistler, I 208
Wilde, I 208
winter, I 182, 183, 231

Winterthur, II 208, 384
Wittumspalais, II 28
woman, I 70; home-filled, I 139; return to, I 140
women, I 109, 110, 169, 228, 281, 282, 332, 340—II 173, 186, 256; as artists, I 70, 286, 345; and love, II 46-49; meeting, II 84, 96, 335; old (Paris), I 109 ff.; understanding, I 181
womb, II 169
words, II 136, 165, 168; and music, II 127, 128; poetic, II 340, 393; spoken vs. written, II 210, 393
work, I 144, 159, 180, 226, 334, 340—II 26, 33, 34; center of life, I 105; daily, I 126, 134; and grow old, I 197; one's own, I 312; real, I 268, 315; transition, I 290
world, I 268, 335, 360—II 67, 72, 75, 76, 163, 285
Worpswede, I 44, 45, 49, 50, 54, 55, 72, 81, 95, 97, 116, 184, 215, 216
writer's material, I 276
"writing in French," II 381 ff.
not writing, II 15, 26, 49-50
Wunderly-Volkart, Herr, II 394

Yasnaia Poliana, I 39 ff.—II 354, 355

Zeno, II 15, 58
Zionism, II 306
Zola, I 306, 307
Zuloaga, Ignacio, I 127, 131, 160—II 356
Zurich, II 198, 205, 208

In the Norton Library

LITERATURE

Austen, Jane *Persuasion* Intro. by David Daiches N163

Brace, Gerald Warner *The Garretson Chronicle* N272

Browning, Robert *The Ring and the Book* Introduction by Wylie Sypher N433

Burgess, Anthony *A Clockwork Orange* Afterword by Stanley Edgar Hyman N224

Burgess, Anthony *Tremor of Intent* N416

Burney, Fanny *Evelina* N294

Conrad, Joseph *The Arrow of Gold* N458

Conrad, Joseph *Chance* N456

Conrad, Joseph *The Rescue* N457

Edgeworth, Maria *Castle Rackrent* N288

Fielding, Henry *Joseph Andrews* Introduction by Mary Ellen Chase N274

Gaskell, Mrs. Elizabeth *Mary Barton* Introduction by Myron F. Brightfield N245

Gogol, Nicolai V. *"The Overcoat" and Other Tales of Good and Evil* N304

Golding, Arthur, TR. *Shakespeare's Ovid* N336

Gosse, Edmund *Father and Son* N195

Hamilton, Edith, TR. AND ED. *Three Greek Plays* N203

Harrier, Richard C., ED. *Jacobean Drama: An Anthology* Edited with Introduction, Notes, and Variants (Norton Library Seventeenth-Century Series) N434a (Vol. I) and N434b (Vol. II)

Hawthorne, Nathaniel *The Blithedale Romance* Introduction by Arlin Turner N164

Herrick, Robert *The Complete Poetry of Robert Herrick* Edited with Introduction and Notes by J. Max Patrick (Norton Library Seventeenth-Century Series) N435

Homer *The Iliad* A Shortened Version translated and edited by I. A. Richards N101

James, Henry *The Awkward Age* N285

James, Henry *"In the Cage" and Other Tales* N286

Jonson, Ben *The Complete Poetry of Ben Jonson* Edited with Introduction, Notes and Variants by William B. Hunter, Jr. (Norton Library Seventeenth-Century Series) N436

Lawrence, T. E. *The Mint* N196

Lederer, William J. and Eugene Burdick *The Ugly American* N305

Lucian *Selected Satires of Lucian* Edited and Translated by Lionel Casson N443

Lynn, Kenneth S., ED. *The Comic Tradition in America: An Anthology of American Humor* N447

Mackenzie, Henry *The Man of Feeling* Introduction by Kenneth C. Slagle N214

Mish, Charles C., ED. *Short Fiction of the Seventeenth Century* (Norton Library Seventeenth-Century Series) N437

Peacock, Thomas Love *Nightmare Abbey* N283

Reeves, James, ED. *The Idiom of the People* N289

Richardson, Samuel *Pamela* Introduction by William M. Sale, Jr. N166

Rilke, Rainer Maria *Duino Elegies* N155

Rilke, Rainer Maria *The Lay of the Love and Death of Cornet Christopher Rilke* N159

Rilke, Rainer Maria *Letters of Rainer Maria Rilke, 1892-1910* N476

Rilke, Rainer Maria *Letters of Rainer Maria Rilke, 1910-1926* N477

Rilke, Rainer Maria *Letters to a Young Poet* N158

Rilke, Rainer Maria *The Notebooks of Malte Laurids Brigge* N267

Rilke, Rainer Maria *Sonnets to Orpheus* N157

Rilke, Rainer Maria *Stories of God* N154

Rilke, Rainer Maria *Translations from the Poetry* by M. D. Herter Norton N156

Rilke, Rainer Maria *Wartime Letters of Rainer Maria Rilke* N160

Rizal, José *The Lost Eden (Noli Me Tangere)* Translated by Leon Ma. Guerrero N222

Rizal, José *The Subversive (El Filibusterismo)* Translated by Leon Ma. Guerrero N449

Seneca *The Stoic Philosophy of Seneca* Essays and Letters, translated and with an introduction by Moses Hadas N459

Stendhal *The Private Diaries of Stendhal* N175

Tolstoy, Leo *Anna Karenina* The Maude Translation, with an introduction by George Gibian N326

Tolstoy, Leo *Resurrection* The Maude Translation, with an introduction by George Gibian N325

Trollope, Anthony *The Last Chronicle of Barset* Introduction by Gerald Warner Brace N291

Turgenev, Ivan *"First Love" and Other Tales* N444

Whitman, Walt *Leaves of Grass* The Comprehensive Reader's Edition, edited by Harold W. Blodgett and Sculley Bradley N430

Wollstonecraft, Mary *A Vindication of the Rights of Woman* Introduction, Chronology, and Bibliography by Charles W. Hagelman, Jr. N373

EU Authorised Representative:
Easy Access System Europe
Mustamäe tee 50, 10621 Tallinn, Estonia

www.ingramcontent.com/pod-product-compliance
Lightning Source LLC
Chambersburg PA
CBHW020648110726
47901CB00001B/88